Praise for *Arguments Over Genocide*

"This compelling study unravels how nearly two centuries ago, the Supreme Court developed doctrines of Christian discovery that superseded the laws of the time, including existing American law, and laid the foundation for genocidal crimes and what is now considered the legal basis for administering the Indigenous peoples who remain."

Professor Noam Chomsky

"*Arguments Over Genocide* will reward attentive readers whether they are new to the field of U.S. policy toward the Cherokee and other Indigenous Nations, or have studied it for decades. The author, Steven Schwartzberg, provides a framework for discussion using citations from central, well-known sources like the 'Marshall Trilogy,' but that is merely a beginning. He has unearthed a treasure trove of overlooked or seldom cited material from the architects and apologists of U.S. policy that will surprise and inform even people who have spent their lives studying these issues. As a respected and well-trained historian, Schwartzberg does a masterful job of placing the history of Cherokee Removal into a much larger context, including the religious justifications for these laws which may surprise some readers. In doing so he builds on the work of people like Robert A. Williams Jr. not only explaining the issues with this religious connection but also providing thoughtful ideas for moving forward in a more positive way. This should be of interest to people around the globe, since the religious intervention and subsequent legal doctrines have been applied with few changes in most of the nations dominating Indigenous peoples. In the best tradition of authors like Vine Deloria Jr., Schwartzberg is not afraid to expose the greed of policymakers and the evil it caused. In particular, *Arguments Over Genocide* should cause many people to reassess their view of John Marshall's role in both Cherokee Removal and subsequent policy. Schwartzberg argues persuasively that common portrayals of Marshall attempting to render 'justice' within the context of a constitutional crisis are probably better seen as a way to rehabilitate a bankrupt policy and gloss over its true evil. As one of the first major works since the 2020 Supreme Court Decision in McGirt, Schwartzberg places that decision within his overall picture of failed Federal Policy and unjust laws. Though many legal commentators hailed the McGirt ruling as justice long overdue, *Arguments Over Genocide* provides a much more critical and arguably correct view. McGirt actually provides a smoke screen to hide the perpetuation of the worst of the policies, allowing politicians and lobbyists eager to sway them a cover behind which they can smugly feel vindicated."

Thomas "Lee" Hester, Jr., a founding editor of *Ayaangwaamizin: International Journal of Indigenous Philosophy,* and former faculty in the History of Law and Policy concerning Indigenous People at universities in Canada and the United States.

"I am surprised as I write this: the most compelling new work of theology I have read in years is embedded in a historian's exploration of 19th century legal debates. Worthy of its alarming title, *Arguments Over Genocide* is an urgent book that every clergyperson and seminarian should read. In it, Schwartzberg grabs hold of Christian arguments for genocide and drawing from 19th century counter arguments, beautifully refutes them, on Christian terms. In so doing, he indicts every American Christian, pulls Christian thought out of its pious cul-de-sac, suggests a new way to write history, and places the Christian origins of the genocide of Native Americans under the withering light of truth. The remarkable thing is that his argument is on fire with hope. Such hope does not come cheaply. Centuries of violence against Native Americans can be traced directly to Christian convictions. Schwartzberg shows that Christian legal arguments for genocide have never lost the ascendancy they gained in the 1830s, and continue to kill today. Are there 'sufficient intellectual and moral resources within the Christian tradition to do successful battle with its capacity to believe that one is being benevolent while committing genocide?' The story Schwartzberg has unearthed throws this question down with force. It cannot be ignored. The integrity of American Christianity rides on the answer. More importantly, so do human lives."

Matt Fitzgerald, Senior Pastor, St. Pauls, United Church of Christ, Chicago.

"On December 1, 1790, the new United States summarily informed the Ohio Iroquois that it had them in their hand, by the 'closing' of which, they 'could crush' them to 'nothing.' To prevent the crushing, the invader 'demanded … a great County,' Ohio, as 'the price of that peace' thus offered. It was as if, said the Seneca chiefs Gaiänt'wakê, Gahgeote, and Kiandochgowa, 'our want of strength had destroyed our rights.' That was precisely the invader's presumption, articulated at the birth of U.S. Indian Affairs and continuing into the present. It is what Steven Schwartzberg examines legally in *Arguments over Genocide: The War of Words in the Congress and the Supreme Court over Cherokee Removal*. Neither was the weakness of the proposition unrecognized at the time by a loud minority in Congress, even as the State of Georgia obviated the new Constitution by unilaterally evicting the Cherokee from their homeland. As critics lay supine, the Supreme Court under John Marshall crafted the 'Marshall Trilogy'—*Johnson v. McIntosh* (1823); *Cherokee Nation v. Georgia* (1831), and *Worcester v. Georgia* (1832)—gutting James Wilson's carefully crafted, legal premises of 1787. Despite Marshall's legalized genocide in embracing the antique, papal doctrine of discovery and its corollaries of conquest, the Trilogy to this day forms the basis of 'Indian law,' with its 'dependent domestic' definition of Indigenous nations as 'wards' of the U.S. Examining Marshall's premises, Schwartzberg demolishes them, one by one, demonstrating their honeyed lethality and urging a principled revision of American jurisprudence."

Barbara Alice Mann, Professor of History, University of Toledo, and author of *Iroquoian Women: The Gantowisas* (2006)

"We all, indigenous people and settler descendants, have become trapped in the tangled web of the Doctrine of Discovery and a legal system that practices denial of justice and historical facts. Too often these themes deliver a message of despair and hopelessness. However, Steven Schwartzberg's *Arguments Over Genocide* transcends the darker themes of indigenous history by shedding a light of reason and moral clarity onto our nations' colonial history. When I refer to "our nations' history" I refer to my own Potawatomi ancestry and also our family's French Canadian voyageur origins that became entangled as two nations and civilizations encountered one another in the 18th century. I think it is no coincidence that Steven lives on, writes from, and in many ways writes about the history of my tribal homeland in and around Chicago. This place is obviously speaking to him, and he listens. Throughout his book, and particularly in his magnificent climactic Epilogue, Steven writes in a voice that expresses respect for the aspirations both of indigenous people and of our other than human kin in a manner that is rare amongst those with no Native American ancestry. This book is more than a mere scholarly exploration. It is a gift. Hopefully, it is part of a roadmap forward."

Randy Kritkausky is an enrolled tribal member of the Citizen Potawatomi Nation.

"The unique contribution of *Arguments Over Genocide* is its interweaving of spiritual and constitutional discourses to help us see the deep dynamic of the debate over 'Indian Removal'. Removal was about land, no doubt; but it was also about a claimed 'right of domination' of Christians over 'heathens and pagans'. On one side, it was a brutal brew of racism and religion in service of economic 'development' (read, imperial expansion). On the other side, it was a blend of pity and religion in aid of a campaign for co-existence of peoples. Schwartzberg demonstrates that these competing perspectives fought within the frameworks of the US Constitution and the Christian religion. For their most virulent enemies, the goal was 'removal' of Indigenous peoples from the 'path of civilization,' whether accomplished by extermination or wagons. For their most sympathetic friends, the goal was 'civilization' of Indigenous peoples, accomplished *in situ* with the aid of missionaries. Both sides of the debate claimed Christian right; both claimed Constitutional authority."

Peter d'Errico, Professor Emeritus of Legal Studies, University of Massachusetts at Amherst, from the Afterword.

"This is a bracing, learned, and eloquent study of words and actions that mattered -- that still matter -- and the relationship between them. I learned much. Steven Schwartzberg has taken the trouble to be scholastically, morally, and politically rigorous, and he has produced a book that will have lasting value."

David Waldstreicher, Professor of History, The Graduate Center, City University of New York

Arguments over Genocide

The War of Words in the Congress and the Supreme Court over Cherokee Removal

By Steven J. Schwartzberg

Arguments over Genocide: The War of Words in the Congress and the Supreme Court over Cherokee Removal

By Steven J. Schwartzberg

This book first published 2023

Ethics International Press Ltd, UK

British Library Cataloguing in Publication Data

A catalogue record for this book is available from the British Library

Print Book ISBN: 978-1-80441-107-0

eBook ISBN: 978-1-80441-108-7

I dedicate this book to all whose righteous demand for LandBack must be accepted for the beloved community to emerge and to all I have hurt or neglected through a patriarchal masculinity

"All Christendom seems to have imagined that, by offering that immortal life, promised by the Prince of Peace to fallen man, to the aborigines of this country, the right was fairly acquired of disposing of their persons and their property at pleasure."

Senator John Forsyth of Georgia, 15 April 1830

"Is the Indian right less a right because the Indian is a savage? Or does our civilization give us a title to his right? A right which he inherits equally with us, from the gift of nature and of nature's God. The Indian is a man, and has all the rights of man. The same God who made us made him, and endowed him with the same rights; for 'of one blood hath he made all the men who dwell upon the earth.'"

Senator Asher Robbins of Rhode Island, 21 April 1830

"I do not think any subject ever discussed in Congress has drawn forth a more splendid display of talent in each house of the national legislature than this, or is more worthy of the deliberate consideration of the government and of the nation."

Supreme Court Chief Justice John Marshall, 5 June 1830

"For verily there is no savage nation under the Cope of Heaven, that is more absurdly barbarous than the Christian World."

Thomas Traherne, 1636-74
Centuries of Meditations

"We all know how often individuals feeling connected to someone through the process of cathecting insist they love the other person even as they are hurting or neglecting them. Since their feeling is that of cathexis, they insist that what they feel is love."

bell hooks, 1952-2021
All About Love

"What gives us elbow room, what gives us space to grow and become ourselves, is the love that comes to us from another. Love is the space in which to expand, and it is always a gift."

Herbert McCabe, 1926-2001
God Matters

"When you can't see how that rock on the ground has as much vitality and as much presence as any other entity, tensions will inevitably rise. When you feel like there's nothing to learn from others, including the porous rock, and you have all the answers, and in the process of getting where you want to be, you will kill me to get there, then the soldier of love in me will fight, defend, care, and tend simultaneously with the rock and for the rock. This tension lives throughout Formless Formation *and that's why we move from artists mobilizing the aesthetic to how the militarization of the police mobilize it. There's this ongoing interplay throughout the book: a constant call and response, a move forward and a move back, tango, a careful hustle. I am always trying to understand how I am in them, and how everything that I see as two is also one, and how the most important thing I'll ever be able to hear and say is thank you—to them, to myself, to the rock, to the frog, to you. But I don't know that I'm there, because too much brutality, not thoughtfulness, is our everyday. It's a cycle created and perpetuated by racial misogynist colonial capitalist logics and I want to get someplace else."*

Sandra Ruiz, October 2021

https://www.e-flux.com/journal/121/423318/resonances-a-conversation-on-formless-formation/

TABLE OF CONTENTS

Preface and Acknowledgements

With love and hope for what Martin Luther King, Jr. called the beloved community—and with trust in the grace any effort to help realize that community requires—we will reimagine and radically revise our relations to the land and to each other including to all of the peoples on whose land we abide. "We have no right over the Indians, whether within or without the real or pretended limits of any Colony," the Pennsylvania jurist James Wilson told the Continental Congress in July 1776: "Grants made three thousand miles to the eastward, have no validity with the Indians."[i] This book tells a story that indicates why we must return U.S. law to such a stance and that explores in depth the arguments that we will have to overcome to do so—the arguments *for* genocide that have helped determine the law, policy, and conduct of the United States toward the Native Nations for centuries.

The simple fact is that the arguments advanced by men guilty of horrific evil—the arguments advanced by the advocates of genocide and their appeasers—triumphed in the 1830s and have never since lost the ascendency. These historic arguments for genocide—or for a "right" to commit genocide—support present-day assertions of U.S. domination in the structure of what the American Bar Association calls "federal Indian law." The arguments of the opponents of the genocide of the 1830s, meanwhile, have largely been forgotten, at least among non-Native people. These arguments center on the proposition that the Native Nations are independent foreign states, as the Cherokee Nation told the Supreme Court in 1831, "not owing allegiance to the United States, nor to any state of this union, nor to any other prince, potentate, or state, other than their own."[ii] This is the truth that the advocates of genocide and their appeasers—then and now—have united in denying.

The "extravagant pretension" whereby the Supreme Court sought to lay claim to this continent in *Johnson v. McIntosh* in 1823—the pretension of "discovery" by representatives of a "Christian people" centuries earlier—is not, as is commonly claimed, either a legal fiction or a historical fact.[iii]

Rather, it is a treaty-violating fantasy that is repugnant to the Constitution as well as to the truth of the past. It is a fantasy that ignores the Treaty Supremacy Clause and presents the title to their lands of the Cherokee Nation, Choctaw Nation, Chickasaw Nation, Muscogee Nation (and hundreds of others) as a mere right of occupancy rather than as a treaty-guaranteed and treaty-relationship guaranteed dominion, well established both in constitutional law and in the law of nations as it was understood by the framers of the Constitution.[iv] The doctrine of "discovery" is a fantasy at odds with the intentions of the framers, with the meaning of the text, and with the international moral and legal order under which the American people claim their own rights.

The Supreme Court's consequent denial in *Cherokee Nation v. Georgia* in 1831 of the Cherokee Nation's right to defend their dominion in the courts of the United States—a wrongly decided opinion that paved the way for the Trail of Tears and for subsequent genocides and land thefts—is an even more stark violation of constitutional law. It simultaneously represents the single worst expression of the Supreme Court's long-standing bad faith interpretive stance toward the treaty obligations of the United States to the Native Nations and brought that stance into existence in the first place with its denial of Cherokee treaty rights. According to this anti-democratic and anti-constitutional interpretive stance, treaties and the law of nations (even including the prohibition against genocide) are deemed binding upon "the sovereign" only to the extent that the federal government deigns to so consider them. Because of the nature of precedent in legal structures, this bad faith interpretive stance has warped and twisted *every* decision that has ever been made in the Supreme Court regarding the national rights of a Native Nation, depriving each and all of them of what is rightfully theirs in *American* law to say nothing of what they are entitled to in the laws and usages that prevailed on Turtle Island before the eurochristian invaders arrived.[v]

The Supreme Court derives its denial of the binding character of treaty obligations, and its repudiation of sovereign equality, from the doctrine of "Christian discovery."[vi] This doctrine made possible the Supreme Court's assertion, in *Cherokee Nation v. Georgia*, that the Cherokee Nation "is not a foreign state in the sense of the Constitution, and cannot maintain an action in the Courts of the United States."[vii] The doctrine of Christian discovery, in turn, rests on the claim that sovereignty resides not in "we the people"—as a right of self-government claimed by the American people under an international moral and legal order mandating respect for the equal rights of all peoples—but rather derives from some Christians setting eyes on the land and so acquiring ownership of it and authority over those living on it. The doctrine involves a claim to "title" to the land—a title that originates in a treaty-violating fantasy—and a claim to an "ultimate dominion" over other peoples that is equally and utterly repugnant to the Constitution.[viii]

As the Supreme Court has built on this doctrine of Christian discovery—this assault on the lands and authority of others conducted behind a fog produced by the allegedly benevolent intentions of a "Christian people"—it has added a "trust doctrine" and an explicit claim to a "plenary power" in the Congress to its arsenal. But the entire "trust relationship" between the United States and the Native Nations is simply a secularized expression of the doctrine of Christian discovery in which the word "trust"—like the words "Christianity" and "civilization" before it—is designed to sound good in many American ears as a source of motivation and effectively disguises reality. In terms of what my friend Steve Newcomb (Shawnee, Lenape) calls "the view from the shore" before the European invaders arrived, these words—as the Supreme Court uses them—are merely code words that sustain what Steve has shown at length—in *Pagans in the Promised Land*—is a system of domination and dehumanization.[ix]

There is reason to think that we are on the cusp of another moment like *Brown v. Board of Education* when a system of institutionalized racism and bigotry—embodied in what the Supreme Court had claimed for decades was the law of the land—was revealed to the general public as at odds with the Constitution, with human rights, and with the global common good.[x] After this book—and especially after my friend Peter d'Errico's recently published volume: *Federal Anti-Indian Law: The Legal Entrapment of Indigenous Peoples*—there should be no remaining doubt as to why "federal Indian law" is another such system of domination and dehumanization; no remaining doubt as to why it is a system that is racist and bigoted to its core.[xi]

In *Vasquez v. Hillery,* in 1986, the Supreme Court suggested, in an opinion by Associate Justice Thurgood Marshall that precedent to be overturned must be shown to be "outdated, ill-founded, unworkable, or otherwise legitimately vulnerable to serious reconsideration." [xii] The precedents on which "federal Indian law" rests *are* outdated, ill-founded, unworkable, and a violation of the intentions of the framers of the Constitution and the meaning of the text. They are also violations of Native law and of Native understandings of the meaning of treaties signed with the United States. They are precedents that allowed the genocide of the 1830s to take place, as well as subsequent genocides and land thefts, and that function as an obstacle to lawful conduct on the part of the United States to this day. This book will make clear how these precedents were adopted in violation of the obligations upon the Supreme Court that are inherent in the Constitution's having made treaties the supreme law of the land, including those obligations deriving from the explicit grant to plaintiffs of the right to compel states to accept the original jurisdiction of the court in all cases arising under treaties in which a state is a party to the case.

The land I am seeking to write in harmony with—the land that all law must ultimately draw upon—i want to acknowledge as sustaining the traditional homelands of the nations of the Council of the Three Fires—the Potawatomi, the Odawa, and the Ojibwe—as well as the nations of the Illinois Confederacy—including the Peoria and the Kaskaskia—and others including the Miami, Menominee, Kickapoo, Ho-Chunk, Sauk and Meskwaki nations, near and including what is currently Chicago. Native Nations throughout Turtle Island—throughout this continent—continue to adopt various approaches to resist the ongoing dispossession, colonization, genocide, and erasure begun by the Spanish, English, French, Dutch, and other European powers, and continued by the United States. [xiii] That genocide is the accurate term is made clear at the beginning of the Introduction to this book. If you are a member of one of the Native Nations, you already know the most important part of what I want to convey far better than I do, although I hope you will find here some new and useful information. Together the Native Nations are—as they always have been and always will be—what the theologian Vine Deloria, Jr. (Standing Rock Sioux) calls the "spiritual owner of the land."[xiv] This is, always has been, and always will be, Native Land. The United States lacks, as this work will make clear, a valid legal claim to title.

I am profoundly indebted to Steve Newcomb, the co-founder and co-director of the Indigenous Law Institute, to Peter d'Errico, an emeritus law professor at the University of Massachusetts at Amherst, and to JoDe Goudy (Yakama Nation), a former chairman of the tribal council of the Yakama Nation and the guiding light behind the deeply informative website: www.redthought.org. Entering into the conversations they have been having for decades has been a great honor and delight from which I have learned much more than I can put into words, especially about the doctrine of "Christian discovery" and the American form of the domination and dehumanization system that has been built with the tools that doctrine provides. I have also learned more than I can say from Steve Russell (Cherokee) whose book, *Sequoyah Rising*, first convinced me that the injustice of "federal Indian law" required going to the root of the problem and not being satisfied with correcting the numerous low hanging evils that Steve identified that might be addressed by Congressional action. In the copy of his powerful memoirs that he sent to me, before his untimely death from cancer in 2021, he wrote: "For my friend Steve, for whom I will write words we'd both like to see in *U.S. Reports*: 'Wherefore, premises considered, *Cherokee Nation v. Georgia* ought to be, and is hereby, REVERSED.'"[xv]

I would like to single out for special thanks my parents, Hugh and Joanne Schwartzberg, and my sister, Jenny Schwartzberg. My mother, in particular, offered helpful comments on what must have seemed an interminable stream of drafts. My sister proof-read the penultimate version. The work is also better for comments from, and/or conversations over the years with: Margo and John Arbogast, Cindy Ball, Bruce Beavis, Diane Bell, Thalia Bell, Matt Bergman, Joanna Blad, Bill Borden and Allan Heinemann, Carrie Bruggers, Betsy Burnam (Lakota), Ingrid Burnett, Guy and Erika Burton, Willie and Carol Cade, Jeff Carlson, Peter Choi, Liz Clark, Mark Clark, Rick Conason, Taylor Culver, Rick D'Loss, Kurk Dorsey, Bill Eilfort, Joe Fendt, Matt and Kelli Fitzgerald, Joan Flanagan, David Frisk, Joel Gawlik, Alan Gilbert, Walter and Celia Gilbert, David Hacker, Kurt Hansen, Brian Hastings, Scott Hibbard and Tara Magner, Konan Houphoue, Akira Iriye, Michael Koenigsknecht, Gil Klapper, Carolyn

Schmidt and Randy Kritkausky (Potawatomi), Frank Labaty and Kevin Malone, Gerry Lang (Chowanoke Nation), Frank Lackner, Barb Lloyd, Fred Logevall, Julie Fudala Loprieno, Karen Lyons, Dean Martin, Deirdre McCloskey, Liz McPike, Paul Metzger, Heather Miller (Wyandotte Nation), Brendan Minard and Erika Burton-Minard, Greg Mooney, Christoph Mueller, Shawna Bluestar Newcomb (Shawnee-Lenape-Azteca), Andrew and Shannon Page, Rick Peterson, Steve and Betsy Peterson, Sam Peterson, Anthony Redmond, Joan and Toby Roberts, Marilynne Robinson, Patrick Levine Rose, Paul Saenger, Galen Schwartzberg, Pattie and Tom Sokol, Gaddis Smith, Katie Spero, Mary Stainton, Charles Stewart and Sena Leikvold, Steve Tamayo (Sicangu Lakota), Tink Tinker (wazhazhe/Osage), John Tuohy, Anthony Vaccaro, Helen Valkavich, Irene Voros, Clark Wagner, Jeff Wagner, Mark and Kathy Watson, Jon Welsh, Jack Womack, and Cheryl Woodson.

Three churches have been spiritual homes to me while writing this book: St. Pauls, a UCC church in the Lincoln Park neighborhood in which I live in Chicago, the Lighthouse Church of Chicago, another UCC church that meets in the same building as St. Pauls, and Church of Our Saviour, an Episcopal church in Lincoln Park. I would also like to mention the monthly meditations and Dharma talks by the Rev. angel Kyodo williams that I have been blessed to attend. I am indebted as well to the Chicago Literary Club, whose members graciously received and commented upon several of my papers, and to my students at DePaul University. And I am grateful also to the many people I met and talked with about these issues while campaigning for Congress in the Illinois 5th District in 2018.[xvi]

The conduct of the United States has consistently fallen short of American democratic ideals. We are far from ever having had a government of all of the people, by all of the people, and for all of the people. Not only has the United States fallen short, but at times some of its ideals—most obviously "assimilation" or even "integration"—have been genocidal in their implications. It is in the nature of systems of domination that they can take any word or ideal and twist it to genocidal purposes. There is a sense, moreover, in which all states—by their nature—constitute systems of domination. The claim of "democracy" is that despotic power—sovereign power—resides in the people within a legal context that respects the political rights and civil liberties of the citizenry and that this makes democratic states distinctive among states. This book shows some of the limits of such a perspective, especially when it comes to the United States.

Here it is necessary to make a comment not about the invader state, but about the people who see themselves as loyal to that state or as loyal to the United States Constitution, and who still acquiesce in that state's conduct toward the Native Nations. This is a comment about who the American people has been in its conduct—not in its aspirations, but in its history. What needs to be said is that this is a people whose state has committed both genocide and attempted genocide; a people whose state has consistently broken the people's word. This is a people, in other words, that over the centuries has not only been murderous—in the conduct toward the Native Nations that it has tolerated—but a people that appears incapable of maintaining trustworthy, reciprocal, and consensual relationships with the Native Nations to this day.

I am not trying to talk about all of the reasons why this has been the case: the desire for domination, the greed, the religious bigotry, the racism, the belief in "superiority" however defined—(especially among those who think of themselves as benevolent)—but just the part of the story that concerns the collective amnesia of this people when it comes to the arguments of those Americans who were opposed to the genocide of the 1830s. I do not claim that if everybody in America knew these arguments the American people would suddenly wake up and become a trustworthy people seeking consensus and reciprocity in their relationships with the Native Nations and adhering to all of the requirements of their treaties with these nations. I do not imagine that they would immediately and effectively oppose their government's spurious claims of jurisdiction and plenary power over the Native Nations. But I think knowledge of these arguments against genocide—although they are rooted in Eurochristian culture—may be helpful in the struggle for justice. And by justice, I mean the right of the Native Nations to their original free and independent existence.

Here are two of these Eurochristian arguments against genocide. I would ask readers to keep them in mind as they read through the text. The first is from Senator Asher Robbins of Rhode Island in the debate in the United

States Senate in 1830 over the Removal Bill: "The Indian is a man, and has all the rights of man. The same God who made us made him, and endowed him with the same rights; for 'of one blood hath he made all the men who dwell upon the earth.'"[xvii] The second is from the lawyer, publicist, and Congregationalist Jeremiah Evarts whose "William Penn" essays were read by perhaps half a million people in 1829-1830 in a country with a total population of less than thirteen million: "The people of the United States are bound to regard the Cherokees and other Indians, as *men*; as human beings, entitled to receive the same treatment as Englishmen, Frenchmen, or ourselves, would be entitled to receive in the same circumstances."[xviii]

This book begins with the central premise of these arguments against genocide—the truth that the Native Nations are entitled to be treated just the same as all nations—and builds from that foundation. The Introduction presents the most refined arguments in support of the genocide of the 1830s—those of the House Committee on Indian Affairs—the first chapter then develops the larger structure of this book's argument, the second chapter reviews the debate in the Senate, the third chapter reviews the debate in the House of Representatives, the fourth and fifth chapters explore and critique the Supreme Court's decision in *Cherokee Nation v. Georgia* in the context of what I refer to as "Marshall's War" against the rights of the Native Nations in his entire "trilogy," the sixth chapter provides a brief account of the immediate aftermath of that decision for the Cherokee Nation, the seventh chapter provides an examination of the jurisprudence of the constitutional framer James Wilson, the eighth chapter emphasizes the rupture with the rhetoric and some of the practices of the founding generation, and then there is an Epilogue that looks to the future.

Native voices speak in this work primarily through quotations—especially from the Cherokee Nation's bill before the Supreme Court, in 1831, that I present in chapter four—rather than through paraphrases. The argument that the Cherokee Nation made was valid then and remains valid now. This is the argument that the Cherokee Nation's treaty-rights as an independent and sovereign state should be respected as a matter of *American* constitutional law. That argument is at one with the argument made by the Yakama Nation in 2018, in an *amicus* brief, in the case of *Washington State Department of Licensing v. Cougar Den, Inc,* calling on the Supreme Court to "repudiate the doctrine of Christian discovery and its racist foundations as the basis for federal Indian law."[xix] Noting that the true foundation of the United States' relations with the Yakama Nation is a treaty, the Yakama Nation charged the courts of the United States with systematically attempting to undermine the Yakama Nation's treaty rights by imposing an imaginary prior relationship sourced in the doctrine of "Christian discovery." [xx] The Supreme Court, the Yakama Nation argued, has "judicially manufactured an extra-constitutional congressional plenary authority to abrogate treaties and regulate Native Nations. This manufactured authority rests on the false assertion that our sovereignty and free and independent existence were 'necessarily diminished' upon Christian European arrival on the North American continent."[xxi]

The bad faith interpretive stance that the Supreme Court ultimately derives from the doctrine of Christian discovery is repugnant to who any people wants to be and repugnant to the Constitution. It is foulness generating worse foulness. It would be repugnant even if it had not led directly to genocide. And yet it remains the interpretive stance that the Supreme Court uses to this day with two modifications. The Court adds two significant additional lies to its foundational dishonesty about treaties not being binding on "the sovereign": first, it proclaims that the United States is in some sort of "trust relationship" with the Native Nations and, second, it proclaims that it is interpreting treaties as they would have been understood by these nations when they were signed. In fact, the trust in any *treaty relationship* is the trust that the treaty will be adhered to and this is precisely what the "trust relationship" as the Supreme Court defines it denies whenever "the sovereign" wishes to deny it. The original Native understanding of any treaty was that it was to be adhered to on both sides in good faith. There was no understanding that the American side thought that it could lie its way out of any of its commitments by appealing to the doctrine of Christian discovery and the "ultimate dominion"—the sovereignty or "plenary power"—it supposedly conveys.

At times, over the course of the book, we will circle back to examine points previously made in a new light. A handful of vital quotes—of particularly powerful evidence—will probably become familiar to attentive readers by the end of the work. There is also a larger circling back in the structure of the book as we return, after the discussion of the debates in the Congress and the Supreme Court, to an examination of James Wilson's revolutionary jurisprudence as a contrast to John Marshall's reactionary jurisprudence and then to another exploration of how and why the United States came to break with the positions of the founders of the United States and the framers of the Constitution in the genocide of the 1830s. This exploration emphasizes the importance of the initial resistance—followed by appeasement—with which President John Quincy Adams met Georgian aggression and suggests that "removal" would have been attempted even if Adams had been reelected and Andrew Jackson had never won the presidency.

I pay little attention to James Wilson's and John Marshall's role as large land speculators whose personal economic interests had a direct bearing on the positions they advocated.[xxii] Wilson wanted to establish that private individuals could purchase land directly from the Native Nations, as land companies that he was involved with had sought to do, especially with regard to vast territories in what would come to be called Illinois, and Marshall wanted to establish that the United States had some sort of "title" to lands still in the possession of the Native peoples, particularly in what would come to be called Kentucky, where he and his family had acquired substantial claims that had originally been articulated without first even beginning to approach the Native owners. It is Wilson's and Marshall's conflicting ideas, rather than their conflicting economic interests, that will provide a focus of our attention. These ideas had (and have) a life of their own and won support among those less directly engaged in their economic consequences. It remains true that every American was affected by the choice between Wilson's jurisprudence and Marshall's; a choice which acted as a switch between radically different trajectories of history and economic organization for the American people and for all of the peoples of Turtle Island. From the perspective of those on the shore when the invaders from Europe arrived, all American land speculators were encroaching on lands that did not belong to them and appeared motivated, to a greater or lesser extent, by genocidal visions of a future territory in which the Native Nations would have no part.[xxiii]

* * *

When faced with the history of American genocidal conduct—to foreshadow the Epilogue—I urge rejecting any efforts to make excuses for the past, or for failing to do the right thing going forward, such as "sometimes real justice is impossible." Rather we should hold that real justice is always deemed impossible under the terms of this world and recognize that the call of justice can lead to a rejection of these terms as a pernicious illusion of scarcity and can lead instead to the embrace of the truth that we are each unique expressions of everything else in the universe and are created to communicate abundant love as embodied ideas born of the love with which God extends God's Self in creating the space and time in which all creation either reciprocates God's love with spaciousness and grace toward *all* or else sustains the terms of this world. In the arguments over genocide that are still ongoing we either oppose genocide or we acquiesce in and even support it. It is a subject on which there can be no middle ground.

Introduction

That the United States deliberated so publicly over "ethnic cleansing" before embarking upon it surely makes the genocide of the 1830s distinctive among the world's genocides. That the genocide of the 1830s was a genocide, or rather a series of genocides, is made clear in the next few pages. The administration of President Andrew Jackson knew full well—in advance—that the Trail of Tears would be utterly horrific for the Native Nations with great sufferings to be encountered and many people expected to perish along the way. In September 1831, Jackson was expressly, if ineffectually, warned by his Secretary of War, Lewis Cass, that without adequate preparations: "great sufferings must be encountered upon the journey, and many will doubtless perish."[24] Beyond the callous indifference to human life that the Jackson administration demonstrated by failing to make "adequate preparations"—a callous indifference itself suggestive of genocidal intent—it is clear that *every* argument and action that was taken in support of removal occurred in the context of Georgia's express intention to see the Cherokee Nation destroyed. Georgia's Senator John Forsyth was explicit in publicly claiming that his state had a right to destroy the Cherokee Nation without any interference on the part of the United States: "If their separate existence as a tribe is destroyed by State legislative enactments, the control of the Government of the United States, even over the commerce with them is at an end."[25]

Whatever the self-deluded self-righteousness of many of those who supported removal—whatever their pathetic fantasies that they were acting in the "best interests" or even simply in "the interests" of the Native Nations—the fact remains that *all* of the advocates of removal were effectively assisting Georgia in its pursuit of its admittedly genocidal intentions; in its efforts to completely eradicate any Indian political presence from what it claimed (falsely) was its territory by seeing the Cherokee Nation "destroyed" as a prelude to getting rid of some or all of its nationals.[26] The laws by which Georgia expressly sought to destroy the Cherokee Nation's "separate existence as a tribe" were emulated by the states of Alabama and Mississippi as they also "extended" the jurisdiction of their states over territories that were guaranteed to Native Nations—including the Cherokee, Creek (Muscogee), Choctaw, and Chickasaw Nations—by treaty.[27] All this was common knowledge. There was thus no way to pursue "ethnic cleansing" that did not also pursue genocide. No way to seek removal that did not also aid Georgia, Mississippi, and Alabama in their efforts to destroy Native Nations in violation of the treaty commitments of the United States to these nations.

Even if vast numbers had not died on the Trail of Tears, the genocide of the 1830s would have been both "ethnic cleansing" and genocide. The express Georgian intention—and this is the key point—was to destroy, in whole or in part, the Cherokee Nation. The Congress is guilty of genocide for choosing to support Georgia in violation of the law. And the whole country, as Congressman Henry Storrs of New York noted at the time, "must bear the crime and the shame."[28] The Congress' action was also, as Congressman George Evans of Maine noted before it was taken, proposed initially as a straightforward violation of the good faith of treaties: "We are called to pass a law exchanging land with private individuals, when we have guaranteed the possession of that land to the Cherokee nation, as common property; so that we are not only to stand by, and see Georgia violate our faith, but to pass a bill—which very bill expressly violates it."[29] The bill, Congressman Edward Everett of Massachusetts observed, "provides the means for co-operating with the States of Georgia, Alabama, and Mississippi, in removing the Indians within their limits.... It is a joint policy. We are to do part, and the States to do part. We are to furnish money, and a portion of the machinery. The great principle of motion proceeds from the States. They are to move the Indians. We are to pay the expense of the operation."[30] As Supreme Court Chief Justice John Marshall wrote in a letter to Everett—thanking him for his speech—"You have shown, what is certainly true, that they are parts of the same system, and that Congress completes the coercive measures begun by the states."[31] But, rather than denounce the unconstitutionality of this crime, Marshall would lead the Supreme Court to join this genocidal "system" and help complete "the coercive measures begun by the states" with his opinion in *Cherokee Nation v. Georgia* before disguising what the Supreme Court had done with his opinion in *Worcester v. Georgia* the following year.

Georgia's intentions were genocidal in the strictest sense of the term for both the United Nations' convention on the subject of 9 December 1948, and Article 6 of the Rome Statute of the International Criminal Court of 16 January 2002, define genocide in terms of "acts committed with intent to destroy, in whole or in part, a national, ethnical, racial or religious group, as such."[32] This genocidal intention was effectively embraced, unavoidably, by every advocate of removal. Those who claimed to be "saving" the Cherokee Nation by supporting removal were doing something that made no sense and that remained genocidal: helping destroy the Cherokee Nation (at least in part) in order to "save" it: severing the nation from its roots in its territory and depriving it of the exercise of self-determination through almost all of its established institutions; annihilating or greatly disrupting all of the rights, privileges, powers, and relations which the Cherokee Nation had previously enjoyed as a distinct and independent community.[33] The deaths brought about by driving the Cherokee Nation and its neighboring nations onto the Trail of Tears also constitute an effort to destroy (at least in part) the nations involved but given the self-deception of so many Americans—then and now—the genocidal intentions may seem less clear to some; may appear as merely a callous acceptance of "collateral damage" rather than direct genocidal intent.

It was Georgia's intentions that drove the course of events in the late 1820s and the early 1830s, that qualify beyond the shadow of a doubt as genocidal, and that unquestionably identify this episode as a genocide in the history of international law. Georgia passed an Act on 19 December 1829 that promised to extend its jurisdiction over the territory of the Cherokee Nation—an Act that sought to destroy the existence of the Cherokee people as a distinct people. "And be it further enacted," the seventh article read, "That after the first day of June next, all laws, ordinances, orders and regulations of any kind whatever, made, passed, or enacted by the Cherokee Indians, either in general council or in any way whatever, or by any authority whatever of said tribe, be, and the same are hereby declared to be null and void and of no effect, as if the same had never existed."[34]

To coercively deny a peaceful people, or a group of peaceful peoples, their dominion by "legally" destroying their governments, invading their homelands, and depopulating them is sufficient to justify the term genocide and would be even if the deaths of large percentages of these peoples' populations were not involved. That some of the Native Nations "agreed"—under extreme duress—to "remove" across the Mississippi should not obscure the reality of the genocide of the 1830s.

The law professor Gary Clayton Anderson in his book, *Ethnic Cleansing and the Indian*, has claimed that genocide is "difficult to prove" and maintained that "the conflicts with Indians hardly resemble the mass killings of millions that occurred in Europe."[35] This ignores both the more revealing comments of what the perpetrators of the genocide of the 1830s said were their intentions and the lived experience of numerous Native Nations for whom losses of twenty percent or more of their nationals were common. The contrast between the ruthless workings of the bureaucratic and financial machinery of expulsion—well illuminated in a book titled *Unworthy Republic* by the historian Claudio Saunt—and the rosy picture of removal painted by some of its advocates in 1829-1830 could not be more striking. The loss of life and the sums involved in what soon became a coercive federal effort to extirpate 80,000 people from their homelands are staggering. In 1836, removal consumed more than 40 percent of the federal budget and would again in 1838.[36] According to Saunt: "The federal government expended about $75 million to expel Native peoples from their homelands, equivalent today to a trillion dollars, or about $12.5 million for each deportee."[37] Put in relative proportional population terms, the "removal" of 80,000 people from a territory containing a total U.S. population of less than 13 million in the 1830s, would be the equivalent of "removing" more than two million people today out of a territory containing a total population of around 328 million—and seeing something like 400,000 of them die.[38] Had it been the American people, today, who suffered the kinds of losses that the Native Nations experienced on the Trail of Tears, the numbers of the dead would have exceeded sixty million.[39]

The genocide of the 1830s stretched on for years after the horror was widespread knowledge as nation after nation to the east of the Mississippi was driven west. Before the issue returned to the Supreme Court, in *Worcester v. Georgia*, in 1832, the term a Trail of Tears had already begun to reverberate in the northern press.[40] This was a result of the Choctaw

Nation's horrific experience in accepting the United States' "offer" and a comment from a Choctaw chief to an *Arkansas Gazette* reporter about the journey as far as Little Rock. It had been, he said, "a trail of tears and death."[41] As the historian A. J. Langguth notes, rough calculations show that one in five Choctaw nationals, perhaps more, did not survive.[42] Alexis de Tocqueville, who personally witnessed some of the Choctaw Nation crossing the Mississippi in late 1831, wrote in *Democracy in America*: "I was the witness of sufferings which I have not the power to portray."[43]

* * *

The language of the late eighteenth and early nineteenth centuries can be difficult to follow. Nevertheless, and for a variety of reasons, I have chosen to let the historical actors speak in their own voices rather than in paraphrased summaries to a great extent. The vile brutality of an advocate for removal such as Senator John Forsyth of Georgia cannot really be appreciated in summary. Nor can the eloquent decency of an opponent of removal such as Congressman Henry Storrs of New York. The comments in the debate are generally presented in chronological order so that it is possible, at least to some extent, to perceive the flow of criticisms and responses on both sides. Although the debate proper began in the Senate on 9 April 1830, the report of the House Committee on Indian Affairs of 24 February 1830 is an essential part of the background and will be examined first.

* * *

Presenting the report titled, "Removal of Indians," to the House of Representatives, on 24 February 1830, Congressman John Bell of Tennessee began by pointing out that beyond the great interests involved, "many entertain the opinion that the honor and character of the country are, also, in an eminent manner placed in the keeping of Congress, at this juncture."[44] The report observed the division of opinion and explicitly noted that whether those who were opposed to removal "can claim to have been the most judicious friends of the Indians, remains to be tested by time."[45] With the advantages of hindsight, it is clear not only that the claims of the opponents of removal have been vindicated but also that the claims of the advocates of removal to be advancing the interests of the Indians have proved hollow and part of a grotesque and morally bankrupt genocidal policy. Given this retrospective clarity, the question naturally arises as to how such a horribly evil policy triumphed, and what would have been required to defeat it. Here it is essential to stress the self-deception of the advocates of removal and to note the power of the sense of self-righteousness and seeming sophistication with which they made their claims. The committee's report addressed the moral criticisms leveled by the opponents of removal head-on:

> Principles of natural law, and abstract justice, are appealed to by some, to show that the Indian tribes within the territorial limits of the States, ought still to be regarded as the owners of the absolute property in the soil they occupy, and that they are to be regarded as independent communities, having all the attributes of sovereignty, except such as they have voluntarily surrendered. All civilized nations acknowledge the validity of the principles appealed to, according to their understanding of what they are, and profess to be governed by them in their intercourse with the rest of mankind. That the interpretation of these principles, as developed in the practice of nations, should vary with the progress of general science, is natural, and agreeable to the truth of history. What, at one period, was held to be just and reasonable, in a succeeding age is condemned as cruel and oppressive. The errors of society, committed in the early stages of it, generally admit of correction, when detected by more enlarged and just views; but it is not always so. It often happens, that they become so closely connected with the very foundations of society itself, that any attempt to eradicate them would involve a dissolution of its bonds, and the destruction of all order—an extremity, forbidden by the very principles, the recognition of which pointed to the original mischief.[46]

The only remedy to the original mischief, the report suggested, was "to have abandoned the continent to the undisturbed possession of the Indian."[47] The authors of the report explicitly recognized the existence of a moral order that "all civilized nations" professed to be "governed by," and then proceeded to argue that its apparent obligations could not be realized in this case without undermining "the very foundations of society itself." This rhetorical maneuver depended for its persuasiveness on an understanding of "society itself" that derived from an extremist conception of states' rights in which there could be no challenge to the sovereignty of a state from within its chartered limits—no autonomous Native Nations with full rights of sovereignty and ownership of the soil within those limits or, better said, on their own territories which were, in fact, outside the actual limits of any state and of the United States. Framed somewhat differently, states' rights—as a legal claim and as a legal concept—is really code for stealing lands and authority from the Native Nations on the basis of an "inheritance" from some Christians gazing at the land and lacks a coherent account of its origins without reference to the doctrine of Christian discovery. This "inheritance" was, to be sure, a claim on untrammeled authority allegedly acquired from "the Crown" by revolution, but the Crown (which certainly did not possess such untrammeled authority under the British constitution) allegedly derived what untrammeled authority it had in the Americas from discovery.

From the perspective of the authors of the report, what were important were not any "abstract" moral principles, but rather their own interpretations of the "actual practices" and maxims of those "civilized nations" that settled the Americas. They were, in short, although they did not use either term, "positivists" and "realists." Rather than look to the natural law principles of the Declaration of Independence, or those that informed the revolutionary jurisprudence underlying the Constitution, they looked instead to the history of communities founded on a Christian supremacist nationalism:

> The foundations of the States which constituted this Confederacy were laid by Christian and civilized nations, who were instructed or misled, as to the nature of their duties, by the precepts and examples contained in the volume which they acknowledged as the basis of their religious rites and creed. To go forth, to subdue and replenish the earth, were received as divine commands, or relied on as plausible pretexts to cover mercenary enterprises, by the governments which gave the authority, and the adventurers who first discovered and took possession of the new world. Whether they

> were right or wrong in their construction of the sacred text, or whether their conduct can, in every respect, be reconciled with their professed objects or not, it is certain that possession, actual or constructive, of the entire habitable portion of this continent, was taken by the nations of Europe, divided out, and held originally by the right of discovery as between themselves, and by the rights of discovery and conquest as against the aboriginal inhabitants. In the Spanish provinces, the Indians became the property of the grantee of the district of country which they inhabited; and this oppression was continued for a considerable period. Although the practice of the Crown of England was not marked by an equal disregard of the rights of personal liberty in the Indians, yet their pretensions to be the owners of any portion of the soil were wholly disregarded.[48]

This dishonest vision of the past—the vision of "Christian discovery"—had, somehow, to account for several hundred years of treaties in which land was purchased from the Indians. The rhetorical mechanism whereby this history was made an irrelevancy was the claim that such purchases were a matter of expediency not law—in other words that the treaties signed were signed on the part of the colonists in bad faith. There was, the report's authors asserted, a religious feeling that forbade thrusting the Indians out of the land with violence and, besides, trade with them was profitable. This soon brought the colonists to perceive the advantages of cultivating peaceable relations:

> This interest, however, was found, in the progress of the new societies, to be opposed to another great interest; which was, that their resources should be increased, and the demands of the cultivator supplied, by appropriating the wild land within their limits as speedily as possible. The difficulty that was felt in reconciling these two interests, lies at the foundation of the policy which was adopted in relation to the Indians; and the expedients which were resorted to, in order to effect an object so important, constitute the evidence of what the policy of the country was, from that time up to the formation of the Constitution. One of those expedients was, to appear to do nothing, which concerned the Indians, either in the appropriation of their hunting grounds, or in

> controlling their conduct, without their consent. It is not intended to be asserted that this device was employed by all the colonies, from their first settlement. It came, however, to be a general principle of action, upon this subject, at some period or other of their progress, and was adhered to, when found practicable, and in any degree consistent with their interests; but, in several instances, some of which occurred at an early, and others at a later period, the public interests were believed to require a departure from it; but in all the acts, first of the colonies, and afterwards by the States, the fundamental principle, that the Indians had no rights, by virtue of their ancient possession, either of soil or sovereignty, has never been abandoned, either expressly or by implication.[49]

This is essentially an explicit version of the position John Marshall articulated more subtly with his claim of an "ultimate dominion" derived from "discovery" by a "Christian people" in *Johnson v. McIntosh* and which formed the basis for his conclusion in *Cherokee Nation v. Georgia* that: "If it be true that the Cherokee Nation have rights, this is not the tribunal in which those rights are to be asserted."[50] In contrast, Congressman George Evans of Maine, in the debate in the House of Representatives in 1830, made it clear that the rights the Native Nations derived from their treaties were binding law and that the attempt to weasel out of them was dishonorable as well as illegal. He stressed that there is a moral obligation beyond all treaties to keep promises in good faith in the day of our strength and power that were made in the day of our weakness:

> Sir, it is a well known rule in morals and in common sense, that every one making a promise is bound by it in the sense in which he knows the other party to understand it. When Georgia, therefore, laid by, and saw and knew the promises which this Government was making to the Indians, and yielded her assent, shall she be precluded from asserting that either she or we are not bound, according to the sense we then knew the Indians put upon those promises? By this rule our guarantee is to be measured; and I, for one, will never move an inch to relieve a State which thus lies by, and permits us to enter into engagements, and receives the benefit of our contracts, and at last comes forward with the complaint that we had no right to make

> them. I say to Georgia, if we had no right without your consent, your consent has been obtained. It is too late. You are estopped.[51]

For the House Committee on Indian Affairs, there could be only one sovereign within the chartered territories of any of the states and it was these states—"succeeding as they did to the sovereignty over all the lands within the limits of their respective charters"—that had the right to extinguish Indian title: "Thus, the practice of buying Indian title is but the substitute which humanity and expediency have imposed, in place of the sword, in arriving at the actual enjoyment of property claimed by the right of discovery, and sanctioned by the natural superiority allowed to the claims of civilized communities over those of savage tribes."[52]

The treaties made with turbulent and warlike bands of Indians were made, the report claimed, because there was no way of governing them by regular law: "These treaties were, therefore, but a mode of government, and a substitute for ordinary legislation."[53] As the Indians declined in strength, and were enclosed by the white population, a transition took place between conciliating by treaty to controlling by regular laws. Adverting to Georgia's recent promise to extend its laws over Cherokee territory, the report sought to minimize what was different about this action from all previous state action, but still acknowledged something of the difference: "It is true, that the legislation in most of the States, has been simple, and intended rather for the protection than the restraint of the Indians."[54] That Georgia had a right to impose such "restraint," the authors of the report had no doubt. The guarantee extended by treaty to the Cherokee Nation of their lands, the House Committee on Indian Affairs turned into a guarantee of a boundary that had caused trouble in the past as a result of white intrusions across it: this guarantee, they maintained, "was probably a device, adopted more for the intimidation of the whites, than for any effect it was likely to have on the Indians themselves."[55]

In accordance with their vision of states' rights, the committee asserted that "The superior right of the State to the control of every inhabitant within its territorial limits, whether citizen or alien, must prevail over every inferior or inconsistent claim."[56] Georgia's extension of its laws, they suggested, would be a positive good for the Cherokee people. The chiefs of the

Cherokee Nation would be the "principal sufferers." But the committee suggested that their alleged "avarice" and a "corrupt love of power" made them fitting targets as against a middle class that would benefit—"A middle class, which is composed chiefly of a mixed race, will become good citizens, or be permitted to enjoy their property and liberty, with no other restraint than is imposed in the natural obligation to respect the rights of others."[57] The real difficulty concerned the poor since—in the claim of the committee—"an Indian cannot work."[58] Recognizing that its account of the poor among the Southern Indians "will be almost incredible to those who have formed their opinions of the Cherokees from the inflated general accounts found in the public journals of the day," the committee sought to suggest that these accounts only applied to a mixed-race upper and middle class and not to the mass of the population.[59] If the condition of the poor among the Southern Indians were taken seriously, the report's authors insisted, the course of action they advocated would be adopted:

> The true nature of the calamity which threatens them, and from which some power competent to save them is invoked, by so many considerations of generosity and pity, will be partially understood, when the fact, which, to many, must be incomprehensible is stated, that, out of a population of 60 or 65,000 souls in the enjoyment of twenty-five or thirty millions of acres of fertile land, 50 or 55,000 Southern Indians may be said to have no property at all, and that a large portion of them are in fact below the condition of common paupers among the whites. The Southern tribes do not present the case of a few hundred, or even a few thousand Indians, who may have remained on a reservation enclosed by the white population of other States: they present the *materiel* of a future mass of wretchedness and degradation, which, to those who have duly considered the Indian character, and the causes which have heretofore, and, under similar circumstances, will continue to depress and debase their condition, must appear truly frightful.... If the Committee have not wholly misstated the condition of the Southern Indians, it will be apparent, that the common feelings of humanity, besides the obligations incurred in the past intercourse of the Government with them, require, that whatever means may be constitutionally employed, should be liberally applied for their

> relief. If they remain where they are, the experience of two centuries has shown, that they eventually must perish.[60]

The boldest argument of the American advocates of genocide has always been the paradoxical claim that unless the action they advocated was adopted, the Native peoples would suffer or even perish. Challenge any opponent of recognizing and respecting the independent national existence of the Native Nations today—any opponent of ceasing the United States' lawbreaking activities—and the immediate claim will be that these nations could not "survive" without the "assistance" provided by the United States. This argument is patently an excuse for a desire to continue to dominate the Native Nations. It ignores all previous excuses and attempts to dominate these nations—and the horrific consequences that this desire to dominate has *always* wrought. All this will become evident after a detailed examination of the record of these arguments in the Congress and the Supreme Court.

The original free and independent existence of the Native Nations was far closer to the social values Christianity alleges it favors than the societies of Christendom and its successors have been. This is a simple factual statement. Vine Deloria, Jr. makes some arguments along these lines in *God is Red* and I make some others in this book, especially in the Epilogue.[61] But, as far as I am concerned, it is not a controversial observation. What may be controversial is to suggest to Christians, in part on the basis of this observation, that the "body of Christ" has been mostly misconceived within the Christian tradition as something consisting of Christians rather than as a cosmic reality with which all people may seek to be in harmony. This mystical body, from my perspective, is constituted by the community formed by all living beings; by the entire web of life whose unity and diversity is well conveyed in the phrase "all our relations." So many Christians believing that they were somehow enlarging the body of Christ has been a large part of the ability of these Christians to engage in genocide while seeing themselves as benevolent; an ability that has persisted among their secular successors in the name of expanding "civilization" or even extending "democracy."

Whether there are sufficient intellectual and moral resources within the Christian tradition or its secular successors to do successful battle with this capacity to believe that one is being benevolent while committing genocide is an open question. The Sikh thinker and social justice advocate Valarie Kaur has written a book, *See No Stranger*, in which she suggests that we should see every new individual we meet as a part of ourselves whom we do not yet know.[62] I think the Christian tradition is capable of something similar; capable of sustaining a belief that one should seek to serve Christ in everyone and seek to avoid judging lest we be judged. A Dominican theologian, Herbert McCabe, who has contributed to my thinking, once defined love as the space in which to expand; I would add, the space in which to become more of one's true self (understanding our true self as a unique and embodied expression of everything else in the universe). Such love is, he noted, always a gift.[63] Stealing space and depriving others of space is what the societies of Christendom and its successors have done for centuries. That this is at odds with what Christians and their secular successors avow and should understand love to be would seem obvious but their vision has frequently been obscured by their misplaced faith that a culture and a politics of domination can create or extend a worthwhile community. This is one of the greatest obstacles to liberation from the domination and dehumanization system that first imposed itself on Indigenous peoples and which is now ubiquitous on the planet in various forms; a system in which all of us confront a profound misunderstanding of who we are and a profound misapprehension of how we are connected.

Chapter 1
Three Claims and Three Levels of Argument in this Book

In the argument about arguments in this book, I make three basic claims. In the first place, I claim that all these old arguments from the 1820s and 1830s—and even some of their antecedents from the fifteenth century—are all still with us: as relevant to the law, policy, and conduct of the United States today as they were when they were first articulated; and as relevant to the life of the Native Nations. In the second place, I claim that the premises of the arguments of the advocates of genocide and their appeasers—the assertions of U.S. domination at the foundation of "federal Indian law"—depend for their "authority" on a collective amnesia with regard to the premises of the arguments of those who opposed the genocide. In the third place, I claim that understanding the intentions of the framers of the Constitution, as well as all sides of the debates in the Congress and the Supreme Court in 1829-1832, can dispel that amnesia and facilitate more open communication between the American people and the peoples of the Native Nations—communication on which the emergence of the beloved community depends.

We are obliged, if we truly want to be law-abiding, to respect the international laws and usages that prevailed among the Native Nations of Turtle Island before the European invaders arrived. We are obliged to care for the land as our grandmother Earth and to respect the unity and equality of all living beings in a beloved community for whom the "all" of which the founders of the United States spoke has been transformed into the "all" in the "*all our relations*" of whom the peoples of the Native Nations speak. That would be closer to the true constitutional legal order of this land of which the American Constitution is an inadequately-rooted expression that has so far failed to guarantee equal belonging to all.

The legal theorist James Wilson was one of the most progressive of the founders of the United States and perhaps the single most important architect of the American Constitution. He spoke with hope of the prospects for political and moral improvement in the society as a whole—the prospects for a more harmonious unity; "a more perfect Union." One of the strategies for realizing the beloved community involves grafting our hopes for progress onto the hope that Wilson expressed for an American society in which: "All will receive from each, and each will receive from all, mutual support and assistance: mutually supported and assisted, all may be carried to a degree of perfection hitherto unknown; perhaps, hitherto not believed."[64]

From the perspective of those on the shore when the invaders from Europe arrived, we may all hope to find our way back to the degree of perfection—the balance—that was present before that arrival. Our future as the beloved community involves a restoration of that balance between our ancestors and our descendants, between ourselves and all our relations: a balance that the Eurochristian peoples have yet to know or at least have yet to realize that they have access to within themselves. That is at the heart of what progress and restoration must mean: that deep harmony and the maintenance of balance are realized together for all.

The "war of words" in the Congress and the Supreme Court in 1829-1832 was a far cry from James Wilson's glowing aspirations for progress. This war—with one side explicitly championing bad faith with regard to America's treaty obligations to the Native Nations and even openly advocating the crime that would come to be known as genocide against them—would have been unthinkable to the framers of the Constitution. Some of the framers can be accused of hypocrisy in their dealings with the Native Nations, but even they showed every indication of intending to keep the treaties they had made with these nations—at least to uphold what they saw as the letter of the legal requirements of these treaties if not the spirit of friendship in which they at least sometimes appeared to have been made.[65] Although he was not at the constitutional convention, President Thomas Jefferson's hypocritical approach to American treaty commitments is illustrative. In 1786, he wrote to a friend: "It may be regarded as certain that not one foot of land will be taken from the Indians without their own consent."[66] But within fifteen years, Jefferson was advocating the use of American trading houses as a means of enticing influential chieftains to run up large debts with an eye toward putting them in a position in which they would have to cede lands to the United States to settle their debts.[67]

Dividing North from South, the "war of words" that launched the genocide of the 1830s was a prelude to the Civil War. The victory of the South in this prelude increased the economic and political power of the advocates of slavery and hardened the racism in the nation's arteries.[68] New England's Senators voted 11 to 1 against the Removal Bill; southern Senators voted 18 to 0 for it. The rest of the country was more evenly split: 8 against and 10 for.[69] The outcome in the House of Representatives, which began its debate after the Senate had already voted, was much more closely contested. When the first decisive vote was taken, on an amendment to have an exploratory mission survey Indian opinion and the quality of the land in the West before any further decision was made, the vote was 99 to 98 against the amendment, and the final vote for the bill was 102 to 97.[70] The horrific consequences of these votes were equally far removed from progress and from any restoration of balance.

One way of looking at this war of words is in terms of the question of whether the United States, having received such title as it possessed from the Native Nations, would honor the obligations it had promised to fulfill in return—whether it would respect an "all" that included these nations. The Treaty Supremacy Clause of the Constitution guaranteed that it would.[71] The doctrine of "Christian discovery"—at least the version adopted by the Supreme Court in *Johnson v. McIntosh*—suggested that it would not. According to this doctrine, the colonists and their heirs and successors had acquired "ultimate dominion" over everything the Native Nations owned, and a "right" to a "degree of sovereignty" over them, simply by gazing.[72] Hence, the new nation did not owe them anything in return—except maybe an effort to cultivate or impose "Christianity and civilization" among them as the new nation saw fit, even by driving them a thousand miles across the Mississippi should it decide to do so. This was and remains a doctrine of domination—a doctrine first spelled out in a series of papal bulls whose premises were used in attempts to justify such horrors as chattel slavery, the trans-Atlantic slave trade, and the Trail of Tears.[73]

Perhaps the most famous of these papal bulls was *Inter Caetera* of 3 May 1493 in which Pope Alexander VI—in order "that barbarous nations be overthrown and brought to the faith"—somehow allegedly gave to Spain's monarchs, Ferdinand and Isabella: "the aforesaid countries and islands thus unknown and hitherto discovered by your envoys and to be discovered hereafter, provided however they at no time have been in the actual temporal possession of any Christian owner, together with all their dominions, cities, camps, places, and villages, and all rights, jurisdictions, and appurtenances of the same."[74] The following day this bull was revised to include a specific line one hundred leagues west of the Azores and to grant to Spain exclusive rights to the west of that line.[75] Less well known, but equally important, was Pope Nicholas V's grant to the King of Portugal in *Dum Diversas* of 18 June 1452—reiterated in *Romanus Pontifex* of 8 January 1455—awarding that monarch, Alfonso V, a monopoly of the African slave trade and authorizing him: "to invade, search out, capture, vanquish, and subdue all Saracens and pagans whatsoever, and other enemies of Christ wheresoever placed, and the kingdoms, dukedoms, principalities, dominions, possessions, and all movable and immovable goods whatsoever held and possessed by them and to reduce their persons to perpetual slavery, and to apply and appropriate to himself and his successors the kingdoms, dukedoms, counties, principalities, dominions, possessions, and goods, and to convert them to his and their [Alfonso's and his successors'] use and profit."[76]

At the most basic level, this book seeks to recuperate the arguments of those who were truly opposed to such doctrines—who were truly opposed to the genocide of the 1830s—who maintained that the Native Nations are sovereign and independent foreign states toward whom the United States has binding legal obligations under its treaties, and under constitutional law, and under international law; obligations that require respect for these nations' dominion over their own territories and prohibit genocidal conduct toward them.

The lawyer, publicist, and Congregationalist Jeremiah Evarts provided a clear contemporary understanding of the American conduct that the law of nations required. Building on the arguments and evidence amassed in his essays, Evarts and his allies—particularly in the country's churches—

launched a campaign to flood the Congress with scores of thousands of petition signatures on behalf of the Cherokee Nation, an endeavor that was bitterly resented by Georgia's political leaders.[77]

"Recently great efforts have been made to excite the public mind into a state of unreasonable and jealous apprehension in their behalf," Georgia's Senator John Forsyth declared in April 1830: "The evidences of these efforts are before us in petitions that have been pouring in from different parts of the country. The clergy, the laity, the lawyers, and the ladies, have been dragged into the service and united to press upon us."[78] "An attempt is making in the Eastern States to create a great deal of sympathy for this people;" Forsyth continued, "and the attempt is making, so far as I can discover, by what is termed the 'Christian party in politics.'"[79] Evarts believed that the weight of these petitions had been considerable and almost enough: "A few more spirited memorials, supported by the personal influence of men distinguished in the community for their integrity and patriotism, would probably have defeated the removal bill."[80] There is reason to think this judgement correct. One of the early votes on the issue in the House of Representatives was 113 to 56 on the question of whether to print 10,000 copies of the pro-removal report by the House Committee on Indian Affairs. As we have seen, the final vote on the removal bill itself was much closer.[81] Public pressure, and the course of the debate in the Congress, appears to have made the difference.

Here is Evarts' understanding of the most basic requirement of the law of nations: that all nations—including all the Native Nations—are entitled to be treated as sovereign equals. This is the position from which he argued against genocide in 1830:

> The people of the United States are bound to regard the Cherokees and other Indians, as *men*; as human beings, entitled to receive the same treatment as Englishmen, Frenchmen, or ourselves, would be entitled to receive in the same circumstances. Here is the only weak place in their cause. They are not treated as men; and if they are finally ejected from their patrimonial inheritance by arbitrary and unrighteous power, the people of the United States will be impeached and condemned for treating the Indians, not as men, but

> as animals.... In this matter, we cannot offer even the sorry plea of prescription in crime, as an extenuation of our guilt. The precedents, in our own country, are all against us. For two hundred years the Indians have been treated like other men, as to the acknowledgement of their rights and the interpretation of treaties made with them.[82]

The simple honesty involved in the stance of Evarts and his allies was in sharp contrast not only with the brutal dishonesty of the advocates of genocide but also with the more subtle dishonesty of those, like President John Quincy Adams and Supreme Court Chief Justice John Marshall and their supporters, who chose to engage in an appeasement of Georgian aggression and later sought to cover their tracks by blaming President Andrew Jackson and his supporters for the Trail of Tears as if they themselves had not greatly contributed to it. Adams' later reflection on American conduct toward the Native Nations in the 1830s—in his diary, in 1841—conveys no hint of his personal role: "It is among the heinous sins of this nation, for which I believe God will one day bring them to judgement."[83] We will examine Adams' personal role in chapter eight. As for Marshall, he reportedly praised Evarts' essays as constituting the "most conclusive argument that he had ever read on any subject whatever," and then proceeded to rule against that argument—as we will see in chapters four and five—on the basis of a wrongly decided opinion rooted in the alleged indispensability of expediency.[84]

The role of the state of Georgia—which was the driving force behind the genocide of the 1830s—in undertaking and advocating vicious coercive measures to destroy the Cherokee and other Native Nations in pursuit of what was then known as "removal," is now largely forgotten. The Jackson administration's policy and racist populism have come to the fore instead in the common understanding of the origin of the Trail of Tears. This has obscured the dishonesty of the Congress in seeking to exercise what the Supreme Court would later claim as a Congressional "plenary power" over the Native Nations that the Congress of 1830 knew full well that it did not lawfully possess. Thus the Congress employed treaty-violating coercion—while claiming not to be doing so—by initially relying on the coercion of Georgia's, Alabama's, and Mississippi's brutal anti-Indian laws rather than direct Congressional coercion to achieve its treaty-violating aims. So did the Jackson administration.

Where Georgia's distinctive role is remembered, it is primarily from the case, *Worcester v. Georgia*, in 1832, whose poorly understood majority opinion is still popularly perceived (wrongly) as a vindication (if an ineffectual one) of the rights of the Cherokee Nation.[85] The lie that the lands of the Cherokee Nation belonged to either the state of Georgia or the United States by virtue of "Christian discovery"—and the derivative lie that the Native Nations are "completely under the sovereignty and dominion of the United States" (or, in Georgia's view, the state of Georgia)—is the lie at the heart of both the genocide of the 1830s and the "federal Indian law" that allowed it.[86] Nothing in *Worcester* challenged that lie as far as the claims of dominion for the United States are concerned. It was on the basis of this lie that Senator Forsyth claimed that his state had a right to destroy the Cherokee Nation without any interference on the part of the United States: "If their separate existence as a tribe is destroyed by State legislative enactments, the control of the Government of the United States, even over the commerce with them is at an end."[87] It was on the basis of this lie that John Marshall could write that "If it be true that the Cherokee Nation have rights, this is not the tribunal in which those rights are to be asserted. If it be true that wrongs have been inflicted, and that still greater are to be apprehended, this is not the tribunal which can redress the past or prevent the future."[88]

At the second level, then, this book seeks to illuminate the arguments of those who sought genocide, and those who sought to appease them, showing how their arguments—in both cases—derived from versions of the doctrine of "Christian discovery" whereby the Native Nations were seen to have lost authority over themselves and lost ownership of their own lands—lost an authority and an ownership that was then somehow "inherited" by the states and the federal government. Now the reason why the arguments of the opponents of genocide were defeated by this pernicious nonsense, I maintain, is *not* to be found in the text of a Constitution that promised that *all* treaties were part of the supreme law of the land, but in a betrayal of that Constitution by the executive branch, and by the legislature, and by the judiciary—all at the instigation of the state of

Georgia—and their adoption of the vicious doctrine of Christian discovery in place of the requirements of constitutional law. As Senator Forsyth championed the adoption of their position in 1830, he suggested that the decision had already been taken by the European powers long ago: "All Christendom seems to have imagined that, by offering that immortal life, promised by the Prince of Peace to fallen man, to the aborigines of this country, the right was fairly acquired of disposing of their persons and their property at pleasure."[89] Adopting the religious bigotry and "civilized" arrogance of the potentates of the old world, John Marshall claimed in 1823 that the "religion and character" of the "heathens"—the Native inhabitants—"afforded an apology for considering them as a people over whom the superior genius of Europe might claim an ascendency."[90] Marshall found that these old world potentates had—and he did not disagree with them—"no difficulty in convincing themselves that they made ample compensation to the inhabitants of the new by bestowing on them civilization and Christianity in exchange for unlimited independence."[91]

The importation of this vicious doctrine into U.S. law—as Steve Newcomb has shown in *Pagans in the Promised Land* (and as we will see in our own examination of the text)—was largely Marshall's handiwork in *Johnson v. McIntosh*.[92] Various versions of the doctrine were in political discourse in the centuries that preceded the use that Marshall made of his unique version of the doctrine in his "trilogy," but there was no prior mention of that doctrine in federal law and still less in the Constitution. On the contrary, the Constitution, properly construed—that is construed in terms of respect for treaties as part of the supreme law of the land, and of the interpretation of treaties in terms of the requirements of the law of nations as understood by the framers—requires respect for the sovereignty of the Native Nations as the sovereignty of independent foreign states in American law toward whom the United States has binding obligations that it is not free to independently alter.

Marshall was not as forthcoming as Senator Forsyth when it came to the "right," which the latter explicitly claimed, of "disposing" of the Native persons and their property "at pleasure."[93] Marshall recognized that something that he called the Indian title of "occupancy" stood in the way, but by adopting the mythology of Christian discovery—by claiming a spurious "ultimate dominion" in the United States—he ensured that this Indian title wasn't much of a legal obstacle to genocide.[94] Such title could help constitute a legal obstacle, in Marshall's eyes, to the claim that genocidal conduct on the part of the state of Georgia was that state's right, but was no legal obstacle at all to genocidal conduct on the part of the United States. Much the same could be said with regard to the treaties between the United States and the Cherokee Nation—they were no legal obstacle at all to genocide on the part of the United States as far as Marshall was concerned because the United States had "sovereignty and dominion" over the Native Nations.[95] In the end, Marshall's premises and Forsyth's were much the same. As Forsyth put it: "The lands, the streams, the woods, the minerals, all living things, including the human inhabitants, were all the property of, or subject to, the Government of the fortunate navigator, who, by accident or design, first saw the before unknown country."[96] As Marshall put it in *Johnson*, the mere presence of representatives of a "Christian people" on this side of the Atlantic "necessarily diminished" the sovereignty of the "heathens"—the Native peoples—and gave an "ultimate dominion" to the discoverers whereby they claimed a "title" over the land and a "right" to dominate the Native peoples—a "degree of sovereignty" over them—to be possessed by their government.[97]

In a famous sentence, Marshall claimed that "Conquest gives a title which the courts of the conqueror cannot deny."[98] In fact, far from being unable to deny a fraudulent claim of conquest on the part of the "conqueror," the Treaty Supremacy Clause of the Constitution mandated that the judges of the Supreme Court adopt such a position of denial toward any claim at odds with America's treaty obligations to the Native Nations. The heart of Marshall's fraudulent claim in *Johnson*—a claim adopted in violation of his oath of office—was exclusively a product of Marshall's turgid imagination without foundation in law or fact.[99] This was the assertion that "discovery" somehow *is*" conquest"—that "discovery" somehow "*gave also a right to such a degree of sovereignty as the circumstances of the people would allow them to exercise.*"[100] In other words, that the invaders had a "right" to dominate subject only to a Native capacity for resistance with their "degree of sovereignty" (an absurd and self-contradictory concept) varying accordingly with the strength of that resistance.

As New York Congressman Henry Storrs responded to the same nonsense when it appeared in the 24 February 1830 report of the House Committee on Indian Affairs: "I deny that our English ancestors, who first colonized these States, ever countenanced that disregard of Indian rights, or carried into practice that system of injustice to the Native inhabitants, which has been asserted in the report of the Committee on Indian Affairs." [101] Emphasizing that it was essential to title by conquest to actually make use of the rights granted by the laws of war, Storrs noted that this had *not* been done: "Have we taken away their lands, abolished their governments, and put them in subjection to our government? If this has not been done, (and history shows that it has not,) it is too late now to say that there has been a time when we might have done it."[102] Far from claiming to exercise this right, hostilities had been closed by treaties ever since the United States became an independent government. Moreover, one might add—even if it were true that each of these treaties had been signed in bad faith in an effort to persuade an apparently independent people that they were to be treated as independent when actually the intent was to claim that they were "conquered" and proceed to seek to make that so—once the Constitution was ratified any treaties made became the supreme law of the land and such guarantees to the Native Nations as these treaties contained or implied became binding American law.

What Marshall offered—indeed imposed—on American law, was nothing less than an evil fantasy version of the past that became an accurate description of the genocidal future that this version of the past established. In this fantasy the United States had boldly acquired rights "by the sword" and by "conquest" when, in truth, as Congressman Storrs told the House of Representatives in 1830, the United States had claimed no such right of conquest and instead "have closed our hostilities by treaties ever since we became an independent Government, and both parties were restored to their original condition"—in other words the politico-military situation at the end of every conflict was such that each side was restored with the adoption of a treaty to their original condition as an independent and sovereign foreign state—"except on points which treaties provided for."[103]

And so it is essential to acknowledge that "conquest," as law professor Joseph William Singer has observed, "is not something that happened in the distant past which cannot be corrected." On the contrary, it is something that *never* happened and thus, I would add, is no basis at all for any valid legal claim to title in the United States. Rather, as Singer observes, the Supreme Court is *still* "attempting to conquer Indian nations *now* by its failure to protect tribal property rights and inherent sovereignty."[104] In other words, attempted conquest is the unconstitutional activity that the United States Supreme Court has been engaged in since 1823—the illegal activity that masks itself as "federal Indian law." This attempted conquest is a violation not only of the Constitution but also, as Storrs noted—and even Marshall acknowledged in a backhanded sort of way—of the laws of war themselves.[105] It is a base and cowardly fraud and those Supreme Court justices who participate in that fraud to this day do so because—knowingly or unknowingly—they have accepted the arguments of the advocates of genocide and their appeasers.

In the debate in the United States Congress in 1830, Senator Theodore Frelinghuysen of New Jersey gave voice to an alternative mythology of the past that conflicted with the doctrine of Christian discovery. Like Marshall's account in *Johnson*, Frelinghuysen's account before the Senate was a mythological one. But unlike Marshall, Frelinghuysen offered a version of the past that was compatible with a measure of respect for the national rights of the Native Nations in American constitutional law. Frelinghuysen naively maintained that the United States had dealt honorably with the Native peoples: "It is a subject full of grateful satisfaction, that, in our public intercourse with the Indians, ever since the first colonies of white men found abode on these Western shores, we have distinctly recognized their title, treated with them as owners, and in all our acquisitions of territory, applied ourselves to these ancient proprietors, by purchase and cession alone, to obtain the right of the soil."[106] As Congressman Storrs made the point—in countering Georgia's claims to have acquired its lands by "discovery" and "conquest"—"There is not a foot of land now held by Georgia, for which we cannot produce, from authentic history, her title by purchase from the Indian nations."[107] Much the same argument was made by the plaintiff in *Johnson v. McIntosh*: "In short, all, or nearly all, the lands in the United States, is holden under purchases from the Indian nations."[108]

The treaties by which changes in possession and occupancy of the land had actually taken place, whether by cession as part of a peace settlement after a war, or by cession through "purchase," were claimed by the advocates of genocide (falsely) to have been a matter of expediency not law. In the words of the report of the House Committee on Indian Affairs of 24 February 1830: "These treaties were, therefore, but a mode of government, and a substitute for ordinary legislation."[109] This claim contrasts sharply with the principles, and even some of the practices, of the framers of the Constitution and the administration of President George Washington. As the historian Colin G. Calloway reminds us, "in Washington's day the government dealt with Indians as foreign nations rather than domestic subjects."[110]

That all a foreign state in the sense of the Constitution was to the framers was another state possessing dominion—and that the Indian Tribes qualified as such—is clear from President Washington's successful appeal to the Senate of the United States in 1789 to establish the practice of ratifying treaties made with the Native Nations: "It doubtless is important that all treaties and compacts formed by the United States with other nations, whether civilized or not, should be made with caution and executed with fidelity."[111] The issue, in other words, was simply one of good faith versus bad faith: were treaties with a Native people worth the paper they were printed on? The issue was not obscure to the Senate which agreed to Washington's appeal.

At the third level, then, this is a book about what constitutional law *is* and what it requires with regard to relations with the Native Nations—that it requires, at a minimum, treating these nations the way the opponents of genocide argued that they should be treated rather than as the United States has treated them. My argument is not that the Constitution is some sort of utterly just document. The Constitution can be seen as an expression of the Enlightenment of the eighteenth century. As such it is part of deeper intellectual and political stirrings within Christendom that were both national and European—part of a supremacist expansionism that can be seen to have begun with Henry the Navigator and which involved

Christians coming to see themselves as the heirs and national successors of Israel in their relationships with God and in their conduct toward those outside of the sacred community—outside of Christendom or outside of any particular Christian nation. [112] This is the foundation on which nationality and nationalism have emerged as the principal recognized communities of belonging in the modern world and the principal ideological perspective from which politics are viewed and understood.[113] This supersessionist thinking about European nations, this quasi-secularized religious perspective, was, as the theologian Willie James Jennings has argued, part of the origin of whiteness and white supremacy—the "womb" in which it matured.[114] There is a part of what the Chinese philosopher Tu Weiming calls "the Enlightenment mentality" that struggles with the supremacist expansionism that predominates within it—a part that we might call "democratic."[115] But it struggles on the basis of a provincial and radically inadequate conception of what is "universal"—a conception that can itself be turned to the purposes of supremacist expansionism, the purposes of a politics of domination.[116] The same point applies to European Christianity. Neither democracy nor Christianity have, as yet, really begun to appreciate the societies of the Native Nations of Turtle Island and their original conceptions of what is involved in being a people living in relationship with this land in contrast with what "nationhood" means in Europe or in the countries that Europe has sought to dominate which have experienced a measure of nationalist "decolonization."

European aspirations to scientific universality were both an engine for the penetration of those outside of Europe and a potential source of self-restraint where the nations outside of Europe were seen as equals in their relationship to God or to a common humanity. While the advocates of "self-restraint"—the advocates of respecting the equal rights of others under the same international moral and legal order in which one claimed one's own rights—were rarely in the ascendancy, they exercised a decisive influence on the Constitution's Treaty Supremacy Clause. It was that clause that James Wilson, clarifying the intentions of the framers, would proudly champion in the Pennsylvania ratifying convention: "This clause, sir, will show the world that we make the faith of treaties a constitutional part of the character of the United States; that we secure its performance no longer nominally, for the judges of the United States will be enabled to carry it into effect, let the legislatures of the different states do what they may."[117] In other words, as we will see in greater detail in chapter seven, the framers envisioned—in the Treaty Supremacy Clause—the judicial review of state legislation affecting the United States' treaty-obligations that is inherent in the Constitution's establishing treaties as part of the supreme law of the land, guaranteeing plaintiffs the right to compel states to submit to the Supreme Court under its original jurisdiction in all cases arising under treaties in which a state is a party to the case! They envisioned the United States breaking with the European past and maintaining covenantal relationships with all nations.

The imperial powers of Europe had come to see those outside of Christendom—in the words of Pope Nicholas V's bull—as "Saracens" or "pagans" or "other enemies of Christ" with devastating consequences for other peoples and ultimately for the peoples of Europe as well when the arrogance, hatred, and violence they put out into the world returned in the American Civil War, two world wars, a long cold war, and a "war on terror," each of which also involved still more suffering for non-European peoples. The Eurochristian peoples—including the American people as a Eurochristian people in this regard—themselves have suffered from secularizations of the old supremacist expansionism, such as Communism, fascism, and white supremacy. Communism, it might be noted, presented itself as a form of opposition to the old order while actually embracing the worst aspects of that order's adherence to a politics of domination.[118] Its specific form of dominationist politics—often described as totalitarianism—deeply influenced the totalitarianism of fascism and Nazism as well.[119] This is an approach to politics that remains a powerful cautionary tale against using the tools of the dominant culture in any effort to end domination.

There is some truth to President Bill Clinton's claim, in his second inaugural address in 1997, that during the twentieth century the United States "became the world's mightiest industrial power, saved the world from tyranny in two world wars and a long cold war, and time and again reached across the globe to millions who, like us, longed for the blessings of liberty."[120] The problem with this claim is, first, that it ignored the broader historical context in which these conflicts can all be seen as rooted in western imperialism's culture and politics of domination and its brutal approach to the non-European parts of the world; second, that it ignored the genocides and land thefts and slavery that are part of the foundation of the United States itself and its industrial power; and, third, that it assumed the relative "blessings of liberty" (on those occasions when they were in fact shared and not undermined by American actions) are to be celebrated as if they were part of the "End" of "History" rather than a detour from or a prelude to the recovery and widespread adoption of something closer to the original free and independent existence of the Native Nations—what Peter d'Errico has described as an Indigenous nomos of the earth.[121]

Whether it is possible to reconcile the best of the jurisprudence of the framers of the Constitution (the jurisprudence of James Wilson and his allies) with Indigenous ideas of law is an open question. The latter are based in relationships among all within the web of life whose unity and diversity and equality are a given. The ideas of the former, on the other hand, are based in abstract systems of thought that aspire to recognizing the equality of all under a rule of law designed to protect a global common good that embraces the common good of every nation and every national. In the very act of calling for universal equality, however, these thinkers rearticulate a hierarchical order by implicitly defining an inferior "them" in need of being "raised" to full equality and by insisting on the administration (by elites) of the law everyone is to be "under." In short, a politics of domination is rejected by the one and seems inherent in the other. Perhaps if the global common good is seen as embracing the common good of every entity that exists—and every entity is seen as a unique expression of everything else in the universe—some measure of harmony might be reached.

It is of limited importance whether the "plenary power" that the United States claims over the Native Nations of much of Turtle Island is seen to derive from the doctrine of "Christian discovery"—as articulated in the assertion in *Johnson v. McIntosh* of an "ultimate dominion" in the United States, and a "necessarily diminished" Native sovereignty, consequent on some representatives of a "Christian people" showing up on this side of the Atlantic—or is seen rather as somehow appearing *sui generis* in the subsequent claim in *Cherokee Nation v. Georgia* that the Native Nations are "completely under the sovereignty and dominion of the United States."[122] I do *not* intend to suggest that the doctrine of Christian discovery must be seen as the only possible origin of a politics of domination and dehumanization. But the doctrine of discovery—as Marshall understood it (and he persuaded a unanimous Supreme Court to agree with him)—was certainly the source Marshall began his evil work with and from: the foundation for the system to which the Native Nations have been subject since the Marshall trilogy. Clearly, more recent Supreme Court decisions have dropped any reference to "Christianity" from the doctrine of discovery that the Court continues to enunciate, and continues to appeal to, as a source of "plenary power" over the Native Nations (by continuing to cite *Johnson* and cases that depend on *Johnson*).

This is part of a pattern in "federal Indian law" of the Supreme Court's trying to obscure the foundation of the law by changing the names involved in prior understandings of the law and, indeed, in this dishonest way, to change the law itself from one of binding obligations compatible with James Wilson's revolutionary jurisprudence into a "law" compatible with the licentiousness of John Marshall's reactionary jurisprudence all the while disguising such changes with a series of new names as if constitutional law had not been viciously transformed in the process. In other words, all that was necessary to break faith with the Cherokee Nation and the framers of the Constitution was a willingness on the part of the justices on the Supreme Court to lie—to claim that one can change the terms of an agreement with a foreign nation by unilaterally ceasing to call it "foreign" and calling it "domestic" and "dependent" instead.[123] And then to double down on that dishonesty by eliding the word "Christian" from the rationale for the Supreme Court's grotesque misconduct as if that elision could make the unconstitutional religious rationale for the "doctrine of discovery" somehow secular and innocuous.

Law professor Milner Ball has noted the profound conflict between the untrammeled authority claimed by the United States—"the sovereign"—over the Native Nations on the one hand and the self-understanding that the American people have of their government and Constitution on the other:

> In the hands of the federal government, power over the tribes is said to be plenary in the singular modern sense of "unlimited." With plenary power, Congress and now the Court may dismantle tribes as they wish. No provision of the Constitution sanctions the exercise of a plenary power of this sort. The Court contends it is warranted by superiority. Because we say we have a government of laws and not men, we hold our government to be limited and to have no unlimited power. If the federal government nevertheless exercises unrestrained power over Indian nations, then what we say is not true, and we have a different kind of government than we think we have. And if our government is different in fact in relation to Native Americans, perhaps it is not what we believe it is in relation to other Americans, including ourselves. The Court is regarded as the institution of restraint and a protector of rights. If the Court restrains neither Congress nor itself in taking away tribal rights, then we are confronted by a fundamental contradiction between our political rhetoric and our political realities.[124]

In short, the premises on which the Supreme Court's precedents of *Johnson* and *Cherokee Nation* rest are repugnant to the Constitution as the framers intended it to function and as it should clearly function according to what the text itself says. To break America's treaty guarantees without just cause, as the Supreme Court did in *Johnson*—when it refused to recognize Native sovereign title and the treaty relationships to which it had given rise—and as it did in *Cherokee Nation*—when it denied that nation standing to sue the state of Georgia over Georgia's treaty violations—was a violation of the self-executing aspects of the Treaty Supremacy Clause. It was a refusal to respect the fact that Cherokee sovereign title had been explicitly guaranteed by treaty and therefore was no mere "right of occupancy," but rather a treaty-guaranteed dominion. The refusal to respect the rights of the Cherokee Nation to its dominion was a usurpation on the part of the judiciary of the power to make war and an act of aggression against every Native people over whom the Supreme Court continues to assert (falsely) an American "ultimate dominion."[125] It rests on a refusal to accept the intentions of the framers and the clear meaning of the Constitution's text: "all Treaties made, or which shall be made, under the Authority of the

United States, shall be the supreme Law of the Land; and the Judges in every State shall be bound thereby, any Thing in the Constitution or Laws of any State to the Contrary notwithstanding."[126]

This claim about the United States Constitution and, especially, about the equal rights of the Native peoples as independent foreign states—as the sovereigns of nations who are treaty partners—to make use of the Supreme Court in defense of their national rights (just the same in constitutional law as any other foreign powers) is sustained in this book by the arguments of the Cherokee Nation and of its lawyers before the Supreme Court in 1831, by Associate Justices Smith Thompson's and Joseph Story's dissent in *Cherokee Nation v. Georgia,* by the arguments of the opponents of removal in the Congress in 1830, by a review of two key opinions from the Attorney General of the United States (one in 1821 and the other in 1828), by the jurisprudence of the constitutional framer James Wilson, by the rhetoric (and at least some of the conduct) of the Washington administration, by a review of some of the debates and discussions in the constitutional convention and some of the ratifying conventions as well as by the clear logico-grammatical implications of the text of the Constitution to an informed contemporary reader and by a careful critique of John Marshall's reasoning, especially in his so-called "trilogy"—*Johnson, Cherokee Nation,* and *Worcester*—and including a comparison with his approach in *Cohens v. Virginia* (1821) that demonstrates, as Peter d'Errico puts it, the "incoherence and mendacity in Marshall's refusal to hear the Cherokee case."[127]

Although this book emphasizes the importance of the reactionary jurisprudence of John Marshall and his allies in the genocide of the 1830s, in sharp contrast with the revolutionary jurisprudence of James Wilson and his allies, the sad fact is that even the latter bears some responsibility for the trajectory of the United States' law, policy, and conduct toward Indigenous peoples. In his first law lecture at what would become the University of Pennsylvania in 1790, Wilson boasted: "We have passed the Red Sea in safety: we have survived a tedious and dangerous journey through the wilderness: we are now in full and peaceable possession of the promised land: must we, after all, return to the flesh pots of Egypt? Is there not danger, that when one nation teaches, it may, in some instances, give the law to another?"[128] Some such fear, though perhaps rooted in an understandable desire to be free from antidemocratic British precedents, is at the foundation of the United States'—and the American people's—relative unwillingness to learn from anyone else and, particularly, to learn from the peoples of the Native Nations from whom there is so much to learn. There was a belief, even in the best of American revolutionary thought, that a worthwhile community could be cultivated and extended by benevolent authority rather than a recognition that the beloved community always already exists and that its further realization can only be fostered by love and only obstructed by efforts to "create" unity through a culture and a politics of domination.

* * *

"History furnishes no parallel case of palpable injustice and cruelty, committed, or allowed, by the mass of the inhabitants of a great country, after ample time for deliberation," Jeremiah Evarts wrote in November 1830 on the cusp of the Trail of Tears.[129] "Nothing of this kind has ever yet been done, certainly not on a large scale, by Anglo-Americans," he had observed the year before: "To us, as a nation, it will be a new thing under the sun. We have never yet acted upon the principle of seizing the lands of peaceable Indians, and compelling them to remove. We have never yet declared treaties with them to be mere waste paper."[130] And shall we, Evarts asked in 1830, "in this early age, of our growing Nation, after exhibiting to the world most illustrious examples of public virtue, suddenly cast away, as a worn-out Government, all regard to our national character, all respect for the opinions of mankind, all respect for ourselves, all consideration of our permanent interests, and all fear of God, the Avenger of the oppressed?"[131]

Nearly two hundred years later, Evarts' questions still resound in the ears of attentive listeners. One should come away from this book with a horrified sense of how hard it was for the nation's institutions to "see" clearly what in retrospect is so obvious: the incompatibility of the doctrine of discovery (and, with it, the officially imagined foundations of property law in the United States after 1823) with justice for the Native Nations. One should see clearly the ongoing injustice of American conduct toward these nations in terms of our ongoing violations of the promises of our own

Constitution as well as our ongoing violations of our treaties. One should come away with a bitter awareness of how readily the United States took the decisions that led to genocide, with a detailed knowledge of the considerable opposition to genocide—in both public and elite opinion—and with a detailed sense of specific junctures at which other courses were available to those with sufficient decency and courage to choose them, as well as some of the choices that remain at this day. For the situation of "federal Indian law" in the United States at the present day is analogous to a situation that can hardly be imagined—a Germany today in which the anti-Semitic Nuremberg laws were still on the books and enforced. One should finish this book with a firm grasp of the arguments on all sides, premises as well as conclusions.

Chapter 2
The Debate in the Senate

When the removal bill reached the floor of the Senate, on 9 April 1830, with its provision for an exchange of lands with the Indians residing in any of the states or territories, and their removal west of the Mississippi river, New Jersey Senator Theodore Frelinghuysen offered an amendment that struck at the heart of Georgia's program of coercion: "That, until the said tribes or nations shall choose to remove, as by this act is contemplated, they shall be protected in their present possessions, and in the enjoyment of all their rights of territory and government, as heretofore exercised and enjoyed, from all interruptions and encroachments." And that the Indians' rights, "shall be stipulated for, secured, and guaranteed, by treaty or treaties, as heretofore made."[132]

Speaking in support of his amendment, Frelinghuysen argued that the very character of the United States was at stake: "We, whom God has exalted to the very summit of prosperity—whose brief career forms the brightest page in history; the wonder and praise of the world; freedom's hope, and her consolation; we, about to turn traitors to our principles and our fame—about to become the oppressors of the feeble and to cast away our birthright! Sir, I hope for better things."[133] Frelinghuysen traced the history of American treaties with the Cherokee people and their solemn guarantees of Cherokee lands, stressing the Indians' ownership of their own lands and the decency with which this ownership had been respected in the past: "It is a subject full of grateful satisfaction, that, in our public intercourse with the Indians, ever since the first colonies of white men found abode on these Western shores, we have distinctly recognized their title, treated with them as owners, and in all our acquisitions of territory, applied ourselves to these ancient proprietors, by purchase and cession alone, to obtain the right of the soil."[134]

Quoting Vattel, Frelinghuysen argued that the rule of international law on the subject of Cherokee political rights was clear: "one community may be bound to another by a very unequal alliance, and still be a sovereign State.

Though a weak State, in order to provide for its safety, should place itself under the protection of a more powerful one, yet, if it reserves to itself the right of governing its own body, it ought to be considered as an independent State."[135] The Southern Indians had never relinquished this right, and it had always been recognized by the United States. Quoting the text of the Treaty of Hopewell, he noted that any American citizen resident on Cherokee lands six months after ratification of the treaty forfeited the protection of the United States "and the Indians may punish him or not as they please."[136] Under the Constitution of the United States, these treaties were declared "to be the supreme law of the land, any thing in the constitution or laws of any state to the contrary notwithstanding."[137] In the words of the Treaty of Holston, "The United States solemnly guarantee to the Cherokee nation all their lands not hereby ceded."[138] These treaties were submitted to the Senate, and Georgia, "by her able representatives in the Senate, united in the ratification of these same treaties, without, in any single instance, raising an exception, or interposing a constitutional difficulty or scruple."[139] How can Georgia, after all this, Frelinghuysen asked, desire or attempt, and how can we quietly permit her, to invade the property, rights, and liberty of the Indians? "How can we tamely suffer these States to make laws … for the avowed purpose of inflicting the gross and wanton injustice of breaking up their Government—of abrogating their long cherished customs, and annihilating their existence as a distinct people?"[140]

> Sir, our fears have been addressed in behalf of those states whose legislation we resist: and it is inquired with solicitude, would you urge us to arms with Georgia? No, sir. This tremendous alternative will not be necessary. Let the General Government come out, as it should, with decided and temperate firmness, and officially announce to Georgia, and the other States, that if the Indian tribes choose to remain, they will be protected against all interference and encroachment; and such is my confidence in the sense of justice in the respect for law, prevailing in the great body of this portion of our fellow-citizens, that I believe they would submit to the authority of the nation. I can expect no other issue. But if the General Government be urged to the crisis, never to be anticipated, of appealing to the last resort of her powers; and when reason, argument, and persuasion

> fail, to raise her strong arm to repress the violations of the supreme law of the land, I ask, is it not in her bond, sir? Is her guarantee a rope of sand? This effective weapon has often been employed to chastise the poor Indians, sometimes with dreadful vengeance, I fear; and shall not their protection avail to draw it from its scabbard?....Let such decided policy go forth in the majesty of our laws now, and, sir, Georgia will yield. She will never encounter the responsibilities or the horrors of a civil war. But if she should, no stains of blood will be on our skirts; on herself the guilt will abide forever.[141]

Georgia's Senator John Forsyth began his response, on 15 April 1830, by noting that Frelinghuysen clearly intended the Indians in New York, New England, Virginia and elsewhere to be left to the tender mercies of those states while the arm of the federal government was to be extended to protect the Choctaw, Chickasaw, Creek, and especially, the Cherokee Nation from the anticipated oppressions of Mississippi, Alabama, and Georgia. To the claim that the bloodshed would be on Georgia's head if the Executive were to adopt the course recommended by Frelinghuysen, Forsyth replied that "although we dread no responsibility, I have so much kindness for the Senator as to wish to satisfy him, that there is no occasion for an assault upon us, notwithstanding he displayed so little sympathy for the whites—a circumstance not wonderful, however—having exhausted all his sympathy upon the red men, none for the whites could be reasonably looked for from him."[142] A more sympathetic view of Georgia's position, Forsyth suggested, would be sufficient to vindicate it.

Quoting the Treaty of Hopewell, Forsyth maintained that the United States had obtained the power of legislation over the Cherokee Nation: "For the benefit and comfort of the Indians, and for the prevention of injuries or oppressions on the part of the citizens or Indians, the United States in Congress assembled, shall have the sole and exclusive right of regulating trade with the Indians, and managing all their affairs in such manner as they think proper."[143] This power, he then argued, the United States had ceded to Georgia in the compact of 1802. According to that compact, the United States "cede to the State of Georgia, whatever claim, right or title, they may have to the jurisdiction and soil of any lands, lying within the United States, and out of the proper boundaries of any other State, and situated south of the Southern boundaries of the States of Tennessee, North Carolina, and South Carolina and east of the boundary line herein above described."[144]

As to Frelinghuysen's claim that the Cherokee Indians were the owners of the soil, Forsyth responded that he had thought the "European doctrine of the right conferred by the discovery of new countries, inhabited by barbarous tribes" was well known. "The lands, the streams, the woods, the minerals, all living things, including the human inhabitants, were all the property of, or subject to, the Government of the fortunate navigator, who, by accident or design, first saw the before unknown country."[145] Forsyth argued that under the Constitution the Congress was not intended to have any special authority over those Indians that were taxed and subjected to State laws, but rather only to regulate commerce with tribes of Indians not taxed, and contended that "If their separate existence as a tribe is destroyed by State legislative enactments, the control of the Government of the United States, even over the commerce with them is at an end."[146] Forsyth then came to an equally twisted, brutally dishonest, and absolutely essential part of his argument:

> That the President has made, with the advice and consent of the Senate, various contracts with Indians and called them treaties, is not to be denied. That various contracts have been made with Indians, by States and individuals, under the superintendence of the United States, is certain; they have been submitted, too, to the Senate, voted upon as, and have been called, treaties. What I assert is, that these instruments are not technically treaties, supreme laws of the land, superior in obligation to State constitutions and State laws. Can it be believed that the stern jealousy of the State Governments gave to the United States the power to use a miserable fragment of the population of a State, to extend, indefinitely, their authority, and narrow that of the State Government?... How, then, can a contract made with a petty dependent tribe of half starved Indians be properly dignified with the name, and claim the imposing character of, a treaty?[147]

As for those who would make claims on behalf of the Cherokee government, that government was of no consequence except as it operated to improve the Indians moral, physical, and intellectual conditions. But in fact it sanctioned polygamy, allowed horse thieves to be put to death by the rightful owner in the heat of passion, and interfered, by severe penalties, with the personal rights of its people, to remain or to remove at their pleasure, to sell or retain their improvements at their own discretion.

> It is for this Government, he desires to compel the President to make war upon a State. For disputing its authority and annulling its laws, he calls down upon Georgia the thunder of Divine wrath. Verily, sir, it requires the exertion of some forbearance, to dismiss this subject without farther remarks upon the opinions and sentiments which the gentleman has expressed. For his misapplied, and, if successful, mischievous efforts, I trust he will receive the appropriate reward: that not the poor Cherokees who remove to the West, only, may look back to bless him, but that he may receive the blessings of all the Cherokees, of those who remain and those who remove. For his prejudiced examination, and unjust condemnation of our cause, our curses will not follow him. Charitably believing in the purity of his motives, giving him credit for honest but mistaken zeal, if unable to correct, we can at least pardon his errors.[148]

Noting that Forsyth's strong language and triumphant tone had made "an evident impression upon the members of the Senate," Maine's Senator Peleg Sprague suggested that Forsyth's arguments be carefully examined.[149] The power given to the United States by the Treaty of Hopewell was strictly personal and fiduciary. To illustrate the point, Sprague drew an analogy. By the Constitution, "Georgia has given the United States the right to legislate, in certain cases, over her citizens, for their benefit; for example, to organize, arm, discipline, and call forth her militia. Can the United States transfer this right to South Carolina, or any other sovereign?"[150] As for the right of discovery under international law, it "confers no claim or right against the Natives, the persons discovered, but only as between discoverers."[151]

> We are next told that the constitution recognizes the right of the respective State Legislatures to pass their laws over, and annihilate these communities, by that clause in the first article, which provides that an enumeration of inhabitants, as a basis for representation, shall be made "excluding Indians not taxed"…. By what imaginable process could these words "Indians not taxed," produce the magical effect of annulling the Treaty of Hopewell, then existing in full force? Let us substitute the word aliens for Indians. The clause would then exclude "aliens not taxed." Will it be contended that foreigners existing as a nation, with whom we had treaties as such, would be subject to the laws of a State? Would it not apply exclusively to the aliens, who had separated themselves from the nation and mingled with our citizens?[152]

As for the idea that treaties with Indians were not treaties, Sprague contended that this amounted to nothing less than the assertion "that every President and every Senate have been guilty of usurpation, in extending the treaty-making power beyond its legitimate objects: for if these contracts are not treaties, within the true meaning of the constitution, they could be made only by the authority of Congress" as a whole.[153] To the claim that Georgia was being unfairly singled out and the repeated question as to why it could not extend its laws over the Indians as other states had done, Sprague replied: "our treaties—our treaties. The Indians object, and the United States have solemnly promised, to interpose at their request. In no other instances have they opposed State legislation, and demanded our interposition. This is a sufficient answer."[154]

> Sir, we cannot wholly silence the monitor within. It may not be heard amidst the clashings of the arena, in the tempest and convulsions of political contentions; but its 'still small voice' will speak to us—when we meditate alone at eventide—in the silent watches of the night—when we lie down and rise up from a solitary pillow—and, in that dread hour, when, 'not what we have done for ourselves, but what we have done for others' will be our joy and our strength; when—to have secured, even to the poor and despised Indian a spot of earth upon which to rest his head—to have given him but a cup of cold

> water, in charity, will be a greater treasure than to have been the conquerors of kingdoms, and lived in luxury upon their spoils.[155]

While Sprague had attempted to deflect Forsyth's claim about the Treaty of Hopewell giving the United States the power over the Cherokee Nation of "managing all their affairs," there was a much more powerful answer which remained unspoken in the Senate debate. John Marshall would give it voice in *Worcester v. Georgia* in 1832:

> To construe the expression "managing all their affairs" into a surrender of self-government would be, we think, a perversion of their necessary meaning, and a departure from the construction which has been uniformly put on them. The great subject of the article is the Indian trade. The influence it gave made it desirable that Congress should possess it. The commissioners brought forward the claim with the profession that their motive was "the benefit and comfort of the Indians, and the prevention of injuries or oppressions." This may be true as respects the regulation of their trade and as respects the regulation of all affairs connected with their trade, but cannot be true as respects the management of all their affairs. The most important of these are the cession of their lands and security against intruders on them. Is it credible that they should have considered themselves as surrendering to the United States the right to dictate their future cessions and the terms on which they should be made? or to compel their submission to the violence of disorderly and licentious intruders? It is equally inconceivable that they could have supposed themselves, by a phrase thus slipped into an article on another and most interesting subject, to have divested themselves of the right of self-government on subjects not connected with trade. Such a measure could not be "for their benefit and comfort," or for "the prevention of injuries and oppression." Such a construction would be inconsistent with the spirit of this and of all subsequent treaties, especially of those articles which recognise the right of the Cherokees to declare hostilities and to make war. It would convert a treaty of peace covertly into an act, annihilating the political existence of one of the parties. Had such a result been intended, it would have been openly avowed.[156]

Attempting to deflect the implication that the advocates of the bill were unfriendly to the Indians, Mississippi Senator Robert Adams insisted that they wished the Indians to make a free and voluntary choice. "The friends of this measure do not wish to vest power in the President of the United States to assign a district of country west of the Mississippi, and, by strong arm, to drive these people from their present abode, and compel them to take up their residence in the country assigned to them."[157] But the idea that the Indian title could be awakened from its "sleep of ages" and urged as "prior and paramount to that of civilized nations" Adams rejected. Those who were convinced that civilized man had lawlessly usurped the territory and dominion of the barbarian should show some consistency and "call them back from the deep wilderness to which they have been driven."[158] That they had left by treaty and by cession was poor excuse: "for I am sure that, if the history of these transactions could be truly known, it would appear, that, if the one originated in force, the other was obtained by fraud."[159] This was how barbarians were dealt with. "Whilst the tribes were warlike and powerful, no matter what were the stipulations of treaties; no matter how much those treaties infringed the legislative rights of the States; all acquiesced: all submitted. But as soon as they became reduced to a handful; as soon as their power was lost, and they were no longer formidable, they fell from the cognizance of the General Government, and became subject to the control and legislation of the States."[160]

To this vision of inveterate savages who enjoyed rights relative to civilized people only when powerful, as a temporary expedient, Rhode Island's Senator Asher Robbins replied with an appeal to international and natural law and the binding legal character of treaties:

> It is said … that the Indian is an inveterate savage, and incapable of civilization. Admitting this to be the fact, which I by no means do admit, what has it to do with the question, whether his nation is *sui juris*, and competent to make a treaty. Is the Indian right less a right because the Indian is a savage? Or does our civilization give us a title to his right? A right which he inherits equally with us, from the gift of nature and of nature's God. The Indian is a man, and has all the rights of man. The same God who made us made him, and endowed him with the same rights; for "of one blood hath he made all the men

> who dwell upon the earth." And if we trample upon these rights, if we force him to surrender them, or extinguish them in his blood, the cry of that injustice will rise to the throne of God and there, like the blood of Abel, will testify against us. If we should be arraigned for the deed before his awful bar, and should plead our boasted civilization in its defence, it would, in his sight, but add deeper damnation to the deed, and merit but the more signal retribution of his eternal justice. As to the civilization of the Indian, that is his own concern in the pursuit of his own happiness; if the want of it is a misfortune, it is his misfortune; it neither takes from his rights nor adds to our own.[161]

These were the basic arguments that emerged in the Senate. The final vote was not even close. First Frelinghuysen's amendment was voted down and then, by 28 to 19, the removal bill was approved.[162] The vote in the House would be much more closely contested. Indeed, as a matter of their honor, it is worth stressing that about one in five Southern Congressmen voted against the bill, including Davy Crockett who would later lose his Congressional seat in part as a result.[163]

Chapter 3
The Debate in the House

The lead speaker in the opposition to the removal bill in the House was Congressman Henry Storrs of New York. He began his argument, on 15 May 1830, by saying that if he believed the real object of the bill was to provide a country west of the Mississippi for Tribes who freely wished to move there, he would support it. But as he was convinced that it was chiefly intended to assist the efforts of Georgia, Alabama, and Mississippi in their measures to remove the Indians, "and finding a purpose so unjust to these people, and so mischievous to the reputation of the country, lurking under it, I cannot give it any countenance or support."[164] The unwillingness of the Jackson administration to defend the Cherokee people from Georgia's pretensions, and indeed its acceptance of much of Georgia's arguments, Storrs charged, had "virtually abrogated" treaties made by every administration going back to the first organization of the government.[165] The friends of "State rights," he suggested, were making a serious mistake. They had heard the alarm sounded and "rushed to the standard with an alacrity which leaves us no reason to doubt that they have really believed their favorite doctrines to be in jeopardy."[166] But what was really going on was a usurpation on the part of the President. It was the treaties that expressed the will of the States, "and not the capricious inclinations or the pleasure of the Executive Department."[167] If the President had followed his duty, he would have submitted the matter to Congress instead of seeking to extend executive prerogative. If the Congress yielded up the power over treaties claimed by the President, Storrs warned, one had only to look at history and read the fate of "all republics that have gone before us and perished; or, if we are not admonished by the past, to look around us, and see what is passing in the world in our own day."[168] What was now the condition of South America, in whose emancipation we felt so deep an interest, Storrs asked: "Disunion has blasted our hopes. Slavish Congresses have there betrayed their country, and the power of that whole continent is swayed by bands of reckless despots."[169]

The report of the Committee on Indian Affairs, Storrs charged, had projected theories the history of the country would not sustain. In particular, the report held that "'possession, actual or constructive, of the entire habitable portion of this continent, was taken by the nations of Europe, divided out and held originally by the right of discovery as between themselves, and by the right of discovery and conquest as against the original inhabitants;' that 'although the practice of the Crown of England was not marked with an equal disregard' (as that of Spain) 'of the rights of personal liberty in the Indians, yet their pretentions to be the owners of any portion of the soil were wholly disregarded;' that 'in all the acts, first of the colonies and afterwards by the States, the fundamental principle that the Indians had no rights, by virtue of their ancient possession, either of soil or of sovereignty, has never been abandoned either expressly or by implication.'"[170] Before proceeding to deal with these theories, Storrs challenged the entire enterprise of the Committee on Indian Affairs, both its rationality and its purpose:

> It would be much easier to get rid of our treaty obligations by assuming, at once, that Christian nations were not bound to keep their faith with infidels; and plentiful casuistry can be found for that, too. This matter is not to be disposed of in that way; nor will it be hereafter. It is too late for us to deny our claims to be considered a civilized people; that we are willing to acknowledge the public and social law of the human family, and to be bound by that code of universal morality which is confessed by every Government which feels it honorable to stand within the pale of Christian nations. It is not a trifling thing for us to start any principles, at this day, on which we may claim to absolve ourselves from the obligation of that faith which we have pledged in all our Indian treaties. The question is too solemnly settled.[171]

In the age of Columbus, Storrs asserted, "when the human mind was darkened by bigotry," it was not difficult to silence conscience and even enlist the religious feeling of mankind in favor of schemes of avarice and ambition.[172] But as moral and political science became emancipated from superstition and intolerance, the situation changed. Before the beginning of the eighteenth century, that great civilian and Christian moralist, Hugo

Grotius, had already given the true foundation of all original title: We have the right to take that which others have not already appropriated to themselves, but we have no right to take away our neighbor's property. "I deny that our English ancestors, who first colonized these States, ever countenanced that disregard of Indian rights, or carried into practice that system of injustice to the Native inhabitants, which has been asserted in the report of the Committee on Indian Affairs."[173] In point of fact, Storrs claimed, "There is not a foot of land now held by Georgia, for which we cannot produce, from authentic history, her title by purchase from the Indian nations."[174]

There were those, Storrs acknowledged, even commissioners to the Native Nations, who had maintained a claim along the lines of that propounded by the Committee on Indian Affairs, but that position had been explicitly repudiated by the Washington administration. In an effort to avoid war, in 1793, Secretary of War Henry Knox stressed precisely this point in his message to the Native Nations then confederated against the United States:

> Brothers—The commissioners of the United States have formally set up a claim to your whole country southward of the great lakes, as the property of the United States, grounding this claim on the treaty of peace with your father, the King of Great Britain, who declared, as we have before mentioned, the middle of those lakes, and the waters which unite them, to be the boundaries of the United States. Brothers—We are determined that our conduct shall be marked with openness and sincerity. We therefore frankly tell you that we think those commissioners put an erroneous construction on that part of our treaty with the King. As he had not purchased the country of you, he could not give it away. He only relinquished to the United States his claim to it. That claim was founded on a right acquired by treaty with other white nations, to exclude them from purchasing or settling in any part of your country, and it is this right which the King granted to the United States.... Brothers—We now concede this great point. We, by the express authority of the President of the United States, acknowledge the property or right of soil of the great country above described to be in the Indian nations, so long as they choose to occupy the same.[175]

Having addressed the claim of "discovery," Storrs turned his attention to the claim of "conquest." Emphasizing that it was essential to title by conquest to actually make use of the rights granted by the laws of war, he noted that this had not been done: "Have we taken away their lands, abolished their governments, and put them in subjection to our government? If this has not been done, (and history shows that it has not,) it is too late now to say that there has been a time when we might have done it."[176] Far from claiming to exercise this right, hostilities had been closed by treaties ever since the United States became an independent government. Why, then, had the laws of Georgia, Alabama and Mississippi been extended, Storrs asked, and what did this mean for the bill before the Congress?

> We are told that this bill is only to come in aid of their voluntary emigration. But you have had their answer to that for years. Your table is covered by their memorials and protests against it. You have made large appropriations before now to effect that object, and have failed. Why, then, are you repeating these appropriations at this particular time? They are at your door, and tell you they will not accept them. Is there not reason, then, to believe that they are to be removed against their real consent and inclinations, though no force is meditated in any quarter? Individuals may doubtless be found to surrender the lands of the nation which they happen to occupy. These lands then pass to Georgia. The nations are to be put at variance among themselves. Their social institutions are to be destroyed. The laws of the States have done that effectually. The lands surrendered are to be covered with white men. Can the Cherokees then live there? Is this the protection which you have promised? Is that the execution of your solemn guarantees? Is that your dealing with your plighted faith and national honor?[177]

Storrs declared that he would "not consider a treaty made with them in their present wretched and forsaken condition, as morally binding upon them."[178] Free them from all restraint and return them to perfect liberty and then make a treaty with them, if they wish. In such an event, he declared, "The treasure of the nation shall flow like water, and the people of this country will bear any burden rather than suffer the honor of their government to be stained with perfidy."[179] Let the feeling and judgement of the whole country be consulted. Once the bill was passed, Storrs told his fellow Congressmen, the matter would be beyond our reach and theirs. The memorials on your table "ought not to be lightly trifled with."[180] This was not something to be done in a corner. It affected the security of the social law of all mankind, which all nations are interested to maintain. These nations might not have a right to interfere, but they certainly had a right to sit in judgement. And ultimately, the judgement of history would have to be faced as well.

> But, sir, we must stand at last at the bar of posterity, and answer there for ourselves and our country. If we look for party influence to sustain us now, it will fail us there. The little bickerings in which we now bustle and show off our importance, will then have ceased and been forgotten, or little understood.... Our country will be brought by the historian—*custodia fidelis rerum*—to that standard of universal morality which will guide the judgment and fix the sentence of posterity.... You may not live to hear it, but there will be no refuge for you in the grave. You will yet live in history; and if your children do not disown their fathers, they must bear the humiliating reproaches of their names. Nor will this transaction be put down in history as a party measure. Our country, too, must bear the crime and the shame.[181]

On 17 May 1830, Congressman Wilson Lumpkin of Georgia began his response by denying that motives of concern for the material effects that might be produced on any of the interested states were anywhere near as important to him as solicitude for the condition of the Indians. The states could, at least to some extent, take care of themselves:

> But to those remnant tribes of Indians whose good we seek, the subject before you is of vital importance. It is a measure of life and death. Pass the bill on your table, and you save them. Reject it, and you leave them to perish. Reject this bill, and you thereby encourage delusory hopes in the Indians, which their professed friends and allies know will never be realized. The rejection of this bill will encourage and invite the Indians to acts of indiscretion and

> assumptions which will necessarily bring upon them chastisement and injury, which will be deplored by every friend of virtue and humanity.[182]

The only difference between the removal bill and past practice, Lumpkin claimed, was that the bill provided "greater security and benefits to the Indians."[183] The Cherokee had been going under the treaty of 1817, and would continue to go until not one real Indian will be left behind, if only they were "permitted to express their own true feelings, unawed by the tyrannical enactments of their mixed blood chiefs."[184] Noting that treaties had already been made with the Choctaw and the Creek, assigning to them countries west of the Arkansas and Mississippi, he claimed that the Chickasaw were "anxious to emigrate thither" and that the Seminole "are also desirous" to join their Creek brethren in the West.[185] It was surprising, Lumpkin repeated, to hear the removal bill described as novel and fraught with danger and ruin to the Indian given the records, laws, and treaties of the country. "I feel assured, if the good people who have been memorializing us through the winter were in possession of the facts which are within the reach of every member of this committee, they would change their politics, and unite with the friends of Indian emigration."[186] This was no new measure, Lumpkin insisted. President Jefferson gave it its first official impulse and presidents Madison, Monroe, Adams and Jackson had all sustained the principles and policy of the bill. A majority of Senators and Representatives had done so repeatedly. "We have been inundated with memorials, pamphlets, and speeches, made at society and town meetings," Lumpkin complained. "But, sir, let it be remembered that weak minorities always make the most noise. Contented majorities, conscious of their strength, are never found praying for a redress of grievances."[187] Those who were making a false plea of inability founded on the words "reasonable and peaceable" were engaging in "pettifogging quibbles" and deserving of pity and contempt: "No man is fit to be a Congressman, who does not know that the General Government might, many years ago, upon both reasonable and peaceable terms, have removed every Indian from Georgia."[188]

Lumpkin complained that the Cherokee Nation received "large annuities" from the American government, had a "rich treasury," and had turned these resources over to "northern intruders": "But for these annuities, we should not have been encumbered, throughout the session, with memorials from Maine to Steubenville, in Ohio. These self-interested reporters of the state and condition of the Cherokee Indians tell you that they are already a civilized and Christianized people."[189] But the principle part of Cherokee accomplishments, Lumpkin claimed, were confined to the blood of the white man, either in whole or in part: "few, very few of the real Indians participate largely in these blessings. A large portion of the full-blooded Cherokees still remain a poor degraded race of human beings."[190] The northern "intruders" and "fanatics" divided the spoil with the Cherokee rulers and left the common Indians to struggle with want and misery, "without hope of bettering their condition by any change but that of joining their brethren west of the Mississippi."[191] These western Cherokee were flourishing and enjoying the blessings of their emigrating enterprise. Lumpkin stressed that they included Sequoyah, whom he praised as "The Cadmus of the Cherokees."[192]

Congressman William Ellsworth of Connecticut prophesied in response that not twenty-five years would pass away before those who had moved west "will be in some white man's way."[193] And he directly challenged the claims to humanitarian motivation made by the advocates of the removal bill and their presumption in assuming that they knew what was best for another people:

> It has been said that the Indians in the southern States will soon become extinct—that humanity dictates their removal. Sir, why not leave the Indians to judge for themselves in this matter? They have the deepest interest in it, and they are sufficiently intelligent to discover what is best for themselves. Sir, I confess that I do not like this parade of humanity. Nor, if there be a willingness on the part of the Indians, would Georgia need to pass her extraordinary laws. But, sir, who constituted us judges over them? We may as well set ourselves up as judges for any other people—for Spain or France, for instance, and force upon them republican Government, if we thought it would be better for them.[194]

Cognizant of the depth of public opinion on the other side, Congressman Thomas Foster of Georgia sought to find a way to avoid its conclusions in his remarks. "We cannot shut our eyes to the fact that there is a strong and powerful feeling in favor of the Indians," he acknowledged, "which pervades an extensive portion of this country, the influence of which is very perceptible in this House." But it was "the very kind of feeling which is most calculated to mislead the judgment."[195] Free of such feeling, Foster suggested, it was clear that the right of discovery had eliminated Indian sovereignty. No one doubted that the discovering nation had a right to prohibit the Indians from disposing of their territory to any other nation or individuals. "And will it be pretended that a people who were denied the privilege of disposing of their own property, either as a nation or as individuals, and that by a foreign power, were sovereign? What kind of sovereignty is this which is subject to be thus qualified and controlled?"[196] In support of this position, he invoked the authority of the chief justice of the Supreme Court, John Marshall, in the 1823 case of *Johnson v. McIntosh*: "While the different nations of Europe respected the right of the Natives, as occupants, they asserted the ultimate dominion to be in themselves; and claimed and exercised, as a consequence of this ultimate dominion, a power to grant the soil, while yet in possession of the Natives. These grants have been understood by all, to convey a title to the grantees, subject only to the Indian right of occupancy."[197]

Armed with the conviction that the Cherokee people were not sovereign, Foster professed that the guarantee to the Cherokee nation in the Treaty of Holston was no problem: "Here the Cherokees have planted their standard, and run up the flag of independence, with 'UNITED STATES GUARANTY,' inscribed in staring capitals. Sir, I am not alarmed by this guaranty, imposing as it may be considered. I shall contend, and trust be able to show, that the United States had no right to make it; and, if so, Georgia certainly is not bound by it."[198] Portraying the federal government as possessed of a disposition to increase its powers, Foster then claimed that under the constitution it had the power only "to manage the affairs of the Indians, so that the legislative rights of the States should not be violated."[199] Georgia's legislative power was set at complete defiance by the Treaty of Holston, Foster maintained, adding that there could have been no thought that the guarantee in that treaty was designed "to authorize the

Cherokees to organize or establish an independent government."[200] Storrs' argument that there was something "arbitrary and despotic" about the way Andrew Jackson had interpreted the Treaty of Holston, Foster rejected:

> Whenever the execution of a treaty is confided to the President, he is necessarily clothed with the power of construing it; and so long as the executive chair is filled by our present Chief Magistrate, that power will be exercised. And whenever you attempt to compel him to adopt a construction of a treaty entrusted to his execution, which he believes to be unconstitutional, and then require him to act on that construction, he will tell you: "No, I cannot. If you choose to impeach me do so. Drag me to the bar of the Senate, and accuse me before that august tribunal; but I will not go to the bar of God with the damning sin upon my conscience of having openly and knowingly violated that great charter of our Government which I had solemnly sworn to support and defend."[201]

As for Storrs' quotes from Jefferson, Foster acknowledged the words: "the Indian tribes possess entire and unlimited sovereignty as long as they chose to keep it, and this might be forever."[202] He simply maintained that Jefferson could not have meant what those words import, for Jefferson also claimed that the United States have the right of "preventing other nations from taking possession of the Indian lands, and defeating our expectancy."[203] Georgia, Foster insisted, was determined to maintain its jurisdiction over all the territory within its chartered limits. Was it to be supposed, he asked, that she will submit to be restrained from the exercise of her rights by the arm of the general government? "No, sir, I assure you that she will not—her course is determined on, and she will pursue it with a resolution which no threats can intimidate, but with a justice and moderation which will leave no cause for reproach."[204]

Congressman George Evans of Maine found cause for reproach in any effort to deceive the Indians as to the nature of their rights or intimidate them into an acquiescence with our wishes. Is there, he asked, an objection from any quarter unless it be to a removal to be accomplished "by coercion, or force, or withholding from them that protection that we are bound to afford?"[205]

> The guarantee in the treaty of Holston is a guarantee to the Indians as a nation. No individual ownership is therein recognised; and when individuals leave the tracts on which they have resided, those tracts revert, not to the United States, nor to the Government, nor to anybody else but to the nation as a nation. But this bill contemplates a separate negotiation with individuals, and it declares that all the land abandoned by individuals who become emigrants, reverts not to their tribe, but to the State of Georgia. We are called to pass a law exchanging land with private individuals, when we have guaranteed the possession of that land to the Cherokee nation, as common property; so that we are not only to stand by, and see Georgia violate our faith, but to pass a bill—which very bill expressly violates it."[206]

As for the argument that the United States had no right to make the treaty of Holston, Evans noted that this right flowed from the delegation by the States to the United States of the power to make peace and war. The states had a power to repel invasion or imminent danger of invasion, but they had no power at all to make peace. The United States alone could do so. This was the foundation of the treaty of Holston.[207]

> Sir, it is a well known rule in morals and in common sense, that every one making a promise is bound by it in the sense in which he knows the other party to understand it. When Georgia, therefore, laid by, and saw and knew the promises which this Government was making to the Indians, and yielded her assent, shall she be precluded from asserting that either she or we are not bound, according to the sense we then knew the Indians put upon those promises? By this rule our guarantee is to be measured; and I, for one, will never move an inch to relieve a State which thus lies by, and permits us to enter into engagements, and receives the benefit of our contracts, and at last comes forward with the complaint that we had no right to make them. I say to Georgia, if we had no right without your consent, your consent has been obtained. It is too late. You are estopped.[208]

There was, Evans continued, a moral obligation beyond all treaties to keep promises in good faith in the day of our strength and power that were made in the day of our weakness. Yet the head of one of the committees of this

House has claimed that these engagements were mere "expedients" to obtain peace and get the Indian lands. "I am not," Evans declared, "willing to commit the honor of this nation to the gentlemen's keeping."[209]

> The great object of the gentleman is to procure the removal of the Indians; and to obtain their consent, he proposes in the bill that the President shall "solemnly guarantee"—the very words of the treaty of Holston—solemnly guarantee to them the country to which we propose to send them. The gentleman says that the guarantee in that treaty was "probably a device for the intimidation of the whites." Well, sir, let the project be executed, and, within a period that the gentleman may live to see, the whites will again press upon them, and say you must go—move further west. When the Indians inquire for what cause, the same reasons will be given then that are given now. All history shows that if you remain near us you will be destroyed. The red man cannot live in contact with the white. Humanity and your own interests require your removal. Besides, we have a right to the land. Our ancestors discovered it. Are we not civilized? And has not civilization a right to prevail over savage life? Suppose it be so, reply the Indians, but we were sent here not by our consent but by your power; and did you not "solemnly guarantee" to us these limits? Very true; but were you so ignorant as not to know that our guarantee was only an expedient? only a device? Had you not sagacity enough to perceive that it was only a plan to get rid of you? Were you not told by us at the time, that "Indian treaties were only a species of legislation?".... Sir, I have no doubt that the gentleman is sincere in the guaranties he proposes to give, and intends to bind the nation in all future time. If he should live to see his assurances thus explained and chaffered away, he will feel something of the emotion which Washington and the fathers of the country would have experienced, could they have anticipated that their solemn assurances are to be thus lightly regarded.[210]

Clearly stung by the line of argument, the chairman of the House Committee on Indian Affairs, Congressman John Bell of Tennessee, interrupted to say that the report had not been correctly understood—that he did not contend that the guarantee was not binding. Replying graciously, Evans offered to read any part of the committee's report that could clear up any misrepresentation. Bell declined to indicate any portion of the committee's report that could be read in response and Evans continued. He stressed Cherokee accomplishments: "They till the earth; they have mechanics' shops and trades, schools and churches; cultivated fields and flocks—have made great advances in civilization—formed a written code of government—established a press."[211] Where in history was there any indication that the condition of such a people could be improved by expelling them into the forest? The claim of Congressmen Bell and Lumpkin that the great mass of the Southern Indians were willing and anxious to remove, but were restrained and kept in awe by their chiefs, was presented without evidence. There was, however, testimony on the subject available from the missionary Samuel Worcester:

> It is said abroad that the common people would gladly remove, but are deterred by the chiefs and a few other influential men. It is not so. Nothing is plainer than that it is the earnest wish of the whole body of the people to remain where they are. They are not overawed by the chiefs. Individuals may be overawed by public opinion, but not by the chiefs. On the other hand, if there were a chief in favor of removal, he would be overawed by the people. He would know that he could not open his mouth in favor of such a proposition, but on pain, not only of the failure of his re-election, but of popular odium and scorn. The whole tide of national feeling sets, in one strong and unbroken current, against a removal to the West.[212]

If the bill was to pass in its present form, Evans concluded, it would stand on the same page of injustice as the blotting out of Poland from the map of nations at the close of the last century. It would stand by those enormities that England had practiced in India, and if no Edmund Burke were found to hold up the picture of the wrongs done to the Cherokee people to the execration of mankind, they would ultimately find "a higher tribunal, where sophistry cannot delude, and where the humblest Indian will be equal to his proudest oppressor."[213]

Speaking also against the bill, Congressman Isaac Bates of Massachusetts summarized his point of view succinctly: "My positions are, that the

Cherokees are not the tenants of Georgia, nor subject to her jurisdiction; but they are the sole proprietors of the territory they occupy, whether as hunting grounds or otherwise, and are sovereign; and that the United States are pledged to defend their boundary, to protect them in the enjoyment of all their rights and privileges as a nation."[214] Bates' fellow Congressman from Massachusetts, Edward Everett, stressed that the only constitutional way of acquiring title to Indian land was by cession after a war or by amicable agreement to purchase. He attacked the actions of Georgia, Alabama and Mississippi: "Here, then, the States step in with the novel, and, as I regard it and deem it fully proved in this debate, the unconstitutional and illegal extension of their ordinary civil and criminal jurisdiction over these tribes, accompanied with enactments peculiarly operative and oppressively binding on them."[215] It was force that was being used, claimed Everett, or else there was no force used against the Huguenots by the revocation of the Edict of Nantes.[216] The advocates of the removal bill were imagining a march of youthful Indian warriors, penetrating the forest with their accustomed vigor. It would be no such thing.

> They are to go in families, the old and the young, wives and children, the feeble, the sick. And how are they to go? Not in luxurious carriages; they are poor. Not in stage coaches; they go to a region where there are none. Not even in wagons, nor on horseback, for they are to go in the least expensive manner possible. They are to go on foot; nay, they are to be driven by contract.... A community of civilized people, of all ages, sexes, and conditions of bodily health, are to be dragged hundreds of miles, over mountains, rivers, and deserts, where there are no roads, no bridges, no habitations, and this is to be done for eight dollars a head; and done by contract.[217]

Everett asked his fellow Congressmen to imagine how they would stand if they were to go home and tell their constituents that they were to be removed, whole counties of them, to a distant desert beyond the Arkansas. That the money was voted and flying from the wrath of insupportable laws, go they must.[218] And what would the Indians do when they arrived across the Mississippi? "Can any man, on his responsibility, say, they will find wood and water, and soil, and access to market, and convenience of navigation, like what they have left?"[219] The Shawnees and Delawares of Cape Girardeau were doing well twenty years ago with good houses, little farms, and stocks in abundance. Now, after removal, they are in distress, roving the country in pursuit of subsistence. "I adjure you, sir, to re-cede; there is no disgrace in it. Other States, more powerful than Georgia, have re-ceded, on points where their honor and interest were equally involved."[220]

Congressman Richard Wilde of Georgia claimed in response that there were millions who were "silent and satisfied" with the course of the government. The feeling that had emerged on behalf of the Indians, if it was deep, was as sudden as it was deep.

> The Indians had nearly disappeared from eleven of the thirteen old States. They had perished, or removed, or been absorbed into the mass of the population. A few yet lingered—ghosts of old habits and lost dialects—dim shadows of departed tribes. Heretofore their gradual disappearance has produced no violent sensation. The legislation of the country, its arts, its agriculture, its commerce, its institutions, had all proceeded quietly on their march toward maturity and greatness, without alarm or remorse. Our population had advanced upon the wilderness with almost incredible rapidity, and no one was shocked when the hunter and his game retired before the hardy pioneers of Christianity and civilization.[221]

Like Mississippi Senator Robert Adams, Wilde sought to cast doubt on the idea that purchases of land from the Indians were anything more than "a legal or a pious fraud."[222] While disclaiming any disposition to enter into abstract or speculative doctrines on the subject of Indian title, he thought those who were would probably say that all property was founded on utility—on its tendency to sustain a greater portion of life, promote the happiness of human beings, and develop the intellectual and moral faculties of man.[223] "No treaty explicitly guaranties the sovereignty and soil to the Indians," he insisted: "The title guarantied is merely the occupancy, which, so far as he knew, was not proposed to be disturbed by the bill before them."[224] Then there were constitutional issues:

> By the constitution, a basis of representation is agreed on, and "Indians not taxed" are to be excluded. He was at a loss to conceive why this provision was necessary, or how it was applicable, unless the States had a right to include and tax them. In addition to this, the constitution guaranties to every State a "republican form of Government," and engages to protect them against invasion and domestic violence. How is this consistent with the existence of an Indian Government within the heart of a State independent of her laws? Moreover, "no new State shall be formed or erected within the jurisdiction of any other State."[225]

The Cherokee constitution, in Wilde's opinion, had barbarism distinctly stamped upon it. Its fundamental principle was that the land was to remain common and inalienable whereas separate property in land was the basis of civilized society. "This constitution was the work of white men and half breeds. Its object was to throw the power of the tribe, the lands, the offices, the annuities of the tribe, into their hands."[226] It was vain to say that the Cherokee Nation did not wish to go: "There is one argument which is conclusive: when was it found necessary to punish, by cruel and sanguinary punishments, any people for leaving a country which they had no mind to leave?"[227] As for the claim that the United States was discharged from its obligation to Georgia under the compact of 1802 because Cherokee title could not be extinguished "peaceably and on reasonable terms," Wilde said: "You are not discharged if the impossibility is of your own creating.... If you or your agents encouraged them to stay, when you ought to have induced them to go, you are not discharged."[228] If the treaty of 1817 had been faithfully executed, this part of the discussion would not be an issue:

> About six thousand Cherokees did emigrate to Arkansas. They did not ride in coaches there, to be sure: neither did they starve; nor have the other Indians massacred them; nor did they attack the white settlements; nor was the treasury ruined by the expense of their removal. Those were days of economy, too, sir. There they now are; and, by all we can learn, quite as well or better off than the bulk of their countrymen in Georgia.[229]

It was said that the race of Indians would perish, Wilde noted. But what was history, save the obituary of nations? Whose fate do we lament? The present generation of Indians? They will perish like the present generation of white men, he declared:

> And if it were possible to perpetuate the race of Indians, what would be the consequence? Why, that a hundred or a thousand fold the number of white men would not be born, because the Indians would roam over and possess, without enjoying, the land which must afford the future whites subsistence. And if our far-sighted, prospective humanity must weep over distant contingent generations, is it not as fair a subject of grief to lament the millions of whites who will never exist, in the one case, as the thousands of Indians who will not receive life, in the other?[230]

But there was another issue, Wilde suggested, which was what exactly the advocates of preserving the Indians meant to preserve? It was not their mode of life, they were to be converted from a hunting to an agricultural people. It was not their barbarous laws and customs, they were to be prevailed upon to adopt habits like our own. It was not their language, they were to be taught English. It was not their religion, they were to be converted to Christianity. What, then, was the identity of that race which we were so anxious to preserve? Was it the more copper color of the skin? "It is the order of nature we exclaim against. Jacob will forever obtain the inheritance of Esau. We cannot alter the laws of Providence, as we read them in the experience of ages. The earth was given for labor, and to labor it belongs. The gift was not to the red, or to the white, but to the human race—and the inscription was, to the wisest—the bravest—to virtue—and to industry!"[231]

Congressman John Test of Indiana suggested that what made for Indian identity was sovereignty. What is sovereignty? It is that power and dominion that man has over all created things. "It extends to the lives, liberties, and fortunes of all those over whom it exerts its influence. It is that, and that only, which gives the tenure by which nations hold the property they possess. It is that, and that only, which gives them a name and a being as a nation."[232] If it was true, as Georgia maintained, that the

Cherokee Nation were not sovereign, then they could not hold the lands and Georgia has them "without money and without price"—the land and the Indians also. "And such being the state of the case, Georgia can have no claim upon the United States, and the passage of this bill, as to her, would be perfectly nugatory."[233] To understand the true situation, it was necessary to note that the compact of 1802 clearly established that the Cherokee people held title to their lands and that the United States were not obliged to go to war with the Indians for them, or to violate treaties, or to trample upon established principles, or to tear up the foundation of a settled policy the government was pledged to maintain. It was President Jackson's telling Georgia, Alabama and Mississippi that they had the right and the power that had led them to embark on their bold experiment. It was only after General Jackson had told the Cherokee Nation that he could not protect them that those states took upon themselves to extend their laws over the Indians within their borders. "I say, it is evident that they were emboldened to do so by the language which General Jackson held toward those Indians; for they had never before presumed to do so, nor until he had announced to these tribes that the protection of the United States should be withdrawn from them; thereby inviting the States to do what they did."[234] And it was remarkable that Jackson should have taken this stance after having negotiated with the Cherokee people the treaty of 1817. For the preamble of that treaty indicated that its object was to divide or separate the nation into two parties—one to remain where they were, having made much more progress than their brethren toward civilization, and being disposed to pursue the arts of husbandry, quit the hunter's life, and "to establish among themselves fixed laws and a regular form of Government"—and the other, being disposed to pursue the hunter's life, to sell their lands and remove over the Mississippi.[235]

> Here, sir, is a treaty entered into with the Cherokees by General Jackson, now President of the United States, and a distinguished citizen of the State of Georgia, by and with the consent of Georgia; those distinguished gentlemen acting under the solemn obligations of an oath to support the constitution of the United States making a treaty with the Cherokee Indians, a large portion of whom reside in Georgia; which, in its solemn stipulations, recognizes the following facts: "that the Indians who remain on this side of the Mississippi,

> either in Georgia or Alabama, are not citizens of the United States," because it provides for their becoming such; that they have the right, and intend "to establish fixed laws for themselves, and a regular form of Government of their own," separate, distinct, and independent of the United States, of Georgia, of Alabama, and of all the world. I say that it is not a little remarkable that, after those solemn engagements, recognizing these high sovereign rights, they should be told by General Jackson himself, holding in his hand the power and prerogative of a mighty nation, that they could not be maintained in them; that they must go to the desert, or yield to the encroachments of the States in which they reside.[236]

The most prominent feature of the bill before the House, Test continued, was that it placed the whole business in the hands of the President, to be disposed of according to his discretion. No treaty is to be made. Instead, the President is to lay off the districts of land, the President is to exchange lands, the President is to do and cause to be done everything proposed by the bill. "If, sir, I had the most implicit confidence in the discretion, the energy, and firmness of the President, I would withhold from him this vast power and patronage."[237] It was not to be presumed that the President would, in person, make all the exchanges. It will have to be trusted to agents, perhaps deeply interested Georgians seeking to obtain the best possible terms. "This is putting it on the best and most honorable grounds. The laws of Georgia have annulled and abrogated all the decrees and edicts of the tribes, thereby rendering them perfectly powerless, and giving to the vile and perfidious among them liberty of expressing, with perfect impunity, the basest fraud and treachery, and, to cap the climax, doom to the penitentiary for six years, at hard labor, any Indian in their nation who shall attempt to prevent them."[238]

Test concluded that he had always been in favor of colonizing the Indians as well as the Negroes. But in a manner agreeable to them and on correct principles:

> I say, therefore, give him a country that he may call his own; take him under your kind protection; fix his title to it upon principles that shall satisfy him that it is to be his forever; do not drive him hence,

> but make it his interest to go, and he will go voluntarily; and, instead of bearing in his bosom the feelings of hatred and revenge, he will carry with him the pleasing recollections of your beneficence and kindness. Instead of pouring fourth the curses of his injured country, he will breathe the aspirations of kindred affections. But, sir, if you drive him away with unprovoked wrongs, visit upon him the evils with which this bill is fraught, surround him with insuperable difficulties, till he is forced to yield to their pressure; send him away in that spirit, and he will war with you till he reaches the shore of the Pacific; and, when he has no longer a clod of earth upon which to set his foot, you will hear his curses (not his sighs) wafted back upon the returning gale; and not his only, but the curses of pitying nations who shall sympathize in his wrongs and his sufferings. You will be told of your broken faith, violated treaties, unprovoked wrongs inflicted upon the poor Indian, when he (as eloquently expressed by the gentleman from Georgia) shall not be extinct, but sunk in the vast ocean of oblivion.[239]

Denying that the bill conferred upon the President "alarming powers," Congressman Henry Lamar of Georgia maintained that it was in no way a departure from previous policy. Under the administration of President John Quincy Adams, it was supposed there was a union of all hearts and heads on this subject. It was only within the last twelve months, and after some extraordinary changes of opinion, that a campaign of hostility was waged against this favorite policy of former administrations. Opposition had been justified on the grounds that Georgia had extended her laws over the Cherokee Nation:

> But while gentlemen oppose the policy proposed in the bill, and acknowledge the condition of the Indians to be an evil, why do they not condescend to suggest to us some other plan to relieve the objects of their benevolence, and to free the States where they are from the inconvenience? The gentlemen from New York [Mr. Spencer] made the nearest approach to it, by an amendment proposed in the Committee of the Whole. It asserted the independence of the Indians, denied the right of the States to subject them to their laws, and probably instructed the President as to his duty in carrying into effect

> subsisting treaties. But it was no sooner read, than it was rejected by a decided vote of the committee, and it will scarcely be revived in any other shape. Let me then inquire, will the rejection of the bill aid the Indians? Will the operation of the State laws over them be arrested? No, sir. Yet, while the gentlemen raise the cry of oppression, and inveigh largely against the laws of Georgia, they will not contribute their aid to remove the Indians beyond the reach of that tyranny they profess so much to deprecate. The amount of the argument is this—that because Georgia, in their opinion, has done wrong, they will not do anything to accomplish what most of them believe to be an act of pure benevolence.[240]

Adding his voice to support for the removal bill, Congressman Dixon Lewis of Alabama also argued that many of those who had indicated opposition to the bill had supported its principles in 1826 under a previous administration. He "inferred from that, that the opposition to it was a party opposition to the administration, and to the South; that as this bill was known to be the leading measure of the present President, it was an object of great solicitude with the opposition to defeat it; and therefore called on those who avowed themselves supporters of the administration, to sustain this measure; that, if they did not, they would be faithless, and traitors to their party."[241] Congressman James Wayne of Georgia, attempting to raise the moral tone of advocacy on the bill's behalf, spoke of the future historian who will be forced to write of "the short-sightedness and perverseness of that hostility which so perseveringly seeks to defeat a scheme so full of national disinterestedness and of moral grandeur, for the alleviation of human misery." [242] He also took issue with what he claimed was the inconsistency involved in saying nothing about New York's extension of its laws over the Indians within its boundaries while protesting against Georgia for doing so:

> I will content myself with remarking that no state in the Union has more positively insisted upon her sovereignty over Indians, and their lands within her limits, than New York; and that her civil jurisdiction over their persons, both by the decisions of her courts and her statutes, is affirmed in the strongest terms, as well over those Indians who have not ceded their lands to that State, as over those

> who have; and this, notwithstanding the establishment by the Indians of a Government for themselves, claiming to be independent of the State, as the Cherokees do of Georgia, and the existence of treaties between those Indians and the United States, containing the same assurances of protection and guaranties of territory, which, it is said by a gentleman on this floor, make the Cherokees a distinct and independent nation. Nor, sir, should we have heard a denial of the jurisdiction of the States over Indians within their limits, if the too zealous anxiety of gentlemen to defeat the administration, in this prominent point of its policy, had not caused an oblivion in their minds of the political history of the country.[243]

Seeking to establish some sort of middle ground, Congressman Joseph Hemphill of Pennsylvania proposed a substitute for the bill that would provide for the appointment of three commissioners by the President and Senate, not to be residents of any of the States immediately interested. These commissioners would go through the Indian Tribes east of the Mississippi and ascertain their disposition to emigrate and then explore the country west of the Mississippi and ascertain the quality and the extent of the country that could be offered to the Indians, and the terms on which they would make the exchange, dispose of their improvements, and remove. The commissioners would then issue a report to the President to be laid before the Congress at its next session. Thirty thousand dollars was to be appropriated to carry the provisions into effect.[244]

Speaking in support of his substitute amendment, Hemphill argued that the question was too important to be placed on party grounds and claimed that the President had no more sincere friends in the United States than those of his party who prefer this amendment to the original bill. It was vital to convince the world that action was not being taken under circumstances that leave the Indians no choice. And American opinion was also to be considered:

> It appears to me that the people of this country are not prepared for this question; they have not as yet had an opportunity to reflect upon it. We all know that no petitions have been presented to us in favor of the measure. We know, too, that remonstrances against it from

> many parts of the country are numerous. The honorable gentlemen from Georgia [Mr. Wilde] made, as I thought, an unsuccessful attempt to weaken this state of the case. He said, if I rightly understood him, that the excitement was partial, and that the silent speculators ought to be considered as acquiescing in the proposed measure. This is not the practice of the people of this country. An excitement on one side always rouses the other, (if there be any other). The silence, therefore, which is claimed as acquiescence on this occasion, is rather to be considered as a solemn warning that we ought to act with the greatest caution and circumspection.[245]

Congressman Wiley Thompson of Georgia demanded the previous question, which would supersede Hemphill's substitute amendment. The vote was 98 to 98. The Speaker of the House, Andrew Stevenson of Virginia, then cast the deciding vote in the affirmative. Congressman Daniel Miller of Pennsylvania made one more effort to arrest the measure by moving to lay the bill on the table. His motion was defeated 103 to 94. The previous question—"Shall the main question now be put"—was then voted upon. The vote was 99 to 99 and the Speaker of the House again cast the deciding vote in the affirmative. The main question—"Shall the bill be read a third time"—was then put. It was approved 102 to 97.[246] With this vote, it seemed that while Hemphill himself would vote against the removal bill, four of the Congressmen he had lined up to vote for his substitute amendment would vote with the Jackson administration, at least they had done so on the vote for the third reading of the bill.[247] These four were Henry Dwight of Massachusetts, and James Ford, William Ramsey, and John Scott of Pennsylvania. But the following day there was again a tie—96 to 96—on a motion to put the previous question (and supersede a motion of Hemphill's to recommit the bill to the Committee of the Whole for further discussion). And although that motion was approved by Stevenson's deciding vote, the House then voted against putting the main question by 99 to 98 with Dwight, Ford, Ramsey and Scott all voting with the opposition to the bill.[248] The day after that, on 26 May 1830, Congressman John Gilmore of Pennsylvania moved the previous question in another effort to supersede Hemphill's motion to recommit. A roll was called and 200 members were present.[249] The vote for Gilmore's motion was 98 to 96. Since the ayes and nays were not divided on Gilmore's motion, the six members present who chose not to vote cannot be identified. The previous question—"Shall the main question now be put"—was then decided in the affirmative 101 to 97. And the question—"Shall the bill pass"—was then approved 102 to 97 with Dwight, Ramsey, and Scott voting for the bill and Ford abstaining.[250]

The final text of the Act did contain one important victory for the opponents of removal—in the midst of their overall defeat—as well as a hypocritical reference to the Native peoples' treaty rights and some obfuscatory language about their relationship to the President of the United States. Whereas the draft of the bill in the House Committee on Indian Affairs' report of 24 February 1830 had sought to authorize the President to deal with "any tribe, or the individuals thereof," the final Act referred exclusively to dealing with "any tribe or nation."[251] It claimed, "That it shall and may be lawful for the President to have the same superintendence and care over any tribe or nation in the country to which they may remove, as contemplated by this act, that he is now authorized to have over them at their present places of residence: Provided, That nothing in this act contained shall be construed as authorizing or directing the violation of any existing treaty between the United States and any of the Indian tribes."[252] It is worth noting that this alleged "superintendence" of the President to which the Congress appealed for authority is perfectly good evidence that the Congress did not possess any "plenary power" over the Native peoples and knew this perfectly well.

The "plenary power" that the Supreme Court would later explicitly claim for the Congress in *Lone Wolf v. Hitchcock* (1903), is rooted in the "ultimate dominion" that the Court claimed for the United States in *Johnson*—as well as in the "complete sovereignty and dominion" over the Native Nations that the Court claimed for the United States in *Cherokee Nation*—but it was only fully expressed as "plenary power" after, and as a result of, the Trail of Tears and subsequent genocides and land thefts.[253] It was only after something of what the Congress and the Executive had done—with at least the tacit sanction of the Supreme Court—became a tradition that the delusion that they had a right to act in that way emerged into full articulation. The contention that the rights of the Kiowa Nation were protected by treaty, the Supreme Court held in *Lone Wolf*, "in effect ignores the status of the contracting Indians and the relation of dependency they bore and continue to bear towards the government of the United States. To uphold the claim would be to adjudge that the indirect operation of the treaty was to materially limit and qualify the controlling authority of Congress in respect to the care and protection of the Indians, and to deprive Congress, in a possible emergency, when the necessity might be urgent for a partition and disposal of the tribal lands, of all power to act, if the assent of the Indians could not be obtained."[254]

In early 1831, there still seemed to be reason to think that the Supreme Court might honor the supreme law of the land by issuing an injunction against Georgia's genocidal aggression and so put an end both to that aggression and to the federal efforts at genocide by indicating that the Cherokee Nation's dominion over its own land was guaranteed by treaty and that the Cherokee Nation had a right to enforce respect for their dominion in the courts of the United States. The beginnings of the bad faith interpretive stance that would guide the Supreme Court in its violations of American treaty obligations and of the Constitution had already been established in *Johnson*. They had yet to be cemented into place in a racist and bigoted structure of oppression and exploitation, and yet to be disguised by a "trust relationship," as they would be in *Cherokee Nation*. They had also yet to be further obscured by the slap at Georgian aggression—and its attendant largely meaningless rhetoric about some of the traditional and "natural" as opposed to legal rights of the Cherokee Nation—in *Worcester*. There was, in short, still reason in early 1831 to hope that the Supreme Court might uphold the law as the framers intended and as the text of the Constitution mandates.

Chapter 4
Marshall's War: *Cherokee Nation* in Context, part 1

Placing hope in the Supreme Court, the Cherokee Nation hired William Wirt, a former Attorney General of the United States whose gifts of oratory were sufficient for him to have been chosen to deliver the eulogy of Thomas Jefferson and John Adams before a joint session of Congress in 1826, and John Sergeant who would later run for vice-president on Henry Clay's National Republican ticket in 1832.[255] Wirt himself would run for president in that election, on the Anti-Masonic Party's ticket, and receive nearly 8% of the vote. Georgia's officials, in keeping with their exaggerated view of their state's rights, refused to appear before the Supreme Court to present oral arguments.

There were seven members of the Supreme Court in 1831. Gabriel Duvall, who in his long career on the court, disagreed with Marshall very rarely, was absent for the term.[256] This left six men to decide *Cherokee Nation v. Georgia*: John Marshall, John McLean, William Johnson, Henry Baldwin, Joseph Story, and Smith Thompson. Appointed by Andrew Jackson in 1829, John McLean voted with Marshall both in *Worcester* and in *Cherokee Nation*. Absent the political strength of Marshall's sleight-of-hand with the word "foreign" in *Cherokee Nation*—swapping the political for the geographical meaning of the word and distracting attention from the supremacy of treaties in constitutional law with an argument relying on the "ultimate dominion" of the United States that *Johnson* had created out of whole cloth—McLean might well have supported the plaintiff in 1831. William Johnson, who had been somewhat respectful of Indian rights to the soil in *Fletcher v. Peck* in 1810, had reversed his earlier opinion by the time of *Johnson*, and so must be considered as possible but unlikely to have been persuadable to support a different course.[257] Appointed by Andrew Jackson in 1830, Henry Baldwin was perhaps the most hostile to Cherokee rights of any member of the court, although he did wind up authoring a unanimous opinion in *Mitchel v. United States* in 1835 that spoke of Indian rights to the soil they had occupied since time immemorial and said that "their right of occupancy is considered as sacred as the fee simple of the whites."[258] Joseph Story and Smith Thompson offered an interpretation of constitutional law that respected the law of nations and the intentions of the framers and sided with the plaintiff in 1831.

At the very beginning of their Bill before the Supreme Court, the Cherokee Nation made intellectual mincemeat of the idea that "discovery" or "conquest" had any bearing on their situation and their rights:

> Respectfully complaining, show unto your honours, the Cherokee nation of Indians, a foreign state, not owing allegiance to the United States, nor to any state of this union, nor to any other prince, potentate, or state, other than their own: That, from time immemorial, the Cherokee nation have composed a sovereign and independent state, and in this character have been repeatedly recognized, and still stand recognized by the United States, in the various treaties subsisting between their nation and the United States. That long before the first approach of the white men of Europe to the western continent, the Cherokee nation were the occupants and owners of the territory on which they now reside; deriving their title from the Great Spirit, who is the common father of the human family, and to whom the earth belongs. That on this territory they and their ancestors, composing the Cherokee nation, have ever been, and still are, the sole and exclusive masters, and governed, of right, by no other laws, usages and customs, but such as they have themselves thought proper to ordain and appoint.[259]

The European monarch who affected to grant this territory, the Bill continued, had no title to it whatsoever. The only pretended title was what has been called a title by first discovery, a title that was not true in point of fact as the Cherokee and other Native Nations had discovered and occupied it long before the first European ship had ventured to cross the Atlantic Ocean. Indeed, the land belonged to them probably far beyond the period when the British islands, themselves the residence of heathen savages and barbarians, became prey to a heathen conqueror from Rome. Even this pretended title by discovery has never been claimed, by the

European sovereigns themselves, to give a right to oust the Indian proprietors from their possession. The utmost length to which they have carried the unjust pretensions derived from their alleged discovery has been the claim that the first European discoverer has the prior and exclusive right to purchase these lands from the Indian proprietors, as against all other European sovereigns; "a principle settled among themselves for their own convenience, in adjusting their mutual accounts of rapine on the western world; a principle to which the Indian proprietors have never given their assent, and which they deny to be a principle of the natural law of nations, or as in any manner obligatory on them."[260]

As for this wild and chimerical title by discovery, it was never alleged by George II, or by his grantee, the Georgia company, in 1732, or at any time since, that the charter gave to that company any right to disturb or question the exclusive right of possession by the Indians or to interfere in any manner with their own self-government within their respective domains. On the contrary, they entered into treaties that acknowledged and treated with the Cherokee Nation as a sovereign and independent state within boundaries changed by successive cessions but always acknowledging their right of governing themselves without any right of interference on the part of any one of the states of the United States. These treaties explicitly recognized the right of each side to make war and specifically called for a prior declaration of hostilities before any future resort to arms. Any citizen of the United States attempting to settle on Cherokee land was explicitly placed under the authority of the tribe after the Treaty of Hopewell had been in effect for six months. Moreover, the eleventh article of the Treaty of Holston explicitly admitted that the territory of the Cherokee Nation was not within the jurisdiction of either the states or the territorial districts of the United States. And by the seventh article of that treaty, "the United States solemnly guaranty to the Cherokee nation all their lands not hereby ceded."[261]

Having disposed of arguments by "discovery" or "conquest," the Cherokee Nation turned to speculative objections to their title rooted in an alleged lack of civilization:

> Under the promised "*patronage, aid,* and *good neighborhood*" of the United States they have become *civilized, Christians,* and *agriculturalists,* and have no more land than is sufficient for their subsistence and that of their posterity, and this land they hold under repeated, solemn, and still subsisting guarantees by treaty with the United States. They do not mean to allege, that they have all become perfectly civilized, nor all public professors of Christianity, nor all agriculturalists: but in all these respects they are willing that a comparison shall be instituted between them and their white brethren around them, and they are very little apprehensive of suffering by such comparison when instituted before this honorable court. If practicing justice, and the doing to others as we would have them do unto us, be the tests of civilization and Christianity, and the proportion of the cultivators of the soil to the whole number of the population be the test of the agricultural character of a nation, with reference to the theory in question, they apprehend that they have at least as little reason as their white brethren around them to shrink from such tests.[262]

As for the Compact of 1802, the Cherokee bill noted that it contained an implicit admission, on the part of Georgia, "that the Indian title was a subsisting title, which remained to be extinguished, and that it could be properly extinguished only *peaceably* and on *reasonable terms, by the United States.*"[263] Since then, the Cherokee Nation have "reduced their territory into as small a compass as their convenience would bear."[264] The state of Georgia, after having gained from a series of land cessions over a series of treaties "now affected to treat these measures; consecrated as they were by the names of the best patriots of the United States, and sanctioned by herself; as a tissue of hypocritical pretenses of benevolence and philanthropy, which had no other object in view than to disappoint her own just hopes of engrossing to herself all the Indian lands within her remaining limits."[265]

Acting on unjust and unlawful pretensions, Georgia had sought to extend her laws by compulsion over Cherokee territory. Applying to the present chief magistrate of the United States to make good on the protection and guarantee pledged to them by treaty, they have received the answer that the United States has no power to protect them from the laws of Georgia.[266] As for the Congress of the United States, it had passed an act offering to exchange Indian lands east of the Mississippi for other lands to its west. As a sovereign and independent state, the Cherokee Nation could simply decline the offer, but they wanted their reasons to be known:

> In the first place, the territory which they now inhabit is well known to them, and has been found well adapted to all their wants. It has been opened, improved, settled, built upon and placed in a condition for agriculture, which they are prosperously carrying on. It is well supplied with wood and water, enjoys a salubrious climate, and every convenience of commerce and intercourse suited to a civilized people, composed of farmers, planters, mechanics and herdsmen. The ports of the United States are all within reach of those exchanges which their pursuits make necessary for their prosperity. They have schools established for the education of their children, and means of furnishing them with instructors from among the citizens of the United States: they have places of religious worship established, in which the Christian religion is peaceably taught by missionaries and pastors, easily supplied from the United States, and the word of God is prospering among them; they have learned to relish the manners and pursuits of civilized life; and, if their treaties with the United States shall be faithfully executed, they have continually brightening prospects of becoming, speedily, as civilized, as enlightened, and as Christian as the best portion of their white brethren. This country, too, so fraught with every convenience and advantage to them; and so endeared to them by the great and multifarious benefits which they have already received and are still receiving from it; is consecrated in their affections from having been, immemorially, the property and residence of their ancestors, and from containing now, the graves of their fathers, relatives, and friends. Such are the grounds of their attachment to this country, and of their unwillingness to relinquish it.[267]

Hoping that Georgia's laws were merely a form of terrorism designed to persuade them to exchange their lands, a threat that would be ended upon their firm refusal, they have found instead that "that state has declared its determination to continue to enforce them upon these complainants and upon their territory, so long as these complainants shall continue to occupy that territory."[268] They thus begged leave to humbly and respectfully suggest to the Supreme Court that by the constitution and laws of the United States, "original jurisdiction is conferred on this court in controversies between a state and a foreign state," and that this provision manifestly contemplated "every case in which the claims or conduct of a single state towards a foreign state may jeapord the peace, safety, and good faith of the United States."[269]

"That your complainants are a foreign state, is not only evident by the only test which can be properly applied to such a question, the test of allegiance, but has been again and again, and still is unequivocally admitted by the United States, by the fact of their being acknowledged and treated with, in that character, by the properly constituted authorities of the United States."[270] Accordingly, the bill the Cherokee Nation presented to the Supreme Court, together with a supplemental bill enumerating the Georgians laws in question, asked that "the said state of Georgia, her governor, attorney general, judges, magistrates, sheriffs, deputy sheriffs, constables, and all her other officers, agents, and servants, civil and military, may be enjoined and prohibited from executing the laws of the state within the boundary of the Cherokee territory, as prescribed by the treaties now subsisting between the United States and the Cherokee nation…"[271]

* * *

One of the deepest flaws in the founding documents of the United States may not be immediately apparent to everyone in the texts—this is the fact that "we the people" did not include *all* of the people. Generations of reformers and revolutionaries have sought the full and equal inclusion of people of color, women, working people, and poor people in all American institutions and many of their heirs and successors are still struggling toward such goals. The founding documents upon which they have attempted to build emerged from a culture still grappling—as ours is today—with the implications of its own supremacist expansionism, and, in particular, with the implications of slavery, the slave trade, and previous efforts at colonization. This conflicted culture (again very much like our own) can be seen, on the one hand, as aspiring to "do better" in its relations with the Native Nations and, on the other, as sustaining a system of ideas designed to destroy the original free and independent existence of these nations on their own lands and territories for the benefit of an American empire, which was believed destined by "God" to possess the continent from "sea to shining sea."[272] Until American culture can no longer sustain such a genocidal system of ideas, the beloved community will remain an unfulfilled aspiration in the womb of time. For this community, if we succeed in realizing it, will involve much more than inclusion and equal belonging for individuals. Among other things, it will also involve all of the many independent and interdependent nations on this continent sharing this land (and this world) on the basis of trustworthy, reciprocal, and consensual conduct toward one another—on the basis of shared respect, equal rights, and equal belonging for each and all.

There are three large and competing legal orders on this continent among whom the same term—"tribal sovereignty"—has at least two radically different meanings. The first is the legal order inherent to the land of Turtle Island—the international laws and usages that are rooted in the cultures and traditions of the Native Nations, that are valid in the life of this continent, and that were valid long before the European invaders arrived. In this legal order, the land is cared for as our grandmother Earth and there is respect for the unity and equality of all our relations and for the maintenance of trustworthy, reciprocal, and consensual relationships to help sustain a cosmic and social balance. In this legal order "tribal sovereignty" (if the concept of "sovereignty" is even used) refers to the original free and independent existence of the Native Nations: their full and free national self-determination.[273] Within this legal order and sustaining it—within this way of life—are the legal orders of each of the Native Nations and the ethical framework formed by the stories they share and the guidance these stories provide.

Each of the three large legal orders on this continent (ignoring for the moment the Mexican and the Canadian) is associated with a path that the American people could have followed with regard to the Native Nations; paths that still persist. The first path is a path barely imagined: the path of seeking to learn from the Native peoples what they considered sacred rather than seeking to "teach" them what the newly independent republic's citizens considered sacred. This is the path of seeking to live with them on their lands according to their laws and to act and be in a world informed by their worldview. It involves conduct that the peoples on the shore might reasonably have expected of the invaders—conduct along the lines of "when in Rome, do as the Romans do." Those who saw themselves as Christians among the invaders were largely unwilling to do this. Their heirs and successors may yet acknowledge that the societies of the original free and independent nations of Turtle Island were far closer to the social values Christianity alleges it favors than the societies of Christendom and its successors have been.[274] They may also acknowledge—if civilization is defined in terms of moral and political decency and not in terms of material comfort and technological gadgetry—the far greater civility of these peoples.[275] If civilization is defined—in contrast—as simply a form of domination disguised by material comfort and technological gadgetry, the far greater liberty of the Native peoples as free peoples and of Native societies as free societies should be perceived.

The second large legal order on this continent is the legal order manufactured by the United States Supreme Court in which "tribal sovereignty" is allegedly subject to the supposedly superior sovereignty of "the sovereign" and can be overridden or destroyed by "the sovereign" at pleasure because the Native Nations are—in the words of John Marshall's opinion in *Cherokee Nation v. Georgia*—"completely under the sovereignty and dominion of the United States."[276] The ubiquitous cultural intrusiveness that this legal order sustains must feel, in the lived experience of the Native Nations, essentially totalitarian in character—a continuous immersion in a deeply alien culture whose needling insistence as to its alleged superiority is coercively reinforced at the whim of an "authority" exercising completely unconstrained "plenary power." In this legal order, "tribal sovereignty" refers to whatever "the sovereign" allows the Native Nations to retain in the way of self-government. "The Indian wars are not in your historical rearview mirror if you are Indian," comments the jurist Steve Russell in *Sequoyah Rising*, "You see what little you have being quietly chipped away every year."[277]

The path associated with this legal order is the path taken. This is the path that led to the genocide of the 1830s and to all of the land thieving and all of the genocides that have followed since. This is the path of the reactionary reversion to a particularly pernicious version of the doctrine of "Christian discovery" as the claimed basis of land title in the United States and of an alleged American authority over the Native Nations.[278] This was the path taken by John Marshall and a unanimous Supreme Court in *Johnson v. McIntosh* in 1823 and reiterated—after its premises were challenged by the Cherokee Nation—in *Cherokee Nation v. Georgia,* in 1831, and reiterated again in *Worcester v. Georgia,* in 1832. These three cases, taken together, are known as the "Marshall trilogy." They should be known as "Marshall's War" against the rights of the Native Nations—a war the Supreme Court continues to wage.

Those opponents of what would become known as the Trail of Tears who embraced Marshall's decision in *Worcester* because it seemed a slap at Georgian aggression—and those who do so to this day—are unwittingly embracing the premises of the advocates of genocide and their appeasers, and embracing the system of domination and dehumanization to which their efforts gave rise. They are asserting, often without realizing it, that it is the federal government rather than individual states that has the "right" to destroy the Native Nations. Even as acute an observer as the historian Claudio Saunt has mistakenly described *Worcester* as "a complete legal victory for the Cherokees."[279] And the equally perceptive law professor Stuart Banner has claimed that "Marshall's opinion vindicated the Cherokees' position on virtually every point."[280] In fact, Marshall's opinion in *Worcester* was just as much a denial of the Cherokee Nation's legal right to their own treaty-guaranteed dominion over their own land as *Johnson v. McIntosh* and *Cherokee Nation v. Georgia*; just as much a reaffirmation of the doctrine of Christian discovery and a discourse of "power" and "conquest." *Worcester* did speak of some of the traditional and "natural" rights of the Cherokee Nation and in this way obscured the Supreme Court's continued denial of the Cherokee Nation's legal rights.

As the law professor Robert A. Williams, Jr. (Lumbee) has noted, the "legal rules and principles of federal Indian law set down by Marshall in *Johnson v. McIntosh* and its discourse of conquest ensured that future acts of genocide would proceed on a rationalized, legal basis."[281] *Cherokee Nation v. Georgia* provided the Supreme Court with an opportunity to correct its mistakes and abide by the Constitution, which it refused to take. The unwillingness of John Marshall's hagiographers, and the Supreme Court's apologists generally, to accept the Court's responsibility for grotesque misconduct is a striking feature of their literature. Charles Hobson, the editor of Marshall's papers, for example, claims that Williams "grossly misconstrues the meaning of the opinion" in *Johnson* and asserts—against Williams' reasoned analysis and evidence—that Marshall had somehow "placed Indian property rights on a firm foundation."[282] As we will see in this chapter and the next—and as should be evident to anyone familiar with *Tee-Hit-Ton v. United States*—Hobson's claims and assertions in this regard are groundless.[283] Marshall's position was, though more subtle in its dishonesty, every bit as monstrous as President Andrew Jackson's.

Marshall did not exactly agree with Jackson's hope—expressed already in 1821—"that the absurdity in politics may cease of an independent sovereign nation holding treaties with people living within its territorial limits."[284] Had Marshall been directly challenged on the point, he would surely have denied that treaties with the Native Nations were meaningless. But the rights of "conquest" to which Marshall appealed rested upon a reactionary jurisprudence for which that was a logical conclusion. As Williams conveys the central idea of this jurisprudence, "the Crown was presumed to be at perpetual war with infidels, who were, in turn, presumed to be incapable of conforming their laws or conduct to natural law. Thus English discovery of infidel-held territories amounted to a declaration of war on the Crown's perpetual enemies and imposed on the Crown the duty to subjugate the infidels and provide them with the Christian faith and civilization."[285] Although Williams does not say so, the clear implication of this jurisprudence is that treaties with infidels are merely truces with perpetual enemies and have no more validity than that: they can never lead to friendship.

The professions of friendship in so many treaties with the Native Nations either reflected the good faith that these treaties were meant to be kept or they were—as they have been by means of the Supreme Court's interpretive stance since the Marshall "trilogy"—a lie resting on bad faith and, at best, constitute a form of self-deluded self-righteousness. As American Indian Studies professor Dina Gilio-Whitaker (Colville Confederated Tribes) has noted, when American representatives proclaimed that their commitments would be honored "as long as the grass grows" they were making pledges that their heirs and successors would fail to keep—pledges that the Native peoples have nevertheless used in their struggles for justice not only for themselves but for all our relations.[286]

The third large legal order on this continent is associated with the path not taken. This is the legal order intended to be recognized by the United States Constitution in which "tribal sovereignty" is the same as the sovereignty of any independent foreign state with whom the United States has treaty relations and in which the rights that a foreign nation derives from its treaties with the United States are respected as part of "the supreme law of the land."[287] As Supreme Court Associate Justices Smith Thompson's and Joseph Story's dissent in *Cherokee Nation v. Georgia* made clear, "any distinction" between treaties made with the Native Nations and treaties made with any other foreign powers is without foundation in the Constitution.[288] In consequence, the Cherokee Nation had a right to an injunction to protect its dominion from unconstitutional aggression and the United States' denial of the Native Nations' treaty-guaranteed dominion over their own lands—a denial that persists to this day—persists in opposition to constitutional law properly construed.

Albert Beveridge, Marshall's biographer, acknowledged more than a hundred years ago that Marshall "could easily have decided in favor of the wronged and harried Indians, as the dissent of Thompson and Story proves."[289] If their treaty-guaranteed dominion had been respected by the Supreme Court—as it easily could have been—the Cherokee Nation and its Native neighbors might still be on their ancestral lands. The horrible lie of "Manifest Destiny"—including the false claim that the genocidal brutality of the United States' expansion was somehow inevitable and not a series of deliberate murderous choices—might have been avoided.

The third path is the path that the new nation more or less started out along. This is the path informed by the American revolutionary jurisprudence of the constitutional framer James Wilson and his allies—the path of acknowledging the national rights of the Native Nations. In a famous political pamphlet in 1774, Wilson declared that "All men are, by nature, equal and free" that "no one has a right to any authority over another without his consent" and that "all lawful government is founded upon the consent of those who are subject to it."[290] Wilson recognized that the Native Nations had never consented to be governed by the United States and that the United States therefore had, as he put it in 1776, "no right" over them.[291] He believed that the American people had claimed such powers as they asserted a right to exercise under the law of nations—an expression of natural law—while recognizing the equal right of all other nations, including the Native Nations, to do likewise. This is what the sovereignty of "we the people" meant to Wilson: that we were answerable to the international moral and legal order under which we claimed our rights—and ultimately answerable to God—for our conduct. He made this perfectly clear in his law lectures in 1790-1791:

> [When] I say that, in free states, the law of nations is the law of the people; I mean that, as the law of nature, in other words, as the will of nature's God, it is indispensably binding upon the people, in whom the sovereign power resides; and who are, consequently, under the most sacred obligations to exercise that power, or to delegate it to such as will exercise it, in a manner agreeable to those rules and maxims, which the law of nature prescribes to every state, for the happiness of each, and for the happiness of all. How vast—how important—how interesting are these truths! They announce to a free people how exalted their rights; but at the same time, they announce to a free people how solemn their duties are.[292]

According to his biographer, Charles Page Smith, Wilson played the leading role in the early formulation of Indian policy in the Continental Congress: "If the positions he held and the frequency with which he appeared on committees concerned with Indian affairs are an index, he was until his departure from Congress in 1777 the most active and influential single delegate in laying down the general outline that governed the relations of Congress with the border tribes."[293]

By 1787, Wilson's position was close to the consensus view. "At the time the Constitution of the United States was drafted," as the judge and legal historian Robert N. Clinton (Winnebago) has noted, "the Framers generally accepted the notion that the Indian tribes constituted separate sovereign peoples who were totally self-governing within their territory and who relied on the federal government solely for external relations, i.e., diplomatic representation with foreign governments and protection from foreign foes and citizens of the United States."[294] "At the establishment of the federal government under the present Constitution of the United States," President John Quincy Adams observed with regard to the Native Nations in 1828, "the principle was adopted of considering them as foreign and independent powers and also as proprietors of lands."[295] "The theory of the colonial governments," according to the historian Ulrich Phillips in his 1902 book, *Georgia and State Rights*, "had been that these tribes were independent communities with the rights and powers of sovereign nations. During the Revolution and in the period of the Confederation the central government adhered to that theory."[296] It was the Supreme Court, first in 1823, and then more clearly in 1831, that repudiated this approach to the national rights of the Native Nations and in so doing sanctioned the genocide that the state of Georgia, the Jackson administration, and a majority in Congress sought to conduct.

* * *

Of the two lawyers for the Cherokee Nation in 1831, William Wirt and John Sergeant, Sergeant addressed the Supreme Court first. The record of their presentations to the court comes to 121 pages in Supreme Court reporter Richard Peters' published volume.[297] In general—with one vitally important exception—they elaborated on the arguments made in the Cherokee bill and among the opponents of genocide in the Congress. Noting that the judicial power extended to all cases arising under treaties, that a state of the union was a party to the case, and that the character of the other party was of no consequence as to whether the case merited the attention of the highest tribunal, Sergeant asked if there could be any reason for excluding the case. As Supreme Court Associate Justice Stephen Breyer notes, this question went unanswered by Marshall in the court's opinion.[298] Sergeant, after showing that the court clearly had original jurisdiction, continued with yet another key question:

> Why should the constitution which says expressly that, in all cases where a state is a party, the supreme court shall have original jurisdiction, be made to say by implication, that in this case, where a state is a party, it shall not have original jurisdiction? To what jurisdiction would they [the Cherokee Nation] be referred. The same argument which took away the alien character of the nation would equally destroy the alien character of the individuals composing it. They certainly are not citizens; and if they be not aliens, what are they? Outlaws. Declared outlaws, without a nation, and without protection. Public law abhors such a state of existence. It is not more essential in municipal arrangements that everything capable of ownership should have a legal and determinate owner, than it is in the great society of nations that every man should be bound by some allegiance, should be a member of some community. The Cherokee Indians are willing to be so. They are so. They are more so now than they were at any former period.[299]

This was an argument that Marshall would seek to answer in the only way possible: by ignoring it. Wirt, too, when he addressed the court, would offer an argument to which there was no answer:

> There is I know not what vague idea among us, that these nations cannot be states, because they are Indians, ignorant savages, wild and wandering hordes, mere heathens, very little if at all superior to the beasts which they chase. This is a remnant of that superstition which led Pizarro and Cortez to hunt down Mexicans with blood hounds; and which proved them (Christians though they styled themselves) to be far worse *savages* than those whom they persecuted under that name. It is not the tincture of a skin by which the rights of these people are to be tested. We are beginning to recover from our mistake on this ground, with regard to another unfortunate race. Let us not create for ourselves, and place in the hands of a just God, a new scourge of a similar description. However variously colored by differences of climate or other adventitious causes, the human beings

> who people this globe belong to the same family, and derive from their common Parent equal rights. We see them, all over the earth, formed into nations of different hue, without the slightest question of their sovereignty on this ground. And as to their being savages, heathens, and ignorant wandering tribes, even if this were still the case, which we know it is not, it would not detract from their independence and sovereignty *as states*; nor weaken in the slightest degree the obligation of those treaties which we have thought proper to form with them.[300]

The one vitally important exception, in which the Cherokee Nation's lawyers failed to follow up effectively on the Cherokee Nation's lead was the apparent unwillingness of Sergeant and Wirt to explicitly challenge the essential premises of *Johnson v. McIntosh* and especially Marshall's interpretation of the doctrine of "Christian discovery" as providing the United States with an "ultimate dominion." [301] Where the Cherokee Nation's Bill had mocked the ridiculous character of the doctrine of discovery—the Cherokee Nation's lawyers failed to drive this essential point home by attacking the premises of what was novel and distinctive in Marshall's dishonest version of the dishonest doctrine of "Christian discovery" in comparison with the traditional understanding of "discovery" in a British or American context. For what was novel in Marshall's position was a reactionary reversion to some of the worst of the original Spanish versions of the doctrine. Read carefully, Marshall's version of "discovery" was as twisted as John Forsyth's.

Sergeant did ask the key question, apparently rhetorically, without realizing that Marshall had actually sought to answer it for *all* Native Nations in *Johnson*. Observing that the Cherokee people existed as an independent nation from the first settlement of the country, and that they never became incorporated with the European settlers, or subjected by them, Sergeant asserted that it was for those who claimed that they were no longer an independent nation to show when and how this had happened: "The *history* of the case is in this respect the *law* of the case. In what part of their history is it to be found?"[302]

The answer to Sergeant's question, as he should have known and contested, was in John Marshall's turgid imagination: in his unique version of the doctrine of Christian "discovery" with its seeming acknowledgement that it was all an "extravagant" pretension—"opposed to natural right, and to the usages of civilized nations" and perhaps to "reason" itself—and his actual insistence that an "ultimate dominion" and a "right" to dominate derived from the conversion of "discovery" into "conquest" was "indispensable" to U.S. property law.[303] Not only could "discovery" be converted into "conquest" as far as Marshall was concerned, "discovery" somehow "*gave also a right to such a degree of sovereignty as the circumstances of the people would allow them to exercise.*"[304] In other words, they—the discoverers and their heirs and successors—had a "right" to dominate subject only to a Native capacity for resistance with their "degree of sovereignty" varying accordingly with the strength of that resistance. *Johnson* denied any semblance of justice toward the Native peoples in the name of expediency—in the name of an injustice that was allegedly "indispensable":

> However extravagant the pretension of converting the discovery of an inhabited country into conquest may appear; if the principle has been asserted in the first instance, and afterwards sustained; if a country has been acquired and held under it; if the property of the great mass of the community originates in it, it becomes the law of the land and cannot be questioned. So, too, with respect to the concomitant principle that the Indian inhabitants are to be considered merely as occupants, to be protected, indeed, while in peace, in the possession of their lands, but to be deemed incapable of transferring the absolute title to others. However this restriction may be opposed to natural right, and to the usages of civilized nations, yet if it be indispensable to that system under which the country has been settled, and be adapted to the actual condition of the two people, it may perhaps be supported by reason, and certainly cannot be rejected by courts of justice.[305]

The popular alternative to Marshall's position in *Johnson* also had two basic principles that also concerned authority and land, principles that might have been expected to have been upheld instead by a court alleging to be one of justice and taking a position perhaps "supported by reason." The first principle was that, as Rhode Island Senator Asher Robbins put it in 1830: "The Indian is a man, and has all the rights of man. The same God who made us made him, and endowed him with the same rights; for 'of one blood hath he made all the men who dwell upon the earth.'"[306] The second principle—which would be given voice by New Jersey Senator Theodore Frelinghuysen and New York Congressman Henry Storrs, among others in 1830—was that all property title vested originally in the Native Nations. Far from being "indispensable," in other words, grants made three thousand miles eastward had "no validity with the Indians," as James Wilson put it in 1776, and the United States had "no right" over the Native Nations.[307]

Deliberately or not, both Sergeant and Wirt coddled the Chief Justice's ego in the deference that they showed to his opinion in *Johnson*. Both claimed that the Supreme Court's ruling in *Johnson* actually supported the Cherokee Nation's position. Had they first demolished the premises of that ruling, turning around and saying that even if those premises had been accepted the Cherokee Nation's position would have been vindicated, would have been a viable approach. It was not the approach they took.

Wirt, to his credit, did mock the absurdity of Pope Alexander affecting to divide a great part of the world between the crowns of Spain and Portugal. He also did a fine job of trashing the doctrine of discovery in the abstract, just not the version that Marshall had articulated. He began by noting that the Cherokee Nation were in no way parties to Georgia's charter and then asked:

> What right had the king of England to grant to his subjects the lands which the common father of the human family had previously assigned to their people? Was it the right of *discovery*? But in what chapter of the law of nations shall we find any such right recognized with regard to a country which was previously inhabited? The first discoverer of a *desert island* or *country* may acquire a right to take possession of it, on the principle of treasure found of which there is no prior owner. But no such right is acquired as to a country which is previously possessed by another nation.[308]

Rather than engage in a discussion of "the abstract question of right," as between the European discoverers and the Native inhabitants—which could have supplied some of the strongest possible arguments that could have been employed—Sergeant instead simply stated that "the claim of Great Britain never asserted the incorporation or subjection of the native inhabitants within her discovery."[309] He then cited *Johnson* as having made only a "limited claim" and insisted that "the Cherokee nation of Indians is the same nation now, that it was when the soil of their country was first pressed by a European."[310]

Sergeant never explored, or refuted, the "limited claim," he asserted Marshall made in *Johnson*. In fact, of course, Marshall's claim was effectively unlimited—"ultimate dominion" as a result of the conversion of "discovery" into "conquest" and into an unnamed "right" to dominate qualified only by "circumstances"—and thoroughly anti-Constitutional and unhistorical in character.[311] Marshall's later effort to cover his tracks in this regard is evident in his assertion in *Worcester* that "The United States succeeded to all the claims of Great Britain, both territorial and political, but no attempt, so far as is known, has been made to enlarge them."[312] Wirt appears to have noticed that Marshall had made just such an enlarging claim with his version of the doctrine of Christian discovery in *Johnson* and then insisted it was not "for the courts of the country which asserts this kind of title" to dispute.[313] "But," said Wirt, "since the title is not to be found in the law of nations; has no foundation in natural justice; and exists only in *the assertions of the monarchs* of Europe, the courts of the country will not extend it *beyond their assertion*."[314] This was as close as Wirt came to directly attacking Marshall's interpretation of the past. Whether Wirt and Sergeant did not see how much farther beyond the assertions of the monarchs of Europe Marshall had gone in his assertions in *Johnson*, or wanted to avoid taking his argument apart piece by piece, they failed to mount the defense of their client's position that they should have mounted. Had they not wanted to attack Marshall directly, they could have used the arguments of the House Committee on Indian Affairs report of 24 February 1830 as a partial proxy and even relied on Congressman Henry Storrs demolition of that report to do most of their work for them. First, however, they had to understand Marshall's complex and dishonest argument.

In effect, Marshall claimed that it was legally possible to convert "discovery" into "conquest," and into a "right" to dominate qualified only by "circumstances," as if the laws of war allowed the systematic use of deceitful and fraudulent treaties signed in bad faith as a substitute for directly governing a "conquered" population composed of nations who still saw themselves (accurately) as completely independent and who had been seen as completely independent by American officials including James Wilson and Thomas Jefferson.[315] And, as if that wasn't dishonesty enough, Marshall had the gall to state that this system was valid "conquest" by "the sword" in conjunction with unspecified "principles" even if the laws of war didn't allow it, because "Conquest gives a title which the courts of the conqueror cannot deny."[316]

Far from being unable to deny a fraudulent claim of conquest on the part of the "conqueror," the Treaty Supremacy Clause mandated that the judges of the Supreme Court adopt such a position of denial toward any claim at odds with America's treaty obligations to the Native Nations. The heart of Marshall's fraudulent claim in *Johnson*—a claim adopted in violation of his oath of office—was exclusively a product of Marshall's imagination without foundation in law or fact. [317] This was the assertion that "discovery" *is*" conquest" in combination with his repudiation of Native sovereign title and the relationships to which the treaties governing the sales of some of such sovereign lands had given rise. Here is the most elegant and persuasive formulation of Marshall's absurd position in his own words in *Johnson*:

> The United States, then, has unequivocally acceded to that great and broad rule by which its civilized inhabitants now hold this country. They hold and assert in themselves the title by which it was acquired. They maintain, as all others have maintained, that discovery gave an exclusive right to extinguish the Indian title of occupancy either by purchase or by conquest, *and gave also a right to such a degree of sovereignty as the circumstances of the people would allow them to exercise.* The power now possessed by the government of the United States to grant lands, resided, while we were colonies, in the Crown, or its grantees. The validity of the titles given by either has never been questioned in our courts. It has been exercised uniformly over

> territory in possession of the Indians. The existence of this power must negative the existence of any right which may conflict with and control it. An absolute title to lands cannot exist at the same time in different persons or in different governments. An absolute must be an exclusive title, or at least a title which excludes all others not compatible with it. All our institutions recognize the absolute title of the Crown, subject only to the Indian right of occupancy, and recognize the absolute title of the Crown to extinguish that right. This is incompatible with an absolute and complete title in the Indians.[318]

Here we see Marshall's dishonesty in trying to claim that the Crown had an "absolute title" to land—however qualified by Indian rights—and an "absolute title" to "extinguish" the "Indian right of occupancy" when in fact it had no such title and no right to do anything of the kind without a Native Nation's consent. "An absolute must be an exclusive title," Marshall acknowledged without seeming to notice that the United States' "title" was not exclusive as—even in his imagination—it specifically depended on Native consent to come into fruition and had no meaningful existence without such consent. If there were any truth to Marshall's position, there would never have been any treaties with the Native Nations as there would have been no point to them (except, of course, for purposes of deception). Moreover, there could be no validity to Marshall's make-believe if treaties were recognized as the supreme law of the land. The effort to construct a "legal fiction" giving the United States an "absolute title" was and remains repugnant to any good faith approach to the United States' treaty obligations to respect the treaty-guaranteed dominions of the Native Nations. The original, sovereign, and exclusive title of the Native Nations remains valid under the law of nations as it was understood by the framers of the Constitution and—because of the Treaty Supremacy Clause—remains valid under constitutional law properly construed, except where sales took place whose terms were and have continued to be complied with (if any such can be found).[319]

That Marshall's supposed "title" depended for its "consummation" on a "right" to purchase land from the Native Nations—a right that was meaningful if and only if these nations were willing to sell—Marshall himself would acknowledge in *Worcester* where he specifically referenced "the universal conviction that the Indian nations possessed a full right to the lands they occupied until that right should be extinguished by the United States with their consent."[320] Even then Marshall sought to obscure the truth by tacking "with their consent" onto the end of the sentence and by writing their "right to the lands they occupied" instead of their "right to the lands they possess as sovereign and independent foreign states."

What Marshall was engaged in throughout his war against the rights of the Native Nations—in his opinions from *Johnson* through *Worcester*—was a systematic effort to mar these nations' original, sovereign, and exclusive title with spurious claims to titles and authority that the United States did not possess and an attempt—especially at key junctures—to suppress the truth that without Indian consent the United States had nothing. Or, as Thomas Jefferson put it in 1793: "I consider our right of preemption of the Indian lands, not as amounting to any dominion, or jurisdiction, or paramountship whatever, but merely in the nature of a remainder after the extinguishment of a present right, which gave us no present right whatever but of preventing other nations from taking possession and so defeating our expectancy: that the Indians had the full, undivided and independent sovereignty as long as they chose to keep it and that this might be forever."[321]

Perceiving the kind of make-believe at the heart of Georgia's pretensions, Wirt lampooned it. He should have done the same with Marshall's pretensions in *Johnson*. Marshall's treaty-violating make-believe was no more sound than Georgia's. Indeed, both rested their pretensions on the same premises. Noting that the first company that crossed the Atlantic under the charter by which Georgia claimed its rights was led by General Oglethorpe, and arrived in 1733, Wirt proceeded to mock Georgia's pretensions with a telling piece of authentic history drawn from a book that Marshall himself had authored. Wirt could and should have used it against Marshall's pretensions directly:

> According to the present claim of Georgia, all the lands within the limits of that charter belonged to these colonists; and they had nothing more to do than to take possession and to claim the

> allegiance of the Indians as a conquered people, and a part of the subjects of his Britannic majesty. Had any such arrogant pretension been set up, *this conquered people*, the lords of the forest, could, and probably would have crushed the puny colony with as much ease as they could have crushed the serpents' eggs around them. But General Oglethorpe understood the charter as his sovereign understood it. "*A treaty* was held with *the Creek Indians, to whom the lands were admitted to belong, and the cession of a considerable tract was obtained from them*." 1 Marshall's Life of Washington, 226.[322]

Marshall must have been stung by this evidence of his dishonesty with regard to treaties with the Native Nations—and the reason for them in the need to acquire land lawfully from its rightful owners—for in a subsequent edition of the work the phrase: "to whom the lands were admitted to belong" was dropped from Marshall's text.[323] Unfortunately, neither Wirt nor Sergeant subjected Marshall's pretensions in *Johnson* to the analysis and the skewering they deserved. In a letter to James Madison of 5 October 1830, Wirt did indicate that he thought the doctrine of *Johnson* "the strangest absurdity. It is said they have no other title than that of having chased their game over them."[324] But he did not demolish this absurdity before Marshall's face. He was too polite to hammer on the glass jaw of that doctrine until it shattered. That Wirt had the knowledge to pursue such a pugilistic approach is clear from two of his key opinions as Attorney General, one from 1821 and the other from 1828. In the first opinion, addressing competing New York and Massachusetts claims on the Seneca Nation's lands, Wirt explained why these lands belonged to the Seneca Nation; why that nation has sovereign title and what sovereign title means. The Secretary of War had asked Wirt's opinion as to the right of citizens of Massachusetts to enter upon these lands and make a survey. Wirt replied:

> So long as a tribe exists and remains in possession of its lands, its title and possession are sovereign and exclusive; and there exists no authority to enter upon their lands, for any purpose whatever, without their consent. Of the admission of this principle, the treaty above referred to [the Treaty of Canandaigua of 11 November 1794 between the United States and the Six Nations (Haudenosaunee)] furnishes a proof. The United States stood in need of a road through

> the lands of the Senecas from Fort Schlosser to Lake Erie; yet, inasmuch as they had no authority to enter upon the lands of the Senacas, even for the purpose of passing through them, without their consent, their right of way became the subject of compact. Although the Indian title continues only during their possession, yet that possession has always been held sacred, and can never be disturbed but by their consent. They do not hold under the States, nor under the United States; their title is original, sovereign, and exclusive.[325]

Wirt could, on the foundation of this truth, have attacked the dishonesty in Marshall's claiming in *Johnson* that the British Crown had—and that the United States had inherited—an "absolute title" to the land and an "absolute title" to "extinguish" the Indian "right of occupancy."[326] Wirt could have pointed out that this was a position incompatible with the Treaty Supremacy Clause that made the treaty guaranteed dominion of the Cherokee Nation part of the supreme law of the land. He could have emphasized that it was not an improvement on the fantasy "title" derived from discovery, much less a "clear" or "absolute" title, but rather merely an alleged capacity to "extinguish" someone else's title—a capacity that could in fact only be exercised with that someone else's consent—as it is the Indian title to the land that is "original, sovereign, and exclusive."[327] Marshall, in short, was deliberately seeking to disguise a reality that vitiated his argument, to protect his spurious claim that the United States possessed some sort of "clear title" to the land as a result of an "ultimate dominion" allegedly acquired by Christian discovery.

It is worth noting that even Wirt, mistakenly, spoke at times of the European conquerors of the country rather than to stress, as Congressman Henry Storrs would in 1830, that the United States had broken with any claim to exercise a right of "conquest" and "have closed our hostilities by treaties ever since we became an independent Government."[328] But whatever Wirt meant by "the European conquerors of this country," he certainly did not mean anything capable of adversely affecting Native sovereign title or the treaty relationships to which sales of such title gave rise.[329] The central importance of treaties, and of these treaty relationships, Wirt would address eloquently. Writing to President John Quincy Adams in 1828 about the state of Georgia's effort to reopen old and settled

Georgian claims against the Creek (Muscogee) Nation, Wirt tackled head-on Georgian claims that there was some sort of significance to their assertion that the Creek Nation was not an independent nation. Wirt began by noting that whatever Georgia intended to mean by this assertion it could not mean that the Creek Nation was not *sui juris* for Georgia itself had entered into treaties with the Creek Nation before the Constitution.

> If they are independent for the purpose of treating, they have all the independence that is necessary to the argument. If they are competent parties to this species of contract called a treaty, the construction of the contract must be governed by the same rules of reason which govern the contracts of all other competent parties; for the rules which govern the construction of treaties are not *technical* and *artificial*, as seems to be assumed by the Georgia memorial; on the contrary, they are the mere dictates of reason and common sense, which apply to the transactions of all rational beings, of whatever nation, color, or religion. The point, then, once conceded, that the Indians are independent to the point of treating, their independence is, *to that purpose*, as *absolute* as that of any other nation. Being competent to bind themselves by a treaty, they are equally competent to bind *the party who treats with them*. Such a party cannot take the full benefit of the treaty with the Indians, and then deny them the reciprocal benefits of the treaty, on the ground that they are not an independent nation to all intents and purposes. It would require no technicality to perceive and to expose the injustice of such an attempt. It would lie open to the reprehension of the plainest understanding.[330]

And yet taking the benefit of our treaties with the Native Nations and denying them the reciprocal benefits they are entitled to anytime "the sovereign" wishes to do so is the very definition of the "federal Indian law" John Marshall and a majority of the Supreme Court established with *Johnson* and *Cherokee Nation*. It is the legal foundation of the Trail of Tears and all of the genocides and land thefts that have followed in its wake. It is an organized system of robbery and oppression built on delusions of conquest and delusions of the different treatment to which "domestic" and "dependent" nations are supposedly entitled in comparison with foreign states when it comes to their treaty rights in constitutional law.[331] It rests precisely on an attempt to claim that the principles that should govern the United States' treaty relationships with the Native Nations under constitutional law are "*technical* and *artificial*" rather than "the mere dictates of reason and common sense, which apply to the transactions of all rational beings, of whatever nation, color, or religion."[332]

Worcester masked the Supreme Court's bad faith interpretive stance toward the treaty-obligations of the United States to the Native Nations with pleasant-sounding observations about treaties and "natural" and traditional Cherokee rights that had already been violated by Marshall's refusal in *Cherokee Nation* to recognize and respect the corresponding treaty-obligations on the United States—and in particular on the Supreme Court—that these treaties and the Cherokee Nation's attendant treaty-rights entail. One would never know from reading some of the passages in *Worcester* that a majority of the Supreme Court considered the Native Nations as being completely under the "sovereignty and dominion" of the United States.[333] One would never know that a majority of the Supreme Court viewed these nations as having allegedly surrendered their "unlimited independence" in "exchange" for "civilization and Christianity."[334] The dishonesty with which Marshall claimed to be treating the Native Nations the same as all the other nations of the earth is truly breathtaking after he had just—the year before in *Cherokee Nation*—insisted that they cannot maintain an action in the courts of the United States because they were different—"domestic" and "dependent."[335] Here is the language in *Worcester* with which Marshall tried to cover the lie in *Cherokee Nation* that the Native Nations were "different" while simultaneously continuing to obtain the benefit of that lie for "the sovereign":

> The Indian nations had always been considered as distinct, independent political communities, retaining their original natural rights as the undisputed possessors of the soil from time immemorial, with the single exception of that imposed by irresistible power, which excluded them from intercourse with any other European potentate than the first discoverer of the coast of the particular region claimed, and this was a restriction which those European potentates imposed on themselves, as well as on the

> Indians. The very term "nation," so generally applied to them, means "a people distinct from others." The Constitution, by declaring treaties already made, as well as those to be made, to be the supreme law of the land, has adopted and sanctioned the previous treaties with the Indian nations, and consequently admits their rank among those powers who are capable of making treaties. The words "treaty" and "nation" are words of our own language, selected in our diplomatic and legislative proceedings by ourselves, having each a definite and well understood meaning. We have applied them to Indians, as we have applied them to the other nations of the earth. They are applied to all in the same sense.[336]

The dishonesty of Marshall's claim in *Worcester* to have treated the Indians fairly—to have treated them the same as "the other nations of the earth"—is evident in even a cursory examination of *Worcester* in the context of *Johnson* and *Cherokee Nation*. Nothing in *Worcester* repudiated the claim of an "ultimate dominion" or a complete "sovereignty and dominion" over the Native Nations that Marshall had claimed for the United States in the earlier cases; a claim that the United States made with regard to no other nations in the world. Nothing in *Worcester* repudiated Marshall's claim that the Native Nations were "domestic" and "dependent." Nothing in *Worcester* respected the right of the Cherokee Nation as an independent foreign state to maintain an action in the courts of the United States. Nothing in *Worcester* respected the right of the Cherokee Nation—as a Tribe (a legal entity specifically mentioned in the Constitution)—to maintain an action in the courts of the United States simply because the United States had guaranteed them their dominion as part of the supreme law of the land and that treaty-guaranteed dominion was being violated by a state of the union.

Worcester allowed Marshall—after he had, in effect, repudiated the Treaty Supremacy Clause in *Cherokee Nation*—to pretend to embrace treaties as the supreme law of the land. Here it is essential to stress that Marshall's claim in *Worcester* is that the Cherokee Nation are at the "rank" of treaty partners and *not* that they have *any* rights that they can enforce in the courts as a consequence of their treaties or as a result of their "rank." Their "rank" and their treaties might have meaning for the executive branch, or for the legislative branch, but, somehow—and this is the essential point that must be perceived if the Supreme Court's bad faith interpretive stance is to be understood at its origin—the judiciary is under no obligation to uphold constitutional law over these other branches when it comes to the treaty rights of a Native Nation. This is because these nations, in *Cherokee Nation,* were held (falsely) to be completely under the sovereignty and dominion of the United States and stripped—on that pretext (and in the worst of bad faith)—of their right as a foreign state to maintain an action in the Supreme Court under its original jurisdiction and stripped of their right to do so even on the obvious grounds that they were parties to a case that arose under a treaty in which a state of the union was a party.

Like so many with an aggressive intention toward others, Marshall projected the aggression he felt onto these others and then presented himself and what he saw as his side as the ones being threatened. The Tribes of Indians inhabiting this country during the period of British colonial rule, according to Marshall's opinion in *Johnson,* were fierce savages whose occupation was war and whose subsistence was drawn chiefly from the forest:

> To leave them in possession of their country was to leave the country a wilderness; to govern them as a distinct people was impossible because they were as brave and as high spirited as they were fierce, and were ready to repel by arms every attempt on their independence. What was the inevitable consequence of this state of things? The Europeans were under the necessity either of abandoning the country and relinquishing their pompous claims to it or of enforcing those claims by the sword, *and by the adoption of principles* adapted to the condition of a people with whom it was impossible to mix and who could not be governed as a distinct society, or of remaining in their neighborhood, and exposing themselves and their families to the perpetual hazard of being massacred.[337]

Marshall ignored the possibility that treaties with the Native Nations could serve as a path to friendship and coexistence. To the end of his life, he failed to acknowledge, much less explain, how the Native Nations, in his own words, were "fierce savages" in his account of the colonial past in *Johnson* and sovereign equals in the treaty with the Delaware in 1778 that he correctly cited in *Worcester*.[338] As for the "principles" he advocated in *Johnson*, he did not spell out what these "principles" were, simply noting later in that opinion that they included a "rule" which somehow had the effect of "converting" discovery into conquest: "That law which regulates and ought to regulate in general the relations between the conqueror and conquered was incapable of application to a people under such circumstances. The resort to some new and different rule better adapted to the actual state of things was unavoidable."[339] The "new and different rule" that Marshall came up with was "the pretension of converting the discovery of an inhabited country into conquest."[340] In other words, the true "actual state of things" was that the Native Nations were here first—and in lawful and original possession—and the "new and different rule" was to act towards them with dishonesty, malice, and treaty-violating brutality as if they somehow had been conquered with a glance:

> According to the theory of the British Constitution, the royal prerogative is very extensive so far as respects the political relations between Great Britain and foreign nations. The peculiar situation of the Indians, necessarily considered in some respects as a dependent and in some respects as a distinct people occupying a country claimed by Great Britain, and yet too powerful and brave not to be dreaded as formidable enemies, required that means should be adopted for the preservation of peace, and that their friendship should be secured by quieting their alarms for their property.[341]

"Quieting their alarms," although Marshall does not explicitly say so, meant establishing treaties with them; treaties of "friendship" that, in Marshall's interpretative stance toward treaties, were implicitly all signed in bad faith—adopted for reasons of "national policy" and not in order to acquire land lawfully.[342] In other words, these treaties were not what the Native Nations thought they were and were not really meant to respect these nations' independence and guarantee their property—far from it—merely to quiet their alarms.

For Marshall (or anyone else) to maintain good faith with regard to the treaty obligations of the United States to the Native Nations, they would have to recognize Indian title as original, sovereign, and exclusive and to recognize the sovereignty of these nations as the sovereignty of independent foreign nations—to recognize their having dominion. That is something these nations possess by natural right—their dominion as independent foreign states. This was powerfully demonstrated by the Cherokee Nation in its bill before the Supreme Court in 1831. It was also powerfully demonstrated by figures like Asher Robbins and Jeremiah Evarts in their arguments in 1829-1830. This right of these nations to their dominion is also a right that they possess under constitutional law—properly construed—derived from treaty guarantees and the requirements of treaty relationships entered into and maintained in good faith under the same international moral and legal order in which the American people have claimed their own right to self-government.

Instead of illuminating and attacking Marshall's premises in *Johnson*, Sergeant seems to have mistakenly assumed that everyone knew that the doctrine of discovery—as it was understood in a British or American context—had no bearing on the Cherokee Nation's existence as a sovereign and independent foreign state: "The European claim of discovery never asserted their [the Native peoples] subjection or extinguishment as its consequence. It asserted nothing in respect to them. It only fixed the limits of the pretensions of different European states or sovereigns between themselves; each maintaining an exclusive right to what he had discovered, and within his discovery to deal with the natives according to his own will, without interference by others."[343]

There was plenty of reason for Sergeant to believe this. The law professor David E. Wilkins (Lumbee), and his colleague and Indigenous Studies professor K. Tsianina Lomawaima (Muscogee) have argued at length that there were three major versions of the doctrine of discovery. The third, for which they claim the best historical and legal support, is closest to Sergeant's understanding.

> First, the expansive definition of discovery asserts that indigenous nations have an occupancy or possessory right to lands, but that they

> are incompetent to manage those lands and require a benevolent guardian who holds full legal title to native lands. This definition invokes a sense of the "benevolent paternalism" supposedly exercised toward tribes by European, and later the U.S., governments. Second, the absolute definition of discovery equates discovery with complete conquest. It denies any possibility that indigenous nations possessed aboriginal title, or even use and occupancy rights, to their lands. This definition implies no need for U.S. respect for native land rights. Finally, a third definition of discovery, as a preemptive doctrine granting an exclusive right of first purchase, is argued for as the legally and historically most authentic understanding of the term.[344]

The problem is that *none* of these three definitions of the doctrine of discovery capture *Marshall's* understanding (although the "absolute" definition comes closest as Marshall deliberately conflated "discovery" and "conquest"), and both Sergeant and Wirt ought to have known this and argued accordingly—they ought to have dispelled Marshall's illusions and taken apart his arguments and assertions.

Near the heart of Marshall's illusions was the stubborn belief that the United States had acquired all the rights of the British Crown, including all the rights allegedly derived from Christians first gazing at the land, regardless of the American revolutionary jurisprudence on the basis of which the colonists had actually acted, and that this British inheritance had somehow given the United States something like "clear title" to the land.[345] This remained Marshall's express belief from *Johnson* through *Worcester*. Marshall's whole idea that arbitrarily selected episodes of prior conduct hundreds of years earlier—a few steps or a glance by representatives of a "Christian people"—should determine the law for a new and revolutionary nation is problematic and would be even if Marshall's history of the implications of that conduct were not fraudulent and built on a studious unwillingness to consider treaties as binding law. As it was, Marshall's "history" could only be defended by eliding the truth—at key junctures in his argument—that the consent of the Native Nations was necessary to "extinguish" their title—a title which Marshall also could not admit was original, sovereign, and exclusive—and by ignoring the fact that the dominion of these nations over their own land was guaranteed by the United States by treaty and by treaty relationships established in accordance with the law of nations. Even without explicit treaties of guarantee, or promises of perpetual friendship, there is no way under the law of nations—as it was understood by the framers—for one nation to conquer another and take its land without just cause; a cause Marshall never even pretended to have on any grounds other than expediency.

The heart of *Worcester* remains Marshall's spurious conversion of discovery into conquest—and especially his unique view of the way that discovery *is* conquest—in his particularly pernicious version of the doctrine of discovery; a version hidden in the word "power" in *Worcester*: "But power, war, conquest, give rights, which, after possession, are conceded by the world, and which can never be controverted by those on whom they descend.... *To avoid bloody conflicts which might terminate disastrously to all*, it was necessary for the nations of Europe to establish some principle which all would acknowledge, and which should decide their respective rights as between themselves. This principle, suggested by the actual state of things, was 'that discovery gave title to the government by whose subjects or by whose authority it was made against all other European governments, which title might be consummated by possession.'"[346] Note that the Native Nations are not included in the *all* to whom this alleged "principle" for sparing *all* from disaster applied: "power," "war," and "conquest" were to be applied to them, just not to the Europeans among themselves. These Native Nations were specifically, and with gross immorality, excluded from Marshall's conception of the global common good—from what was good for *all*.

And yet, Marshall acknowledged something of the true state of things at the commencement of the Revolutionary War: "*Far from advancing a claim to their lands, or asserting any right of dominion over them,* Congress resolved 'that the securing and preserving the *friendship* of the Indian nations appears to be a subject of the utmost moment to these colonies.'"[347] Moreover, Marshall acknowledged that in a treaty signed with the Delaware (Lenape), in September 1778, the terms used were of equality between the Delaware and the United States: "The language of equality in which it is drawn evinces the temper with which the negotiation was undertaken and the opinion which then prevailed in the United States."[348] How and when, then, had the "opinion which then prevailed" changed? How and when had the supposed "power," "war," and "conquest" acquired the attendant "rights" which "can never be controverted by those on whom they descend?" How had what was merely potential in 1778 been "consummated" and "possession" realized? How had it come to be that the Native Nations allegedly were, or so Marshall claimed in *Cherokee Nation v. Georgia*, not friends, but rather "completely under the sovereignty and dominion of the United States."[349] How had the "degree of sovereignty" and the "ultimate dominion" referred to in 1823 become the complete "sovereignty and dominion" of 1831? The answer is that this had happened exclusively in Marshall's turgid imagination in his formulations in *Johnson* and *Cherokee Nation*—especially in his dishonest version of the dishonest doctrine of the law of conquest and his equally dishonest version of the dishonest doctrine of discovery and in his consequent fantasy of a "ward" to "guardian" relationship between the Native Nations and the United States. In this fantasy, treaties signed with a Native Nation were not really treaties because a spurious American "dominion" meant that they were ultimately not binding, but rather a form of deception designed to convince trusting peoples that good faith in sovereign equality was present where it was not and that their ownership of and authority over their land was recognized—indeed guaranteed—when the intention was to dispossess them as soon as it was feasible. This is what the "power" that Marshall asserted in *Worcester* boiled down to: the power to deceive.

Aside from those sentences about "power," "discovery," and "conquest" in *Worcester*, almost everything in the majority opinion gives the impression that the Cherokee Nation is a sovereign and independent foreign state—it appears, in other words, to recognize the truth of Cherokee self-government, and the truth of an obligation to respect it, without actually doing so. There is an obligation not to intrude on Cherokee lands placed on the state of Georgia, but no such obligation is acknowledged for the United States. Associate Justice John McLean's concurrence was less coy: "At no time has the sovereignty of the country been recognized as existing in the Indians, but they have been always admitted to possess many of the attributes of sovereignty. All the rights which belong to self-government have been recognized as vested in them. Their right of occupancy has never been questioned, but the fee in the soil has been considered in the Government. This may be called the right to the ultimate domain, but the Indians have a present right of possession."[350]

This was a treaty-violating claim to the "fee in the soil" on McLean's part that was articulated in a passive voice without any effort to present argument or evidence to support it: a claim to deny the Native Nations their independence and sovereignty as foreign states derived from some Christians gazing at the land—a claim first made as a matter of American "law" in 1823 long *after* treaties were signed guaranteeing many of these nations their domains. McLean's opinion also contains a reference to the "vested" rights of the Cherokee Nation that was articulated after the Supreme Court had already made it clear in *Cherokee Nation* that any such rights—*if they even existed*—could not be enforced by the Cherokee Nation in the Supreme Court; that "an Indian tribe or Nation within the United States is not a foreign state in the sense of the Constitution, and cannot maintain an action in the Courts of the United States."[351] Nothing in *Worcester* changed that basic denial to the Cherokee Nation of its right under constitutional law to defend its treaty-guaranteed dominion over its own lands in the Supreme Court. Out of that basic bad faith denial—emerging from *Johnson v. McIntosh* and confirmed by *Cherokee Nation*—the Supreme Court's bad faith interpretive stance toward the treaty obligations of the United States to the Native Nations was born. By means of that interpretive stance, the Supreme Court sanctioned the genocide of the 1830s as licit behavior for "the sovereign," just not for the state of Georgia, regardless of the treaty obligations of the United States.

If Wirt and Sergeant had been able to ask Marshall how and when "the opinion which then prevailed in the United States" had changed from that of the founding generation, Marshall's answer—if he had been honest—would have had to have been in his own mind—in particular in his own interpretation of the Treaty of Paris of 1783 as presented in *Johnson*. In that interpretation in *Johnson* he asserted:

> By the treaty which concluded the war of our revolution, Great Britain relinquished all claim not only to the government, but to the "propriety and territorial rights of the United States" whose

> boundaries were fixed in the second article. By this treaty the powers of government and the right to soil which had previously been in Great Britain passed definitively to these states. We had before taken possession of them by declaring independence, but neither the declaration of independence nor the treaty confirming it could give us more than that which we before possessed or to which Great Britain was before entitled. It has never been doubted that either the United States or the several states had a clear title to all the lands within the boundary lines described in the treaty, subject only to the Indian right of occupancy, and that the exclusive power to extinguish that right was vested in that government which might constitutionally exercise it.[352]

This interpretation of course took place in Marshall's mind in 1823 and could not account for any alleged change in American "opinion" any time before 1823, much less as early as 1783. It is an evil fantasy of the past designed to secure "clear title" where no such title existed. Far from having anything like "clear title," as Secretary of War Henry Knox acknowledged in 1793, on the express authority of President Washington, "the property or right of soil of the great country above described"—the "whole country southward of the great lakes"—is "in the Indian nations, so long as they choose to occupy the same."[353] Moreover, the lands of the Cherokee Nation and the Creek Nation and the Choctaw Nation and the Chickasaw Nation and many others were explicitly guaranteed to them by treaty.[354] Marshall's ignoring such facts is perhaps most strikingly evident in his claim that the Indian title was a mere "right of occupancy" instead of what should have been acknowledged in truth: that the Indian title is original, sovereign, and exclusive, and far more accurately to be considered "clear title" or "absolute title" with only United States pretensions based on fantasy and dishonesty to mar it. Moreover, it is title expressly guaranteed by the United States by treaties and treaty relationships and the good faith on which they were based. We are speaking here, if we are to be true to the historical record, not about a mere right of "occupancy" but rather of a treaty-guaranteed dominion.

There is a more subtle aspect to Marshall's dishonesty that should also be stressed. This is the false claim that the "exclusive power to extinguish that right ["the right of occupancy"] was vested in that government [the British or American government] which might constitutionally exercise it."[355] In fact, the only one with the "exclusive power" to "extinguish" that right was a Native Nation itself and there was no right "vested" in any British or American government to do so without a Native Nation's consent. The impression that Marshall left by eliding that fact was a particularly contemptible lie.

The report of the House Committee on Indian Affairs of 24 February 1830 was almost as coy as Marshall when it came to treaties—treaties and treaty obligations that are potentially a legal basis for opposition to genocide if viewed as the supreme law of the United States—but in the end proved more explicit in their dishonesty. This, then, is the "rule" by which "discovery" is converted into "conquest"—the "principle" that treaties with the Native Nations are but a "mode of government" and a "substitute for ordinary legislation" and have been signed with the Native Nations in bad faith for hundreds of years![356] The trick, as the House Committee explained, "was, to appear to do nothing, which concerned the Indians, either in the appropriation of their hunting grounds, or in controlling their conduct, without their consent."[357] That is what the report of the House Committee on Indian Affairs boils down to. That is what *Johnson* boils down to. In other words: we will seem to sign treaties with you in good faith, but actually we are just biding our time until we can rule over you directly regardless of your lack of consent. We will calm your alarms over your property now, so as to better be able to separate you from it later. We will enjoy a small "degree of sovereignty" over you today (at least in our own minds), while you are powerful, but tomorrow we will enjoy a greater "degree of sovereignty" until we can finally overwhelm you. This is the "conquest" that Marshall claimed the courts of the "conqueror" could not deny—the attempted "conquest" by the lies and deceit of "federal Indian law," in violation of the Constitution, of the continuing independent sovereignty of the peoples of the Native Nations and their treaty-guaranteed dominion over their own lands. This is a "conquest" that Congressman Henry Storrs, with truth and justice on his side, denied had ever taken place as a matter of both law and history. It represents an interpretive stance toward the treaty obligations of the United States to the Native Nations that Wirt denounced as implying that President

Washington, and the Senate that ratified the Treaty of Holston, were guilty of the grossest and basest fraud.[358] It is a position that could only be taken in ignorance of, or in opposition to, the Treaty Supremacy Clause (and Marshall certainly knew that clause). It rests on a deceitful doctrine of domination. Genocide is its almost predictable result. The Georgians held this doctrine with regard to Georgia. Marshall and a unanimous Supreme Court held this doctrine with regard to the United States. This pretended "ultimate dominion" was at odds with the history of the country, with generations of treaties with the Native Nations, and, especially, with the Treaty Supremacy Clause. As Sergeant spelled out the matter in succinct and lucid terms:

> These, then, are treaties made in pursuance of the constitution. They are in full force. They stand in the statute book, with all the sanctions of treaties with foreign states; and *we* are in the possession and enjoyment of the benefits derived from them. Can we under these circumstances deny that which they necessarily import? [In other words, can we deny that we have already received land and that our treaty-partners have a right to hold us to what we promised in return, namely such benefits as the guarantee of their remaining land?]. Can we, consistently with any right rule of interpretation, or with the common obligations of good faith, call in question the character of the party, announced and admitted on the face of the instrument itself especially when by so doing we impair or take away from [them] the stipulated advantages of [their] compact? [In other words, can we cast doubt on the fact that the Cherokee Nation are a sovereign and independent foreign state with whom we have a treaty relationship when we have established a treaty with them that indicates that they are? And can we deny them the standing to pursue their rights in court simply by calling them something other than an independent foreign state?] If it were morally or politically admissible, is it *judicially* possible, while the government acknowledges, as it continues to do, the existence and binding obligations of these treaties?[359]

The answer to Sergeant's questions should have been a resounding: "No." Under Marshall's leadership, the Supreme Court, in effect, answered all these questions: "yes." With that decision, the moral character of every treaty that had ever been signed in good faith with a Native Nation was betrayed. Henceforth these treaties were to be seen by the advocates and apologists for "federal Indian law"—much as the House Committee's report had claimed—and in violation of the Constitution—as "but a mode of government, and a substitute for ordinary legislation."[360] Far from being what they had been intended by the framers to be—part of the supreme law of the land—they became part of an elaborate lie veiling a system of domination with the appearance of a "trust relationship" and further obscuring the fact that Native title is original, sovereign, and exclusive with an elaboration of a fantasy about some Christians setting eyes on the land. This was most clearly evident after the Supreme Court's opinion in the *United States v. Kagama* (1886) upholding an unconstitutional Congressional exercise of authority over the Native Nations—noting with approval that "after an experience of a hundred years of the treaty-making system of government, Congress has determined upon a new departure -- to govern them by acts of Congress."[361]

Dispelling the lies behind "federal Indian law" with the truth—including the truth of constitutional law—and abolishing the system of domination that "federal Indian law" sustains, is an urgent task. The "trust" in the relationship between the United States and any Native Nation was to be found in the belief, on both sides, that the other would keep their word in any treaty signed. This is precisely the genuine trust that the "trust relationship" as the Supreme Court defines it denies whenever "the sovereign" wishes to deny it. Since the combination of the Supreme Court's opinions in *Johnson* and *Cherokee Nation,* the United States has grounded "federal Indian law" in a bad faith rejection of genuine trust masked by what is called a "trust relationship" and what has been, in fact, a sustained effort to weasel out of the United States' treaty obligations by making use of a bad faith interpretive stance toward these obligations. Perhaps the best way of viewing the "trust relationship" is as a secular expression or extension of the doctrine of Christian discovery that shares its essential features: masking an assault on the lands and authority of others behind a cloak of rhetoric about one's allegedly benevolent intentions. In this rhetoric, these allegedly benevolent intentions function as both the justification for oppression and exploitation—for stealing Native lands and denying Native authority—and as the source of the "benefits" that the Native Nations supposedly receive "in exchange" for their lands and authority. In the original doctrine, these nations supposedly received "Christianity and civilization" from the invaders "in exchange" for their formerly "unlimited independence," even though they never agreed to such an exchange and what was received, in practice, made Christianity and civilization into code words for domination and dehumanization.[362] In the secular expression of the doctrine of Christian discovery, these nations receive the spurious "trust" in the "trust relationship" which serves to disguise the same domination and dehumanization, a "trust" that they first received in *Cherokee Nation* in exchange for their treaty-guaranteed dominion over their own lands and at the additional price of physical genocide.

Chapter 5
Marshall's War: *Cherokee Nation* in Context, part 2

The use of Marshall's opinion in *Johnson* on behalf of Georgia's pretensions, in the debate in the Congress, was allegedly a source of dismay to the Chief Justice.[363] Wirt was careful to argue that this decision, which he quoted at length, actually supported the Cherokee position. The Cherokee Nation, according to this interpretation, "were not to be constrained to sell. No actual or moral force was to be applied to constrain them to that conclusion. For as they had *a legal as well as a just right to retain the possession as long as they pleased, and to use the land according to their own discretion*; it would have been as illegal and unjust to place them under any moral coercion to sell by disturbing and annoying them in the enjoyment, as to wrest it from them by force."[364] But Georgia, moved by cupidity, "chooses to consider a future contingent title, as a present, absolute one, a mere possibility, as a certainty: and boldly assuming this novel construction as an obvious truth, she proceeds to act on it, in entire and open disregard of all the treaties, as well as the laws and constitution of the United States, to which she is herself a party."[365]

The Constitution, Wirt noted, seems to have contemplated the very case which is presented by the Bill.[366] The motive for enabling the Supreme Court to act as an international tribunal was clear: "can a more lofty spectacle be contemplated among men, than such a tribunal holding the balance of justice with a steady hand, between contending states and nations, and thus superseding the horrors of war, and performing the work of a God of peace, on the earth."[367] The president of the United States, Wirt suggested, might be waiting for such a decision to justify his taking action.[368] Wirt had taken the liberty of approaching Marshall before the case began via an intermediary to sound him out on his central argument and had received a noncommittal reply, though one that bewailed Jackson's policy.[369] One can speculate that this weakened the Cherokee Nation's case in Marshall's eyes as it suggested that Wirt lacked confidence in his own argument.[370] One can also speculate that Wirt might have approached Jackson in advance as well and perhaps had received an answer to wait for the Supreme Court's decision.

Certainly, Wirt told the Court, it was part of the sworn duty of the president of the United States to "take care that the laws be faithfully executed."[371] Unless the government be false to the trust which the people have confided to it, Wirt continued, "your authority will be sustained. I believe that if the injunction shall be awarded, there is a moral force in the public sentiment of the American community, which will, alone, sustain it, and constrain obedience. At all events, let us do our duty, and the people of the United States will take care that others do theirs. If they do not, there is an end of the government, and the union is dissolved."[372]

> It is with no ordinary feelings that I am about to take leave of this case. The existence of this remnant of a once great and mighty nation is at stake, and it is for your honors to say, whether they shall be blotted out from the creation, in utter disregard of all our treaties. They are here in the last extremity, and with them must perish forever the honor of the American name. The faith of our nation is fatally linked with their existence, and the blow which destroys them quenches for ever our own glory: for what glory can there be of which a patriot can be proud, after the good name of his country shall have departed? We may gather laurels on the field and trophies on the ocean, but they will never hide this foul and bloody blot upon our escutcheon. 'Remember, the Cherokee nation' will be answer enough to the proudest boasts that we can ever make—answer enough to cover with confusion the face and the heart of every man among us in whose bosom the last spark of grace has not been extinguished.[373]

Approaching the writing of his decision in *Cherokee Nation v. Georgia*, Marshall faced what must have seemed to him a grim choice. On the one hand, taking on the state of Georgia, and the president of the United States, and a majority of the Congress, on a highly charged issue in the name of the law of the land, at a time when the advocates of "states' rights" were already seriously threatening the fabric of the Union. On the other hand,

Marshall had, in October 1828, written to Supreme Court Associate Justice Joseph Story recognizing and regretting something of the historic injustice of American conduct toward the Native peoples and aspiring to do better:

> It was not until after the adoption of our present government that respect for our own safety permitted us to give full indulgence to those principles of humanity and justice which ought always to govern our conduct towards the aborigines when this course can be pursued without exposing ourselves to the most afflicting calamities. This time however is unquestionably arrived; and every oppression now exercised on a helpless people depending on our magnanimity and justice for the preservation of their existence, impresses a deep stain on the American character. I often think with indignation on our disreputable conduct (as I think it) in the affair of the Creeks of Georgia…[374]

The "disreputable conduct" to which Marshall referred was the conduct of the Adams administration—resistance followed by appeasement—when confronted with an earlier instance of Georgian aggression. It will be examined in chapter eight. Marshall himself would engage in "disreputable conduct" in *Cherokee Nation* less than three years after this letter to Story. Marshall seems never to have realized the severity of the "disreputable conduct"—indeed the grotesque oppression and exploitation—that he himself engaged in against the Native Nations in *Johnson v. McIntosh* and the way this shaped the future course of events. His position at this juncture—in 1828—could perhaps still be seen less as an expression of his dishonesty and more as a form of self-deluded self-righteousness. On the other hand, the fact that Marshall maintained his position in the face of all the arguments and evidence that the opponents of genocide brought to bear against it reveals a closed mind—a closed mind willing to lie on behalf of an "indispensable" expediency as he had done in *Johnson* and would again in *Cherokee Nation*. Much as he might bemoan the genocide of the 1830s—and he surely did not foresee that Jackson would use a fraudulent treaty to achieve his aim with regard to the Cherokee Nation—Marshall seems to have believed that it was not illegal for the president and the Congress to commit that genocide. Marshall perceived the Treaty Supremacy Clause and then adopted a lie about its significance—the lie that the Native Nations are "domestic" and "dependent" such that the Treaty Supremacy Clause does not apply to them. He then doubled down on that lie in *Worcester* by pretending that the Native Nations had been treated fairly by the Supreme Court, and that treaties were still being treated as the supreme law of the land.

Either the United States did not have the military power to conquer and seize Cherokee territory and govern the Cherokee people by American law at the time of the Treaty of Holston in 1791, and was dishonestly "buying time" until it could, or it wished to live in peace with the Cherokee Nation under the law of nations. Those are the options as far as whether there was bad faith or good faith in the establishment of the Treaty of Holston. Once the Treaty was established, however, it became part of the supreme law of the United States. As a result, not only Cherokee territory (Article 7) was guaranteed to the Cherokee Nation under constitutional law, but Cherokee dominion was as well.

Where Wirt and Sergeant argued that American honor was at stake in respecting the treaty rights of the Cherokee Nation, and that as a foreign state the Cherokee Nation had a right to sue the state of Georgia, neither Justice Johnson nor Justice Baldwin agreed. While the Cherokee form of government, Johnson maintained, must be classed among the most approved forms of civil government, "Whether it can yet be said to have received the consistency which entitles that people to admission to the family of nations is, I conceive, yet to be determined by the executive of these states."[375] That this was even possible, Johnson seemed to deny by maintaining that, "It cannot be questioned that the right of sovereignty, as well as soil, was notoriously asserted and exercised by the European discoverers." [376] Certainly, he claimed, there was a consequence that operated greatly against recognizing the Cherokee Nation as a state: "Where is the rule to stop? Must every petty kraal of Indians, designating themselves a tribe or nation, and having a few hundred acres of land to hunt on exclusively, be recognized as a state?"[377] Justice Baldwin likewise warned of "countless tribes, who occupy tracts of our vast domain, who, in their collective and individual characters, as states or aliens, will rush to the federal courts in endless controversies, growing out of the laws of the states or of congress."[378] His solution was simple: "Mere phraseology cannot make Indians nations or Indian tribes foreign states."[379]

Johnson's and Baldwin's opinions, together with Marshall's opinion for the court, for which they and Justice McLean voted, were seen as a great victory by the Georgian advocates of "states' rights." They hailed the majority's refusal to accept jurisdiction and denounced the Cherokee Nation for making the attempt. One Georgia editor declared, "The views of the State, with regard to her entire jurisdiction over the Indians within her limits, are fully sustained.... The Cherokees, therefore, must either submit to our laws or emigrate to the West of the Mississippi."[380] The *Globe* correspondent concluded that the Supreme Court had put an end to "a tremendous storm, attempted to be got up for political purposes, without the slightest injury being done to the Administration or any of its friends."[381] Attempting to reply, the *Intelligencer* claimed that this was a "gross error," that the Court did not mean to give confirmation to Georgia's policy, and that it had merely declared it had no power "to interfere in the manner required on the part of the Indians."[382]

Faced with the impact the Court's decision was having on public opinion, Marshall took the highly unusual step of encouraging Justice Thompson and Justice Story to make their views known in a written dissenting opinion.[383] Marshall also supported Richard Peters, the court reporter, in his plan to present the bill of the Cherokee Nation, the whole of the arguments of Sergeant and Wirt, and other matter connected with the case in a separate publication. "As an individual I should be glad to see the whole case," Marshall wrote to Peters: "It is one in which the public takes a deep interest, and of which a very narrow view has been taken in the opinion which is pronounced by the court." The reasoning and eloquence of the arguments involved were something the public had a right to see—these had been "seldom equaled—never surpassed."[384]

Justice Smith Thompson, in his dissent, in which opinion he noted Justice Joseph Story joined him, addressed the questions of whether the Cherokee Nation of Indians was a competent party to sue in the Supreme Court, whether the case in their bill warranted the court in granting relief, and whether an injunction was fit and appropriate relief. He began by noting that a state of the union could clearly be sued by a foreign state under the constitution and that the Supreme Court had original jurisdiction in such cases.

> The terms *state* and *nation* are used in the law of nations, as well as in common parlance, as importing the same thing; and imply a body of men, united together, to procure their mutual safety and advantage by means of their union. Such a society has its affairs and interests to manage; it deliberates, and takes resolutions in common, and thus becomes a moral person, having an understanding and a will peculiar to itself, and is susceptible of obligations and laws.... a weak state, that, in order to provide for its safety, places itself under the protection of a more powerful one, without stripping itself of the right of government and sovereignty, does not cease on this account to be placed among the sovereigns who acknowledge no other power.[385]

Surely the Cherokee people were a foreign nation before the New World was discovered by Europeans: "And if the Cherokees were then a foreign nation; when or how have they lost that character, and ceased to be a distinct people, and become incorporated with any other community?"[386] As for their lands, their occupancy belongs to them by right and is not a mere indulgence. "They cannot be disturbed in the enjoyment of it, or deprived of it, without their free consent; or unless a just and necessary war should sanction their dispossession."[387] As to whether they were foreign in the sense of the constitution or not, "it is their political condition that constitutes their *foreign* character, and in that sense must the term *foreign*, be understood as used in the constitution."[388]

"What is a treaty as understood in the law of nations? It is an agreement or contract between two or more nations or sovereigns, entered into by agents appointed for that purpose, and duly sanctioned by the supreme power of the respective parties. And where is the authority, either in the constitution or in the practice of the government, for making any distinction between treaties made with the Indian nations and any other foreign power?"[389] The terms "nation" and "tribe" were frequently used indiscriminately in the journals of the old congress, and as importing the same thing. As for an effort to distinguish nations from tribes in the commerce clause or elsewhere, "it appears to me of too doubtful import to outweigh the considerations to which I have referred to show that the Cherokees are a foreign nation."[390]

> No very important conclusion I think, therefore, can be drawn from the use of the term "tribe" in this clause of the constitution; intended merely for commercial regulations. If considered as importing the same thing as the term "nation," it might have been adopted to avoid the repetition of the word *nation*. Other instances occur in the constitution where different terms are used importing the same thing. Thus, in the clause giving jurisdiction to this court, the term "foreign states" is used instead of "foreign nations," as in the clause relating to commerce. And again, in article 1, section 10, a still different phraseology is employed. "No state, without the consent of congress, shall enter into any agreement or compact with a 'foreign power.'" But each of these terms, nation, state, power, as used in different parts of the constitution, imports the same thing and does not admit of a different interpretation.[391]

The Cherokee Nation's rights of property, Thompson observed, are guaranteed to it by several treaties. "It is immaterial whether this interest is a mere right of occupancy, or an absolute right to the soil. The complaint is for a violation, or threatened violation, of the possessory right."[392] The treaty guarantee is to the Cherokee people in their national capacity. "Their land is held in common, and every invasion of their possessory right is an injury done to the nation."[393] That the Cherokee Nation of Indians have, by virtue of these treaties, an exclusive right of occupancy of the lands in question, and that the United States are bound, under their guarantee to protect the nation in the enjoyment of such occupancy, was undoubtedly the case. "The laws of Georgia set out in the bill, if carried fully into operation, go the length of abrogating all the laws of the Cherokees, abolishing their government, and entirely subverting their national character."[394]

Justice Thompson concluded that the Cherokee people composed a foreign state within the sense of the constitution, constituted a competent party to maintain a suit against the state of Georgia, and that their bill presented a case for consideration to which an injunction was a fit and proper response that should be awarded to prevent the further exercise of Georgian laws violating the laws of the United States and treaties made under their authority.[395] Written after Marshall wrote his opinion, Thompson's dissent reads in part as a direct critique of Marshall's decision.

As Marshall approached the writing of his decision in *Cherokee Nation v. Georgia*, a Cherokee national named Corn Tassel was undoubtedly in his thinking. In the summer of 1830, Georgia arrested Tassel for a murder that had taken place on Cherokee territory. Wirt and Sergeant sought to make his defense a means of championing the Cherokee cause and, after pursuing the issue in the Georgia courts, filed an appeal with the United States Supreme Court. The notice of appeal should have stayed Tassel's execution, but Georgia's Governor George Gilmer called an emergency session of the Georgia legislature and declared that the Supreme Court did not possess jurisdiction because Georgia's state constitution vested criminal jurisdiction exclusively in its Superior Court. The legislature agreed and passed a resolution advising the governor and every other officer of the state to disregard any instruction from the Supreme Court for the purpose of arresting the execution of any of the criminal laws of the state. The state of Georgia, the legislature declared, would never compromise her sovereignty as an independent state. Tassell was promptly hanged.[396]

On the evening of 4 January 1831, John Quincy Adams, now a member of Congress, wrote in his diary that the *Telegraph*—then still seen as a Jackson administration mouthpiece, and soon to be seen as a mouthpiece for South Carolina nullificationist John Calhoun—was publishing, with approval, the resolutions of the Georgia legislature defying the Supreme Court. "The Constitution, the laws and treaties of the United States are prostrate in the state of Georgia," Adams wrote: "Is there any remedy for this state of things? None. Because the Executive of the United States is in League with the State of Georgia… This example… will be imitated by other States, and with regard to other national interests—perhaps the Tariff… The Union is in the most imminent danger of dissolution… The ship is about to founder."[397]

This was the context in which Marshall had to write his decision in *Cherokee Nation v. Georgia.* Claiming that he was relying on American maps, geographical treatises, histories, and laws—although certainly not examining treaties as the supreme law of the land—Marshall claimed that the Indian territory was admitted to compose a part of the United States and maintained that the Indians were "within the jurisdictional limits of the United States."[398] Like the Georgians, Marshall had no difficulty in coming up with a novel elaboration of the "discovery" myth he had expressed in *Johnson* to justify his position; an elaboration that ignored the reasons why treaties had been made part of the supreme law of the United States and denied the Cherokee Nation the exercise of its rights under its treaties and under the Constitution:

> Though the Indians are acknowledged to have an unquestionable, and, heretofore, unquestioned right to the lands they occupy, until that right shall be extinguished by voluntary cession to our government; yet it may well be doubted whether those tribes which reside within the acknowledged boundaries of the United States can, with strict accuracy, be denominated foreign nations. They may, more correctly, perhaps, be denominated domestic dependent nations. They occupy a territory to which we assert a title independent of their will, which must take effect in point of possession when their right of possession ceases. Meanwhile they are in a state of pupilage. Their relation to the United States resembles that of a ward to his guardian.[399]

The "title independent of their will" was, of course, nothing more than the "title" derived from "Christian discovery" created, as a matter of American "law," out of whole cloth in *Johnson v. McIntosh* and maintained by the Supreme Court in violation of treaties that are the supreme law of the land according to the Constitution. It was a "title" that Marshall, had he been honest, would have had to acknowledge was meaningless without Native consent: a claim to a capacity to "extinguish"—if and only if a Native Nation consented—that nation's title to some of its land and that nation's right to the "occupancy" thereof.

Claiming that the idea of appealing to an American court of justice for an assertion of right or a redress of wrong, had, at the time of the framing of the Constitution, perhaps never entered the mind of an Indian or of his tribe, Marshall asserted that their appeal was "to the tomahawk, or to the Government."[400] In fact, he was quite mistaken in this—and in seeking to ignore away the fact of existing treaties—as Indians and Indian Tribes had been using colonial courts since the seventeenth century.[401]

Marshall placed great emphasis on the distinction, in the language of the commerce clause of the Constitution, between "foreign nations, the several states, and Indian tribes."[402] The Cherokee Nation's lawyers had already shown how the language of this clause emerged from an effort to remove any doubt about the exclusive authority of the Congress to regulate commerce with the Indian Tribes given the obscurities in the analogous section of the Articles of Confederation.[403] "This may be admitted," Marshall wrote, "without weakening the construction that has been intimated." And here we reach the seeming heart of Marshall's argument: "We perceive plainly that the constitution in this article does not comprehend Indian tribes in the general term 'foreign nations;' not we presume because a tribe may not be a nation, but because it is not foreign to the United States."[404] That twisted piece of reasoning—presenting the geographical as if it were the political meaning of the word "foreign"—appears to constitute the "perception" and the "presumption" on which Marshall's claim that the Cherokee Nation was not a foreign state in the sense of the Constitution rested. That claim was not merely false but irrelevant as Sergeant had shown by explicitly noting that the Supreme Court had jurisdiction in *all* cases arising under treaties, and in *all* cases in which a state of the union was a party the Supreme Court had original jurisdiction, and that the character of the other party was of no consequence.[405]

Here we arrive at what law professor Peter d'Errico has called the "incoherence and mendacity in Marshall's refusal to hear the Cherokee case."[406] Here we arrive at the bad faith approach to the question of jurisdiction with which Marshall established the bad faith interpretive stance toward the treaty obligations of the United States to the Native Nations that serves as the foundation of "federal Indian law" to this day; a bad faith interpretive stance rooted in the doctrine of Christian discovery as it supposedly sustains a "necessarily diminished" sovereignty for the Native Nations, an alleged authority for "states' rights," and a pretend "ultimate dominion" in the United States. Here we arrive at, or at least very near, the belly of the beast, sharpened wooden stake in hand. The animal—seemingly innocuous rather than vicious beyond belief—has fled to its last redoubt: the thicket of a case that came before the Supreme Court in 1821 on appeal. This case only matters for *Cherokee Nation,* it must be stressed, because of Marshall's dishonesty in changing the terms of an agreement by unilaterally changing the name of one of the parties to that agreement: by calling an independent and sovereign foreign state a domestic dependent nation (as if that name change should have any effect on the legal obligations of the United States to that party or that party's legal rights).

In *Cohens v. Virginia* (1821), Marshall chose to opine on the Supreme Court's original as well as its appellate jurisdiction. Unfortunately, his "poorly thought out dicta" in that case, as law professor James E. Pfander has observed, "have become bedrock limits on the scope of the Court's original jurisdiction." [407] In *Cohens,* the state of Virginia—on "states' rights" grounds—challenged the propriety of the Supreme Court hearing the case. This case thus presents something of an analogue for the state of Georgia—on "states' rights" grounds—refusing to even show up to make oral arguments before the Supreme Court ten years later in *Cherokee Nation*. Both Virginia, and later Georgia, in the first case by explicit argument and in the second case by conduct, maintained that "a sovereign independent State is not suable except by its own consent."[408]

Virginia also maintained—on genuinely constitutional rather than on spurious "states' rights" grounds—that the Supreme Court's ruling in *Marbury v. Madison,* in 1803, meant that the Supreme Court had original jurisdiction over Virginia's case so that it could not be considered by the Supreme Court under appellate jurisdiction (assuming the impossibility of concurrent original and appellate jurisdiction). Virginia made that argument on the basis of Marshall's literal reading of Article III, Section 2, of the Constitution in *Marbury*. There the question being addressed involved the constitutionality of a piece of Congressional legislation that assumed it was within the power of Congress to alter the definition of the

Supreme Court's original jurisdiction as specified in the Constitution. Marshall's response to Virginia's argument in *Cohens* was to adopt a non-literal reading of Article III, Section 2. Here is the relevant text of the Constitution with the critical clause in italics:

> The judicial Power shall extend to all Cases, in Law and Equity, arising under this Constitution, the Laws of the United States, and Treaties made, or which shall be made, under their Authority;—to all Cases affecting Ambassadors, other public Ministers and Consuls;—to all Cases of admiralty and maritime Jurisdiction;—to Controversies to which the United States shall be a Party;—to Controversies between two or more States;— between a State and Citizens of another State,—between Citizens of different States,—between Citizens of the same State claiming Lands under Grants of different States, and between a State, or the Citizens thereof, and foreign States, Citizens or Subjects. *In all Cases affecting Ambassadors, other public Ministers and Consuls, and those in which a State shall be Party, the supreme Court shall have original Jurisdiction*. In all the other Cases before mentioned, the supreme Court shall have appellate Jurisdiction, both as to Law and Fact, with such Exceptions, and under such Regulations as the Congress shall make.[409]

In other words, the Congress can make regulations with regard to the appellate jurisdiction of the Supreme Court in all of the cases specified in Article III, Section 2, with the exception of all those cases mentioned in which, if a state shall be a party—or in which ambassadors, or other public ministers and consuls, are affected (or in which any of the "diverse party" controversies specified are involved or the United States is a party)—then the Supreme Court shall have original jurisdiction and Congress has no right to obstruct the constitutional right or obligation of these parties to come into the Supreme Court as plaintiffs or defendants. Here is the relevant text of Marshall's ruling in *Marbury*:

> If it had been intended to leave it in the discretion of the Legislature to apportion the judicial power between the Supreme and inferior courts according to the will of that body, it would certainly have been useless to have proceeded further than to have defined the judicial

> power and the tribunals in which it should be vested. The subsequent part of the section is mere surplusage -- is entirely without meaning -- if such is to be the construction. If Congress remains at liberty to give this court appellate jurisdiction where the Constitution has declared their jurisdiction shall be original, and original jurisdiction where the Constitution has declared it shall be appellate, the distribution of jurisdiction made in the Constitution, is form without substance. Affirmative words are often, in their operation, negative of other objects than those affirmed, and, in this case, a negative or exclusive sense must be given to them or they have no operation at all. It cannot be presumed that any clause in the Constitution is intended to be without effect, and therefore such construction is inadmissible unless the words require it.[410]

In other words, the phrase "*shall have original Jurisdiction*" in the Constitution negates the ability of Congress to deny this original jurisdiction because such a change would leave the clause in which that phrase appears "without effect." Yet Marshall, in *Cohens*, would adopt a non-literal reading of Article III, Section 2, that had precisely the effect of depriving the clause giving original jurisdiction to the Supreme Court in all cases in which "*a state shall be party*" of any operation at all in federal question cases unless what has come to be known as "diverse parties" (such as citizens of different states) are present. This non-literal reading ignores the intentions of the framers who were evidently concerned to protect the laws, and treaties, and Constitution of the United States from infractions by the states in the event that the Congress failed to establish lower federal courts. The framers, as Pfander shows—and as we will see in greater detail in chapter seven—were seeking to secure an original docket for the assertion of coercive federal claims against the states. This is clear not only from a literal reading of the text of Article III, Section 2, but even more so from Pfander's careful review of the historical context, drafting, and ratification debates. The Original Jurisdiction Clause was, as he puts it, essential to" the framers' plan to secure the effective enforcement of federal law against the states."[411]

"It is significant that Wilson wrote the grant of state-party original jurisdiction into Article III," Pfander observes: "Dedicated to a strong national government, Wilson was well aware of the doctrine of sovereign immunity and committed to restricting its application in America. He not only played a central role in drafting language for the Pennsylvania constitution that abrogated sovereign immunity but also argued persuasively in *Chisholm* and in his lectures on law that the British doctrine of immunity had no place in the United States government."[412] As we have already seen, Wilson championed the position that the Supreme Court, under the Treaty Supremacy Clause, would take cognizance of—and had the power to remedy—unconstitutional action by the states when it came to treaty violations: "This clause, sir," he told the Pennsylvania ratifying convention, "will show the world that we make the faith of treaties a constitutional part of the character of the United States; that we secure its performance no longer nominally, for the judges of the United States will be enabled to carry it into effect, let the legislatures of the different states do what they may."[413]

In other words, as I have maintained throughout this book, the Constitution extends the judicial power to *all* cases arising under treaties and insists explicitly that this jurisdiction is original to the Supreme Court in *all* cases in which a state is a party. There were thus no good grounds for avoiding taking the Cherokee Nation's case. Marshall, in *Cohens*, however, had adopted a non-literal reading of Article III that had precisely the effect of depriving the clause giving original jurisdiction to the Supreme Court in all cases in which "a state shall be party" of any operation at all in federal question cases without "diverse parties." Here is the relevant text from Marshall's ruling in *Cohens*:

> Jurisdiction is given to the Courts of the Union in two classes of cases. In the first, their jurisdiction depends on the character of the cause, whoever may be the parties. This class comprehends "all cases in law and equity arising under this Constitution, the laws of the United States, and treaties made, or which shall be made, under their authority." This clause extends the jurisdiction of the Court to all the cases described, without making in its terms any exception whatever, and without any regard to the condition of the party. If there by any exception, it is to be implied against the express words of the article. In the second class, the jurisdiction depends entirely on

> the character of the parties. In this are comprehended "controversies between two or more States, between a State and citizens of another State," "and between a State and foreign States, citizens or subjects." If these be the parties, it is entirely unimportant what may be the subject of controversy. Be it what it may, these parties have a constitutional right to come into the Courts of the Union.... When, then, the constitution declares the jurisdiction, in cases where a state shall be a party, to be original, and in all cases arising under the constitution or a law to be appellate, the conclusion seems irresistible, that its framers designed to include in the first class, those cases in which jurisdiction is given, because a state is a party; and to include in the second, those in which jurisdiction is given, because the case arises under the constitution or a law.[414]

As Pfander comments: "Such a reading makes a hash of the framers' apparent understanding by suggesting that state-party 'cases' may encompass matters that the menu defines as 'controversies' but not those it defines as 'cases.' Yet, paradoxically, the Court itself and most commentators have adopted precisely that reading of the Court's jurisdiction over state-party 'cases.'"[415] This is in spite of the fact that Marshall appears to have returned to a literal reading of Article III, Section 2 in *Governor of Georgia v. Madrazo,* in 1828: "The decree cannot be sustained as against the state, because if the 11th Amendment to the Constitution does not extend to proceedings in admiralty, it was a case for the original jurisdiction of the Supreme Court."[416] All that needs to be noted to appreciate Marshall's capricious inconsistency with regard to the original jurisdiction of the Supreme Court is the fact that "cases" arising under treaties and "cases" arising under admiralty and maritime jurisdiction are in exactly the same category of "cases" in Article III, Section 2.

What d'Errico observes—and this is what is most important to us here—is that even with such a convoluted non-literal reading of Article III, Section 2, as Marshall sometimes engaged in, his approach to his own dicta in *Cohens* could easily have been applied to justify taking the Cherokee Nation's case:

> [Marshall] acknowledged the appellant Cohens framed the issue as "arising under the laws of the United States," which he had already said could only be brought by appellate jurisdiction. He then reconciled that little problem by going through a convoluted *negative* analysis of Article III; he focused on what the text did *not* say. He said, it "does *not* say that ... appellate jurisdiction shall *not* be exercised in cases where, from their nature, appellate jurisdiction is given, whether a State be or be not a party." In other words, Marshall said it didn't matter that a state was a party, even though he had just said a state party called for original jurisdiction. Based on this negative analysis, he rejected Virginia's argument and took the Cohens case. The point here is if Marshall had wanted to take the Cherokee case, he could have gone through the same kind of negative analysis to get around his non-literal reading of Article III. He could have said, "Article III does *not* say that treaty cases shall *not* be brought under original jurisdiction, where, from their parties [*i.e.*, a state is a party] original jurisdiction is given." Such a negative analysis would have provided a basis to accept the Cherokee case. But Marshall was not interested in taking the case. Marshall could also have borrowed another statement he made in *Cohens*, where he said the court must be ready to deal with "cases...of direct legislative resistance...opposing the... government." He said that the government must be able "to protect itself and its laws."[417]

The remarkable intellectual sleight-of-hand with the word "foreign" in John Marshall's wrongly decided opinion in *Cherokee Nation v. Georgia* in 1831 was and remains a powerful juristic illusion: a distraction from the fact that original jurisdiction was inherent as the case arose, as the Cherokee Nation's lawyers had argued, under a treaty and with a state of the Union as a party. Marshall took the geographical meaning of the word "foreign" and substituted it for the political meaning of the word "foreign" with the result that the Cherokee Nation—though explicitly recognized by Marshall as a state with treaty relations with the United States—was somehow seemingly stripped of its international legal personality and effectively denied its rights to its territory as guaranteed to it by the Treaty of Holston of 1791.[418] At a deeper level, Marshall's "geography" was itself dependent on the idea that "discovery" gave everything "ultimate" or "absolute" to the discoverers' government so that nothing "foreign" remained. Hence, the Native Nations that did in fact survive were defined as "domestic" and placed in the category of "wards." All that was necessary to the further betrayal of the Constitution, then, was the construction of the obligations of treaties with "wards" as if they were governed by "*technical* and *artificial*" rules rather than by the "dictates of reason and common sense, which apply to the transactions of all rational beings, of whatever nation, color, or religion."[419] In other words, all that was necessary was a willingness to lie—to claim that one can change the terms of an agreement with a foreign nation by unilaterally ceasing to call it "foreign" and calling it "domestic" and "dependent" instead.

Under Article 7 of the Treaty of Holston, it is clear that "The United States solemnly guarantee to the Cherokee nation, all their lands not hereby ceded."[420] Under Article 11, it is clear that Cherokee territory—whose bounds are specified in Article 4—is quite distinct from the territory of the individual states and territorial districts of the United States and is not under American jurisdiction, much less "ultimate dominion." But under Marshall's interpretation in *Cherokee Nation v. Georgia*, the Cherokee Nation became, along with every other tribe, a "domestic" rather than a "foreign" nation—and a "dependent" state allegedly under the jurisdiction of the United States and without recourse to the Supreme Court. This interpretation was a mechanism for ignoring the meaning of treaties in American constitutional law as well as for forgetting any sort of good faith understanding of the word "treaty" in any language—a mechanism for breaking faith with the framers of the Constitution as well as with the Native peoples and for dodging a direct confrontation with the illegal aggression of the state of Georgia.

What the Supreme Court should have said instead is firstly what Thompson and Story claimed in their dissent in *Cherokee Nation*: that the Cherokee people compose a foreign state within the sense of the constitution, that they constitute a competent party to maintain a suit against the state of Georgia, and that their bill presents a case for consideration to which an injunction is a fit and proper response that should be awarded to prevent the further exercise of Georgian laws violating the laws of the United States and treaties made under their authority.[421] Alternatively, the Supreme Court should have held, as Sergeant had argued, that the judicial power extended to the case because it arose under a treaty and that original jurisdiction was given to the Supreme Court by virtue of the fact that a state was a party to the case so that the character of the other party was irrelevant.[422] The commitment that had been made to respect the Cherokee Nation's dominion was a commitment made to a nation—and not to a name—and that commitment was and remains a law the United States and its courts are constitutionally bound to obey.

Far from Marshall adopting Thompson's and Story's position, Story—by 1833—had adopted Marshall's. In the immediate aftermath of *Worcester*, in 1832, Story wrote to his wife as follows: "Yesterday morning, the Chief Justice delivered the opinion of the Court in the Cherokee case, in favor of the missionaries. It was a very able opinion, in his best manner. Thanks be to God, the Court can wash their hands clean of the iniquity of oppressing the Indians, and disregarding their rights."[423] That Story was far more concerned with the reputation of the Supreme Court than with the rights of the Indians can be seen from the way he treated Indian title—as a "mere right of occupancy"—in his *Commentaries on the Constitution of the United States* the following year: "As infidels, heathens, and savages, they were not allowed to possess the prerogatives belonging to absolute, sovereign, and independent nations. The territory over which they wandered, and which they used for their temporary and fugitive purposes, was, in respect to Christians, deemed, as if it were inhabited only by brute animals."[424] Not only did Story reaffirm the Court's dishonest and treaty-violating position in *Johnson*, he essentially started his *Commentaries* with it: beginning with Columbus' discovery of the New World, and the doctrine of Christian discovery, and borrowing heavily from the Court's language in *Johnson* to do so. Together, Story's and Marshall's popular works—the *Commentaries* and the *Life of Washington* (which also started with Columbus and the doctrine of Christian discovery)—contributed to an imagined community that looked less to the Declaration of Independence and the Constitution and more to a white Christian supremacist nationalism as the foundation of the country; at least their contributions were much more in this direction than those of a figure such as James Wilson.[425]

On 29 May 1830, a day after the removal bill passed the Congress, Massachusetts Senator Daniel Webster wrote to former secretary of state Henry Clay that the bill would weaken Jackson in both Pennsylvania and New York in the 1832 election.[426] On 12 December 1831, the National Republicans met in convention, selected Henry Clay and John Sergeant as their ticket, and issued an address that condemned Jackson on a number of grounds: "most important" among them his approval of "inhumane and unconstitutional outrages" against the Indians.[427] In the event, however, Cherokee hopes were before the public primarily through the case of *Worcester v. Georgia,* and that case, in the words of historian Edwin Miles, played "only a minor role in the presidential canvass." [428] Jackson biographer Donald Cole has argued that Jackson's victory in 1832 was a personal one in which the issues were not particularly relevant to his victory and in which even his support for Cherokee removal worked only somewhat to his disadvantage:

> Jackson's Indian policy also hurt a bit but was hardly decisive. Van Buren later recalled that Indian removal had cost the Democrats 8,000 to 10,000 votes in New York. He remembered receiving "a spirited denunciation" from his niece in western New York, "where the pro-Cherokee feeling had been lashed to a great height." The same feeling proved costly in Pennsylvania and Ohio as well. Still, Jackson won the three states. In Georgia, Alabama, and Mississippi, which Jackson would have carried anyway, his removal policy endeared him to settlers, who were eager to take over the vacated lands. He lost some of that support in Alabama when he sent troops to remove white squatters intruding on Creek land.[429]

Had the Supreme Court ruled for the Cherokee Nation in *Cherokee Nation v. Georgia,* the issue would have dominated public and elite discussion in the deepening constitutional crisis and might well have led to Jackson's defeat in the 1832 elections. Jackson, it is true, would claim that Marshall's decision in *Worcester v. Georgia,* was "still born," but no such claim could have been made of a decision calling on him to uphold the law of the land and enforce an injunction on the state of Georgia.[430] As Charles Hobson, the editor of John Marshall's papers notes with regard to *Worcester,* "Scholarship has long since laid to rest the myth that President Jackson refused to enforce the decision."[431] And Jackson might well have complied with a Supreme Court ruling for the plaintiff in *Cherokee Nation*. Had the Supreme Court ruled for the Cherokee people in *Cherokee Nation*, the choice before the American people would have been clear and at the center of American politics.

It is difficult to appreciate how much John Marshall changed the meaning of the words we use by his decision in *Cherokee Nation v. Georgia*. He almost single-handedly altered the very language in which we think. It would be a rare non-Native person nowadays who thinks that the Indian Tribes are foreign states in the sense of the Constitution. Yet the fact of their constituting foreign states was a common position among the Congressional opponents of genocide in 1830, one for which they demonstrated that they had the sanction of both constitutional law and international law. By denying the applicability of the adjective "foreign" to what he admitted was the Cherokee state, Marshall effectively severed the attachment of the word "state" from ascription to the Native Nations. Rather than reestablish an honest approach to the question of relations with the Native peoples, Marshall's decision in *Worcester* established a second-class "sovereignty"—what came to be known as "tribal sovereignty"—that simultaneously obscured the full rights of the Native peoples to be treated as treaty-partner equals in constitutional law, and recognized as independent and sovereign foreign states, and Marshall's own role in the denial of respect for these rights in *Cherokee Nation v. Georgia*.

The slicing cut of Marshall's juristic knife—"If it be true that the Cherokee nation have rights, this is not the tribunal in which those rights are to be asserted"—was in full operation for about a year before seeming to be partially withdrawn in *Worcester v. Georgia* in 1832. That was sufficient. To be a state under international law is to be a member of the society of nations, to have an international legal personality. By treating the Cherokee Nation as outside of that society—which Marshall did when he claimed they were not foreign—he denied the very grounds of their statehood and sought to sever them from it. This linguistic and juristic removal would prove as devastating to the indigenous peoples of America as the physical removal to which it was a prelude. The change in the meaning of the words: "state," "sovereignty," and "treaty rights" that Marshall helped unleash at the federal level, as applied to the Native Nations, effectively stripped from these nations recognition of their membership in the society of nations, it stripped from them recognition of their international legal personality as a matter of "positive" international law. [432] It placed them under the "jurisdiction" of the United States as if they were a "ward"—a status in which they would be abused for centuries and continue to see the erosion of their exercise of their rights to this day.

In seeming to acknowledge that the Cherokee Tribe constituted a sovereign state in *Worcester v. Georgia,* Marshall would quote Vattel:

> A weak state, in order to provide for its safety, may place itself under the protection of one more powerful without stripping itself of the right of government and ceasing to be a state. Examples of this kind are not wanting in Europe. "Tributary and feudal states," says Vattel, "do not thereby cease to be sovereign and independent states so long as self-government and sovereign and independent authority are left in the administration of the state." At the present day, more than one state may be considered as holding its right to self-government under the guarantee and protection of one or more allies. The Cherokee nation, then, is a distinct community, occupying its own territory, with boundaries accurately described, in which the laws of Georgia can have no force, and which the citizens of Georgia have no right to enter but with the assent of the Cherokees themselves, or in conformity with treaties and with the acts of Congress.[433]

But by this point the damage had already been done. Nor was it undone as Marshall rejected only Georgia's spurious claims of jurisdiction over the Native peoples "within" its boundaries and not Marshall's own spurious claims of an "ultimate dominion" over the Native peoples "within" the boundaries of the United States. Marshall's decision in *Cherokee Nation v. Georgia* effectively gave the Cherokee people the international legal status of refugees in their own country. And it did the same to every other indigenous people as well. It was a brutal act of unconstitutional aggression on a par, and in its own way even worse, than Georgia's extension of its jurisdiction over Cherokee territory. In fact, it was an extension in the American collective self-consciousness of American jurisdiction over what had formerly been recognized as foreign states, or, more comfortably to modern ears, as foreign powers. This former recognition was clear not only in the positions articulated by the opponents of genocide in the debate in the Congress in 1830, but in the very language Marshall first embraced in *Cherokee Nation v. Georgia,* before arguing that it be discarded as of no consequence in American law. A more insidious abuse of the language, and of the Constitution, is not easy to imagine. Marshall first conceded the fundamental truth of the situation, and then took that concession away with a linguistic sleight of hand rooted in a spurious question:

> So much of the argument as was intended to prove the character of the Cherokees as a state, as a distinct political society, separated from others, capable of managing its own affairs and governing itself, has, in the opinion of a majority of the judges, been completely successful. They have been uniformly treated as a state from the settlement of our country. The numerous treaties made with them by the United States recognize them as a people capable of maintaining relations of peace and war, of being responsible in their political character for any violation of their engagements, or for any aggression committed on the citizens of the United States by any individual of their community. Laws have been enacted in the spirit of these treaties. The acts of our government plainly recognize the Cherokee nation as a state, and the courts are bound by those acts. A question of much more difficulty remains. Do the Cherokees constitute a foreign state in the sense of the constitution?[434]

In *Cherokee Nation v. Georgia,* Marshall claimed that when "the term 'foreign state' is introduced [in the Constitution], we cannot impute to the [constitutional] convention the intention … to comprehend Indian tribes within it unless the context force that construction on us. We find nothing in the context, and nothing in the subject of the article, which leads to it."[435] In fact, a moment's reflection on why the framers granted foreign states the right to sue states of the United States will suffice to force precisely that construction. The intention was to improve the faith and credit that foreign nations could place in the United States to keep its word and to hold the country to its promises. It was a matter of virtue, honor, and a self-interest centering on the establishment of a new mechanism with which to contribute to prosperity, and to the maintenance of peace, by upholding established agreements and resolving international controversies through the American judiciary. Indeed James Wilson—whom one might have suspected on the warmth of his language alone to have been the primary author of this part of the Constitution—defended its purpose in his law lectures at the College of Philadelphia in 1790-1791 with particular enthusiasm for the new era of moral and legal conduct that it had allegedly ushered in:

> With regard to the government of the United States, they have engaged that the judicial power of the United States shall extend "to controversies between two or more states; between a state and the citizens of another state; between citizens of different states; between citizens of the same state claiming lands under grants of different states; and between a state, or the citizens thereof, and foreign states, citizens, or subjects." ... In all these different enumerated cases, the tribunals of the United States have judicial authority to decide. By what law shall their decisions be governed? Before the establishment of the national government, controversies happening in those enumerated cases, if determined at all, must have been determined by the principles and rules of the law of nations.... Hitherto that great law has been applied and administered by the force or by the pleasure of the parties in controversy: in the United States, it can now be applied and administered by impartial, independent, and efficient, though peaceful authority. This deduction, if properly founded, places the government of the United States in an aspect, new, indeed, but very conspicuous. It is vested with the exalted power of administering judicially the law of nations, which we have formerly seen to be the law of sovereigns.... To every citizen of the United States, this law is not only a rule of conduct, but may be a rule of decision. As judges and jurors, the administration of this law is, in many important instances, committed to their care. What a beautiful and magnificent prospect of government is now opened before you! The sluices of discord, devastation, and war are shut: those of harmony, improvement, and happiness are opened! On earth there is peace and good will towards men![436]

Treaties with a Tribe are treaties: they are valid instruments that the framers intended to have championed by the judiciary and by the American people as against any state of the Union's attempt to violate them and, for that matter, any attempt to violate them on the part of the United States. Unwilling to live within the constraints of the Constitution, and possessed of a fanatic vision of their state's rights, the Georgians pushed for genocide until it was achieved. The Cherokee Nation's rights under the Constitution should have been effectively protected and defended in the administration, in the Congress, and in the Supreme Court but were not. The Cherokee Nation's statehood John Marshall acknowledged while simultaneously seeking to destroy its foundation: the membership of the Cherokee Nation in the society of nations as a state with an international legal personality (as any state with one or more treaties with another state certainly is). The violation of the rights that a state derived from such treaties by the Supreme Court itself was a problem that James Wilson did not address. The common law speaks of a writ of attaint. There is no way of presenting John Marshall with such a writ. However, to the extent that we—the American people—continue to assert that we have jurisdiction over the Native peoples we might be presented with such a writ ourselves.

Chapter 6
Breaking Faith with the Cherokee Nation

Writing in the bilingual English and Cherokee newspaper that he edited, the *Cherokee Phoenix*, Elias Boudinot had his hands full, in early April of 1831, trying to blunt the celebrations of the Georgian press over the Supreme Court's refusal to accept jurisdiction in *Cherokee Nation v. Georgia*:

> Does the Court say that the Cherokees have no property in the soil, but are merely tenants at will? That they have no right of self-government, but are subjects of the states? That treaties are not binding, and the intercourse law unconstitutional? These are the views of Georgia. Now does the opinion of the Court sustain them? Far from it. No language can be plainer than the following: "So much of the argument," says the Court, "as was intended to prove the character of the Cherokees as a state, as a distinct political society, separate from others, capable of managing its own affairs and government itself, has in the opinion of the majority of the judges, been completely successful." If this sustains the views of Georgia and General Jackson (for we are told he also considered his views sustained by the Court) then we have all along been utterly ignorant as to what these views were.[437]

The following week, however, Boudinot was clearly discouraged and wrote in the *Cherokee Phoenix* that it was more blessed to suffer than to be the oppressors: "If the white man must oppress us—if he must have the lead, and throw us penniless upon the wild world, and if our cries and expostulations will avail nothing, let it be so. We are in the path of duty, and the Judge of all the earth will vindicate our cause in his own way and in his own good time."[438] Chief John Ross maintained his faith in American justice: "Upon the whole, I view the opinion of the Court as regards our political character & the relations we sustain towards the United States, as being conclusively adverse to the pretended rights which have been asserted by Georgia over us, under the countenance of the President.... I sincerely believe that a foundation is laid upon which our injured rights may be reared & made permanent."[439] And if a Supreme Court decision was all it took to establish the law of the land in the United States, John Ross' belief in American justice would have been somewhat vindicated in 1832.

Refusing to take an oath of loyalty to Georgia as a condition for working on Cherokee territory, the missionaries Samuel Worcester and Elizur Butler were arrested by the Georgians and sentenced to four years at hard labor. When their case reached the Supreme Court, Marshall's opinion rang out in seemingly clear tones that obscured his own violation of international law and of American constitutional law the year before without rectifying the illegality of his decision in *Cherokee Nation v. Georgia.* Here is a famous part of his opinion in *Worcester v. Georgia*:

> The Cherokee nation, then, is a distinct community occupying its own territory, with boundaries accurately described, in which the laws of Georgia can have no force, and in which the citizens of Georgia have no right to enter, but with the assent of the Cherokees themselves, or in conformity with treaties, and with acts of congress. The whole intercourse between the United States and this nation, is, by our constitution and laws, vested in the government of the United States. The act of the state of Georgia, under which the plaintiff in error was prosecuted, is consequently void, and the judgment a nullity.... the acts of Georgia are repugnant to the constitution, laws, and treaties of the United States. They interfere forcibly with the relations established between the United States and the Cherokee nation, the regulation of which, according to the settled principles of our constitution, are committed exclusively to the government of the union. They are in direct hostility with treaties, repeated in a succession of years, which mark out the boundary that separates the Cherokee country from Georgia; guarantee to them all the land within their boundary; solemnly pledge the faith of the United States to restrain their citizens from trespassing on it; and recognize the pre-existing power of the nation to govern itself.[440]

This seemed an almost complete vindication of the Cherokee position vis-a-vis Georgia, but while rejecting Georgia's spurious claims of jurisdiction over Cherokee territory, it mistakenly maintained Marshall's spurious claims that the United States itself possessed such jurisdiction and began to introduce the warped fantasy that the Native Nations were somehow subject to "acts of Congress." As we have seen, the heart of Marshall's position in *Worcester* was perfectly compatible with his tacit approval of the genocide that the legislature and the executive branch wished to conduct; tacit approval that Marshall had given in his decision—almost explicitly—in his conclusion in *Cherokee Nation*: "If it be true that the Cherokee Nation have rights, this is not the tribunal in which those rights are to be asserted. If it be true that wrongs have been inflicted, and that still greater are to be apprehended, this is not the tribunal which can redress the past or prevent the future."[441] By opposing in *Worcester*, even if ineffectually, the genocide that the Georgians sought to conduct, the Supreme Court gave itself a patina of "good intentions" with which to mask the domination and dehumanization system of "federal Indian law" and its sanctioning of the genocide of the 1830s behind the veil of a "trust relationship."

Worcester v. Georgia provided nothing in the way of practical relief for the Cherokee Nation. The superior court was ordered to reverse its decision and free Worcester and Butler. But even this proved too much for that court which refused to do so, claiming that the Supreme Court of the United States had exceeded its authority. Georgia's new Governor, Wilson Lumpkin, was more blunt, claiming that he would hang the missionaries rather than "submit to this decision made by a few superannuated *life estate* Judges."[442] The Supreme Court, without waiting to find out whether the superior court had obeyed its mandate, adjourned on 17 March 1832.[443]

I said earlier that if a Supreme Court decision was all it took to establish the law in the United States then John Ross' belief in American justice might have been somewhat justified in 1832. This is because Georgia was the driving force behind the genocide of the 1830s and if it had chosen to cease its genocidal campaign out of respect for the Supreme Court's position, the air might well have gone out of the federal effort at genocide, at least as far as the Cherokee Nation was concerned. In that event, even though the Cherokee Nation could not in legal practice claim what Marshall called its "rights," its interests vis-a-vis Georgia would have been partially preserved through Worcester's and Butler's endeavor, at least until the federal government decided otherwise. The Cherokee Nation's true rights as a sovereign foreign state, Marshall obscured, having claimed (falsely) that the Native Nations are "completely under the sovereignty and dominion of the United States."[444]

A major reason why there has yet to have been another mass mobilization of U.S. activists and of U.S. public opinion on behalf of the national rights of the Native peoples since the early 1830s appears to be because the Supreme Court's position in *Worcester* became the outer limit of "progressive opinion." After it was ignored by the state of Georgia, it became a heroic statement of the rights of the Native Nations. Inadequate as it was, it seemed to be something. Even the framers of the Fourteenth Amendment, who certainly hoped to prevent anything like the Trail of Tears from happening again, thought in terms of strengthening the rights of persons not to be dispossessed of their property.[445] Undoing the mistaken assertion of an American jurisdiction over the Native peoples and so respecting their treaty rights was not on the agenda of the most progressive figures in American politics at that otherwise auspicious juncture.

Georgia's insistence on its version of states' rights, in the face of a Supreme Court decision outlining what a majority of the Court considered the law of the land, further discouraged many Cherokee allies. Jeremiah Evarts, who might have urged a more determined stance, had died in May of 1831, and no one had emerged to take his place.[446] Some of the Cherokee Nation's remaining allies, including Senator Frelinghuysen, now began to suggest that they should strike the best deal possible and move west.[447] John Ross, however, would hear none of this and forbade discussion of the possibility of accepting removal in the pages of the *Cherokee Phoenix*, calling for a "unity of sentiment and action for the good of all," and leading Boudinot to resign as editor in August 1832.[448]

Earlier in 1832, the Secretary of War, Lewis Cass, had outlined the terms of a treaty of removal to a visiting Cherokee delegation. The National Council had overruled Ross and agreed to hear the terms when the delegation returned. But the Council also voted to suspend elections and declare themselves, and Chief Ross, legitimate until such time as Georgia's proscription was ended. John Ridge, who had intended to challenge Ross in the coming election, became increasingly opposed to Ross' leadership. John Ridge and his father, Major Ridge, together with Boudinot, formed a faction known to be resigned to a removal treaty. Georgia, meanwhile, began to survey Cherokee land assigning numbers to each plot for use in a lottery. By November 1832, "fortunate drawers" were swarming into the nation. As the historians Theda Perdue and Michael Green have observed, "This was theft authorized by state law, but theft nonetheless, of millions of acres of land."[449] Our people are being "robbed and whipped by the whites almost every day," John Ridge wrote to Ross in February 1833, "we all know, upon consultation in Council, that we can't be a Nation here, I hope we shall attempt to establish it somewhere else!"[450]

Meanwhile, as John Quincy Adams had foreseen in January 1831, the "states' rights" ideology that was loose in the country would spread from Georgia to other states and to other issues, such as the tariff. On 24 November 1832, shortly after Jackson's reelection, a South Carolina convention claimed that the tariff acts of the United States Congress of 1828 and 1832 were "unauthorized by the constitution of the United States, and violate the true meaning and intent thereof and are null, void, and no law, nor binding upon this State."[451] Andrew Jackson issued a proclamation on 10 December 1832 denying the ability of a state to nullify federal law, claiming that such conduct had for its object "the destruction of the Union," and threatening South Carolina with a federal use of force against it.[452] After this, as the historian Edwin Miles notes, the case of *Worcester v. Georgia* was a potential source of considerable embarrassment to the administration:

> If the President should ask for legislation permitting the use of force against South Carolina, he might also be given unwanted authority to coerce her neighboring state. Such a turn of events would destroy the administrations hopes of isolating South Carolina, for other southern states in addition to Georgia would certainly oppose the measure. In addition, many National Republicans were anxious to support Jackson's vigorous stand against South Carolina in hopes of preventing a dismantling of the protective system and would

willingly abandon the missionaries in order to ensure strong presidential action against South Carolina.[453]

Presented with the argument that continued resistance on their part would strengthen South Carolina's political position and risk the union, and doubtful that continued resistance would be efficacious, Worcester and Butler agreed to accept pardons from Governor Lumpkin in January 1833, whereupon South Carolina Senator Stephen Decatur Miller denounced Georgia for "sneaking out of a fight."[454] By this point, Justice Joseph Story could report that Jackson had asked him to dinner at the White House and add that "what is more remarkable, since his last proclamation and message, the Chief Justice and myself have become his warmest supporters…"[455] The unanswerable question is whether, in the face of South Carolina's threat to the Union, an electorally victorious Jackson might not have sought to mend fences with Story and Marshall even if they had both ruled for the plaintiff in *Cherokee Nation v. Georgia*, and what such a reconciliation might have looked like and done for the Native Nations.

Although receptive to a treaty of removal, even John Ridge and Elias Boudinot were opposed to the fraudulent treaty that John Ross' brother Andrew signed in June 1834, surrendering all Cherokee lands in the east for a twenty-four year annuity of twenty-five thousand dollars a year. And, for once, the Senate of the United States sided with the Cherokee Nation and refused to ratify the treaty when the Jackson administration presented it.[456] Meanwhile, Georgia's Governor Lumpkin had written an open letter to Georgia's Senator Forsyth in which he claimed that "before the close of the year it may become necessary to remove every Cherokee from the limits of Georgia, peaceably if we can, forcibly if we must."[457]

Visiting the Secretary of War in early 1835, John Ross indicated that the Cherokee Nation would accept twenty million dollars, plus losses from earlier treaties, and a guarantee of federal protection for the five years it would take to organize the emigration. But the most that even sympathetic members of the Senate would agree to was five million dollars. The Jackson administration appointed the Reverend John Schermerhorn to travel to the Cherokee Nation and work out a treaty. Schermerhorn met with the Ridge faction and put together a draft, which included five million dollars worth of compensation, but before he could present it to the National Council, Ross said he would like to see Schermerhorn's formal commission. When Schermerhorn couldn't produce one, Ross ruled that he would have to lead a delegation to Washington for negotiations, as no commissioners were present. Then, for good measure, he asked whether those assembled were willing to sell their land for five million dollars and received a rousing "No." Refusing to respect the authority and legal processes of the Cherokee Nation, Schermerhorn organized an unauthorized meeting promising blankets and food to those who came. Only a few hundred people turned up, but among them was the Ridge faction and it agreed to sign Schermerhorn's treaty. "We can die," Boudinot observed, knowing that he was signing his death warrant, "but the great Cherokee nation will be saved."[458]

Ross met this betrayal with yet another effort to persuade the Senate of the United States to reject a fraudulent treaty, an effort that included a petition signed by nearly every Cherokee national in the East. When the fraudulent treaty came before the Senate in May 1836, former President John Quincy Adams called it an "eternal disgrace upon the country."[459] But the Senate voted thirty-one in favor and fifteen opposed, ratifying by one vote more than the two-thirds needed.[460] Under the terms of the treaty, the Cherokee Nation had until 23 May 1838 to depart. Engaging in a mixture of peaceful resistance and continued negotiation, Ross saw the Senate increase appropriations for removal to $6,647,067 but continue to reject his appeal for an extension of the deadline. When President Martin Van Buren agreed to Ross' appeal, and sought to move the deadline to May 1840, Georgia's Governor George Gilmer threatened to call out his state militia of two thousand men and let "the consequences" be on Van Buren's head. Van Buren backed down.[461]

Meanwhile, in 1837, the size of the Supreme Court was expanded, and two Congressmen who had voted for the Removal Act—Philip Barbour of Virginia and John McKinley of Georgia—were added to it.[462] There was to be no help from that quarter. On the contrary, its worst biases were strengthened.

Arriving in Cherokee territory with two thousand soldiers, in 1838, Brigadier General John E. Wool sought to encourage the Cherokee people to enroll to move west: "Why not abandon a country no longer yours? Do you not see the white people daily coming into it, driving you from your homes and possessing your houses, your cornfields and your ferries?"[463] But he got nowhere with his efforts and reported that it was futile to talk with the overwhelming majority of the Cherokee people who were "almost universally opposed to the treaty and who maintain that they never made such a treaty."[464] Even his offers of food and clothing were refused because to accept them could be interpreted as accepting the treaty. Ultimately, Wool requested a transfer as his duties violated his sense of honor.[465] General Winfield Scott replaced him.

Three days after the treaty's deadline, Scott's troops began to coerce the Cherokee people into thirty-one forts, beginning what missionary Daniel Butrick described as "that work which will doubtless long eclipse the glory of the United States."[466] Making a claim for abandoned property in 1842, a widow named Ooloocha recounted her experience: "The soldiers came and took us from home. They first surrounded our house and then they took the mare while we were at work in the fields and they drove us out of doors and did not permit us to take anything with us not even a second change of clothes, only the clothes we had on, and they shut the doors after they turned us out."[467] Many who had been well off were reduced to abject poverty overnight. Some had the shock of seeing Cherokee graves dug up by thieves in search of silver jewelry. Scott wrote later of how the Cherokee people had "obstinately" refused to prepare for removal: "Many arrived [at the forts] half-starved, but refused the food that was pressed upon them. At length, the children, with less pride, gave way, and next their parents."[468]

Conditions in the forts were terrible, and those in the camps that replaced them, much the same. American soldiers debauched and raped Cherokee women. And dysentery and fever, whooping cough and measles, led to premature deaths.[469] "The terror that the soldiers spread as they moved through the nation can only be glimpsed through fragmentary records," Claudio Saunt reports: "They seized individuals who were engaged in the routine tasks of daily life, visiting friends, tending to livestock, and farming. They shot dead a deaf and dumb man, who tried to flee at the sight of armed intruders. They drove two hundred children, women, and men through the torrential rain with scarcely a blanket to protect them. One soldier leveled a gun at a father and ordered him to board a barge, though the man had asked to wait for his young son."[470]

Finally, in July 1838, the Cherokee National Council passed a resolution placing Ross and his Washington delegation in charge of the removal effort. Scott agreed to give Ross until November to get ready. Cherokee leadership made removal less vicious than it might have been, but it was still brutal beyond belief. Among those who died was John Ross' wife, Quatie, having given her blanket, so the story goes, to another.[471] Ross supervised the departure of 13,149 Cherokee nationals, by his count. Arrivals in Indian Territory, as counted by an American official there, came to 11,504. The difference—the lower end estimate of 1,645 who did not survive the journey—does not include those who died in the camps in the summer of 1838 or those in the groups removed by the army before Ross took over. Measured in contrast with at least 16,542 Cherokee nationals in the east—the 1835 census figure—the upper end estimate for deaths is thousands higher.[472]

Chapter 7
James Wilson's Jurisprudence

The choice between James Wilson's revolutionary jurisprudence and John Marshall's reactionary jurisprudence was the choice on which the implicit legal sanction for the genocide of the 1830s depended. It was a choice that might have gone the other way at numerous junctures. One of these was in the 1790s when Wilson petitioned the Congress on behalf of land purchases made directly from some of the nations of the Illinois Confederacy—including the Kaskaskia—as well as from the Piankashaw Nation by what became the United Illinois and Wabash Land Companies.[473] Some of these purchases would ultimately form the basis for the claims which the plaintiff made in *Johnson v. McIntosh*. Wilson persuaded the committee of the House of Representatives to which the matter was referred, but failed to persuade the corresponding committee of the Senate. In his petition, Wilson claimed that "An empire founded upon conquest, or the visionary donations of papal power, unsupported by previous contracts with the aboriginal lords and occupiers of the soil, was never set up by Great Britain, and the United States have set up no farther territorial rights than they have derived by their independency and succession to the rights of Great Britain in America."[474]

That Marshall and Wilson were speaking in diametrically opposed terms is clear from the one claiming that the doctrine of Christian discovery had *never* been challenged in the courts of the country and the other claiming that it had *never* been set up. In history—whatever the fifteenth century legal theories that Marshall drew upon; theories spun by the London-based advocates of the would-be English empire in America—land purchases from the Native Nations were traditional practice among the colonists. But legal theories, particularly reactionary ones, are not innocuous and the meaning of centuries of traditional practice—or rather the lack of meaning thereof—was established by the Supreme Court in violation of the understandings of the Native Nations who had perhaps seen these land purchases as a lawful way the colonists could obtain the use of the land and who had undoubtedly believed that the guarantees of their remaining land meant something—perhaps even that they had been made in good faith—and would be adhered to. The Native Nations, whose treaty-guaranteed dominion over their own lands was secured by the fact that the United States Constitution made treaties part of the supreme law of the land, had already suffered oppression and horrific injustice. They did not dream of the nightmare scale of what was coming in terms of the deliberate actions of their neighbors as distinct from the horrific consequences of their neighbors' diseases or wartime crimes and brutality. The advent of a president and a Congress who would actively choose to support genocide—and the Supreme Court's establishment of a bad faith interpretive stance toward the treaty obligations of the United States—was unthought of not only by the Native Nations but also by the founding generation of the United States and the framers of the Constitution who imagined that the United States was embarked on a new and democratic way of doing things.

Of all the advocates of democratic self-government among the founding generation—the advocates of that aspect of Enlightenment thinking that struggles with the politics of domination that predominates within it—James Wilson stands alone in the consistency and clarity with which he presented a democratic vision to the country.[475] The support that his ideas won gave a great impulse to America's future. He was the only one in the constitutional convention to advocate for the direct popular election of the President.[476] Although the continuity tells against the enthusiasm for progress that animated Wilson's progressivism, he remains a progressive figure to this day not only in terms of the culture of his time but in many ways of our own as well.

Reflecting, at the turn of the twentieth century, on James Wilson's popular 1774 pamphlet denying the British parliament any authority over the American colonies—a pamphlet that can be seen as the beginning of American revolutionary jurisprudence—Supreme Court Associate Justice John Marshall Harlan argued that, "Wilson disclosed the broad ground on which his political faith rested, by declaring that all men—not some men, not men of any particular race or color, but '*all* men are by nature equal and free'—the same great principle subsequently embodied in the Declaration of Independence."[477] In light of the grotesque brutality with which an elected Congress has treated the Native Nations, Wilson's opposition to being ruled by an overseas elected Parliament makes perfect sense.

From the perspective of Wilsonian jurisprudence—a jurisprudence that provides a context in which the intentions of the framers of the Constitution can be understood—there was an obligation on all nations, as on all individuals, to respect the international moral and legal order under which the equal rights of every nation and every national are claimed to be upheld. The equality of all international persons, Wilson made clear in his law lectures in 1790-91, is what membership in the society of nations is all about: "Of that great society, equality is the basis and the rule. To this equality, the inferiority of subjection and the superiority of command are, alike, repugnant."[478] "This equality of nations is the great and general foundation of national rights," Wilson continued: "In this matter no regard is had to names. Of the great theater of the world, empires, kingdoms, commonwealths, principalities, dukedoms, free towns, are all equally imperial. A society, which, without subordination to any other, exercises within itself all the essential powers of society, is sovereign, and has all the rights of a sovereign and independent state; however narrow its territories; however small its numbers may be."[479] Like the great Swiss jurist Emerich de Vattel, Wilson held that if a weaker state had, by an unequal alliance, formed a connection with another more powerful state, it was still, as long as it maintained the right of self-government, a sovereign state. To the weaker state, the unequal alliance may secure the most assistance; on the stronger, it may reflect the most honor; but it leaves both at the same rank among the society of nations.[480]

The contrast between John Marshall's jurisprudence and James Wilson's could hardly be more stark. A disregard for the binding character of treaties and engagements, a disregard for the rights of others, was, Wilson maintained in his law lectures, weak as well as wicked. It is a truth certain in the law of nature, Wilson insisted, that he who has made a promise to another has given to that other a perfect right to demand the performance of the promise: "A state, which violates the sacred faith of treaties, violates not only the voluntary, but also the natural and necessary law of nations; for we have seen that, by the law of nature, the fulfillment of promises is a duty as much incumbent upon states as upon men."[481]

In *Foster & Elam v. Neilson*, in 1829, Marshall provided perhaps the clearest window onto his very different approach when it came to treaties and the Constitution:

> In a controversy between two nations concerning national boundary, it is scarcely possible that the courts of either should refuse to abide by the measures adopted by its own government. There being no common tribunal to decide between them, each determines for itself on its own rights, and if they cannot adjust their differences peaceably, *the right remains with the strongest*. The judiciary is not that department of the government to which the assertion of its interests against foreign powers is confided, and its duty commonly is to decide upon individual rights according to those principles which the political departments of the nation have established. If the course of the nation has been a plain one, its courts would hesitate to pronounce it erroneous. We think then, however individual judges might construe the Treaty of St Ildefonso, *it is the Province of the Court to conform its decisions to the will of the Legislature if that will has been clearly expressed*."[482]

In other words: might makes right in dealings with other nations and Parliament (or in this case the Congress) is sovereign. Once Congress voted for the Removal Bill, or so it appears, Marshall considered the treaty-violating genocide that bill authorized as licit behavior for "the sovereign." So much for the judicial review of state and even federal legislation conflicting with the United States' treaty-obligations that is inherent in the Constitution's establishing treaties as part of the supreme law of the land and guaranteeing plaintiffs the right to compel states to enter the Supreme Court under its original jurisdiction in all cases arising under treaties in which a state is a party (or, for that matter, to compel the United States to do so)! The rejection of such judicial review is at odds with the jurisprudence on which the new nation was founded with its claim that "we the people" are sovereign under the Constitution that helps unite us and which makes provision for the rights of foreigners to be respected. According to this jurisprudence, neither the Congress nor the states inherited the powers of the British Crown or the British Parliament—including any of the imaginary powers allegedly derived from "discovery."

Rather "we the people" articulated such powers as "we the people" wanted to claim under the law of nations and distributed them institutionally as "we the people" wished.

We did not inherit British jurisprudence rather we established a revolutionary American jurisprudence and on the basis of it broke away from Great Britain and established a new nation. At the heart of that jurisprudence is an individualist conception of national popular sovereignty—a conception foreign to British jurisprudence, or at least foreign to the ideas about the sovereignty of Parliament championed by William Blackstone and other leading luminaries of British jurisprudence.[483] American society championed the sovereignty of the people, even if not yet *all* of the people. We claimed a decent respect for the opinions of mankind in our Declaration of Independence and, in our Constitution, promised that our word in our treaties would be—not the whim of the Congress—but the supreme law of the land.[484] It may be objected that the "decent respect to the opinions of mankind" in the Declaration did not include the opinions of those later referred to in that document as "merciless savages" or those people enslaved by the states who were later counted as three fifths of a person. Perhaps not. But, as we will see, a review of the ratification debates over the Constitution leaves no doubt that the Treaty Supremacy Clause was intended by the framers to apply to treaties with the Native Nations.

Speaking in the Pennsylvania Ratifying Convention, in 1787, James Wilson made the constitutional convention's thinking clear on the relationship of the United States to its treaties:

> The judicial power extends to all cases arising under treaties made, or which shall be made, by the United States. I shall not repeat, at this time, what has been said with regard to the power of the states to make treaties; it cannot be controverted, that, when made, they ought to be observed. But it is highly proper that this regulation should be made; for the truth is,—and I am sorry to say it,—that, in order to prevent the payment of British debts, and from other causes, our treaties have been violated, and violated, too, by the express laws of several states in the Union. Pennsylvania—to her honor be it

> spoken—has hitherto done no act of this kind; but it is acknowledged on all sides, that many states in the Union have infringed the treaty; and it is well known that, when the minister of the United States made a demand of Lord Carmarthen of a surrender of the western posts, he told the minister, with truth and justice, 'The treaty under which you claim these possessions has not been performed on your part; until that is done, those possessions will not be delivered up.' This clause, sir, will show the world that we make the faith of treaties a constitutional part of the character of the United States; that we secure its performance no longer nominally, for the judges of the United States will be enabled to carry it into effect, let the legislatures of the different states do what they may.[485]

The Treaty Supremacy Clause is what James Madison was referring to in the Virginia ratifying convention when he said: "The general policy of that clause, is to prevent all occasions of having disputes with foreign powers."[486] The Supreme Court, in Wilson's and Madison's vision, was to function at times as a quasi-international tribunal deciding on behalf of foreign powers when these powers were in the right, and against the states of the United States when these states were in the wrong, and so maintaining peace and prosperity.[487] The good faith that the United States would show in keeping its word would deepen the faith and credit that foreigners could place in the promises of the United States to the advantage of all. The example of honest and considerate straight-forward dealing that it would set could eventually be followed by all.

It was the Treaty Supremacy Clause that Benjamin Rush—who had served as the Surgeon General of the Continental Army—had in mind when he suggested to the ratifying convention in Pennsylvania that the only treaty in history that had ever been upheld before was the one between William Penn and the Indians: "I believe, Mr. President, that of all the treaties which have ever been made, William Penn's was the only one, which was contracted without parchment; and I believe, likewise, it is the only one that has ever been faithfully adhered to."[488]

To deny the applicability of the Treaty Supremacy Clause to treaties with the Native Nations is to claim that those in the ratification debates over the

Constitution who were opposed to this clause *because* of its support for Indian rights were foolishly afraid that judges would take their oaths seriously. In an article in the *Virginia Independent Chronicle* of 18 June 1788—under the pseudonym "Many"—Arthur Campbell specifically questioned the arguments of those asserting that "*treaties* should be made part of the *supreme* law of the land." Campbell's very criticism, however, is evidence of the fact that the Treaty Supremacy Clause was seen as applying to treaties with the Native Nations:

> Since the year 1776, the United States, by commissioners acting under their authority, have made a variety of treaties, with different nations of Savages; some of them if considered as law, will destroy the private rights of individuals without an hearing; infringe the sovereignty of States, are contradictory with one another; and in not a few instances manifestly unjust. Can the Indians give us constitutional security for the observation of stipulations on their part? What embarrassments must the Judges of the federal courts be under, when they come to pronounce, what is *the supreme law of the land*. They are either to be accessaries to a multiplicity of wrongs, or endure the imputation of trifling with the obligations of a solemn oath.[489]

The international moral and legal order that Wilson championed, as Vine Deloria, Jr. has suggested when considering equality under the law in the abstract, is ultimately rooted in a vision that is expressed "in the concepts of equality of opportunity and justice equally administered under the law. Equality under the law, however, was a secularized and generalized interpretation of the Christian brotherhood of man—the universal appeal of individuals standing equally before God now seen as people standing equally before the law and secular institutions."[490] This secularized and generalized interpretation of the Christian brotherhood of man can be seen as in conflict—both in its roots within European Christianity and in its branches within the Enlightenment—with the doctrine of "Christian discovery" (as well as with the existence of slavery).

Wilson's jurisprudence provides a way to think about what is, what might have been, and what yet may be in American constitutional law with regard to the Native peoples. This jurisprudence centered on the individualist conception of national popular sovereignty that was the foundation both of the Declaration of Independence and of the work of the constitutional convention. This jurisprudence held that just government rests on the consent of the governed and that sovereignty resided in the body of the people as a "harmony" of united individuals rather than in the thirteen states.[491] It held, in the words of Wilson's opinion in *Chisholm v. Georgia* in 1793, that the American people are meant to be "sovereigns without subjects"—that the citizens of America are "equal as fellow citizens, and as joint tenants in the sovereignty."[492] It held that "Georgia is NOT a sovereign State" and rejected the claim that it was beneath Georgia's dignity to be sued by the estate of a South Carolina merchant alleging that Georgia had never paid for clothing delivered during the Revolutionary War.[493] A dishonest state—bound by a treaty or a contract—that refused to honor its agreement was, Wilson insisted, no different from a dishonest merchant: "The latter is amenable to a court of justice. Upon general principles of right, shall the former, when summoned to answer the fair demands of its creditor, be permitted, Proteus-like, to assume a new appearance, and to insult him and justice by declaring 'I am a Sovereign state?' Surely not."[494]

The law professor Randall E. Barnett, noting something of the progressivism of Wilson's individualist conception of national popular sovereignty, has suggested a major reason why *Chisholm* is not in the cannon, even though it was clearly the Supreme Court's first great decision, is the simple fact that law professors and the Supreme Court alike have deemed this decision too radical in its implications: "If nothing else, *Chisholm* teaches that the concept of sovereignty as residing in the body of the people, as individuals, was alive at the time of the founding and well enough to be adopted by two Justices of the Supreme Court, who were also influential Founders. Likewise, *Chisholm* shows that the bold assertion that states inherited the power of kings (subject only to express constitutional constraints) was rejected by four of the five Justices when the issue first arose."[495]

Wilson's contributions to the Constitution would be a fit subject for several books. His vision of the individualist national popular sovereignty of the

American people, on which the federal government and the individual state governments rest, can be considered as the foundation of the convention's work and, certainly, of his own work on the Committee of Detail which gave birth to the Supremacy Clause (including the Treaty Supremacy Clause), the Necessary and Proper Clause (including the All Other Powers Provision), the enumeration of *some* of the powers of the Congress and of the federal government, much of the structure and shape of the presidency, and the jurisdiction of the national courts. An examination of the origins of the Treaty Supremacy Clause adds strength to the interpretation, given recently by law professor John Mikhail, that the Necessary and Proper Clause includes federal and Congressional powers not specifically enumerated.[496] It does so by reviewing the drafting history of the Treaty Supremacy Clause with an eye toward the convention's concern to protect the treaty rights of foreigners, a review that agrees with Mikhail's suggestion that the "harmony" of the United States—in Wilson's sense of the term—was the guiding principle in the Convention's mandate to the Committee of Detail, and of the committee's work.

The confederation, Wilson maintained in 1785, was not intended to weaken or abridge the powers and rights of the United States—powers acquired under the law of nations (the natural law of sovereigns)—or to transfer any of those powers or rights to the individual states. It was only the union of the individual human members of the United States that vested powers and rights which did not previously exist in the body politic. The case—Wilson quotes the Swiss jurist Jean Jacques Burlamaqui as writing—"is here very near the same as that of several voices collected together, which, by their union, produce a harmony, that was not to be found separately in each."[497] This may be called the "harmony principle" of Wilson's individualist conception of national popular sovereignty: it was the individual inhabitants of the colonies, coming together in revolutionary union, that were collectively sovereign and out of the harmony of their unity gave birth to the individual states and the federal government, with their attendant rights and powers, to serve the people's purposes. It was the people's rights—expressly claimed as such under the law of nations in the Declaration of Independence—that Wilson championed: all of the acts and things "which Independent States may of right do."[498]

For Wilson and his allies, the American people were ontologically, chronologically, and legally prior to and supreme over the federal government and the states they had called into being to serve their purposes. Wilson was a staunch opponent of "states' rights" and, in a very real sense, his intentions (and those of his fellow framers)—as embedded in various clauses of the Constitution—had to be defeated by the state of Georgia and its allies for the genocide of the 1830s to take place. On 8 June 1787, Wilson suggested that a mistaken belief in states' rights was at the foundation of what the constitutional convention was called upon to correct:

> Among the first sentiments expressed in the first Congs one was that Virga is no more, that Masts is no [more]. That Pa is no more &c. We are now one nation of brethren. We must bury all local interests & distinctions. This language continued for some time. The tables at length began to turn. No sooner were the State Govts formed than their jealousy and ambition began to display themselves. Each endeavored to slice from the common loaf, to add to its own morsel, till at length the confederation became frittered down to the impotent condition in which it now stands. Review the progress of the articles of Confederation thro' Congress & compare the first and last draught of it. To correct its vices is the business of this convention. One of its vices is the want of an effectual controul in the whole over its parts. What danger is there that the whole will unnecessarily sacrifice a part? But reverse the case, and leave the whole at the mercy of each part, and will not the general interest be continually sacrificed to local interests?[499]

* * *

Writing to James Madison about the constitutional convention before it began, on 31 March 1787, George Washington adverted to the importance of maintaining the good faith of treaties:

> From the acknowledged abilities of the Secretary for Foreign Affairs, I could have had no doubt of his having ably investigated the infractions of the Treaty on both sides—Much is it to be regretted

> however, that there should have been any on ours. We seem to have forgotten, or never to have learnt, the policy of placing ones enemy in the wrong. Had we observed good faith on our part, we might have told our tale to the world with good grace; but compl[ain]ts illy become those who are found to be the first aggressors.[500]

Replying, on 16 April 1787, Madison noted that without a federal veto of state legislation: "The States will continue to invade the national jurisdiction, to violate treaties and the law of nations and to harass each other with rival and spiteful measures dictated by mistaken views of interest."[501] It was precisely because Madison and his allies were unable to secure a federal veto of state legislation in the constitutional convention that they turned to the judiciary to enforce federal law—including treaties (and the law of nations by which they were to be construed)—upon the states.

Addressing the issue of treaties in the constitutional convention itself, on 13 May 1787, Governor Edmund Randolph of Virginia sought both to specify the need for the convention to act on this and other issues and recommend that it do so first by adopting a general principle as a placeholder for details to be worked out later by what would become the committee of detail. Introducing a resolution that was adopted unanimously, according to delegate Robert Yates' notes,

> Gov. Randolph observed the difficulty in establishing the powers of the judiciary—the object however at present is to establish this principle, to wit, the security of foreigners where treaties are in their favor, and to preserve the harmony of States and that of the citizens thereof. This being once established, it will be the business of a sub-committee to detail it; and therefore moved to obliterate such parts of the resolve so as only to establish the principle, to wit, that *the jurisdiction of the national judiciary shall extend to all cases of national revenue, impeachment of national officers, and questions which involve the national peace or harmony.*[502]

This was the origin of what would become the Treaty Supremacy Clause—"all Treaties made, or which shall be made, under the Authority of the

United States, shall be the supreme Law of the Land; and the Judges in every State shall be bound thereby, any Thing in the Constitution or Laws of any State to the Contrary notwithstanding" in Article VI—in conjunction with the right of foreign nationals and foreign nations to sue states of the union in Article III's grant of jurisdiction to the judiciary in *all* cases "arising under ... Treaties," and made explicitly original jurisdiction in the Supreme Court in *all* cases to which a state of the Union is party.

Much the same procedure as applied to the judicial power, John Mikhail has argued, served as the foundation of the Necessary and Proper Clause of Article I. This can be seen in Resolution VI of the Virginia Plan, as amended—the "harmony" language of which the convention adopted by a vote of six to four, on 17 July 1787:

> Resolved that each branch ought to possess the right of originating Acts; that the National Legislature ought to be impowered to enjoy the Legislative Rights vested in Congress by the Confederation and *moreover to legislate in all cases to which the separate States are incompetent, or in which the harmony of the United States may be interrupted by the exercise of individual Legislation*; to negative all laws passed by the several States, contravening in the opinion of the National Legislature the articles of Union; and to call forth the force of the Union agst. any member of the Union failing to fulfill its duty under the articles thereof.[503]

John Mikhail has argued that, in contrast to the Forgoing Powers Provision of the Necessary and Proper Clause—drafted initially in the handwriting of Edmund Randolph and South Carolina's John Rutledge—the All Other Powers Provision of that Clause appears to have been James Wilson's handiwork. In the Constitution as it stands, the Necessary and Proper Clause (of Article 1, Section 8) reads: "The Congress shall have Power... To make all Laws which shall be necessary and proper for carrying into Execution the foregoing Powers, and all other Powers vested by this Constitution in the Government of the United States, or in any Department or Officer thereof."

As Mikhail observes this can be seen as a powerful implied power in the Necessary and Proper Clause to promote the general welfare and has been seen as such at critical junctures in the nation's past. Here is the case in summary:

1. The Necessary and Proper Clause implies that the Constitution vests powers in the government of the United States that are not identical or coextensive with the powers it vests in its departments or officers.
2. The United States of America is a legal corporation.
3. A legal corporation is vested with the implied power to fulfill its purposes.
4. The purposes of the United States include promoting the general welfare.
5. The Constitution vests the government of the United States with the implied power to promote the general welfare (from 1, 2, 3, and 4).
6. The Necessary and Proper Clause gives Congress the express authority to carry into effect the powers vested by the Constitution in the government of the United States.
7. The Constitution authorizes Congress to make all laws which are necessary and proper to carry into effect the implied power of the United States to promote the general welfare (from 5 and 6).[504]

This reasoning, Mikhail maintains, was drawn on by Benjamin Franklin when he called on Congress to abolish slavery, and by Alexander Hamilton in defense of the first Bank of the United States, and by Frederick Douglass when he called on the United States to abolish slavery. Theodore Roosevelt embraced it at the turn of the twentieth century and Franklin D. Roosevelt affirmed it at the height of the New Deal. It also appears to have informed the opposition of various anti-federalists to the Constitution.[505]

It is worth noting that while the Necessary and Proper Clause was subject to something of a tussle in the drafting (and afterwards in the convention where an unsuccessful effort was undertaken to strike the All Other Powers Provision), the Treaty Supremacy Clause was the product of a complete consensus. Not only was the "harmony" language of Randolph's motion of

13 May 1787 accepted unanimously when it came to the judiciary (as opposed to the six to four vote in favor of such language when it came to the legislature), there was consensus in the drafting process, and in the convention's response as well.

In part, the consensus around the Treaty Supremacy Clause derived from a previous division among the delegates about giving the Congress the power to veto state legislation and not simply override it with national legislation. Although such a power was part of the Virginia Plan, it was rejected in the constitutional convention on 17 July 1787. Immediately following its rejection, the convention voted unanimously to approve the following motion by Maryland's Luther Martin: "that the Legislative acts of the U.S. made by virtue & in pursuance of the articles of Union, and all treaties made & ratified under the authority of the U.S. shall be the supreme law of the respective States, as far as those acts or treaties shall relate to the said States, or their Citizens and inhabitants— & that the Judiciaries of the several States shall be bound thereby in their decisions, any thing in the respective laws of the individual States to the contrary notwithstanding."[506] The final version of the Supremacy Clause would be stronger and more lucid, and specifically mention the Constitution itself as being supreme law over the states and over their constitutions, but the continuity of basic elements is striking. As James Pfander has observed, "the framers viewed the judicial negative as an alternative to legislative control of the states."[507] Wilson and Madison would make one more effort, on 23 August 1787, to secure a Congressional veto of state legislation; an effort that came within one vote of succeeding, but in the end had to be satisfied with the judicial negative on unconstitutional state conduct.

The judicial negative, however, faced practical problems of its own as the convention was divided on whether to establish lower federal courts directly in the text of the document or to leave their creation to the Congress. The decision to pursue the latter course meant, as Pfander notes, that "the framers could not rely on the appellate power of the Supreme Court to assure state compliance with federal law."[508] It was possible that the Congress would not even establish lower federal courts and that the judiciaries of the states would present obstacles to cases being heard by the

Supreme Court on appeal. If the judicial negative was to have meaning, this problem would have to be addressed.

The Original Jurisdiction Clause as we now know it was first formulated in a late draft of Article III in the Committee of Detail and appears designed to deal with precisely this problem of controlling state conduct. This clause, Pfander observes, changed relatively little with the convention's further deliberations: "Drafted by James Wilson, the clause conferred jurisdiction on the Court to hear originally ambassador cases, state-party cases, and impeachments. The power to try impeachments was later transferred to the Senate, but the two remaining grants of original jurisdiction survived essentially as Wilson wrote them. A variety of factors suggest that the paramount purpose of the state-party grant was to secure an original docket for the assertion of coercive federal claims against the states."[509]

On 23 August 1787, Rutledge moved that "This Constitution & the laws of the U. S. made in pursuance thereof, and all Treaties made under the authority of the U. S. shall be the supreme law of the several States and of their citizens and inhabitants; and the Judges in the several States shall be bound thereby in their decisions, any thing in the Constitutions or laws of the several States, to the contrary notwithstanding."[510] This was agreed to by the convention without dissent. And Pennsylvania's Gouverneur Morris moved to strike "to enforce treaties" from Congress' list of enumerated powers as such power was inherent in the fact that treaties were laws. This, too, passed without dissent.[511] Four days later, Rutledge moved to insert the words "and treaties made or which shall be made under their authority." This was a way of ensuring that treaties which had already been signed with the Native Nations were expressly included. It passed without dissent as well.[512]

This review makes it clear that the Treaty Supremacy Clause was one of the *least* controversial features of the convention's handiwork and that, from the beginning, it appears to have been understood by all in the convention—without the slightest hint of dissent—that this meant that even individual foreign subjects could sue states of the union for violation of their treaty rights. In addition to Wilson, framers who spoke explicitly to the right of individuals to sue states included Alexander Hamilton, James

Madison, and Edmund Randolph.[513] It was a triumph of the progressivism of Wilsonian jurisprudence that, in this regard and at this juncture, this was the consensus position of the framers. But this capacity of individuals to sue states under the plan of the convention was not without its critics among the advocates of "states' rights" outside of the convention, convinced, as some of them were, that their states were somehow full sovereigns and possessed of "sovereign immunity."

Wilson's opinion in *Chisholm* that "Georgia is NOT a sovereign State" contributed to the Eleventh Amendment to the Constitution with its insistence that "The Judicial power of the United States shall not be construed to extend to any suit in law or equity, commenced or prosecuted against one of the United States by Citizens of another State, or by Citizens or Subjects of any Foreign State."[514] Where honor for Wilson, and for the Constitution's framers generally, had been seen to flow from keeping one's word, many of the supporters of the Eleventh Amendment had implicitly or explicitly maintained that it was beneath Georgia's dignity to be sued by the estate of a South Carolina merchant alleging that Georgia had never paid for clothing delivered during the Revolutionary War. Even after the Eleventh Amendment it remained possible for a "foreign state" to sue a state of the Union, but the same underlying political conflict and question would recur: did honor come from upholding one's treaties or did honor come from being "above" being sued?[515] As the judge and legal historian John J. Gibbons has shown, however, it was precisely the ability for a foreign state to sue a state of the Union that the framers of the Eleventh Amendment wished to preserve as a means of enforcing the peace treaty with Great Britain. "The amendment's specific wording derives not from some muddled and essentially meaningless original understanding of state sovereign immunity, but from the desire of the Federalists to assuage the Republican clamor over the Supreme Court's decision in *Chisholm v. Georgia* while guaranteeing the enforceability against the states of the controversial peace treaty with Great Britain."[516]

* * *

It was the foundations of the framers' vision that Wilson sought to articulate in his law lectures. These, too, are worthy of review in the interests of understanding how severely America broke with the principles of the founding in the genocide of the 1830s and how much it remains at odds with those principles in its spurious "federal Indian law" today.

The entire House of Representatives and Senate of the United States—and the entire Pennsylvania House of Representatives and Senate as well—attended the first of Wilson's law lectures, as did the President and Martha Washington, and the Vice President and Abigail Adams, and they are a marvel to read.[517] These lectures provide an authoritative context in which to understand the intentions of the framers of the Constitution in terms of the revolutionary American jurisprudence that helps inform it and which has in the past enabled reform movements to appeal to the Constitution as if it were a "promissory note."

Even Alexander the Great, Wilson noted at the beginning of these lectures—when Alexander was master of the world—envied the good fortune of Achilles, who had a Homer to celebrate his deeds. When some future Xenophon or Thucydides shall arise to do justice to the virtues and actions of the United States, Wilson prophesied, "the glory of America will rival—it will outshine the glory of Greece."[518] And, of course, it would outshine the glory of England as well. For the principles of the American constitutions and governments and laws were superior to those of England. The vital and animating principle of American constitutions and laws was that "the supreme or sovereign power of the society resides in the citizens at large"—a principle that Blackstone explicitly rejected.[519] For Wilson, government existed to serve society and not the other way around:

> By some politicians, society has been considered as only the scaffolding of government; very improperly in my judgment. In the just order of things, government is the scaffolding of society: and if society could be built and kept entire without government, the scaffolding might be thrown down, without the least inconvenience or cause of regret. Government is, indeed, highly necessary; but it is highly necessary to a fallen state. Had man continued innocent, society, without the aids of government, would have shed its benign influence even over the bowers of Paradise.[520]

A deep sense of moral purpose rooted in religious faith animated Wilson's view of the law as he presented it in these lectures. Remember, he told his students, "that, in a free government, every honor implies a trust; that every trust implies a duty; and that every duty ought to be performed."[521] The idea that the will of a superior was the origin of obligation in human laws, Wilson refuted and discarded. Rather the true origin of such obligation was to be found in the consent of those whose obedience the law requires. Magna Charta, in this sense, was made, in a mode of expression that had long been used in England, "by the common assent of all the realm."[522]

The law of nature, Wilson argued, was a gift of the all-wise Author of our existence. On inquiry, he suggested, "We shall probably find that, to direct the most important parts of our conduct, the bountiful Governor of the universe has been graciously pleased to provide us with a law; and that, to direct the less important parts of it, he has made us capable of providing a law for ourselves."[523] God has not left himself without a witness in our own breasts, nor us without a guide. As a rational being, man is subject to reason: as a creature of God to his supreme will. These two principles must be united to form a complete system of morality, of internal and external obligation.[524]

For some writers, Wilson observed, the cause of obligation was laid in utility. For others, sociability, or the care of maintaining society properly, was the foundation of every obligation and every right. "From this principle the inference is drawn, that every one is born, not for himself alone, but for the whole human kind." [525] Many authors derived an obligation to observe the law of nature from instinctive affections, or an innate moral sense by which we perceive the moral qualities in actions and distinguish right from wrong.

> The power of moral perception is, indeed, a most important part of our constitution. It is an original power—a power of its own kind; and totally distinct from the ideas of utility and agreeableness. By that power we have conceptions of merit and demerit, of duty and moral obligation. By that power, we perceive some things in human conduct to be right, and others to be wrong. We have the same reason to rely on the dictates of this faculty, as upon the determination of

> our senses, or of our other natural powers. When an action is represented to us, flowing from love, humanity, gratitude, an ultimate desire of the good of others; though it happened in a country far distant, or in an age long past, we admire the lovely exhibition and praise its author. The contrary conduct, when represented to us, raises our abhorrence and aversion.[526]

The existence of the moral sense had been denied by some philosophers, its authority attacked by others, and the certainty and uniformity of its decisions complained of by others still. The claim was made that it varied in different countries, and different ages, and under different governments and religions, some going so far as to assert "that it is as much the effect of custom, fashion, and artifice, as our taste in dress, furniture, and the modes of conversation."[527] For Wilson, as for Aristotle, a key was to consider human nature in its supposedly most improved forms. But even in the most uninformed savages, Wilson maintained in prejudiced and patronizing language, we find the common notions and practical principles of virtue: these same savages have in them the seeds of the logician, the man of taste, the orator, the statesman, the man of virtue, and the saint. It was only for want of exercise and culture, and in some cases perhaps the presence of unfortunate institutions, that they were not cultivated. "It will certainly be sufficient for our purposes to observe, that the dictates of reason are neither more general, nor more uniform, nor more certain, nor more commanding, than the dictates of the moral sense."[528] People always maintain that an approved action will promote their own interest, or be conducive to the public good, or is required by the Deity. In truth, it may have all the contrary properties. But, if so, to what cause is this to be traced? "Does it prove the nonexistence of a moral sense, or does it prove, in such instances, the weakness or perversion of reason? The just solution is, that, in such instances, it is our reason, which presents false appearances to our moral sense."[529]

> The law of nature is universal. For it is true, not only that all men are equally subject to the command of their Maker; but it is true also, that the law of nature, having its foundation in the constitution and state of man, has an essential fitness for all mankind, and binds them without distinction. This law, or right reason, as Cicero calls it, is thus

> beautifully described by that eloquent philosopher. "It is, indeed," says he, "a true law, conformable to nature, diffused among all men, unchangeable, eternal. By its commands, it calls men to their duty: by its prohibitions, it deters them from vice. To diminish, to alter, much more to abolish this law, is a vain attempt. Neither by the senate, nor by the people, can its powerful obligation be dissolved. It requires no interpreter or commentator. It is not one law at Rome, another at Athens; one law now, another hereafter: it is the same eternal and immutable law, given at all times and to all nations: for God, who is its author and promulgator, is always the sole master and sovereign of mankind."[530]

A nation, according to James Wilson, should aim at its perfection. And nations, when they can, ought to give to one another not only the assistance necessary to their preservation, but also the assistance consistent with their pursuit of their perfection. The advantage and improvement of the citizens are the ends proposed by the social union. Happiness is the center, to which men and nations are attracted. The education of youth, the arts, the sciences, philosophy, virtue, and religion all contribute to happiness and should all receive the encouragement of the nation. The first and most necessary duty of nations, as well as of men, Wilson wrote, was to do no harm. But they were also commanded to do good to one another. Sociability was part of the law of nature for nations as well as individuals. The expression natural enemies, which had helped spill oceans of blood, was an unnatural expression: "for natural enmity forms no title in the genuine law of nations, part of the law of nature. It is adopted from a spurious code."[531]

> It may, perhaps, be uncommon, but it is certainly just, to say that nations ought to love one another. The offices of humanity ought to flow from this pure source. When this happily is the case, then the principles of affection and friendship prevail among states as among individuals: then nations will mutually support and assist each other with zeal and ardour; lasting peace will be the result of unshaken confidence; and kind and generous principles, of a nature far opposite to mean jealousy, crooked policy, or cold prudence, will govern and prosper the affairs of men.... The love of mankind is an

> important duty and an exalted virtue. Much has been written, much has been said concerning the power of *intellectual* abstraction, which man possesses, and which distinguishes him so eminently from the inferior order of animals. But little has been said, and little has been written, concerning another power of the human mind, still more dignified, and, beyond all comparison, more amiable—I may call it the power of *moral* abstraction.[532]

Wilson's name for this capacity for benevolence and sociability did not catch on. In our own day one of my mentors, the social theorist Edward Shils, has proposed the term *civility*, by which he means, at least as a first approximation, the virtue of the citizen: the virtue of concern for the common good.[533] But for Wilson, this alternative would have been acceptable only if it was understood that the citizen in question was also a citizen of the world. The power of moral abstraction was "not confined to one sect or to one state, but ranges excursive through the whole expanded theater of men and nations."[534] It was as necessary to the progress of exalted virtue, as the power of intellectual abstraction was to the progress of extensive knowledge. By this power, the commonwealth of a state, the empire of the United States, the civilized and commercial part of the world, and the inhabitants of the whole earth become the objects of the warmest spirit of benevolence. By this power, even a minute, unknown and distant group of individuals may become a complex object that will warm and dilate the soul. By this power, people otherwise invisible are rendered conspicuous and become known to the heart as well as to the understanding.

> This enlarged and elevated virtue ought to be cultivated by nations with peculiar assiduity and ardour. The sphere of exertion, to which an individual is confined, is frequently narrow, however enlarged his disposition may be. But the sphere, to the extent of which a state may exert herself, is often comparatively boundless. By exhibiting a glorious example in her constitution, in her laws, in the administration of her constitution and laws, she may diffuse reformation, she may diffuse instruction, she may diffuse happiness over this whole terrestrial globe.[535]

That this whole terrestrial globe was in need of the "happiness" the Constitution of the United States could provide is a position that can be challenged, particularly by the Native Nations of Turtle Island and by the enslaved people coercively held inside the new American states and outside of the equal rights and equal belonging of the supposedly truly human. For them, the supremacist expansionism underlying this vision of diffusing happiness—the politics of domination with which this effort was (and is) inextricably bound up—meant that not joy but a challenge to their very existence and relationship to reality was inherent in even the best intentioned version of the aspirations informing the invader state's constitution in the aftermath of the American Revolution.

* * *

The law professor and Wilson scholar William Ewald, in an essay on "James Wilson and the American Founding," writes:

> Of all the delegates to the 1787 Convention, Wilson is the one whose constitutional views approximate most closely to the one-man-one-vote frontier democracy that was to emerge in the nineteenth century. That is the world we associate with Andrew Jackson and Abraham Lincoln. The other framers—Washington, Hamilton, Adams, Jefferson, Madison, Dickinson, and the rest—were gentlemen of the 18th century, and they thought like gentlemen of the eighteenth century. So did Wilson. But Wilson, unlike the others, at times can seem to have one foot planted in the century that was to come.[536]

It might be added that while he would have been at home in the democracy that was to come, Wilson would have seen Andrew Jackson, with his initial commitment to "states' rights," and his treaty-breaking, as a betrayal of the framers' vision of the Constitution and seen Abraham Lincoln, with his commitment to the Union and to Emancipation, as moving toward its fulfillment while also being horrified at Lincoln's treaty-breaking. Wilson would also have been revolted at the reactionary return to a despotic European jurisprudence with which John Marshall, in effect, repudiated the Treaty Supremacy Clause.

Believing, mistakenly, that their enlightened principles would gradually triumph over slavery, James Wilson and his allies compromised these principles in the constitutional convention. They failed to feel the urgency that ending the injustice of slavery required and they failed to foresee the way the racism in the nation's arteries would harden and the consequent need to take action against such a prospect. The convention did adopt one measure to contribute to the end of slavery—the implicit grant of authority to the Congress to end the importation of slaves in 1808 (Article 1, Section 9, Clause 1), but without appreciating its profound inadequacy.[537] Their failure was largely a consequence of the convention's unwillingness to risk having Georgia and South Carolina reject the Constitution over ending the slave trade then and there.[538]

Just as there is a debate to be understood between the advocates and the opponents of genocide in which the appeasers of the former held the balance of power, so there is a debate to be understood between the advocates of slavery and their opponents in which once again the appeasers of the former—a majority of the constitutional convention that included James Wilson—held the balance of power.

Slavery, Wilson wrote in his law lectures in the 1790s, is unauthorized by the common law and is "repugnant to the principles of natural law."[539] The reasons which are sometimes assigned for the origin and continuation of slavery in any social system were, Wilson maintained, when examined to the bottom, "built upon a false foundation." [540] Well aware of the compromises he had made over the existence of slavery in the constitutional convention, Wilson still looked forward to the future with enthusiasm: "At last, however, the voice of nature, intelligible and persuasive, has been heard by nations that are civilized: at last it is acknowledged that mankind are all brothers: the happy time is, we hope, approaching, when the acknowledgment will be substantiated by a uniform corresponding conduct."[541]

Chapter 8
Breaking Faith with the Founding Generation

Writing to the Cherokee people in 1796, President George Washington urged that they study with the advice and material assistance of a federal agent, "those things which are found good by the white people, and which your situation will enable you to adopt."[542] He particularly emphasized intensive farming, but also mentioned the workings of the American government and stressed that "the experiment made with you may determine the lot of many nations. If it succeeds, the beloved men of the United States will be encouraged to give the same assistance to all the Indian tribes within their boundaries."[543] Washington was convinced that the security and economic interests of the United States and the Cherokee nation alike would be best served by the progress of civilization among both. In this he was expressing the gentler side of a harsh and sometimes genocidal tradition, perhaps first articulated among the English by the naval commander Christopher Carleill in 1583, which spoke of the alleged desirability of "reducing the savage people to Christianity and civility."[544]

In *Surviving Genocide,* the historian Jeffrey Ostler suggests that what I have called American civility is part of the particular genius of the American people and that part of American civility—a part of this genius that was already identified by Tocqueville, is, as Ostler notes—"their ability to inflict catastrophic destruction all the while claiming to be benevolent."[545] Noting the tension between the approach to the Native Nations of the eastern elites and the frontiersmen, Ostler claims that these elites, as "guardians of the nation's purse" and "trustees of its reputation" within the "civilized world" as they defined it, wished to cultivate "expansion" with what they saw as "honor."[546] Aware of their reliance on extreme violence, including what they saw as the distinctly dishonorable violence of the frontiersmen, they sought to obtain "gestures of consent from the dispossessed."[547] That seeking of "consent" can also be seen as an expression of American civility.

By 1809, when a census was taken, the Cherokee people had reversed a century of decline and increased in number to 12,395. This was in addition to a body of about 1,000 Cherokee nationals who had moved west of the Mississippi. The Cherokee people in the east owned some 6,500 horses, 19,000 black cattle, 19,000 swine, 1,000 sheep, 1,500 spinning wheels, 400 looms, and 500 plows. They had cultivated land with numerous houses and barns, 13 gristmills, and 3 sawmills. Modeling their institutions on the institutions of the surrounding white supremacist society, they also exercised brutal domination over 583 enslaved persons.[548] By 1826, there were 13,963 Cherokee nationals in the east plus three to four thousand in the west. The Cherokee Nation owned some 7,600 horses, 22,000 black cattle, 46,000 swine, and 2,500 sheep. They also owned 1,277 slaves.[549] By 1835, the census recorded 16,542 Cherokee nationals in the east of whom 77.27 percent were "full blooded," 201 were intermarried whites, and 1,592 were enslaved. These people raised well over half a million bushels of corn on some 44,000 cultivated acres.[550] Butter and cheese were seen on Cherokee tables, almost every home grew cotton for its own use, and some families grew cotton for export. There were numerous orchards with peach and apple trees as well as quince, cherry, and plum. There were roads, ferries, and trading stores. There was a saltpeter mine and powder mills. Silversmiths, blacksmiths, wheelwrights, carpenters and armorers could be found in the nation.[551] "The mass of the Cherokee people," Samuel Worcester observed, "have built houses and cultivated lands with their own hands. There may be a few families among the mountains who depend mostly on the chase for support, but I know not one of them."[552]

The extraordinary renaissance that the Cherokee Nation came to enjoy in the early nineteenth century was due overwhelmingly to their own efforts and creativity, but in some part to American civility as well, and specifically to the approach of Washington and his allies. This approach recognized the existence of a common good that included the Native Nations, that acknowledged something of the national rights of the Native Nations under international law, and that included treaties with the Native Nations as part of the supreme law of the land. By 1826, Elias Boudinot, soon to become the editor of a bilingual Cherokee and English newspaper could declare: "I can view my Native country, rising from the ashes of her degradation, wearing her purified and beautiful garments, and taking her seat with the nations of the earth."[553] The horrific end of this first Cherokee renaissance, at the hands of the state of Georgia and then of the federal government, is testimony to the incivility, and indeed the grotesque brutality, of which America has proved capable and—like the history of slavery—raises fundamental questions about the moral character of the American people and American leadership and American institutions from the dawn of the new nation onwards.

The theft of so many nations' homelands, and the forced march of so many along the Trail of Tears, is part of a larger effort at domination that has been ongoing with greater or lesser harshness in American relations with the Native Nations ever since, and that has antecedents stretching back for centuries before. It is remarkable that it can be met with the compassionate attitude conveyed in the following comment from the jurist and Cherokee citizen Steve Russell, who, after noting that an almost bottomless well of collective guilt "keeps the modern beneficiaries of genocide from finishing the job," later writes: "We know the colonists could not now go home if they were so disposed. Our lot is intertwined with the colonists as black South Africans are with the British and the Dutch. They have nowhere to go. While they have not historically been the best of neighbors, they are still our neighbors and we must do our best to civilize them."[554]

The United States has done the Native Nations irreparable and ongoing harm. It has done so on the basis of the doctrine of Christian discovery; on the basis of the argument, in John Forsyth's terms, that for the United States (or rather for the state of Georgia)—having citizens whose ancestors had gazed at the land and allegedly informed the Native peoples about Christ's promises—invader state sovereignty and with it the "right" of "disposing" of the Native persons and their property "at pleasure" somehow followed.[555] Or, in John Marshall's terms, that America—having been seen by representatives of a "Christian people"—somehow from this "discovery" the United States acquired an "ultimate dominion" over the Native Nations and "title" to their lands.[556] Such arguments for genocide, or at least for a "right" to commit genocide—are the arguments from which genocide and the appeasement of the advocates of genocide in the 1820s and 1830s followed. They remain the foundation of "federal Indian law." And of an ongoing assault on the authority and lands of others cloaked under a fog of allegedly benevolent intentions.

That Marshall's reactionary jurisprudence was not quite as reactionary and vicious as Forsyth's meant that Marshall could cry about the crimes he was implicitly or explicitly authorizing. Marshall could and probably did shed what may have been genuine and not merely crocodile tears while, in effect, authorizing genocide. "If Courts were permitted to indulge their sympathies," he wrote in *Cherokee Nation*, "a case better calculated to excite them can scarcely be imagined."[557] That, too, remains a characteristic feature of "federal Indian law" in the form of numerous remarks from judges over the years bemoaning the historical mistreatments and injustices the United States has inflicted on the Native Nations while continuing to deny these nations their constitutional rights and while continuing to uphold violations of their rights under their treaties by means of the same bad faith interpretive stance that Marshall established in *Cherokee Nation*. This toxic mixture of imperialist arrogance, in combination with ignorance of the requirements of constitutional law, together with a seeming sympathy for the peoples of the Native Nations, is perfectly captured in Associate Justice Sandra Day O'Connor's majority opinion in *Lyng v. Northwest Indian Cemetery Protective Association* in 1988: "Even assuming that the Government's actions here will virtually destroy the Indians' ability to practice their religion, the Constitution simply does not supply a principle that could justify upholding respondent's legal claims."[558]

That virtually destroying "the Indians' ability to practice their religion" was and remains an unconstitutional act of aggression and war against Native Nations whose dominion over their own lands the United States was and is treaty-bound to respect doubtless never crossed O'Connor's mind. That is no excuse, of course, for believing that the Constitution is compatible with the exercise of untrammeled despotic power toward the Native Nations.

Readers can decide for themselves whether I am correct in asserting that the Supreme Court is lying—is telling deliberate untruths—or is simply engaged in a self-deluded self-righteousness. Citing a 1985 case—*Oneida County v. Oneida Indian Nation*—which, in turn, cited *Johnson v. McIntosh*, Associate Justice Ruth Bader Ginsburg wrote for the majority in 2005, in *City of Sherrill*, explicitly relying on the doctrine of discovery to deny that the Oneida Nation could reacquire sovereignty over lands they had once both owned and possessed by purchasing those lands on the open market. In her first footnote in the 2005 case, she quoted the 1985 case as follows: "fee title to the lands occupied by Indians when the colonists arrived became vested in the sovereign—first the discovering European nation and later the original States and the United States."[559] That this could simply be untrue, and a claim in violation of the Constitution, and at odds with the American revolutionary jurisprudence that informed it, doubtless did not even cross Ginsburg's mind. Note, however, the subtle prejudice involved in choosing to use only the word "Indians" instead of "the Indians" in her opinion as if writing "the Indians" might lead people to think that the rights of someone worthy of the respect implied in the definite article are being violated. This is in contrast with, for example, the alleged rights of "the colonists" (and their heirs and successors) that Ginsburg was bent on upholding at whatever cost in justice. In addition to blatantly racist and bigoted opinions, even the subtleties of the English language are mobilized by the Supreme Court in its efforts to subordinate the Native Nations to its system of domination and dehumanization.

Under this foul system, the Native Nations do not even have a property right in their own soil—their lands can be taken by the United States at will. In the words of the Supreme Court's decision in *Tee-Hit-Ton v. United States* in 1955: "This is not a property right, but amounts to a right of occupancy which the sovereign grants and protects against intrusion by third parties, but which right of occupancy may be terminated and such lands fully disposed of by the sovereign itself without any legally enforceable obligation to compensate the Indians."[560] Although there is nothing subtle about the court's language here, to have used "Indians"—as in *City of Sherrill*—instead of "the Indians"—would have made the rank bigotry and racism of the opinion more apparent.

From 1887 to 1934, under the terms of the Dawes Act, around an additional 100 million acres of Native land was effectively stolen by the Congress—this on top of untold millions of acres taken during the "Indian wars" of the United States' expansion west of the Mississippi.[561] During those years, and even more recently, a system of indoctrination was imposed in "schools" explicitly designed to "kill the Indian in him, and save the man"—explicitly designed, in other words, for cultural genocide.[562]

The Congress of the United States, in the Supreme Court's twisted view of the world, has plenary power and with it can allegedly destroy a Native Nation or break any treaty obligation to any Native Nation, simply on its "say so."[563] That comment—that Congress' "say so" is sufficient—is actually a quote from Associate Justice Neil Gorsuch's widely praised but poorly understood majority opinion in *McGirt v. Oklahoma* in 2020. The Congress' historic exploitation and oppression—and especially its land thieving—continues to this day with the Congress having recently decided to sell sacred Apache land to a copper mining company threatening to destroy what is known as Oak Flat through yet another bad faith interpretation of a treaty.[564] The resulting conflict is illustrative of the central problem in US-Native Nations relations. Even if there was not the corrupt understanding of the "trust relationship" evident in the United States claim to have a right to sell Apache land valued at some $112 billion to Resolution Copper in exchange for some $7 million worth of other land in a "deal" arranged by Senator John McCain via a last minute addition to the National Defense Authorization Act of 2014, even if there was not a bad faith interpretive stance at work in every Supreme Court ruling concerning a Native Nation so that the Apache people were free—as a sovereign foreign state in constitutional law—to reject the sale of their land, the fact of the economic pressure involved in these valuations would remain an enormous threat to Oak Flat and doubtless a challenge to the autonomy and integrity of Apache national resistance to such a sale. Indeed, the logic of such valuations, and of the economic system built on exploiting them, generates an amnesia as to what the real purposes of life are; an amnesia that may eventually destroy human life on the planet as we have known it and that unquestionably stands as a major obstacle to what the interdisciplinary scholar Richard Sclove has presented as psychospiritual progress in his study of the Hindu classic, *The Mahabharata*.[565]

Much the same conflict can be seen over the attempt that is being made to construct the Dakota Access Pipeline. The Fort Laramie Treaty of 1868 set apart particular lands "for the absolute and undisturbed use and occupation of the Indians herein named."[566] It is only by means of still another bad faith interpretation of a treaty that the United States is deliberating over allowing Energy Transfer Partners to build and operate a pipeline across these lands. A good faith interpretive stance toward the

United States' treaty obligations, in contrast, would block not only the Dakota Access Pipeline but also the Thacker Pass lithium mine and for that matter any excavation of sacred Native lands.[567] A good faith interpretation of the treaty rights of the Anishinaabeg to hunt, fish, and gather wild rice would have precluded the Canadian corporation Enbridge's Line 3 pipeline.[568] Indeed, good faith would require respect for the rights of Manoomin—wild rice—as a living species.

As Peter d'Errico has observed, lawyers of the Anishinaabeg, in the courts of the White Earth Nation, have recently sought—on behalf of wild rice—to prevent the Department of Natural Resources (DNR) of the State of Minnesota from giving away the water the Manoomin needs: "Wild rice is understood as a living entity, which of course it is. And as a living entity, as having legal rights. And as a legal right holding entity, it can litigate to protect itself, protect the water it needs, et cetera. So the White Earth case of the Manoomin, as it's said, the wild rice, is a struggle for a way of life, a different way of thinking about who are human beings in this world anyway? What is our relationship to everything else that exists?"[569] The peoples whom the theology professor Tink Tinker calls Eurochristian have had a very different conception of life and of its purposes.[570] For them, the emphasis has been on exercising dominion over the natural world and exploiting its "resources" for "development."

As of this writing, the White Earth Ojibwe Appellate Court has dismissed the Manoomin suit with what might be termed preemptive deference to "federal Indian law." "If we were to allow the case to proceed on its merits in the Tribal Court," the Appellate Court asserted, "and the Court granted a remedy against Appellants, and this Court affirmed such remedy, we believe that a federal court would apply the same case laws we cite to enjoin the remedy and the Tribal Court from further proceedings. We conclude that *Montana v. United States*, 450 U.S. 544 (1981), requires that a plaintiff show that the nonmember defendant engaged in *activities* on the *reservation* to invoke subject matter jurisdiction in tribal court under the second *Montana* exception."[571] This interpretation of the requirements of "federal Indian law" has been challenged in a supplemental brief on behalf of the Manoomin on the grounds that the impacts of the nonmember defendant's conduct off the reservation can be sufficient on the reservation for the second *Montana* exception to apply and that tribal law also confers jurisdiction: "When considering the *on-Reservation* impacts of DNR's activities and conduct, and White Earth Tribal Law conferring jurisdiction over defendants in a case of this type, it is clear that the Tribal Court may properly exercise jurisdiction over this case."[572]

American Indian Studies professor Mark Freeland (Anishinaabe) has stressed the importance of the Native understandings of the treaties they were signing, and the negotiations and the relationships these nations thought they were entering into. These are understandings and relationships that the Supreme Court explicitly recognizes its obligation to interpret the law in accordance with even though it has failed to do so since 1831 at the latest. Commenting on and quoting Robert Williams, Jr.'s observations on the subject of the negotiations from which these treaties emerged, Freeland notes:

> These treaty negotiations practiced Indigenous customs, so that in the early colonial period, "Indians can be witnessed inviting Europeans to make known the 'good thoughts' of peace, to smoke the sacred pipe, to clear the path, to bury the hatchet, to link arms together and unite as one people, to eat out of the same bowl together." These Indigenous concepts all helped to guide both the ceremonies and the relationships that resulted from these meetings throughout this period. One of these concepts is that of renewal. The concept is significant as it is grounded in Indigenous relationships to cyclical time. This meant that upon entering into a treaty relationship, there were expectations of annual meetings to renew and strengthen these bonds created in the treaty ceremony. As Williams explains, "Renewal, in fact, was regarded as a continuing constitutional obligation of treaty partners."[573]

Every treaty signed with a Native Nation was signed under the international laws and usages that prevailed on Turtle Island before the Eurochristian invaders arrived and the United States Supreme Court is obliged to study these laws and usages and to interpret treaties with the Native Nations in terms of the light these laws and usages cast on the intentions of America's treaty partners on this continent in every treaty that they signed. This is the case even with regard to treaties that officials of the United States thought they were dictating. As long as there was an expectation that American treaty partners would exist to perform the obligations of a treaty, the United States was and is bound by its own constitutional law, as well as by the law of nations as it was understood by the framers, to respect these treaty partners' sovereign equality as independent foreign nations except on points specified by treaty. Failure to sustain that expectation, and that respect, is to maintain a genocidal policy that is repugnant to the Constitution of the United States.

While Joseph Story's adherence to Smith Thompson's dissent in *Cherokee Nation v. Georgia* places Story among the American opponents of genocide, the strength of his opposition—and his willingness to persist in it—may be doubted. Commenting on Supreme Court reporter Richard Peters' preparation of a volume of essential documents on the Cherokee Nation's case against the state of Georgia, in 1831, Story did express hope: "The publication will do a great deal of good—the subject unites the moral sense of all New England—It comes home to the religious feelings of our people. It touches their sensibilities, and sinks to the very bottom of their sense of Justice—Depend on it there is a depth of degradation in our national conduct, which will irresistibly lead to better things."[574] Story's hope may be referred to as the "whistling in the dark" theory of opposition to genocide. Even that level of opposition was, however, more than John Marshall had to offer.

To Congressman Edward Everett of Massachusetts, an opponent of removal—and of Georgian aggression on the grounds that it was unconstitutional—Marshall wrote in 1830 of what may be considered as his own opposition to removal on moral, as distinct from "legal" grounds:

> I have received your speech on the bill for removing the Indians from the East to the West side of the Mississippi, and have read it with the deepest interest. I do not think any subject ever discussed in Congress has drawn forth a more splendid display of talent in each house of the national legislature than this, or is more worthy of the deliberate consideration of the government and of the nation. The speeches with which I have been favored, which are indeed all on

> one side, abound in arguments which appear to me to be solid and conclusive, and which do very great honour to the heads and hearts of those who made them.... It has been to me matter of the greatest astonishment that, after hearing the arguments in both houses, Congress could pass the bill.[575]

Under both international law and American constitutional law—properly construed—Cherokee territory was outside the jurisdiction of both the state of Georgia and of the United States. The removal bill was a blatant violation of the law; a blatant reinforcement of Georgia's genocidal and unconstitutional assault on the Cherokee Nation and its treaty-guaranteed dominion. That territory was guaranteed to the Cherokee Nation by treaties with the United States whose very existence constituted recognition of the Cherokee right to self-government, their right to their dominion. This right of indigenous nations to their dominion was explicitly recognized in international law as early as the Dominican theologian Bartolomé de Las Casas' writings against Spanish colonialism in the sixteenth century. At the heart of Charles V's empire—and at the risk of charges of heresy and lèse majesté—Las Casas publicly and persuasively argued that "war against the Indians, which we call in Spanish, *conquistas,* is evil and essentially anti-Christian.... war against the Indians is unlawful."[576] Pope Alexander VI could not have given dominion over the New World to Spain, Las Casas argued, because the New World was outside of the Pope's jurisdiction; dominion there was in the hands of the Native Nations:

> The king of France does not pronounce sentence in Spain nor does the king of Spain dictate laws for France, nor does the Emperor himself, in his travels, use his imperial authority outside the borders of his empire. [In all these cases] there is a lack of that power and jurisdiction which in his indescribable wisdom the author of nature has prescribed within certain limits for each nation and prince so as to safeguard and preserve the common good of each. For this reason jurisdiction is said to be implanted in a locality or territory, or in the bones of the persons of each community or state, so that it cannot be separated from them any more than food can be separated from the preservation of life.[577]

While the brilliance of Las Casas' theological and international legal arguments before a conference of jurists and theologians at Valladolid in 1550-51—many of which are gathered together as *In Defense of the Indians*—are still beginning to be fully appreciated, his philippic against the conquest of the New World—*A Brief Account of the Destruction of the Indies*—has had a global impact for five centuries. According to the historian J. H. Elliott, this latter work, first published in Seville in 1552, "etched itself into the European consciousness as an unsparing record of the barbarous behaviour of his compatriots."[578] In no small measure as a result of Las Casas' work, the early settlers of what would become Britain's American colonies, the founding generation of the United States, the framers of the Constitution, the Washington administration, and the opponents of genocide in the 1830s, would all seek to distance themselves and their country from the precedent of early Spanish conduct and instead recognize something of the rights of the Native peoples. When Walter Raleigh sent a fleet of ships to the New World in 1584, although he did not sail himself, the historian Jill Lepore reports that he provided his expedition with "a copy of Las Casas's 'book of Spanish crueltyes with fayr pictures,' to be used to convince the Natives that the English, unlike the Spanish, were men of mercy and love, liberty and charity."[579] Las Casas came to oppose not only the oppression and exploitation of the Native Nations, but also the slave trade, and ultimately slavery itself.[580] By the end of his life he was arguing that the king of Spain, if he was to save his soul, would have to make restitution to the Incas by restoring their lands to them and by giving back to "the other [Indian] lords" that which was theirs.[581] That a sixteenth century Spanish priest could embrace the call for LandBack says something about the supposed contemporary "leftist" character of that cause.

* * *

At the time of the framing of the American Constitution, the explicit advocates of genocide toward the Native peoples were a distinct minority. The overwhelming majority of the political leadership of the country in both the Constitutional Convention and in the Confederation Congress aspired to the establishment and maintenance of peace and "free trade" with the Native peoples on the basis of a measure of respect for their national independence and their ownership of their lands. At least this is what these political leaders generally told each other and it is consistent with their contemporary votes and arguments against Georgian claims and Georgian aggression.

Having left the Constitutional Convention in late July 1787 for the purpose of urging the Congress to use force on Georgia's behalf against the Creek (Muscogee) Nation—what Georgia's Governor George Handley would later call making "their towns smoke with fire and their streets run with blood"—the Georgians Willian Few and William Pierce were severely disappointed.[582] They were met in early August 1787 by a committee report on Indian affairs in the South presented by Nathan Dane of Massachusetts, Dyre Kearny of Delaware, Edward Carrington of Virginia, William Bingham of Pennsylvania, and Melancton Smith of New York. And by a resolution recommending to the state of Georgia that it adopt all possible means consistent with the principles of the confederation to preserve peace and friendship with the Creek Indians and make liberal cessions of what Georgia claimed as Georgian territory so that this territory could be "governed and disposed of in the same manner as the territory of the United States, northwest of the river Ohio is."[583] This was, of course, a reference to the Northwest Ordinance of 1787 which said in part: "The utmost good faith shall always be observed towards the Indians; their lands and property shall never be taken from them without their consent; and, in their property, rights, and liberty, they shall never be invaded or disturbed, unless in just and lawful wars authorized by Congress; but laws founded in justice and humanity, shall from time to time be made for preventing wrongs being done to them, and for preserving peace and friendship with them."[584]

Although three quarters of the twenty delegates present supported the resolution in August 1787, only seven states were present and the motion needed all seven to pass.[585] Nevertheless, given its depth of support, the reasons laid out in the committee's report are worthy of close attention, particularly as they help to illuminate the thinking of the Constitutional Convention in the actions it was taking on much the same issue at much the same time and for much the same reasons. They also help to illuminate American public opinion at the time as explicit reference is made to what that opinion was.

"An avaricious disposition in some of our people to acquire large tracts of land and often by unfair means, appears to be the principal source of difficulties with the Indians," the committee reported.[586] Moreover, there could be no doubt that settlements had been made on lands secured by treaty to the Cherokee Nation and the Creek Nation.

> Justice and policy as well as the true interests of our citizens, evince the propriety of promoting peace and free trade between them and the Indians. Various circumstances shew that the Indians, in general, within the United States want only to enjoy their lands without interruption, and to have their necessities regularly supplied by our traders, and could these objects be effected, no other measures would, probably be necessary for securing peace and a profitable trade with those Indians.... *The committee conceive that it has been long the opinion of the country, supported by Justice and humanity, that the Indians have just claims to all lands occupied by and not fairly purchased from them....* The laws of the State can have no effect upon a tribe of Indians or their lands within the limits of the state so long as that tribe is independent.... the Indian tribes are justly considered the common friends or enemies of the United States.[587]

The committee recognized that North Carolina and especially Georgia held different views. At the heart of the matter was the interpretation of a clause in the Articles of Confederation (Article 9, Section 4) that read: "Congress shall have the sole and exclusive right and power of regulating the trade and managing all affairs with the Indians, not members of any of the States; provided that the Legislative right of any State within its own limits be not infringed or violated." [588] For the committee, the subordinate clause concerning "legislative right" reflected similar language from colonial times. Just as the king had exclusive authority to make war and peace, establish boundaries by treaty and the like—without infringing on the legislative rights of the colonies with regard to Indians who were not on the territory of independent Tribes—so the Congress now did as well. The Georgians, the committee suggested, seemed to think that Georgia should be able to negotiate treaties, to call upon the forces of the United States at its will, and to see no settlement except according to its wishes.

The committee's preferred solution was to recommend to Georgia that it cede its claims to the lands in question to the United States. The Constitutional Convention's approach was more direct: in Article 1 it prohibited states from making treaties, simply dropped the subordinate clause about legislative rights altogether, and gave to Congress the power "To regulate Commerce with foreign Nations, and among the several States, and with the Indian Tribes."[589] This was done with remarkably little discussion in the convention. Moreover, the convention adopted the Treaty Supremacy Clause and with it the grant of jurisdiction to the Supreme Court in *all* cases arising under treaties and made explicitly original jurisdiction in *all* cases in which a state is a party.

Immediately after ratification, the Georgian House of Representatives seemed hopeful. It explicitly recognized that under the new Constitution the federal government alone had the power to make war and peace, raise and support armies, enter into treaties, and regulate commerce with the Indians. The Georgian House of Representatives indicated that it believed the federal government would obtain "a firm peace with the Indians" that would be a "blessing" to Georgia. As soon as a compromise was reached with the Creek Nation, however, Georgia's resentment, racism, religious bigotry, cupidity, and sense of "states' rights" began to fester.[590] Article 5 of the 1790 treaty stated: "The United States solemnly guarantee to the Creek Nation, all their lands within the limits of the United States."[591]

In his 1902 book, *Georgia and State Rights,* Ulrich Phillips captured the underlying source of tension in language that treated Georgia's position with great indulgence:

> The discord over these unoccupied lands was due to opposing conceptions of the status of the Indian tribes. The theory of the colonial governments had been that these tribes were independent communities with the rights and powers of sovereign nations. During the Revolution and in the period of the Confederation the central government adhered to that theory. But public opinion, following the arguments of the State governments which were involved in Indian problems, reverted to the original European conception that the relations of the tribes to civilized nations were

> merely those of dependent communities without sovereignty and without any right to the soil but that of tenants at will.[592]

The idea that such "reversion" took place in "public opinion" rather than first among a corrupt elite—and the idea that such "reversion" could take place without breaking faith with the founding generation and violating the promises that had been made to the Native Nations in solemn treaties and so violating the Constitution—is an absurdity. Nevertheless, as we will see later in this chapter, John Quincy Adams would also come to support such a "reversion" in appeasement of Georgian aggression—and in violation of the Creek Nation's treaty rights—after first trying, ineffectually, to stand against it.[593] The point applies as well to John Marshall who had already adopted a similar "reversion" in *Johnson v. McIntosh*. Both Adams and Marshall contributed to, and appear to have been influenced by, a new hardening of attitude toward the Native peoples—especially in the aftermath of the War of 1812.[594] All of this predisposed both men to appease Georgian aggression when push came to shove and to find inspiration and seek justification for their cowardly conduct in the doctrine of "Christian discovery."

Belief in human unity and equality, and therefore in respect for the Native Nations' relationship to the soil in terms of their own laws, in which what Eurochristians considered the "right of the soil" could not be purchased, was a position unthought of by the colonists. The closest they came to it was in some versions of "natural rights" and—to a lesser extent—in the aspirations and sometimes even something of the practices of "civilized" nations in which the Native Nation's ownership of sovereign title to their land was at least recognized. A 1757 legal opinion issued jointly by Charles Pratt, the Attorney General for England and Wales, and Charles Yorke, the Solicitor General for England and Wales, maintains the king's subjects carry the law of England with them when they emigrate: "In respect to such places as have been, or shall be, acquired by treaty, or grant, from any of the Indian princes, or governments, your majesty's letters patent are not necessary; the property of the soil vesting in the grantees, by the Indian grants, subject only to your majesty's right of sovereignty over the settlements, as English settlements, and over the inhabitants, as English subjects, who carry with them your majesty's laws, wherever they form colonies, and receive your majesty's protection, by virtue of your royal charters."[595]

A stronger argument for the "natural rights" of the Native Nations to own and sell land in the context of the Americas was articulated in detail in a 1781 book by Samuel Wharton. This book, which James Wilson may have had a hand in composing, is titled *Plain Facts: Being an Examination Into the Rights of the Indian Nations of America, to their respective Countries.*[596] John Marshall was well aware of the case made by this work, and even cites the work, disingenuously, for evidence that the Pratt-Yorke opinion originated in the context of India—so that Marshall could assert (arbitrarily), in his opinion in *Johnson,* that "It is, of course, entirely inapplicable to purchases made in America."[597] The case that *Plain Facts* makes, Marshall ignored and dismissed with an argument from expediency that Marshall himself confessed is "opposed to natural right, and to the usages of civilized nations" and perhaps to "reason" itself.[598]

As *Plain Facts* reveals, Christian faith—whatever limits it places on human solidarity—is capable of deep recognition of the wrongs of Christendom and the rights of humankind. After quoting Las Casas—"That the *Natives* (of America) having their own lawful kings and princes, and a right to make laws for the good government of their respective dominions, *could not* be expelled out of them, *or deprived of what they possess, without doing violence to the laws of God, as well as the laws of nations*"—Samuel Wharton launched a memorable attack on the doctrine of discovery:

> But if the princes and people of Europe, in more ignorant and superstitious ages, were so mislead by the emotions of avarice, ambition, or religious pride, as to believe it justifiable for them to cross the Atlantic, and usurp the possessions of unoffending nations, only because they did not believe in religious doctrines, of which they had never heard, yet the pervading liberal influence of philosophy, reason, and truth, has since given us better notions of the rights of mankind, as well as of the obligations of morality and justice; which certainly are not confined to particular modes of *faith,* but extend universally to Jews and Gentiles, to Christians and Infidels. And, indeed, the injustice of these attempts to usurp the

> aboriginal possessions of so many of our fellow creatures, from a deficit in their religious opinions, was so manifest, that they never could have been suggested by any other than the detestable policy, and unchristian ambition, which for many ages governed the *Papal See.*
>
> "Avides ravisseurs des richesses *des autres*
> Ils quittent *leur* pais, pour inonder les nôtres."
> —Racine
>
> The Divine Author of our holy religion, when on earth, affirmed no temporal dominion or property, but submitted himself on every occasion, even when criminally arraigned, to the jurisdiction and authority of Infidel magistrates, declaring *that his kingdom was not of this world*; and surely none of his disciples can justly arrogate to themselves powers which their great Master has disclaimed, nor pretend, that he has anywhere authorized them to expect earthly dominion or riches as the rewards of piety and virtue; much less can they plead his permission to acquire them by injustice and violence.[599]

Years before the United States would expel the Cherokee Nation from their homeland with injustice and violence in 1838, that nation's Native neighbors had already begun to be driven west. This "journey" would become the United States' most infamous encounter with its own versions of genocide. Here, again, it must be stressed that whatever the self-deluded self-righteousness of the advocates of genocide, it took willful blindness after 1831 for them not to know that they were sending vast numbers of people to their deaths and such ignorance, or feigned ignorance, unquestionably was maintained within a context shaped by what they certainly knew—as of 1830—was a deliberate Georgian effort to destroy the Cherokee Nation.

Seeking to extend its jurisdiction over Cherokee territory in June 1830, the state of Georgia—according to Supreme Court Associate Justice William Johnson—was invading the Cherokee state: "This is war in fact; though not being declared with the usual solemnities, it may perhaps be called war in disguise." [600] John Marshall's ruling in *Cherokee Nation v. Georgia* the following year was "war in disguise" against every Indian nation that was, allegedly, "within" the United States, because it sought to extend American jurisdiction over the Native peoples and the territories belonging to these nations whose dominion over them was specifically recognized in the existence of treaties that under the American Constitution were part of the "supreme law of the land."[601] Without Marshall's imperialist excuse for his illegal war—his characterization of the Native peoples as "domestic dependent nations," and his claiming (falsely) that they were "within the jurisdictional limits of the United States" as, essentially, children whose relation to the United States "resembles that of a ward to his guardian"—removal could never have taken place in the way that it did.[602] To a considerable extent, even before it came into full view, Marshall's War against the rights of the Native Nations had already been concluded in *Johnson v. McIntosh* with its claim of an "ultimate dominion" over "the soil" of these nations derived from Christian Europeans simply gazing at it, and all that remained was a mopping up operation in *Cherokee Nation* with its denial of the Cherokee Nation's challenge to the doctrine of discovery and its elaboration of a claimed "jurisdiction" over the Native Nations. Smith Thompson knew better and Joseph Story, having voted for the fraud in *Johnson*, apparently could not stomach following Marshall in continuing with it in *Cherokee Nation* in the face of Georgia's genocidal aggression (and threat to the Supreme Court's reputation) and so joined Thompson's dissent.

The immediate banner under which the fight against Indian rights took place in the 1820s and 1830s was "states' rights." This was the rallying call of the fight of the state of Georgia and its allies to break the word of the United States in order to break the international (and American constitutional) legal regime that governed relations with the Native Nations and drive them west. Understanding that fact is essential to understanding that fight. The Cherokee Nation and its lawyers knew better—when it came to interpreting the Constitution of the United States—than to believe in the version peddled by the advocates of "states' rights." John Marshall, the great "federalist," did not. The Cherokee Nation's Bill before the Supreme Court, Marshall observed in 1831, "seeks to restrain a state from the forcible exercise of legislative power over a neighboring people, asserting their independence; their right to which the state denies."[603] This Bill, Marshall continued, "requires us to control the legislature of Georgia, and to restrain the exercise of its physical force."[604] An accurate response to this observation in accord with the framers' intentions would have been: "Exactly, here is an injunction." Marshall's answer was: "The propriety of such an interposition by the court may well be questioned. It savours too much of the exercise of political power to be within the proper province of the judicial department."[605]

While genocide required a "forgetfulness" as to the dominant rhetorical positions of the founding generation, and violation of the obligations the framers had written into the Constitution, there were decades worth of antecedents to the positions of the advocates of genocide, particularly in the practices of New York and Georgia. The experience of the Creek (Muscogee) Nation in the 1820s was a prelude to what happened on a broader scale in the 1830s. Particularly as a window onto the legal and political position of the Cherokee Nation in this period, it is worth examining the defense—tentative and soon forsaken as it was—that the administration of President John Quincy Adams made of the rights of the Creek Nation when confronted by Georgian aggression.

After it became apparent that the fraudulent Treaty of Indian Springs of 1825—which was negotiated with a small faction of Creek nationals at the urging of Georgia's Governor George Troup—was bitterly opposed by the Creek Nation, the Adams administration essentially recognized the right of the Creek Nation to repudiate it. As the historian Michael Green has observed, "No Native nation had ever before persuaded the United States to tear up a ratified treaty, and none would ever succeed again."[606] Horrifically, in an effort to appease the state of Georgia, some of the harshest terms of that treaty—which had provided for the removal of the Creek Nation from Georgia—were incorporated in a subsequent Treaty of Washington in 1826. This treaty, it is true, did leave the Creek Nation in possession of its lands "within" Alabama, but still required the Creek Nation to leave its lands "within" Georgia, with the exception of a sliver of 192,000 acres.[607] Enraged at the repudiation of the Treaty of Indian Springs, Troup declared the Treaty of Washington invalid and, with the support of the Georgia legislature, sent surveyors to mark off the land they claimed as Georgia's. This initially led the Adams administration to accept what Secretary of State Henry Clay called "the necessity of protecting the rights of the Indians by force."[608] On 5 February 1827, Adams sent a message to Congress that threatened war if the Georgians would not back down:

> Happily distributed as the sovereign powers of the people of this Union have been between their General and State Governments, their history has already too often presented collisions between these divided authorities with regard to the extent of their respective powers. No instance, however, has hitherto occurred in which this collision has been urged into a conflict of actual force. No other case is known to have happened in which the application of military force by the Government of the Union has been prescribed for the enforcement of a law the violation of which has within any single State been prescribed by a legislative act of the State. In the present instance it is my duty to say that if the legislative and executive authorities of the State of Georgia should persevere in acts of encroachment upon the territories secured by a solemn treaty to the Indians, and the laws of the Union remain unaltered, a superadded obligation even higher than that of human authority will compel the Executive of the United States to enforce the laws and fulfill the duties of the nation by all the force committed for that purpose to his charge. That the arm of military force will be resorted to only in the event of the failure of all other expedients provided by the laws, a pledge has been given by the forbearance to apply it at this time. It is submitted to the wisdom of Congress to determine whether any further act of legislation may be necessary or expedient to meet the emergency of which these transactions may produce.[609]

This threat of force on behalf of the laws of the United States mandating adherence to a solemn treaty was rooted in a vision of "the sovereign powers of the people of this Union"—and a sense of American legal obligations—that the governor of Georgia did not share. Troup had mobilized two divisions of his state's militia before Adams' message to Congress and did not demobilize them after its delivery.[610] At the cusp of violence between Georgia and the United States, the Adams administration turned to the Creek Nation and persuaded them to resolve the issue by surrendering their remaining lands "within" Georgia in the Treaty of Fort Mitchell.[611]

This was the context in which the Cherokee people adopted a new written constitution in July 1827. That constitution begins as follows:

> We the representatives of the people of the Cherokee Nation, in Convention assembled, in order to establish justice, ensure tranquility, promote our common welfare, and secure to ourselves and our posterity the blessings of liberty; acknowledging with humility and gratitude the goodness of the sovereign Ruler of the Universe, in offering us an opportunity so favorable to the design, and imploring His aid and direction in its accomplishment, do ordain and establish this Constitution for the Government of the Cherokee Nation.[612]

The boundaries of the nation, embracing the lands described as solemnly guaranteed and reserved forever to the Cherokee Nation by the treaties concluded with the United States, were defined precisely by Article 1, Section 1, and it was indicated that they "shall forever hereafter remain unalterably the same."[613] Outrage was rampant in Georgia and Georgia's legislature essentially threatened war with the Cherokee Nation. It declared, in December 1827, that while Georgia would not "attempt to improve her rights by violence until all other means of redress fail.... if the United States will not redeem her pledged honor; and if the Indians continue to turn a deaf ear to the voice of reason and friendship, we now solemnly warn them of the consequences. The lands in question *belong* to Georgia. She *must* and she *will* have them."[614]

Georgia's fantasy that the United States was honor-bound to turn over Indian territories to Georgia that neither the United States nor Georgia owned had—to Georgian eyes—a foundation in a compact that Georgia signed with the United States in 1802 (and, before that, in the state's alleged inheritance of the rights of "discovery"). Under the 1802 compact, Georgia ceded its claims to the territories that would become Alabama and Mississippi in return for benefits including $1,250,000 and a commitment on the part of the United States to extinguish all Indian title to lands within the boundaries of the state of Georgia "as soon as the same can be peaceably obtained on reasonable terms."[615] The negotiating history of the 1802 compact shows that Georgia originally asked for the United States to extinguish all Indian title "within fifteen years."[616] Thomas Jefferson might well have believed that the language to which he agreed would allow the Cherokee people to stay on their own lands for as long as they refused to sell them, but if so he did not make that clear to the Georgians. And, as early as the Louisiana Purchase, Jefferson was apparently considering the possibility of an exchange of lands that would involve the Southern Indians moving west of the Mississippi.[617]

As early as 1822, Georgia was memorializing the Congress urging an end to the federal government's policy of seeking to help the Native peoples pursue civilization arguing that: "it will be necessary for the United States to relinquish the policy which they seem to have adopted with regard to civilizing the Indians, and rendering them permanent upon their lands, and changing their title of occupancy into a fee-simple title, at least in respect to the Creek and Cherokee Indians. Their contract with Georgia must remain forever unperformed so long as this policy is pursued."[618]

When the federal government sought to persuade the Cherokee Nation to sell more land, the Cherokee National Committee sent a letter to Washington indicating that they would not meet with the treaty commissioners. Efforts to bribe Cherokee leaders were met with insistence that the promised benefits be put in writing whereupon the efforts were publicized. When commissioners were finally allowed, at a place of Cherokee choosing, they were firmly rebuffed. To demands that they choose between allotment and removal, the Cherokee Nation noted that they had already refused the latter and considered the former specious: "We find opposition, fraud, and every species of injustice" raised against those who accepted allotment. The historian William McLoughlin has summarized what happened next:

> When the commissioners, angry and frustrated, said that the land the Cherokees occupied belonged to the United States by "discovery" and "by conquest," the Council answered calmly: "Our title has emanated from a Supreme source which cannot be impaired by conquest or by treaty" and if the United States had title to it, "why should [it] purchase, time after time, by treaties, lands to which you would wish to convince us we have no title?" Did the treaty

> commissioners' threat of withdrawing protection for Cherokee boundaries mean that the government "will trample justice under foot?"[619]

President James Monroe, to his credit, issued a statement on 30 March 1823 that the Cherokee nation had refused to sell any more: "In their present temper they can be removed only by force,...and there is no obligation on the United States to remove the Indians by force." Moreover, he added, "an attempt to remove them by force would be, in my opinion, unjust."[620] Taking the initiative, the Cherokee Nation then sent a delegation to Washington to reiterate their position and to suggest that the United States compensate Georgia for its claim on Cherokee lands with lands taken from the territory recently acquired in Florida. They insisted that they were "the original inhabitants of America," that they had a right to remain as a separate community as long as they chose, and that they would consider integration once "the whole nation" was completely civilized and not before.[621]

In the spring of 1828, the Adams administration informed the Cherokee Nation that their new constitution did not alter their relationship with the United States.[622] Addressing the Congress for the last time as president, on 2 December 1828, however, Adams reviewed the history of American relations with the Native Nations and called for an unspecified change. "At the establishment of the federal government under the present Constitution of the United States," Adams observed, "the principle was adopted of considering them as foreign and independent powers and also as proprietors of lands."

> As independent powers, we negotiated with them by treaties; as proprietors, we purchased of them all the lands which we could prevail upon them to sell; as brethren of the human race, rude and ignorant, we endeavored to bring them to the knowledge of religion and letters. The ultimate design was to incorporate in our own institutions that portion of them which could be converted to the state of civilization. In the practice of European states, before our Revolution, they had been considered as children to be governed; as tenants at discretion, to be dispossessed as occasion might require;

> as hunters to be indemnified by trifling concessions for removal from the grounds from which their game was extirpated. In changing the system it would seem as if a full contemplation of the consequences of the change had not been taken.... when we have had the rare good fortune of teaching them the arts of civilization and the doctrines of Christianity we have unexpectedly found them forming in the midst of ourselves communities claiming to be independent of ours and rivals of sovereignty within the territories of the members of our Union. This state of things requires that a remedy should be provided—a remedy which, while it shall do justice to those unfortunate children of nature, may secure to the members of our confederation their rights of sovereignty and of soil.[623]

This statement of Adams' was, in effect, an explicit repudiation of the international legal obligations to the Native Nations that the founding generation of the United States had accepted and enshrined in the Constitution by making treaties part of the supreme law of the land. Adams' claim that the state of Georgia enjoyed "rights of sovereignty and of soil"—which in fact it did not possess—over Cherokee territory is directly at odds with the founding generation's approach. Adams made a mockery of the commitments of the framers of the Constitution as well as of his previous defense of the Creek Nation's treaty rights. Either these treaty rights were part of American constitutional law—as Adams had seemed to suggest in his message to Congress of 5 February 1827—or they were not. No middle ground existed. And yet both John Quincy Adams and John Marshall sought desperately to find or create such middle ground or at least the appearance of middle ground—some sort of way of splitting the difference at the expense of the Native peoples—rather than directly confront Georgian aggression head on. Both men understood that American honor was at stake in the promises that had been given to the Native peoples. Both men failed to understand that, under the Constitution, these promises—because they were made in treaties—had the sanction of and were in fact a part of the supreme law of the land and provided the Supreme Court with original jurisdiction in any case arising under them, most explicitly so where a state of the Union was a party to the case. Both men entered a whirlpool of lowering moral standards and helped to drag the nation down with them. Both men eventually took "sovereignty" to be a power inherited from the British—and ultimately from the doctrine of discovery—rather than something that resides in an American people who claimed a right to exercise self-government under the same international moral and legal order that mandated respect for the equal national rights of others, including the Native Nations.

Given Adams' language in late 1828, it is not unreasonable to think that Adams—like Jackson—would have proposed a Removal Bill in the event he had been reelected: a similar "offer" to the Native peoples to relocate their homelands to the West. To be fair, it should be noted that when Jackson's fraudulent Treaty of New Echota came before the Senate in May 1836, Adams called it an "eternal disgrace upon the country."[624] It was in insisting on compliance with this fraudulent treaty that the United States directly employed force and violence to coerce an unwilling Cherokee Nation onto the Trail of Tears in 1838. But Adams, in failing to respect the right of the Creek Nation and the Cherokee Nation and their Native neighbors to be treated as sovereign and independent foreign states with whom the United States had established binding treaties guaranteeing them their dominion, helped pave the way for such grotesque brutality. The "ethnic cleansing" of Georgia of Creek nationals that Adams presided over was itself a major crime and a violation of the Treaty Supremacy Clause of the Constitution. It can be seen as the beginning of the genocide of the 1830s. Adams' later reflection on American policy in the 1830s in his diary, in 1841, is telling: "It is among the heinous sins of this nation, for which I believe God will one day bring them to judgement."[625]

In his initial attempt to justify his policy of siding with Georgia, Andrew Jackson argued that what the Cherokee people had done in establishing their new government was a violation of that clause in the Constitution that declares that "no new state shall be formed or erected within the jurisdiction of any other state" without the consent of its legislature. That the Cherokee Nation was within the jurisdiction of the state of Georgia was a claim with which even John Marshall's Supreme Court would ultimately disagree in *Worcester* (while maintaining, falsely, that it was within the jurisdiction of the United States). But Jackson clearly believed this claim and sought to make it resonate. In his first annual message to Congress, on 8 December 1829, Jackson asked whether the people of Maine would permit the Penobscot tribe to erect an independent government within their state, whether the people of New York would permit each remnant of the Six Nations within her borders to declare itself an independent people under the protection of the United States, whether the Indians could establish a separate republic on each of their reservations in Ohio. And if so, whether it would be the duty of the federal government to protect them in the attempt. Jackson then sought to present his genocidal program as one of generosity and benefit to the Southern Indians:

> the fate of the Mohegan, the Narragansett, and the Delaware is fast overtaking the Choctaw, the Cherokee, and the Creek. That this fate surely awaits them if they remain within the limits of the states does not admit of a doubt. Humanity and national honor demand that every effort should be made to avert so great a calamity.... As a means of effecting this end I suggest for your consideration the propriety of setting apart an ample district west of the Mississippi, and without the limits of any state or territory now formed, to be guaranteed to the Indian tribes as long as they shall occupy it, each tribe having a distinct control over the portion designated for its use. There they may be secured in the enjoyment of governments of their own choice, subject to no other control from the United States than such as may be necessary to preserve peace on the frontier and between the several tribes. There the benevolent may endeavor to teach them the arts of civilization, and, by promoting union and harmony among them, to raise up an interesting commonwealth, destined to perpetuate the race and to attest the humanity and justice of this government. This emigration should be voluntary, for it would be as cruel as unjust to compel the aborigines to abandon the graves of their fathers and seek a home in a distant land. But they should be distinctly informed that if they remain within the limits of the states they must be subject to their laws. In return for their obedience as individuals they will without doubt be protected in the enjoyment of those possessions which they have improved by their industry. But it seems to me visionary to suppose that in this state of things claims can be allowed on tracts of country on which they have neither dwelt nor made improvements, merely because they have seen them from the mountain or passed them in the chase.

> Submitting to the laws of the states, and receiving, like other citizens, protection in their persons and property, they will ere long become merged in the mass of our population.[626]

Looking back, it is painfully clear that three Congressmen voting the other way in the House of Representatives in 1830 would have defeated the removal bill. As we have seen, there were four Congressmen who might well have voted against the bill on grounds of conscience, but who chose to remain loyal to Jackson, or abstain, and this proved decisive to the outcome in spite of the fact that 36 of 135 Jacksonian Congressmen refused to vote for the bill.[627] Georgia might have sought to engage in "ethnic cleansing" on its own, in the event the bill was defeated, but the dynamic in the country would have been different. The so-called "Christian party in politics" would have been energized by its legislative victory—and outraged at such an effort by Georgia—rather than demoralized by defeat and acquiescent.[628] The ascendancy of a different spirit in the country would have had implications for everything from John Marshall's position in *Cherokee Nation v. Georgia*, to the 1832 elections, to the future of slavery.

Unlike the Supreme Court's decision in *Worcester v. Georgia* in 1832, which the Georgians simply refused to accept—a refusal the Supreme Court never had a chance to challenge as the plaintiffs accepted pardons before the start of the court's next term—a decision for the Cherokee Nation in *Cherokee Nation v. Georgia* would have implicitly or explicitly instructed the president of the United States to fulfill his constitutional duty to uphold the law even if this meant threatening or using military force against Georgia to ensure Georgia's compliance with the court's decision. It would have become *the* central issue in American politics in 1831—and probably *the* central issue in the 1832 presidential campaign. It is by no means clear how the deepening constitutional crisis would have played out.

It is conceivable that, faced with the defeat of the removal bill in the Congress, and a different Supreme Court decision in *Cherokee Nation v. Georgia*, Andrew Jackson would have chosen to uphold the law of the land against Georgia, and the Georgians would have backed down. Instead of Georgia Congressman Richard Wilde's deceitful vision of "the hunter and his game" inevitably having to retire before the "march toward maturity and greatness" of "Christianity and civilization," there would have been a measure of compromise with the Native Nations, a measure of respect for their rights, and an American society closer to the Congregationalist Jeremiah Evarts' understanding of Christianity and civilization.[629] The poisonous legal precedent in *Johnson* that set the tone for all subsequent United States relations with the Native peoples would not have been cemented into place. The moral corruption and self-deception involved in embracing a spurious understanding of "discovery" and a fictitious claim of "conquest" as a justification for American action—notwithstanding the fact that no version of either doctrine provided any grounds for the violation of existing treaties—would have been avoided.

Spared the horrible lie of "manifest destiny"—including the false claim that the genocidal brutality the Native peoples experienced during western expansion was somehow inevitable and not a series of deliberate murderous choices—the very character of the country would have been different. The loss of this character, together with the horrors that the Cherokee people and their Native neighbors experienced, was part of the full cost of the decision Congress took in 1830 at the urging of Andrew Jackson to appease Georgian aggression; an aggression which John Marshall violated the Constitution and his oath of office rather than seek to end through an injunction. After that decision, and as a result of it, there was degeneration in the moral character of the United States. This degeneration is particularly evident in the contrast between the debate in 1830, in which all sides felt obliged to deprecate the idea of removal by force and violence (although with many speakers eliding the vicious coercive acts of Georgia, Alabama, and Mississippi), and the conduct of the country following that debate. The winning side, with its express belief in the absence or paltry character of Indian rights, and the pure expediency of "treaties" with Native Nations—once freed from the moral and legal constraint that an organized public opinion had sought to impose—acted accordingly. The Georgians, in particular, became ever more bold in their racism and aggression, but so did the Supreme Court, and so did the country as a whole. Whether the pseudo-scientific racism of the nineteenth century would have grown as strongly as it did without removal is an open question, though it seems unlikely that this would have been the case.

Considering the rise of pseudo-scientific racism in Great Britain in the nineteenth century, the great scholar of slavery and antislavery, David Brion Davis, notes that most British scientists in the early 1800s insisted on the unity and even perfectibility of all human groups. "The historian Seymour Drescher," Davis observes, "makes the extraordinary point that in the parliamentary debates over slave emancipation in 1833, not a single M.P. spoke of any alleged incapacity of the Negroes. But by the 1850s African American visitors in Britain, like Frederick Douglass, sensed a deeply troubling change in attitude even from the mid-1840s."[630] Is it not likely that a brutal American action denying the Native Nations their equal place in the human family, and dismissing and destroying the evidence of the progress they had made, forms a vital part of this story? Is it not likely that the ongoing progress of the Southern Indians, and especially the Cherokee Nation—in the event that the opponents of genocide had been victorious—would have operated as a major obstacle to the hardening of racist attitudes?

Without the Trail of Tears, can one conceive of the biologist Charles Darwin's position in *The Descent of Man*? According to Darwin, "At some future period, not very distant as measured by centuries…the *civilized races of man* will almost certainly *exterminate,* and *replace,* the *savage races* throughout the world. At the same time, the anthropomorphous apes…will no doubt be exterminated. The *break between man and his nearest allies* will then be wider, for it will intervene between man in a more *civilized state,* as we may hope, even than the Caucasian, and some ape as low as a baboon, instead of, as now, between the negro or Australian and the gorilla."[631]

The role of racism in the connection between John Forsyth's fantasy of a doctrine of discovery—in which everything belonged to "the Government of the fortunate navigator, who, by accident or design, first saw the before unknown country"—and Andrew Jackson's claim that it was visionary to suppose that Indians could own the lands in question—"merely because they have seen them from the mountain or passed them in the chase"—is too evident to require much comment. [632] Surely, the alleviation or elimination of racism is part of any worthwhile conception of progress. But the argument that genocide was simply an outgrowth of a traditionally racist and greedy colonialist past is inadequate. It ignores the religious bigotry underlying the doctrine of "Christian discovery" that antedated and helped give birth to modern racism. It also ignores the fact that opposition to racism is by itself inadequate to prevent genocide. Chattel slavery and genocide came first and modern racism followed as an attempt at justification. Underlying all of them is a politics of domination and it is that politics that must be successfully fought and defeated to prevent slavery and genocide.

Blaming a traditionally racist and greedy colonialist past also elides the considerable evidence suggesting that a solid majority of the American people *were opposed* to removal and leaves unasked the very pressing questions of how an allegedly "democratic" United States could descend so quickly into such extreme brutality and what would have been required for that descent to have been avoided. Spreading the blame so widely has the effect of allowing those most culpable to escape the specific responsibilities of their conduct.[633] Finally, by avoiding the specificities of the past in favor of a simple blanket condemnation, it allows those who see themselves as possessed of a "modern" moral sensibility—supposedly free of such intense racism and greed—to imagine that they are in no danger of repeating such horrors. Such "moderns" may want to take note of New York Congressman Henry Storrs' comment in the debate in 1830 as to how much things had changed since the age of Columbus—"when the human mind was darkened by bigotry."[634] They may also wish to observe the efforts—continuing to this day—at cultural genocide and extreme exploitation that the Native Nations have had to cope with since the doctrine of "Christian discovery" first entered European minds and especially since it first became embedded in "federal Indian law."[635]

It is also worth stressing that a horrifically racist set of views did not necessarily prevent, in conjunction with sufficient respect for the law of nations and the Constitution, a willingness—such as Secretary of State Henry Clay expressed in 1827—to use force in defense of "the rights of the Indians."[636] In a Cabinet meeting on 22 December 1825, according to President John Quincy Adams' recollection, Clay had argued that: "it was impossible to civilize Indians; that there never was a full-blooded Indian who took to civilization. It was not in their nature. He believed they were destined to extinction, and, although he would never countenance inhumanity towards them, he did not think them, as a race, worth preserving. He considered them as essentially inferior to the Anglo-Saxon race, which were now taking their place on this continent. They were not an improvable breed, and their disappearance from the human family will be no great loss to the world."[637] But by 1827, as we have seen, Clay was willing to advocate the use of federal force in response to Georgian aggression, and, by 1831, Clay was convinced that the Cherokee Nation would become "a civilized, Christian and prosperous community."[638] By 1836, he was a voice in the Senate against the fraudulent New Echota treaty. Many other Senators failed to see the moral and legal issues at stake in respecting the obligations of existing treaties with the Native Nations and ignored the obvious lessons of the contrast between a century of decline and the new and increasingly visible Cherokee renaissance.

The way Henry Clay was at least partially led out of some of his intense racist views was through respect for the rule of law. Had John Marshall ruled in accordance with the Treaty Supremacy Clause of the Constitution in *Cherokee Nation v. Georgia,* the country as a whole could have been led along the same path in the same direction. As it was, the ascendancy of the advocates of genocide was associated globally not only with a hardening of racist attitudes but with a shift away from natural law based conceptions of international law to more "positivist" conceptions.[639]

The historian Jennifer Pitts, who has traced something of this shift toward "positivism," has noted that the late eighteenth century "stands out in the history of the law of nations as one of striking openness on the part of Europeans to the possibility of shared legal frameworks and mutual obligation between Christians and non-Christians, Europeans and non-Europeans."[640] She particularly stresses the ideas and principles that the British statesman Edmund Burke and his allies developed to try to check the abuses of British power in India.[641] It was Burke, after all, who impeached Warren Hastings—the de facto first Governor General of India—in language that, like the language of Bartolomé de Las Casas, echoes through the ages:

> I impeach him in the name of the Commons of Great Britain in Parliament assembled, whose Parliamentary trust he has betrayed. I

> impeach him in the name of all the Commons of Great Britain, whose national character he has dishonored. I impeach him in the name of the people of India, whose laws, rights and liberties he has subverted, whose properties he has destroyed, whose country he has laid waste. I impeach him in the name and by virtue of those eternal laws of justice which he has violated. I impeach him in the name of human nature itself, which he has cruelly outraged, injured and oppressed, in both sexes, in every age, rank, situation and condition of life.[642]

Something of the same appeal to eternal truths of universal law and morality is inherent in the ideas and principles behind the Treaty Supremacy Clause; ideas and principles that the opponents of genocide in the United States drew upon in seeking to defend the rights of the Native peoples to their dominion over their own lands. The affinity was noted at the time by Congressman George Evans of Maine who held that even if no Edmund Burke were found to hold up the picture of the wrongs done to the Cherokee people to the execration of mankind, they would ultimately find "a higher tribunal, where sophistry cannot delude, and where the humblest Indian will be equal to his proudest oppressor."[643] Such faith in the ultimately divine foundations of justice as established by the author of nature—as Bartolomé de Las Casas or James Wilson might have put it—faced serious erosion with the rise of "positivism" in the nineteenth century; a rise to which the advocates of genocide and their appeasers contributed. These "positivists" seem never to have realized that charges akin to those Burke leveled at Hastings could be leveled at them. But then the American people as a whole have as yet failed to realize that these charges apply to the extreme misconduct of the United States as well.

If Joseph Story could join Smith Thompson in his dissent in *Cherokee Nation,* despite having voted for the majority opinion in *Johnson,* then John Marshall and John McLean could have done so as well. They could, in short, have repudiated Marshall's position in *Johnson,* either in effect or explicitly. In that event, every Native Nation would have retained independent ownership and independent jurisdiction over its lands in American constitutional law. Had *Cherokee Nation* been rightly decided, "Christian discovery" might have become about as significant as the "allodial title" claimed by a British monarch is today in Britain. "Allodial title" in British land law is the fiction that all lands once belonged to the Crown. But under British law, that claim does *not* make it possible for the Crown to acquire an original title to lands that are already occupied. Such a taking would amount to an act of state against British subjects on British soil, something clearly unlawful.[644] The Crown, in short, does not possess a power of eminent domain or compulsory purchase as a result of "allodial title."

In the American context, in the event of a lawful or rightly constructed decision in accord with the United States Constitution in *Cherokee Nation*, the Native Nations' treaty-guaranteed dominion over their own territory would have been upheld. Marshall's claim in *Johnson*—that the mere presence of Christian Europeans in North America "necessarily diminished" the sovereignty of the Native peoples and gave an "ultimate dominion" to what would become the United States—would have been revealed as nothing more than a reactionary and ridiculous expansion of the concept of "preemption"; an "expectancy" that as Secretary of State Thomas Jefferson noted conveyed no present rights whatever over the sovereignty of a Native Nation.[645] In short, no right of eminent domain or jurisdiction or plenary power in the Congress or in the Judiciary or in any state government or in any other legal authority in the United States over any Native Nation. Had the Cherokee Nation's possessory rights under its treaties with the United States been respected in accordance with the Treaty Supremacy Clause, American rights of "preemption" would have been revealed as a legal irrelevancy over any lands that a Native Nation wished to retain. Far from being "roots" of plenary power, they would have shriveled into nothingness in the sunlight of constitutional law.[646]

David Brion Davis has observed that precisely because slavery symbolized the most extreme model of treating people as exploitable objects, attacks on it opened possibilities of successively discrediting the cultural sanctions for every traditional form of exploitation.[647] Something similar can be said for what the extreme mistreatment of indigenous peoples symbolizes: the most extreme model of the violation of the rights of nations as well as extreme violation of individuals. It is hardly surprising that the defense of Indian national rights proved capable of broadening the horizons of those who engaged in such defense. It deepened their awareness and knowledge of an international moral and legal order under which individuals and nations alike could claim their rights and accept their responsibilities.

The historian Mary Hershberger has shown that opposition to removal generally contributed to the civility of those who participated in it, strengthening both abolitionists and advocates of women's rights.[648] One famous abolitionist, Beriah Green, wrote of a friend and fellow abolitionist, James Birney, that "from the Indian to the Negro, the transition was easy and natural. He could hardly fail to see, when the wrong of the Indians had thoroughly aroused him, that the suffering of the Negro flowed from the same bitter fountain."[649] Harriet Beecher, the future author of *Uncle Tom's Cabin*, thrilled at the new world of political activity that her older sister Catherine inaugurated by launching a national petition drive around a circular addressed to "benevolent ladies of the United States," urging both "prayers and exertions to avert the calamity of removal."[650] "Let every woman who peruses it, exert that influence in society which falls within her lawful province, and endeavor by every suitable expedient to interest the feelings of her friends, relatives, and acquaintances, in behalf of this people, that are ready to perish."[651] The English professor Alisse Portnoy, in her study of women's activism in the debates over removal and slavery, also examines the intertwining of these debates. She notes how the American abolitionist and social justice advocate William Lloyd Garrison was moved to convert to abolition from his previous position of support for colonizing freed slaves in Liberia, by the strength of one resolution at a meeting of African Americans in 1831: "we view, with unfeigned astonishment, the anti-Christian and inconsistent conduct of those who so strenuously advocate our removal from this our native country to the burning shores of Liberia, and who with the same breath contend against the cruelty and injustice of Georgia in her attempt to remove the Cherokee Indians west of the Mississippi."[652]

As for the women's circular that Catherine Beecher and her allies circulated, it called on the Congress to "acknowledge these people as free and independent nations, and … protect them in the quiet possession of their lands."[653] The historian Tiya Miles, noting Hershberger's account of the remarkable leap that white middle-class and elite women had taken into the world of national politics with this circular—a leap involving some fifteen hundred women nationwide—has gone on to show how Cherokee women's organized action against Indian removal both antedated this leap and may well have influenced it. One of the representatives of these Cherokee women, Margaret Ann Scott, responded to an earlier effort at removal, in 1817, with words designed to move an American "Christian" audience:

> Our neighboring white people seem to aim at our destruction. They have not the fear of God before their eyes; they seem not to believe in a Savior; they set wicked examples before the poor, ignorant Indians; they insult our poor people who bear it patiently. I cannot help but cease from weeping to our merciful Savior to show mercy to us, and help from the land of our oppressors.... At a time when there is a good prospect that many more will join the few, who have embraced Christianity, we shall be driven away from the land of our fathers, which is as dear to us as our own lives: from our improved farms, from our beloved teachers, into a Land strange to us; yea, into savage life again.[654]

In our own day, law professor Elizabeth Reese (Nambé Pueblo) has appealed not to the alleged principles of an American "Christian" or "civilized" audience, but to a common humanity and what should be a simple desire to know the peoples who live on this land; a simple concern for the well-being of all. In doing so, she has emphasized how far away from the fulfillment of promises the Supreme Court threatens to take us at every turn:

> The victory for tribal jurisdiction in *McGirt* is hopefully as much a rejection of the fear of tribal governance as it is in keeping with the plain text of the law. Time will tell. Every time a case with large implications like *McGirt* reaches the Supreme Court, many people tied to tribal governments in one way or another are quietly afraid. There is always the fear that the Court will make bad (that is, ill-informed) law. But the great, omnipresent fear is that the Court or Congress will finally do away with tribes. The tragedy—and the injustice—would be that after all these years, and all the blood, ink,

> and tears spilled, the United States will nonetheless finally do away with Indian tribes, not because it knows what they are like, but because it doesn't.[655]

In 1978, in *United States v. Wheeler,* the Supreme Court actually claimed that tribal sovereignty "exists only at the sufferance of Congress and is subject to complete defeasance."[656] In *McGirt v. Oklahoma,* in 2020, the Supreme Court reaffirmed this perverse claim that all Congress needs to do to destroy a Native Nation is "say so." The Congress, Justice Neil Gorsuch also wrote, has "authority to breach its own promises and treaties."[657] These two claims are part of an absurd position—full of genocidal brutality and at odds with constitutional law and the law of nations as they were understood by the framers—that has yet to be officially repudiated. This is the position that the United States is bound by neither treaties nor by the law of nations, even as far as the pursuit of genocide is concerned, except to the extent that it may deign to be. And the Supreme Court has the gall to claim that this absurdity—this untrammeled despotic power—is compatible with the Constitution. The Constitution and treaties of the United States are the foundation of covenantal relationships. Those Supreme Court justices who pretend to be loyal to the Constitution while claiming that treaties can be repudiated or revised by "the sovereign" at pleasure are hypocrites of the worst sort. So, often without realizing it, are all those who fail to respect the treaty- and treaty relationship-guaranteed dominion of the Native Nations over their own territories while claiming to be loyal to the Constitution.

The true meaning of treaties in the Constitution, and of the national sovereignty of all other nations relative to the United States, was well-conveyed by Supreme Court Chief Justice John Jay in his charge to the grand jury in *Henfield's Case* in 1793:

> Treaties between independent nations, are contracts or bargains which derive all their force and obligation from mutual consent and agreement; and consequently, when once fairly made and properly concluded, cannot be altered or annulled by one of the parties, without the consent and concurrence of the other. Wide is the difference between treaties and statutes—we may negotiate and

make contracts with other nations, but we can neither legislate for them, nor they for us; we may repeal or alter our statutes, but no nation can have authority to vacate or modify treaties at discretion. Treaties, therefore, necessarily become the supreme law of the land, and so they are very properly declared to be by the sixth article of the constitution. Whenever doubts and questions arise relative to the validity, operation or construction of treaties, or of any articles in them, those doubts and questions must be settled according to the maxims and principles of the laws of nations applicable to the case. The peace, prosperity, and reputation of the United States, will always greatly depend on their fidelity to their engagements; and every virtuous citizen (for every citizen is a party to them) will concur in observing and executing them with honour and good faith.[658]

Epilogue

The story of the genocide of the 1830s is the story of how the "Columbus Mentality"—as that great poet of the People, John Trudell (Santee Dakota), has put it—came to determine American law, policy, and conduct in a decision to pursue domination that persists to this day.[659] The assumptions and arguments of those who advocated this decision in the 1820s and 1830s are the same assumptions and arguments—although dressed up in less religious and more "polite" language—that continue to be offered up by the Supreme Court and by the advocates of "federal Indian law" in the present—the advocates of a "law" that is not made by the Native Nations but rather imposed upon them. This is the "law" that made possible the Trail of Tears and that continues to facilitate extraordinary oppression and exploitation. This is the "law" whose apologists in the present, as in the 1830s, continue to claim (falsely) that they are acting in the "best interests"—or even simply "the interests"—of the Indian peoples. Here is Trudell's succinct explanation as to the reason for their conduct: "So when Columbus got here, he got off the boat, and he said to the first people he saw, 'Who are you?' And the first people he saw said, 'We're human beings.' And Columbus said, 'Oh, Indians.'"[660]

> It's five hundred years later and they still can't see us. We are still invisible. They don't see us as human beings, but we've been saying to them all along that's what we are. We are invisible to them because we are still the Human Beings, we're still the People, but they will never call us that. They taught us to call ourselves Indians, now they're teaching us to call ourselves Native Americans. It's not who we are. We're the People. They can't see us as human beings. But they can't see themselves as human beings. The invisibility is at every level, it's not just that we're tucked away out of sight. We're the evidence of the crime. They can't deal with the reality of who we are because then they have to deal with the reality of what they have done. If they deal with the reality of who we are, they have to deal with the reality of who they aren't. So they have to fear us, not recognize us, not like us. The very fact of calling us Indians creates a

> new identity for us, an identity that began with their arrival. Changing identity, creating a new perceptual reality, is another form of genocide. It's like severing a spiritual umbilical cord that reaches into the ancestral past. The history of the Indians begins with the arrival of the Europeans. The history of the People begins with the beginning of the history of the People. The history of the People is one of cooperation, collectivity, and living in balance. The history of the Indians is one of being attacked and genocide, rather than a history of peace and balance. The history of the People under attack, the Indians, in an evolutionary context, is not very long, it's only five hundred years. The objective of civilizing us is to make Indian history become our permanent reality. The necessary objective of Native people is to outlast this attack, however long it takes, to keep our identity alive.[661]

Those with the slightest doubt as to the accuracy of Trudell's account, need only consider the writings of Juan Ginés Sepúlveda, the court historian in mid-sixteenth century Spain and Las Casas' great rival in the debate within Spain over Spanish colonialism. Sepúlveda described the Indians of the New World harshly: "In prudence, talent, virtue, and humanity they are as inferior to the Spaniards as children to adults, women to men, as the wild and cruel to the most meek, as the prodigiously intemperate to the continent and temperate, that I have almost said, as monkeys to men."[662] The idea that Las Casas knew better was beyond Sepúlveda's imagination and would have seemed to him an affront to the dignity of the crown and of Spain: "Shall we doubt that those peoples, so uncivilized, so barbarous, so wicked, contaminated with so many evils and wicked religious practices, have been justly subjugated by an excellent, pious, and most just King, such as was Ferdinand and the Emperor Charles is now, and by a most civilized nation that is outstanding in every kind of virtue?"[663] To the claim that wars of conquest were impeding the progress of Christianity because the Indians came to hate those who did them harm, Sepúlveda replied, "the madman also hates the doctor who cures him, and the unruly boy hates the teacher who punishes him, but this fact does not negate the usefulness of one nor the other, nor should it be abandoned."[664]

The central assumption of this "Columbus Mentality"—that those on the shore are not equals from whom one can learn in friendship but rather inferiors to be dominated and "taught" by those coming over by boat—was and remains incompatible with the Native Nations' right to the free and independent existence that they enjoyed before Columbus came and that they will enjoy again once the peoples of the world manage to turn from what Trudell calls "tech-'no-logic' civilization" to ways of living in balance with the land, with the planet's ecosystem and environment, and with all our relations (all living beings). The "Columbus Mentality"—and its doctrine of "Christian discovery"—is like a disease unknown to Turtle Island and it is taking some time for the land and the Native peoples to develop immunity and, in conjunction with allies, effective responses.[665]

Memory runs deep and some truths are so deeply rooted in the fabric of reality that they will always be remembered. "No matter what they ever do to us," Trudell has said, "we must always act for the love of our people and the earth. We must not react out of hatred against those who have no sense."[666] As the attorney and historian Roberta Carol Harvey (Navajo) presents the matter in her critique of the doctrine of discovery, *The Earth is Red*: "When I was a child, Daddy told me the Earth was red from the Blood of our People who fought for their land. I told my children the same story so they can tell their children the same story and it will never be forgotten."[667] Unlike the United States, which continues to lack a valid legal claim to title, the peoples of the Native Nations have multiple valid legal claims to title, including claims rooted in the American Constitution.

As the theologian Willie James Jennings has argued at length, the expansionist "civilization" of which the United States forms a leading part is—in great measure—an expression of a potentiality or a distortion within European Christianity that has formed and warped human identity in modernity.[668] It has done this so effectively that what the historian Calvin Luther Martin calls *The Way of the Human Being*—building on the work of the Yupik elder Harold Napoleon—has been effectively obscured from most of contemporary human consciousness.[669] Now that the global crisis of climate change is bringing the illogic of this ever-expanding "civilization" home to all, there is both additional reason for hope and a desperate need for respecting the wisdom and spirituality of the Native peoples.[670] This is particularly true as major efforts are already underway to commodify this wisdom and spirituality and to extract from the cultures of the Native Nations everything and anything that can be made to serve tech-"no-logic" civilization. There is a desperate need for orienting our conduct toward the reality of our shared sociality outside of this "civilization." We are, in some ways, like fish swimming in polluted waters who are largely unaware of the waters in which we swim and will remain so until we sense the cleaner waters that are available for us to move into; until we can navigate in accord with the landscapes that help to form the deeper realities of our way to the home to which we belong.

We are spirit, being, energy, John Trudell notes—we are forms of the Earth—and as such we are part of that unity—we are all made up of the same stuff just arranged differently and have the same relationship to Sun, Sky, Universe.[671] When we are aware of our identity as human beings we have the power that comes from this energy, but this energy can be and is being mined by those who obscure our identity, and seek to have us cooperate in the mining of our own being, leaving behind a toxic residue of our fears, doubts, and insecurities. Confused about our identity, we become vulnerable to being addicted to a perception of our own powerlessness and to seeking to consume material to comfort ourselves. This is the process of "civilization"—in service to the great god technology—which seeks to erase the memory from the human being of being a human being connected to spiritual reality. It leads to an overconsumption that has unbalanced our relations with all living beings. There is, Trudell reminds us with these insights, another path. I am cognizant that in seeking to speak of this path as an American, and to sketch a possible future for all of us on Turtle Island, I run the risk—at best—of placing myself in a position analogous to that of a German with a Nazi past trying to tell Jews how to lead and practice a Jewish way of life and faith as part of some German vision of the beloved community.What I most hope for is a willingness on the part of the American people to listen to the peoples of the Native Nations—and to all our relations—rather than talk so much. This book is largely an attempt to clear away some of the major obstacles to attentive listening; especially the obstacles rooted in "federal Indian law."

To understand the arguments over genocide in the United States in the 1820s and 1830s, one must understand not only the "Columbus Mentality," but also how a militant minority, whose stronghold was the state of Georgia, had its way in the face of appeasement and collapsing resistance—overcoming, in succession, what had been considerable opposition in the executive branch, the Congress, the Supreme Court, and public opinion. It was only then that they could seek to overcome the Native peoples and carry out genocide on a continental scale. The appeasement that Georgia's murderous fanaticism encountered is at the heart of how and why the genocide of the 1830s took place. This appeasement has been obscured for nearly two hundred years because leading "federalists" including President John Quincy Adams and Supreme Court Chief Justice John Marshall participated in it. These "federalists" and their defenders later sought to present themselves and their side as among the virtuous opponents of genocide rather than as the precursors and appeasers that in fact they were. This has led to a widespread failure to remember the arguments of those who were truly opposed to the genocide of the 1830s; to remember the arguments—on Adams' and Marshall's "left" as it were—to which Adams and Marshall were *opposed*. It has led to a failure to even perceive arguments that are directly relevant to whether American relationships with the Native Nations and, indeed, with all nations going forward in the future, are going to be trustworthy, reciprocal, and consensual—whether they will be accountable and so capable of insuring the fluidity and adaptability needed to address the shared problems our world confronts—or not.[672] Above all, there has been a failure to remember the position of those opponents of genocide who recognized (correctly) that the Native Nations are entitled to be treated the same as all nations.

The vision of American global "leadership" that has been a staple of American politics since the beginning of the republic comes with requirements that have rarely, if ever, been met in practice.[673] In the absence of an approach to all nations that is trustworthy, reciprocal, and consensual, American "leadership"—as the wars in Vietnam, Iraq, and Afghanistan have recently demonstrated—can be a powerful curse and not a blessing. This the Native Nations of Turtle Island have known deeply from their lived experience for centuries.

At the present day, the relationship of Monaco and France, and the Vatican City and San Marino and Italy, are illustrative of what could have been and perhaps could still become the relations of the United States and hundreds of Native Nations. With a reopened treaty making process, or perhaps simply with additional negotiated forms of dispute resolution, these nations should be able to proceed as they see fit. Freed of the oppression and exploitation of "federal Indian law"—and any claim of authority over them on the part of the United States—some of these nations might establish "domination-free-zones" on their territories in which to recuperate their original free and independent existence to the benefit of the entire planet. [674] Others might seek more harmonious forms of modernity in which old traditions mesh with new expressions of self-government that could also benefit the entire planet.[675] As a preliminary step forward, these nations could be asked to jointly resume the stewardship and the ownership of the "public lands" of the United States at the expense of the United States—providing a stream of employment opportunities and financial resources to the peoples of these nations and serving the global common good.[676] Related efforts could be undertaken in urban areas with regard to the restoration of traditional waterways and habitats.

In 1977, the International Non-Governmental Organization's conference on "Discrimination Against the Indigenous Populations of the Americas" in Geneva, Switzerland, received a remarkable document, the *Basic Call to Consciousness*. This was at a time when some international gatherings were prevented by certain states from even using the term "Indigenous peoples" lest there be pressure to recognize the equal rights of these peoples as sovereign nations who are entitled to be treated as independent states. Originating in the Mohawk Nation at Akwesasne, drafted by the scholar John Mohawk (Seneca), and carefully reviewed and revised by the Haudenosaunee Council of Chiefs, the *Basic Call to Consciousness* was a wake-up call to humanity. Decades before the climate crisis was on anyone's lips, as Peter d'Errico has observed, Indigenous peoples were warning that industrial exploitation and destruction of the Natural World threatened the survival of life on Earth: "The way of life known as 'Western Civilization' is on a death path, and its culture has no viable answers....The air is foul, the waters poisoned, the trees dying, the animals are disappearing. We think even the systems of weather are changing.... The people who are living on this planet need to break with the narrow concept of human liberation and begin to see liberation as something that needs to be extended to the whole of the Natural World. What is needed is the liberation of all the things that support life—the air, the waters, the trees—all the things that support the sacred Web of Life."[677]

The scientist and climate change expert Kyle Powys Whyte (Potawatomi) provides a window onto the wisdom of the Native peoples—and its relevance to coping with the climate crisis—when he notes that each time the Native peoples moved from place to place, they encountered a new set of ecosystems, a new habitat: "A lot of our stories are actually about encountering a new place. If you try to control it, you're not going to have a lot of success. But if you actually tried to relate to it, learn from it and appreciate the independence of the nonhuman world, as well as the people there, you're going to be able to adapt to that new ecosystem and deal with the changes in the environment you're encountering."[678] Whyte cautions that the sense of urgency surrounding the climate crisis should not lead to a continuation of colonialist efforts to override relationships with Native peoples and their concerns.

As Indigenous scholars have cultivated the traditions of science and western scholarship, the failures of these traditions to come to terms with their own mistaken biases have become more glaring. Mark Freeland reports an experience that he had as part of a class studying environmental conflict resolution at Rocky Mountain National Park. The conflict being discussed was over controlling the elk population with wolves or perhaps by shooting female elk with a hormonal contraceptive. Told that the problem was that the elk do not have any natural predators in the area, Freeland blurted out: "Are you saying that the Arapahoe, Cheyenne, and Ute peoples had not been hunting elk in these valleys for thousands of years?"[679] The framing of the problem, Freeland observes, demonstrated a significant dissonance in scientific ideology whereby humans are not seen as part of the natural environment: "So strong is the Eurowestern belief in the superiority and separation of humans from the natural world as embedded in the logic of dominion that it is evident even in people trained otherwise, who interact with interrelated environments on a daily basis."[680]

There is a profound ongoing tension between the position of what Vine Deloria, Jr. has called "the spiritual owner of the land" and the position of what he has called "the political owner of the land."[681] Even if the United States were to recognize the national independence of each of the 326 land areas that are administered as reservations on about 56 million acres, even if the United States were to turn over the stewardship and the ownership of the 800 million acres of so-called "public lands" to the Native Nations, this tension would remain.[682] This tension, I think, can only be resolved when the "political owner" learns from the "spiritual owner" what the land is for—both in the sense of what the land wants and in the sense of what is involved in right relations with the land. It should be stressed, however, that even if the "political owner" was to adhere to the international laws and usages that prevailed on Turtle Island before the invaders from Europe arrived, this would still not give the United States a valid legal claim to title. The claims to title by "discovery" and by "conquest" made by the United States are not "legal fictions" but treaty-violating fantasies that are repugnant to the Constitution, to the law of nations, and even to the laws of war as these were understood by the framers of the Constitution. They rest on a studious refusal to consider treaties, as the framers had intended they be considered, as the supreme law of the land. The claims to title by purchase require the terms of those purchases to have been adhered to—and their requirements to be complied with—when, in fact, the United States has never met those terms for any great length of time but rather, and certainly so since 1831, continually violated them.

A major reason why it is so difficult to see what should be done is a false sense of our "sovereign territory" that those of us who are Americans all grew up with. We think, if the idea occurs to us at all, that recognition of the rights of the Native Nations would mean making a map of "our" land look like a patchwork of hundreds of distinct territories. But it is not "our" land. It does not belong to us. We share this continent with Native peoples whose legal and moral claim to dominion over it is far stronger than our own. We are essentially guests rather than hosts on this continent and our conduct as guests toward the true hosts has been despicable. Ultimately, the land itself is the truest of our true hosts and the attempt to parcel her out into so many little and big plots for purposes of domination and extraction and exploitation a grotesque course of conduct on our part. With our grandmother Earth—and indeed with all our relations—trustworthy, reciprocal, and consensual relationships are needed and often almost entirely lacking because of the warped approach to reality of the societies of Christendom and their secular successors.

It is striking, that since the 1830s, there has yet to be another mass mobilization in the United States of progressive opinion and activists on behalf of the national rights of the Native peoples of Turtle Island as distinct from rising and falling concern with the civil rights of individuals and minorities within American society. Other causes have waxed and waned and waxed again. But the embers of the fire of concern for the national rights of others have only been stirred into flame for peoples who are seen as outside of what the United States claims (falsely) as its "sovereign territory."[683] As a matter of justice, law, and politics it is high time for this to change, particularly if human life on the planet is to flourish. We must treat all peoples as equals rather than as objects; as not other, not the same, but rather as close relatives—united with us in a shared humanity constituted not in spite of our differences but rather because of the very entanglements our differences involve. And our understanding of humanity must become more porous to make room for all our relations who also help to constitute who we are.

In approaching differences of metaphysical assumptions and religious beliefs—the ultimate markers of differences among peoples—I often find it helpful to replace the word "belief" with the word "trust." This suggests that one of the things we are trusting (that different faiths can all serve the global common good) is indeed the same. We are gathered together, to reinforce the point, because of the entanglements our differences entail—because of the affinities that are all around us and within us—because of the love that we share and rely upon. This is love for an incredible range of concrete particularities, including ultimately the distinctiveness of every individual human body, far more than for generalized abstractions such as the alleged "principle" of "individualism." For the beloved community to emerge from this love, there must be growing awareness of shared affinity, and growing caring energy, for all of the peoples and individuals who live on Turtle Island—indeed, for all our relations—as well as deeper knowledge of the love and care in which we are always already gathered.

For most people, property is seen as a form of security—an extension of and protection for one's ego—and a good thing to have. This was not the view of Lady Poverty, in a thirteenth-century discourse with Saint Francis. She maintained that in Eden, Adam, possessing nothing, "belonged entirely to God."[684] The idea of such vulnerability and security in love does have its advocates. There are also many more who are profoundly dissatisfied with the extreme individualism of René Descartes' *Cogito ergo sum* (I think therefore I am) and its offspring including *Tesco ergo sum*: "I shop therefore I am." [685] Each of us can say instead: "Ubuntu"—the traditional Nguni Bantu word for humanity—a word whose meaning is conveyed by the Kenyan philosopher John Mbiti in the phrase: "I am because we are."[686]

A system built upon trying to extend and protect the ego—to unleash self-interest in the service of a particular vision of the common good involving "development"—has generated both enormous wealth, especially for a few, and intense insecurity for many by taking with reckless abandon from the land that future generations are to live on and by eviscerating the knowledge of our ancestors and their ways in favor of the latest technology.[687] In consequence of this assault on the land, countless lives among our relations, and even large numbers of entire species, have been destroyed. Blind to the unsustainability of the growth of our consumption of energy, and mistakenly imagining that our economic standard of living is the result of our ingenuity and technological development rather than realizing that this development depends on increasing energy consumption, we have burdened future generations not only with a global climate crisis but also with the threat of global economic collapse and extreme scarcities.

There is, in contrast, an abundance associated with what the poet Lewis Hyde has presented as commerce based on gift exchange and what the anthropologist Marshall Sahlins has called Stone Age economics.[688] There are, the anthropologist David Graeber notes, alternative ways in which our world has been organized in the past and might be organized in the future.[689] It is possible to think of all value as rooted not in scarcity in the market, or in the labor that went into its cultivation or production, but rather in the gifts that Heaven and Earth provide us with and those that we share with and give to each other. This is the foundation of the real economy upon which the market economy and the command socialist economy alike tend to be parasitic.

In *The Dawn of Everything: A New History of Humanity*, David Graeber and his colleague, the archaeologist David Wengrow, hold out hope for the ability of human societies to reject a politics of domination precisely because some Indigenous societies have done so successfully in the past.[690] Their view of these societies is not romanticized, and they recognize the incredible range and diversity of Indigenous experience. They reject the evolutionary schemes whereby there is a supposed progression from "simple" to "complex" societies, from egalitarian hunter-gatherers to hierarchical states, or even from small-scale societies to large-scale empires. Instead, they argue that these evolutionary schemes were themselves developed by prideful Europeans as a defense mechanism against what Graeber and Wengrow demonstrate is a powerful Indigenous critique of Western societies and Western culture and Western religion. This critique, they argue, was a major contributing tributary flowing into the Enlightenment.

Brother Gabriel Sagard's early seventeenth century account of the Wendat (Huron), a work that became a bestseller in Europe cited by both Locke and Voltaire, is one of many that Graeber and Wengrow review. According to Sagard: "They [the Wendat] reciprocate hospitality and give such assistance to one another that the necessities of all are provided for without there being any indigent beggar in their towns and villages; and they considered it a very bad thing when they heard it said that there were in France a great many of these needy beggars, and thought this was for lack of charity in us, and blamed us for it severely."[691] The Jesuit missionary Le Jeune wrote of the Montagnais-Naskapi in 1642: "They imagine that they ought by right of birth, to enjoy the liberty of wild ass colts, rendering no homage to anyone whomsoever, except when they like. They have reproached me a hundred times because we fear our Captains, while they laugh at and make sport of theirs. All the authority of their chief is in his tongue's end; for he is powerful so far as he is eloquent; and, even if he kills himself talking and haranguing, he will not be obeyed unless he pleases the Savages."[692]

As Graeber and Wengrow note, when it comes "to questions of personal freedom, the equality of men and women, sexual mores or popular sovereignty—or even, for that matter, theories of depth psychology—indigenous American attitudes are likely to be far closer to the reader's own than seventeenth-century European ones."[693] Unfortunately, Graeber and Wengrow downplay East Asian influences on the Enlightenment, which were also substantial, as well as those positive contributions to the Enlightenment that were rooted in Christianity and Judaism. I have heard—perhaps it is apocryphal—that in debates in the University of Paris, in the Middle Ages, one had to present one's opponent's position to their satisfaction before proceeding to present one's own response. Such roots of more democratic self-government should also be recuperated and nurtured. And the Enlightenment heritage as a whole should be reconsidered in the light of the world's great spiritual traditions and the past few centuries of the experience of life on earth.[694]

Graeber and Wengrow quickly pass over the sixteenth century which would have provided material that would have strengthened their argument, including the possibility that Sir Thomas More had seen the first of Bartolomé de Las Casas' manuscripts on the New World in early 1516 and that this had helped form the basis for More's *Utopia* later that year.[695] They also could have emphasized that the Indigenous critique is ongoing and that the West is just beginning to realize what can be learned from the Native Nations.

A lesson that might be studied especially deeply concerns the ways Indigenous peoples have embodied and still seek to embody cultures of equality and freedom. Writing of the Wendat in 1648, Father Lallemant noted that "They are free people, each of whom considers himself of as much consequence as the others; and they submit to their chiefs only in so far as it pleases them."[696] As Graeber and Wengrow note: "Equality here is a direct extension of freedom; indeed, is its expression. It has almost nothing in common with the more familiar (Eurasian) notion of 'equality before the law,' which is ultimately equality before the sovereign—that is, once again, equality in common subjugation." [697] The very idea of individual freedom in European culture is tied to private property where someone in possession of a thing can do whatever they want with it, except when limited by force or law. This, in turn, implies freedom is essentially a state of exception to be enjoyed only by those at a pinnacle of—or entirely outside of—the legal order.[698] "Our very word 'family' shares a root with the Latin *famulus,* meaning 'house slave,' via *familia,* which originally referred to everyone under the domestic authority of a single *paterfamilias* or male head of household. *Domus,* the Latin word for 'household,' in turn gives us not only 'domestic' and 'domesticated' but *dominium,* which was the technical term for the emperor's sovereignty as well as a citizen's power over private property. Through that we arrive at (literally, 'familiar') notions of what it means to be 'dominant,' to possess 'dominion' and to 'dominate.'"[699] Perhaps it is unnecessary to add, but the emphasis on control of "things" and on a politics of domination under Communism was even stronger in the enforced absence of "bourgeois" private property. The problem is a culture of domination much more than whether the owning and abuse is at the hands of individuals or corporations or states. The alternative of an embodied liberatory culture rooted in the traditions of Indigenous peoples around the world must first be seen to be perceived. This, in turn, requires a deliberate focus of attention—a willingness to look.

The American revolutionary Benjamin Franklin saw something of the truth of the accomplishments of the peoples of the Native Nations in 1783:

> Savages we call them, because their manners differ from ours, which we think the Perfection of Civility; they think the same of theirs.... Having frequent Occasions to hold public Councils, they have acquired great Order and Decency in conducting them. The old men sit in the foremost Ranks, the Warriors in the next, and the Women and Children in the hindmost. The Business of the Women is to take exact notice of what passes, imprint it in their memories, for they have no Writing, and communicate it to their Children. They are the Records of the Council, and they preserve Tradition of the Stipulations in Treaties a hundred Years back, which when we compare with our Writings we always find exact. He that would speak, rises. The rest observe a profound Silence. When he has finished and sits down, they leave him five or six Minutes to recollect, that if he has omitted any thing he intended to say, or has any thing to add, he may rise again and deliver it. To interrupt

> another, even in common Conversation, is reckoned highly indecent.[700]

The culture of domination that has been ascendant in the western world over the course of the last five centuries or so, and which forms its predominant legacy elsewhere on the planet, is deeply related to what the philosopher Iain McGilchrist has referred to as "the Unmaking of the World." [701] For McGilchrist this unmaking, in turn, implicates an overemphasis in our civilization on the kind of attention that the left hemisphere of the brain specializes in providing with its focus on the control and manipulation of distinct parts of graspable reality—what the philosopher Isabel Millar references with the phrase "instrumental masculinity."[702] This is in direct contrast with what might be called the expressive femininity of the kind of attention the right hemisphere of the brain specializes in providing with its openness to the "presencing" of the world and its focus on relationships. Here, again, what is missing in our civilization is balance, but also widespread recognition of the greater accuracy of the right hemisphere's approach to knowing.

The United States is composed not only of states—and other systems of domination—but also of a matrix of affinity among the American people formed in part by shared territoriality and shared democratic and Enlightenment-based narratives. That territoriality and those narratives—together with the Declaration of Independence and the Constitution—have helped sustain the American people's existence. The distinction between the people and the state, and the superiority of the former to the latter, was stressed by James Wilson in *Chisholm v. Georgia* in 1793: "The states, rather than the people, for whose sakes the states exist, are frequently the objects which attract and arrest our principal attention.... Is a toast asked? 'The United states,' instead of the 'People of the United states,' is the toast given. This is not politically correct. The toast is meant to present to view the first great object in the Union: it presents only the second. It presents only the artificial person, instead of the natural persons who spoke it into existence. A state I cheerfully fully admit, is the noblest work of Man. But, Man himself, free and honest, is, I speak as to this world, the noblest work of God."[703]

In terms of the view from the shore before the European invaders arrived, the "noblest work of Man" is the establishment of a socio-political order that does not require the sovereignty of states or a politics of domination to maintain itself and which facilitates the pursuit of inner and social peace. The American experiment—as advocated and fought for by James Wilson and his allies—can be seen as a pale imitation of the Indigenous accomplishment.

Even within the terms of that pale imitation, the Supreme Court has betrayed the American people and their Constitution—and, above all, their Revolution—in service to what it perceives as the United States' interests in stealing Native land and dominating Native peoples. Those times when the Supreme Court has correctly recognized and respected some of the treaty obligations of the United States toward a Native Nation are like those times when a broken clock—at most twice a day—shows the correct time. The significance of these decisions "sometimes" benefiting Native interests—a fact so often stressed by the system's apologists—resembles the claim that the water in separate drinking water fountains benefited "both races" under Jim Crow in a "separate but equal" manner so that the whole white supremacist structure was (allegedly) compatible with the Constitution.

The simple truth of the matter is that the clock is broken and must be repaired or replaced. Repair would involve respecting the full sovereignty of the Native Nations all of the time as independent foreign states in constitutional law toward whom the United States has binding legal obligations in treaties that the United States is not free to unilaterally alter (in other words: repair would involve recognition that the Treaty Supremacy Clause governs the American side of relations with the Native Nations and there is no "plenary power" in the Congress, or in the Executive, or in the Courts, or in any individual state). Replacement might involve the emergence of what Martin Luther King, Jr. called the beloved community—a community of all those on Turtle Island that would sustain not only respect for the essential rights and essential dignity of individuals but also for the equal rights and the equal belonging of all of the many independent and interdependent nations sharing this continent and acting with trustworthy, reciprocal, and consensual conduct toward each other and toward all our relations.

A key question for the future is how to get from here to there. To begin with, how to get those who have inherited a politico-economic system of domination to renounce the claim of a right of domination that they rely upon for their political and economic existence? A subsidiary question is whether the rhetoric of a people claiming a right to self-government under an international moral and legal order that respects the equal right of all other peoples, including the peoples of the Native Nations, to do the same, can be helpful in realizing such a renunciation? American democratic rhetoric has never yet been of much use to the Native Nations—serving rather as cover for American tyranny. But for various oppressed communities such rhetoric has been associated, at times, with at least some temporary movement towards lessening the oppression. Whether such "progress" amounts to very much is a fit subject for debate. I think it has at times prevented markedly worse outcomes for these communities, though it has never abolished the politics of domination.

There are two separate but related issues that bear on whether democratic rhetoric can ever be of material assistance to the Native Nations: first, what can be made palpable to the American people in terms of feeling not merely the ongoing injustice but also the ongoing illegality of the conduct of their state toward the peoples of the Native Nations and, second, what can be done to give the American people hope that the end of their lawbreaking activities and movement toward the realization of justice would include and advance a global common good in which they could participate.

One of the ways in which the American people have traditionally participated in advancing a global common good—at least in their own minds—has been in seeing their country as contributing to democratic progress both within the United States and abroad.[704] The attendant vision of a gradual, if sometimes dramatically punctuated, transition away from an oppressive past to a more just future has been the background against which democratic progress was perceived. But nothing in the vision of enlightened thinking contributing to gradual progress toward justice has had the slightest relationship to reality when it comes to the national rights of the Native Nations of that part of Turtle Island claimed by the United States (falsely) as its "sovereign territory."[705] Whether this vision has had any lasting positive significance for the hopes for justice of other oppressed communities—or might somehow yet do so for the Native Nations—is, as I indicated above, an open question. In *The Enfranchisement of Women*, in 1851, Harriet Taylor Mill gave particularly clear voice to the claim that it will:

> That those who were physically weaker should have been made legally inferior, is quite conformable to the mode in which the world has been governed. Until very lately, the rule of physical strength was the general law of human affairs. Throughout history, the nations, races, classes, which found themselves the strongest, either in muscles, in riches, or in military discipline, have conquered and held in subjection the rest. If, even in the most improved nations, the law of the sword is at last discountenanced as unworthy, it is only since the calumniated eighteenth century. Wars of conquest have only ceased since democratic revolutions began. The world is very young, and has but just begun to cast off injustice. It is only now getting rid of monarchical despotism. It is only now getting rid of Negro slavery. It is only now getting rid of hereditary feudal nobility. It is only now getting rid of disabilities on the ground of religion. It is only beginning to treat any *men* as citizens, except the rich and a favored portion of the middle class. Can we wonder that it has not yet done so much for women? As society was constituted until the last few generations, inequality was its very basis; association grounded on equal rights scarcely existed; to be equals was to be enemies; two persons could hardly co-operate in anything, or meet in any amicable relation, without the law's appointing that one of them should be the superior of the other. Mankind have now outgrown this state, and all things now tend to substitute, as the general principle of human relations, a just equality, instead of the dominion of the strongest.[706]

In *The Undercommons: Fugitive Planning and Black Study*, the social theorists Stefano Harney and Fred Moten present a markedly different vision of both the past and the present. Their narrative, too, contains an alternative to oppression—an alternative to the politics of domination inherent in liberal democratic civilization. Moten and Harney's description of this alternative involves the neologisms the "undercommons" and "hapticality" as well as a complex metaphor—"the shipped"—that carries resonance of the trans-Atlantic slave trade and much else. Their language is both beautiful and somewhat challenging to follow:

> Hapticality, the touch of the undercommons, the interiority of sentiment, the feel that what is to come is here. Hapticality, the capacity to feel through others, for others to feel through you, for you to feel them feeling you, this feel of the shipped is not regulated, at least not successfully, by a state, a religion, a people, an empire, a piece of land, a totem. Or perhaps we could say these are now recomposed in the wake of the shipped. To feel others is unmediated, immediately social, amongst us, our thing, and even when we recompose religion, it comes from us, and even when we recompose race, we do it as race women and men. Refused these things, we first refuse them, in the contained, amongst the contained, lying together in the ship, the boxcar, the prison, the hostel. Skin, against epidermalisation, senses touching. Thrown together touching each other we were denied all sentiment, denied all the things that were supposed to produce sentiment, family, nation, language, religion, place, home. Though forced to touch and be touched, to sense and be sensed in that space of no space, though refused sentiment, history and home, we feel (for) each other. A feel, a sentiment with its own interiority, there on skin, soul no longer inside but there for all to hear, for all to move. Soul music is a medium of this interiority on the skin, its regret the lament for broken hapticality, its self-regulatory powers the invitation to build sentimentality together again, feeling each other again, how we party. This is our hapticality, our love. This is love for the shipped, love as the shipped.[707]

The undercommons is this love, this attachment, this sharedness.[708] It is the refusal of the interpersonal and, by extension, the international, upon which politics is built; a politics that involves a democratization of despotism seeking to operate through the individual and the national. This politics is a regime of improvement formed from the confluence of the bourgeoisie's championing the improvement of oneself and the imperative of colonialism and capitalism to find investment by judging all people and all land by how much more they might improve. This confluence, Harney and Moten note in *All Incomplete*, "reinforces the fictitious idea of the self-improving, self-owning, self-authoring individual precisely through the act of positing the unproductive and under-willed land and people that surround this fiction, which requires massive resources to sustain itself, producing the impoverishment it posited by means of individuated dispossession in the service of ownership." [709] The undercommons, in contrast, is about a sociality not based on the individual. It is not created by individuals who decided to enter into relations with or through the commons. Rather it is a sharedness underneath the commons in which we are already gathered as we are already dispersed and interspersed. To be undercommon is to live incomplete in the service of a shared incompletion: "Black peoples preserve and defend the invaluable for everyone while not fully having access to it themselves."[710] "Blackness is the meaning of life. Partial, held secret, held out to all but not all there for those who hold, not ours and all we got and here it go, all incomplete."[711]

Just as blackness sustains and is sustained by the sociality to which tech-"no-logic" civilization is opposed, so is that sociality strong among the peoples of the Native Nations. Indeed, one can say that this sociality always sustains, and is always sustained by, what John Trudell called clear and coherent human beings. The closer the relationship to this sociality, the more readily—and the more accurately—are right courses of conduct felt.[712] Such sociality is different from forms of apparent solidarity such as whiteness which are cultivated to sustain a culture and a politics of domination. And different from nationality which all too often sustains domination with scarcely less viciousness than whiteness, even if its borders are, thankfully, at least sometimes, more porous. Blackness, in contrast with such forms, sustains an embodied liberatory culture.[713] So does Indigeneity. This is not because the boundaries of either are porous. It is because these boundaries do not enclose hierarchies sustaining a politics of domination.

This is not to suggest that people with white bodies cannot oppose a politics of domination or that people with Black or Indigenous bodies cannot engage in supporting such a politics. Nor is it to claim that I, as a white bodied man, can have much more than a glimmering of what blackness and Indigeneity may mean to people with Black or Indigenous bodies. It is to claim that having been excluded in the culture and politics of white supremacy from what it claims to consider the highest "universal" standards—having been excluded with horrific state violence from being what white supremacy considers "fully" human—the communities so maligned and so falsely defined have better access to the fabric of reality than those propagating or acquiescing in whiteness. In particular, they have better access to the truths of the sociality that does not exclude; the sociality that sustains our unity and equality with all our relations.

"Having everything taken away and yet remaining in everything that has been taken is a long way of saying that this is an unpayable debt," observes the brilliant philosopher Denise Ferreira da Silva: "'Slave labor' is the flesh and blood of capital because labor is nothing more than the transference of that which composes flesh and blood, the elemental components of everything, any and each possible and actual existent. Until our descriptions of existence take this as the point of departure, critical descriptions of the global political architecture will presume that everything that matters originated in and reflects post-Enlightenment white Europe. Since anything can be traced back there, these descriptions will be unable to account for how much that which matters only does so because it is but the materialization of what has been extracted from everywhere else." [714]

I believe that we all have, for those of you who know fish, something akin to the lateral line by which fish feel movement, vibration, and pressure gradients in the surrounding water—an organ that helps us navigate our shared emotional, socio-cultural, and spiritual space both as individuals and as collectivities. I will call this organ, for lack of a better term, our "heart"— though it should not be too closely connected with the pulsing object in all of our chests.[715] Even the microbiome we host—the foreign cells within our bodies—have something of a voice and a vote in the constitution of who we are, what we feel, and how we think.[716] We are embodied beings and the reality of our embodiment as clear and coherent humans—and the access (unique to each of us) to the truths of our sociality that this embodiment presents—is continually being obscured by what Silva calls the "analytics of raciality"—the apparatus of knowledge manufactured by the sciences of man and society.[717] In subtle as well as in blatant scientific and historical narratives, we are continually being told that we are other than who we are.

As for the question of who we are, Silva has presented a wonderful answer: everything in the universe co-existing "in the manner Leibniz (1646-1716) describes, that is, as a singular expression of everything else in the universe."[718] Without *separability*, she notes, there can be no *sequentiality* or *determinacy*. And without these ontological pillars of modern thought, we are free to reimagine this world as we recognize that everything that *is*, *is* actual in its existence (in spacetime) as well as virtual in its existence (in what we might call nonlocality) especially, as far as our sense of reality is concerned, in what I would call sacred times, sacred spaces, and, ultimately, eternity. Without separability, Silva concludes, "difference among human groups and between human and nonhuman entities, has very limited explanatory purchase and ethical significance." [719] In nonlocality, to put a finer point on it, our unity and equality with every entity that exists—our entangled connection to all—is evident and there is "no place" for what the American theologian James Cone described as "people who think that God called them to rule over others."[720] Rather, as the American social justice activist and Sikh thinker Valarie Kaur has suggested in her book, *See No Stranger*, there is recognition of every new individual we meet: "You are a part of me who I do not yet know."[721]

* * *

Faced with centuries of American brutality and illegal conduct, and with its legacies of injustice and genocide, and attempted genocide—as well as ongoing American oppression, exploitation, and outright theft—what can the Native peoples do? In the absence of the rule of law—which for the Native Nations ended with the end of even the pretense of equal rights under the law in 1831—Steve Russell has suggested that each Tribe needs a well ordered militia: "Not a militia in the style of the Sons of Liberty but rather in the style of the Southern Christian Leadership Conference."[722] While Gandhian nonviolence, or *satyagraha*, should not be attempted over ordinary issues that can be negotiated, he notes, its power is evident in the history of the American labor and civil rights movements: "Willingness to die for the truth always holds an advantage over willingness to kill for greed or for the sake of just following orders."[723] These nonviolent militias, if they are to succeed, must draw their strength from the peoplehood of each nation and this, in turn, will require traditions that are "smoldering" to catch fire.[724]

It is to be hoped that the successes of the Native peoples—as they recuperate their original free and independent existence—will reverberate in American society and in the wider world as well. The American people, and indeed all the peoples of the planet, have a vital interest in the successes of the Native Nations' endeavors in this regard. As the "political owners" grow in their understanding of what is sacred to the "spiritual owners"—as they see the societies that the latter (re)build on their own lands, including those lands that had once been claimed to be the "public lands" of the United States, and especially once their rights as sovereign and independent foreign states in American constitutional law are respected—one can expect that the American people will want to adopt and adapt these successes. With hundreds of Native Nations to learn from, and a new willingness to learn, who can doubt that the world as a whole will benefit?

The radical reforms that the United States would have to undergo in order to really respect the national rights of the Native peoples are formidable. Every aspect of American life from property law to criminal justice to healthcare, and from economic organization to education to the ways the very meaning of the common good on this continent are conceived, would have to change. Above all, the adoption of such reforms would require the American people to put seemingly intangible principles such as honesty and spiritual responsibility and the value of trustworthy, reciprocal, and consensual conduct above convenience, expediency, and the "comfort" of being dominated by allegedly democratic, or at least allegedly economically "efficient," authorities and institutions. Movement toward these reforms would require the American people to get in touch with their own spiritual lateral lines so that such grandmother/grandfather teachings as those of the Anishinaabeg—the teachings surrounding love, truth, bravery, humility, wisdom, honesty, and respect—become deeply felt and the resonances of their reality can be sensed in the body politic and not merely be imagined intellectually. Sharing something of what his mentor conveyed, the law professor John Borrows (Anishinaabe) writes in *Law's Indigenous Ethics* of his view that "There was but one abiding principle that guided all life and that was 'to live in harmony with the world and within one's being.'"[725]

As the beloved community emerges, its emergence will help resolve the problem that the theology professor Tink Tinker has identified with the question: "What Are We Going to Do with White People?"[726] The problem is wrongly thought of as a problem of race.[727] Rather it is a problem rooted in the worldview of those Tinker calls Eurochristians. Whether that Eurochristian worldview can be transformed, or at least radically reformed, by something closer to the worldview of the Native peoples, remains to be seen. There is a sense in which American history can be seen as a striving for this beloved community to overcome all odds and emerge.

The contributions, and increasingly the leadership, that Native people who also see themselves as Americans are offering to the older and wider international society of Turtle Island is striking and should be seen with profound gratitude by the smaller and younger American society. So should the leadership of those Native people who do not consider themselves Americans and who are working for the common good of the Native peoples and, especially, of all our relations.[728] They, too, are serving the common good of the wider society. That every Native person who is an American citizen should be able to retain their membership in American society and their citizenship in the United States—should they wish to do so—even if they also choose to be full members and citizens of Native Nations that are respected as sovereign equals of the United States and as independent foreign states in American law—is the very smallest step forward that the American people can take in the struggle for justice. This is also the very smallest step that the American people can take toward recognizing that its society's common good is part—but only a part—of the already existing common good of the wider society of Turtle Island and, ultimately, the already existing and still emerging common good of the wider society of the whole world. The question of who "we" are is perhaps best answered: we are of creation.[729]

I think that the central problem with what I see as the most powerful and undeniable of the American legal defenses of the national rights of the Native Nations—the defenses rooted in an appeal to the international moral and legal order under which the equal rights of every nation and every national are claimed to be upheld and the appeal to the truth of the equal rights of the Native Nations as foreign states in constitutional law that the Supreme Court has betrayed—is that these defenses ultimately rest on an imagined relationship with the original peoples of Turtle Island premised on the alleged superiority of an individualist conception of national popular sovereignty that the Native peoples are expected to adopt. Democracy is a powerful idea, as Vine Deloria, Jr. has noted, "but it has no relationship to the earth on which we walk and the plants and animals that give us sustenance.... Today we are suffering the impact of two thousand years of Christian individualism."[730]

To appeal to international law—even the relatively uncorrupted version of the law articulated by Bartolomé de Las Casas centuries before John Marshall's prevarications so severely warped it—is to risk granting international law an undeserved legitimacy.[731] Claiming rights under such a law—unless it is the international law that prevailed among the free and independent nations of Turtle Island before the European invasion—risks performing what law professor Stephen Young calls a "technology of self" that assimilates and integrates Indigenous peoples into states, whether as subjects within states or as states of their own within a system of states.[732] A similar danger arises with using the constitutional law of the United States even if there is less danger here than with attempting to use the more obviously spurious, oppressive, and effectively rigged "federal Indian law."[733] In all of these cases, there is a potentiality of what the Native Nations can offer the rest of the world that is at risk. As Young explains, "If ever there were collectivities that could generate legal and normative alternatives to rights-based discourses and liberal democratic regimes it is those I have called autochthonous communities."[734]

If American lawbreaking behavior can be brought to an end, with the rescission of the doctrine of "Christian discovery"—and the reversal, premises considered, of *Cherokee Nation v. Georgia*—movement toward justice will have just begun. In this context, it is worth stressing what even

James Wilson and his allies refused to perceive: what justice meant—and means—to the Native peoples. "Indigenous justice," as Peter d'Errico has observed, "is peace-making that allows each community to survive from 'time immemorial.' State institutions are based on a framework of absolute power and such power is generally absent in indigenous communities; indigenous justice is thus a challenge to state sovereignty as the organizing principle of the world.... An indigenous community provides pragmatic interpersonal context for individual life: How will what I do affect others? Who am I in relation to others? This context is immediate, palpable, an awareness in the moment, as opposed to a rationalized conception of 'shoulds' and norms."[735]

I hope the story I have told in this book gets to the heart of why making the pursuit of inclusion into a system based on domination a goal is—to say the least—inadequate for progress or justice. I hope it suggests the problematic character of the very concept of "rights" as a path to the global common good. Surely rights are preferable to their absence or violation, but insufficient. What is needed is more of the sense of avoiding the "palpable injustice" that Jeremiah Evarts felt—and that the American people as a whole should feel—with regard to our historic and present-day despicable conduct toward the Native Nations and toward all of our relations. What is needed is more of what John Trudell calls "responsibility of thought" and the keener feeling of the truth of our shared sociality in all of its emotional, socio-cultural, and spiritual depths that such thought facilitates.[736]

No one has yet succeeded in scolding anyone else out of sin. I do not imagine this book could buck that trend. What is needed is more of a sense, as d'Errico puts it, of what is "immediate, palpable, an awareness in the moment, as opposed to a rationalized conception of 'shoulds' and norms."[737] This will involve replacing the politics of domination with the politics formed by an embodied liberatory culture. In part, this is simply a matter of maturity. In relation to our older brothers and older sisters among the Native Nations—whose faith is thousands of years older than Christianity or Judaism or Islam or Buddhism or Hinduism or Confucianism—we are children who are far from the top of any evolutionary ladder, far from the position of superiority we like to fantasize about. The knowledge that is most important for us to acquire, if we are to cease being immature, is not new knowledge of science and technology, as important as that is, but rather knowledge of how we can help maintain an already existing cosmic and social balance among ourselves and among all living beings—how we can truly pursue both inner and social peace.

Although they are commonly seen as a path to inner and social peace, I have relatively little to say about "forgiveness" and "reconciliation" in this book. Asking for "forgiveness" and "reconciliation" while continuing to break our own law—not to mention Native law—is a certain indication of what the German theologian Dietrich Bonhoeffer called "cheap grace."[738] When Jesus surprised the pariah of a tax collector, Zacchaeus, by indicating that he would eat at his house that night (and so break the social stigma against him), Zacchaeus responded: "Look, half of my possessions, Lord, I will give to the poor; and if I have defrauded anyone of anything, I will pay back four times as much."[739] Zacchaeus was someone who knew something about reparations: that they are given in gratitude as well as remorse and, to be meaningful, must be substantial. A sense of forgiveness received by the sinner without any corresponding change in conduct—a spiritual gift received that is not shared in turn—is what Bonhoeffer meant by "cheap grace." It is "cheap grace" that permeates the religiosity that sustains tech-"no-logic" civilization; a disordered religiosity of which a degenerative capitalism is the primary economic symptom. As Chief Oren Lyons (Onondaga) has cautioned, as a result of the conduct of this "civilization," a great storm is here. His reaction to those who have brought this storm on all of us is striking: "I said I'll help you. I'll be right there. And that's our elders' position. When they ask for help, we better be there."[740]

Whether the adherents of the Christian tradition can find themselves anew within the global context that the Chinese philosopher Tu Weiming calls "spiritual humanism"—and so can help life overcome tech-"no-logic" civilization—remains to be seen.[741] George Manuel (Secwepemc), chief of the National Indian Brotherhood (known today as the Assembly of First Nations), has written that it will be easier to think that Christianity "can take on a shape that more closely resembles the world around us when we receive a sign that the leaders of the church have joined in the dance of life. Perhaps when men no longer try to have 'dominion over the fish of the sea, and over the fowl of the air, and over every living thing that liveth upon the earth,' they will no longer try to have dominion over us. It will be much easier to be our brother's keeper then."[742]

* * *

Whether the atonement of guilt is even possible, or whether it is an illusory hope and all that can be accomplished in time is recognition, is the question at the heart of Christianity's relations with all of the peoples that Christianity has helped oppress.[743] The German Jewish philosopher of religion, Jacob Taubes, has indicated that this is by no means a modern question, though his writings and his life testify to its importance in contemporary German-Jewish relations as well as in contemporary Christian-Jewish relations:

> Religion is a Latin term, which originally designated the civic cult of the Roman polity. Biblical literature does not know the term. Still the congregations whose experience is reflected in the books of the Old Testament as well as in the writings of the New Testament are classified as "religions." This is not a small philological detail, of interest only to the linguist or to the exegete. The fate of Christianity is embedded in this shift of language as in a nutshell. What was once a way of salvation, a hope for the redemption of man, has become an established religion in the realm of the world. In the term *religio* Rome was victorious over the hope of redemption. It is impossible at this stage of history to break the ambiguity in the term religion that comprises two contradictory elements: religion as a civic cult, and religion as a way of salvation, redeeming man from the authority of the powers and principalities of the world.[744]

As members of a highly competitive civic cult, the advocates of Eurochristianity—whatever their nationality—should acknowledge that the free and independent societies of Turtle Island before the European invaders arrived were far closer to the social values Christianity alleges it favors than the societies of Christendom and its successors have been.[745] As the followers of a way of salvation, going forward into the future, all Christians may wish to do more learning rather than teaching, to devote ourselves to listening respectfully before speaking, and to seek Christ in all living beings.[746] Above all, perhaps—and this regardless of the "benevolence" of our intentions—we should stop trying to "fix" problems to the creation of which we have contributed with a continuation of the same approaches that have yielded horrors in the past. If all eurochristians want to be insular rather than venturesome, they might at least read the *First Nations Version* of the New Testament.[747] They might take seriously the American theologian James Cone's admonition that the cross is a paradoxical religious symbol because it *inverts* the world's value system with hope coming by way of defeat and with the last becoming first and the first last:

> That God could "make a way out of no way" in Jesus' cross was truly absurd to the intellect, yet profoundly real in the souls of black folk. Enslaved blacks who first heard the gospel message seized on the power of the cross. Christ crucified manifested God's loving and liberating presence *in* the contradictions of black life—that transcendent presence in the lives of black Christians that empowered them to believe that *ultimately*, in God's eschatological future, they would not be defeated by the "troubles of this world," no matter how great and painful their suffering. Believing this paradox, this absurd claim of faith, was only possible in humility and repentance. There was no place for the proud and the mighty, for people who think that God called them to rule over others. The cross was God's critique of power—white power—with powerless love, snatching victory out of defeat.[748]

After two thousand years, it should be possible for Christians celebrating Christ's victory over death to cease conflating their churches and the mystical body of Christ. It should be possible for Christians to remember the words of the gospel of John in which: "All things came into being through him" and realize that all living beings are as much a part of Christ's mystical body as they themselves and that non-Christians can easily be closer to Christ than his self-professed followers.[749] The simple fact is that human spiritual sociality is not the creation of Christianity, or Islam, or Buddhism, or for that matter any religion. The adherents of all of them can participate in such spiritual sociality in the body of Christ, the Ummah, the Sangha, and myriad other communities.[750] Seeking to exclude anyone from this sociality, or imagining that it is a product of one's religious identity and not ultimately a gift of God or an expression of the truth of the universe, is a major step toward building a politics of domination. The first step in that direction is denying our unity and equality with all our relations.

From both a traditional Jewish and a traditional Christian perspective, reminders of the truths of the people of God—ultimately, from my perspective, a people constituted by the sociality embracing all our relations—have often come from what has been seen as the periphery rather than the center. Within a global context, this suggests that voices holding eurochristians to what is worthy in their professed ideals—or indicating where these ideals are mistaken and need to be changed, or replaced by different ways of guiding conduct, or even transformed by different sources of conduct entirely—are likely to arise at the margins or outside of "the West." Indeed, within a global context, the very concepts of "center" and "periphery"—of "the West" and "the rest"—appear as obstacles to understanding the unity and equality in which we are always already gathered and already gathering. They are part of a politics of domination built on a denial of the reality of a cosmic and social balance among ourselves and all our relations and a betrayal of the promise of the beloved community. That community requires us to somehow choose both, first—the American Constitution over the invader state—and, second—liberation over the politics of domination. It requires us to recognize that the eurochristians—and for that matter every Christian nation—are no more a people of God than any other people or peoples on earth.

In the late eighteenth century, the German philosopher Johann Gottfried Herder was direct and explicit in his condemnation of the cultural world created by Western imperialism and colonialism—the cultural world marked by the politics of domination in which we continue to live:

> What, finally, is to be said of the culture that has been brought by *Spaniards, Portuguese, Englishmen,* and *Dutchmen* to the East and West Indies, to Africa among the negroes, into the peaceful islands of the southern world? Do not all these lands, more or less, cry for revenge? All the more for revenge since they have been plunged for an

> incalculable time into a progressively growing corruption. All these stories lie open to view in travel descriptions; they have also in part received vocal expression in connection with the trade in negroes. About the Spanish cruelties, about the greed of the English, about the cold impudence of the Dutch – of whom in the frenzy of the madness of conquest hero-poems were written – books have been written in our time which bring them so little honor that, rather, if a European collective spirit lived elsewhere than in books, we would have to be ashamed of the *crime of abusing humanity* before almost all peoples of the earth. Let the land be named to which Europeans have come without having sinned against defenseless, trusting, humanity, perhaps for all aeons to come, through injurious acts, through unjust wars, greed, deceit, oppression, through diseases and harmful gifts! Our part of the world must be called, not the wise, but the *presumptuous, pushing, tricking* part of the earth; it has not cultivated but has destroyed the shoots of peoples' own cultures whenever and however it could.[751]

And yet, Herder continued to think of himself as a Christian. His view of Christianity informing and sustaining his anti-imperialism:

> And why should we conceal a norm of the spread of the moral law of humanity that is so obvious for us? *Christianity commands the purest humanity on the purest path.* Humanly and intelligibly for all, humbly, not with proud autonomy, not even as a *law* but as a gospel of hope [*Evangelium*] for the happiness of all, it commands and provides forgiving tolerance, an active love that overcomes bad with good. It does not command this as an object of speculation but provides it as light and life of humanity, through model example and loving deed, through progressively effective *community*. It serves *all* classes and ranks of humanity until in each one of them everything unfavorable withers and falls away in its time of itself. The misuse of Christianity has caused countless evil in the world – a proof of what its proper use can do. Precisely the fact that, as it has thrived, it has so much to make good, to compensate, to indemnify, shows, according to the rule that lies within it, that it must and will do this. The labyrinth of its misuses and errings is not endless; led back to its pure course, it

> cannot but strive to the goal that its founder already expressed in the name chosen by him, "*son of man* [*Menschensohn*]" (that is, man [*Mensch*]), and in the judgment of the last day. If bad morality is satisfied with the proposition, "Each for himself, no one for all!" then the judgement "No one for himself only, each for all!" is Christianity's slogan.[752]

"No one for himself only, each for all" is a slogan that would have been readily understandable and agreeable to James Wilson and Asher Robbins, Samuel Wharton and Jeremiah Evarts, Catherine Beecher and Henry Storrs, and all those that John Forsyth disparaged as the "Christian party in politics" in the United States.[753]

* * *

In St. Paul's—the Episcopal Church in Stockbridge, Massachusetts, in which I was baptized in 2006—I remember listening every Sunday to the words spoken over the Eucharist—the shared meal of thanksgiving that helps to constitute the communion on which that community rests: "On the night he was betrayed he took bread, said the blessing, broke the bread, and gave it to his friends, and said, 'Take, eat: This is my Body, which is given for you. Do this for the remembrance of me.' After supper, he took the cup of wine, gave thanks, and said, 'Drink this, all of you: This is my Blood of the new Covenant, which is shed for you and for many for the forgiveness of sins. Whenever you drink it, do this for the remembrance of me.'" [754] If you listen carefully, as the Dominican theologian Timothy Radcliffe has suggested, you can hear a subtle difference between what is given to the disciples at the last supper and what is offered as well for the "many" outside their walls—"a tension between the gathering into communion of these disciples, Jesus's close and intimate friends, and the reaching out to all, for the fullness of the Kingdom."[755] The disciples in the upper room that night doubtless all thought of themselves as Jews. Little did they suspect that their identity was about to be opened up and remade as the "many" entered in to what would become Christian identity. In our own day, I believe, the Holy Spirit is opening up Christian identity in the same way.

In his fine book on the emergence of the modern moral order, *A Secular Age*, the Canadian philosopher Charles Taylor suggests that secularism's breach with the culture of Christendom was probably necessary "for the impulse of solidarity to transcend the frontier of Christendom itself."[756] "We might even be tempted," he writes, "to say that modern unbelief is providential."[757] While there is much truth in these observations, modern unbelief is also being opened up to what the Rev. angel Kyodo williams calls "Radical Dharma" and to numerous spiritual outlooks and faiths, all of which can be seen as part of spiritual humanism.[758] By spiritual humanism, to provide a secular definition, I mean an approach rooted in many different faith traditions and outlooks, in which each faith and outlook involved advocates what is living within its own heritage, and from its own more particular context, while seeing itself and all the others as seeking to contribute to the well-being and harmony of humanity and to respect the balance of the cosmos as a whole, adopting what Tu Weiming calls an anthropocosmic rather than an anthropocentric perspective. This, in turn, requires mutual recognition that—working together—the ideas and practices of other faiths and outlooks are capable—at least at times—of better serving the global common good than are our own. Such thinking—of our already being gathered together in unity and equality—seems to me in line with the thinking and affinity underlying a recent spiritual humanist document, the global Charter for Compassion.

This global charter is an interfaith effort that includes among its signatories Christians, Muslims, Confucians, Jews, Hindus, Buddhists, and secular folk all seeking "to restore compassion to the centre of morality and religion ~ to return to the ancient principle that any interpretation of scripture that breeds violence, hatred or disdain is illegitimate ~ to ensure that youth are given accurate and respectful information about other traditions, religions and cultures ~ to encourage a positive appreciation of cultural and religious diversity ~ to cultivate an informed empathy with the suffering of all human beings—even those regarded as enemies."[759]

"We are finite beings," Tu Weiming observes in his own definition of spiritual humanism, "but in our finitude, there is the constant presence of infinite divinity. Spiritual Humanism is a faith in Humanity: the task of learning to be fully human is to 'form one body with Heaven, Earth and the myriad things,' for there is intrinsic unity between immanence and transcendence." [760] Or, as Zhang Zai observed a thousand years ago: "Heaven is my father and Earth is my mother, and even such a small creature as I finds an intimate place in their midst. Therefore that which fills the universe I regard as my body and that which directs the universe I consider as my nature. All people are my brothers and sisters, and all things are my companions."[761]

Such spiritual sociality—whether perceived in Confucian terms as forming one body with Heaven, Earth, and the ten thousand things, or perceived in Indigenous terms as the unity and equality that exists among all our relations in the web of life, or perhaps even in Christian terms as harmony with the mystical body of Christ, or in terms of really any perception of the living truth of our equal belonging—has implications for all peoples and for an America and a world that has yet to be, and that is still struggling to be, born. This is a world whose emergence will involve many religions and not merely Christianity being recomposed, as Stefano Harney and Fred Moten have suggested, in "the wake of the shipped."[762] It will involve American identity—our sense of who "we" are as a nation—being recomposed as well. It will involve many new expressions of what Valarie Kaur calls "revolutionary love."[763]

The wider society of Turtle Island can be expected to come into a deeper social self-understanding as the Native Nations continue to recover. As this happens, the collective self-consciousness of the American people can be expected to change in ways whose outline can at most be glimpsed now and which will undoubtedly look different on the other side of the emergence of the beloved community. To a considerable extent, as the Dominican theologian Herbert McCabe has observed, nations and individuals are shaped by the stories they tell themselves and others—especially the stories they tell about their biographies. These biographical stories, in turn, can be radically changed as our sense of who we are deepens: "A creative advance in love so shifts our moral perspective that we are able to see our whole way of life, and thus ourselves and thus our biography, in a new light."[764] The stories of Turtle Island—like the stories of all the continents and all the oceans and islands—are important to far more than nations and individuals, they are important to whether we will maintain trustworthy, reciprocal, and consensual relationships with all life on the planet.

Even in the context of a Native renaissance, it will be difficult for the American people to learn to tell the story of themselves, as the German people has had to do, as the story of a nation that has perpetrated genocide; indeed, of a nation that has perpetrated genocides, as well as sustained slavery and then Jim Crow, over generations.[765] The United States is, in fact, a nation founded not only on democratic ideals and aspirations, but also on some gruesome realities including stolen land, stolen labor, and grotesque brutality toward people of color and poor and working class people more generally. Above all, this has been a nation founded, or if not founded at least "legally" maintained, ever since "Marshall's War," on the denial to other nations—those nations who were here first—of their national rights. That this denial has been in violation of the Constitution can be at most cold comfort to the modern beneficiaries of genocide and of the "federal Indian law" that first allowed genocide and then has ever since sustained a vicious structure of domination and dehumanization within which additional genocides and attempted genocides have taken place. A course must now be steered by the American people that avoids wallowing in guilt and self-hatred as well as any continued immersion in a culture of self-deluded self-righteousness, neither of which does anyone any good, particularly with regard to ending the efforts at erasure and cultural genocide that continue to this day and that will persist as long as the national rights of the Native Nations are denied. This course of conduct for the American people toward living in truth is essential particularly with regard to living into the realization of our aspirations and truly becoming the democratic people of our best dreams and imaginations.

I suggest seeing ourselves—those of us who wish to consider ourselves Americans and as a people as distinct from the state—as having always sought, however tentatively and incompetently, to learn from the land we live on and the people and the peoples who have lived on it before us—and who live on it today—with an eye to serving the global common good as well as ourselves. If that bright thread can be seen by the eyes of faith running through even the darkest chapters of American history, perhaps we all can face the crimes and failures in the past and in the present with honesty and spiritual responsibility. We can also remember some positive American accomplishments such as seeking to turn former enemies into friends after the Second World War.[766] A true accounting will enable everyone's knowledge of the American relationship with the global common good to grow, and our conceptions of the global common good to become more accurate—indeed to change radically. That is a prerequisite for there to be progress toward justice and harmony; toward a restoration of social and cosmic balance. It is a prerequisite to placing a decisive end to the politics of erasure and genocide, bigotry and racism, by ending the politics of domination—an endeavor that will require both a greater willingness to learn from other peoples and faith.

At least from my Christian perspective, Jesus sets the table for everyone who wants to be there and loves those who do not equally and well. At a deeper level than the name of the faith I seek to share, I seek to participate in sharing love—the kind of love that I would define as offering the space in which to expand and become more of one's true self (to become more deeply connected with the ways the love within each of us is part of the love that pervades the universe). In creating space and time God offers all creation a spaciousness and grace with which each of us can reciprocate such love in the graciousness and the invitations into spaciousness with which we treat each other. I see such love in the adherents of many spiritual traditions and practices. Indeed, I am convinced that many non-Christians are far closer to Christ than many of his self-professed followers. I feel about the label "Christianity" as I feel about the label "American"—or for that matter the labels "socialist" or "conservative"—only those who acknowledge the crimes committed under these labels are worthy to claim the virtuous conduct that has sometimes been associated with them as well.

In a blog post of 27 January 2021, the healing justice advocate Susan Raffo recalled an observation that had been shared with her some years back by the West African writer Malidoma Somé.

> He was reflecting on indigeneity and he said something like this: Westerners or non-indigenous people get very confused about indigeneity. We carry this idea that being indigenous is about living in balance with all life, all of the time. He was laughing while he said

> this and he described how we non-indigenous people romanticize indigeneity as a state of perfect balance and connection. He then said, well, of course this isn't true. Indigenous people like all people misunderstand each other, intentionally and unintentionally cause harm, have bad days, and things get out of balance. The difference, he shared, is that being indigenous means that you know that the reason you are here is to attend to relationships. Most of our time, he said, is spent on attending to relationship imbalance, between people, between people and other living beings, between all of the different ways that one life, human and not, impacts and is impacted by another. Being indigenous, explained Malidoma Somé, is about taking relationships and impact seriously and giving the time needed, the attention, to support balance to re-emerge. We create the conditions for those moments when suddenly or not suddenly, there is balance. We feel, together, the truth of our deeper connection, with each other, with all life. And it is here, and it is felt and then something happens, there is impact, and things go out of balance and here we are again.[767]

The world the Native Nations were a part of before the European invasion, and the world they are a part of still, is closer to the truth of life in community than our own traditions.[768] If that world speaks of "respect" where eurochristians more often speak of "love" this is not for a lack of love but for the actual presence of respect as opposed to simply the rhetoric of respect. It is a world that we—in our arrogance, greed, and ignorance—have sought to dominate, exploit, and destroy. The United States—in particular—has done the Native Nations irreparable and ongoing harm; harm beyond the human ability to fathom. If the majority of the American people were opposed to the genocide of the 1830s, the executive, legislative, and judicial branches of the government went ahead anyway—at the instigation of the state of Georgia—and the American people have long since acquiesced in their government's ongoing anti-Indian measures and its spurious "federal Indian law." This raises the question of who Americans actually are. Part of the answer is who we have been: a people whose state has perpetrated genocide; a people whose state has consistently broken our word. Another part of the answer to that question is who we want to be: do we want to be loyal to the invader state that has committed genocide in our name or do we want to be loyal to the Constitution? Are we capable of making a choice for Wilsonian jurisprudence in the face of the Supreme Court's betrayal of constitutional law or can we, perhaps, even make a choice for something better? We are a people in need of more than simply self-restraint. We are a people in need of liberation from domination.

~i, sjs, November 2022

"Out beyond ideas of wrongdoing and rightdoing,
there is a field. I'll meet you there.
When the soul lies down in that grass,
the world is too full to talk about.
Ideas, language, even the phrase "each other"
doesn't make any sense.
The breeze at dawn has secrets to tell you.
Don't go back to sleep.
You must ask for what you really want.
Don't go back to sleep.
People are going back and forth across the doorsill
where the two worlds touch.
The door is round and open.
Don't go back to sleep."

Jalāl al-Dīn Muḥammad Rūmī, 1207-1273
The Great Wagon

Afterword
by Peter d'Errico

Arguments Over Genocide presents an essentially spiritual critique of US laws regarding Indigenous peoples. This is most fitting, since these laws are an expression of a specific religious tradition rooted in fifteenth century Christianity. No doubt, this fact likely surprised many readers. Among those familiar with the history of Christian colonization and imperialism that led to the "discovery" of the "New World", many were likely surprised to learn that "Christian discovery" is not an artifact of history, but an active doctrine in twenty-first century US law. Moreover, a further surprise was in store for those who presumed this strange doctrine was embraced only by "right wing" jurists. Steven Schwartzberg makes amply clear that the Supreme Court "left" is equally comfortable with imposing religious ideas of "superior civilization" on Indigenous peoples today. The task for any reader of this book is to grapple with the consequences of these startling revelations. *Arguments Over Genocide* assists in this task by providing a global spiritual philosophy to show that there is a way toward freeing the world from ideas and structures of domination that have constituted the past 500 years of law, economics, and morality.

The unique contribution of *Arguments Over Genocide* is its interweaving of spiritual and constitutional discourses to help us see the deep dynamic of the debate over "Indian Removal". Removal was about land, no doubt; but it was also about a claimed "right of domination" of Christians over "heathens and pagans". On one side, it was a brutal brew of racism and religion in service of economic "development" (read, imperial expansion). On the other side, it was a blend of pity and religion in aid of a campaign for co-existence of peoples. Schwartzberg demonstrates that these competing perspectives fought within the frameworks of the US Constitution and the Christian religion. For their most virulent enemies, the goal was "removal" of Indigenous peoples from the "path of civilization," whether accomplished by extermination or wagons. For their most sympathetic friends, the goal was "civilization" of Indigenous peoples, accomplished *in situ* with the aid of missionaries. Both sides of the debate claimed Christian right; both claimed Constitutional authority.

The closeness of the debate, at least in the House of Representatives, is a fact too seldom examined. It shows how hot the debate was and how close the US came to taking a very different path. On May 26, 1830, the House vote on the bill, "An act to provide for an exchange of lands with the Indians residing in any of the States or Territories, and for their removal West of the river Mississippi," was 102 Yea to 97 Nay. The Senate vote, a month earlier, had been lopsided, 28 Yea to 19 Nay. At the end of the debate, a difference of four votes determined the outcome.

The key legal issues of Indigenous land ownership and national status were also being debated in another forum, the US Supreme Court. As Schwartzberg explains, Chief Justice John Marshall had already led a unanimous court to decide that "Christian discovery" would become an integral part of US property law. The decision, *Johnson v. McIntosh*, issued March 10, 1823, just seven years before the Removal Act, claimed that the US assumed all the claims of the English Crown, including the claim of land ownership of the continent "discovered" by John Cabot pursuant to his charter from Henry VII. In June 1830, two months after the Removal Act, the Cherokee Nation argued to the court that their treaty with the US mandated federal protection against intrusion and removal. Their case, *Cherokee Nation v. Georgia*, was dismissed, with an opinion by Marshall from which two justices dissented. Marshall said the Cherokee had no place to stand in court because they didn't own their land and thus weren't a "nation" in the full sense of the word. Marshall's third act in the matter, *Worcester v. Georgia*, March 3, 1832, two years after the Removal Act, sounded a note of "sympathy" for the Cherokee and said Georgia had no right to intrude on their lands. But Marshall left no doubt that the Cherokee were subservient to the US. He didn't even mention Indian Removal, though he cited the 1819 Civilization Act, praising its "humane designs for civilizing the neighboring Indians." No wonder Schwartzberg refers to these cases as "Marshall's War". Marshall's rhetoric occasionally sounded like the "sympathetic" faction in Congress, but he upheld the federal power that served the "enemy". No surprise, then, when the court in 1903, in *Lone Wolf v. Hitchcock*, encapsulated the Marshall decisions as a doctrine of "congressional plenary authority" over Indigenous peoples and their lands. To be sure, the court had already said that the US would be "governed by such considerations of justice as would control a Christian people in their treatment of an ignorant and dependent race" (*Beecher v. Wetherby*, 1877).

Schwartzberg argues for overturning the Marshall precedents, just as the anti-Black precedent of "separate but equal" was overturned in 1954. He says the philosophical and constitutional arguments rejected by congress and the court are still available today to support this overturning. Justice Neal Gorsuch recently argued for overturning a related colonial doctrine, attacking the notion of congressional "plenary power" over Puerto Rico, in the case of *US v. Vaello Madero* (2022). He said:

> A century ago in the Insular Cases, this Court held that the federal government could rule Puerto Rico and other Territories largely without regard to the Constitution. It is past time to acknowledge the gravity of this error and admit what we know to be true: The Insular Cases have no foundation in the Constitution and rest instead on racial stereotypes. They deserve no place in our law.

The Insular Cases, like Indian Removal, were the subject of what Gorsuch calls "a fierce debate". In a clear echo of the Removal debate, he says, "At bottom…[the views in favor of plenary power] rested on a view about the Nation's 'right' to acquire and exploit 'an unknown island, peopled with an uncivilized race . . . for commercial and strategic reasons.'"

In short, Schwartzberg's call for a wholesale reappraisal and rejection of "federal Indian law" arrives at a time when such large-scale thinking may be possible, notwithstanding the practical difficulties that would be occasioned. To draw upon Gorusch again:

> To be sure, settling this question right would raise difficult new ones. Cases would no longer turn on the fictions of the Insular Cases but on the terms of the Constitution itself. Disputes are sure to arise about exactly which of its individual provisions applies in the Territories and how. Some of these new questions may prove hard to resolve. But at least they would be the right questions.

Arguments Over Genocide asks the right questions. Moreover, Schwartzberg extends the purview of these questions to show their global "rightness" as a necessary response to the crisis of the planet brought about by "belief in the superiority and separation of humans from the natural world as embedded in the logic of dominion". He says, "The knowledge that is most important for us to acquire...is not new knowledge of science and technology, ... but rather knowledge of how we can help maintain an already existing cosmic and social balance among ourselves and among all living beings—how we can truly pursue both inner and social peace."

Arguments Over Genocide tasks readers with reassembling what in some sense we have always known, namely that systems of domination are "built upon trying to extend and protect the ego" and are therefore ultimately unworkable as *social* systems. One characteristic of Indigenous peoples often noted by missionaries and colonizers was the combination of strong individuality and strong group cohesion. The outsiders, believers in an abstract individualism of "cogito, ergo sum", were puzzled by this complex sociality, which Kenyan philosopher John Mbiti describes as an awareness that "I am because we are." Ultimately, *Arguments Over Genocide* calls us to understand this phenomenon, which will give us a foundation on which to stand as we remake the law.

— Peter d'Errico
Professor Emeritus of Legal Studies
University of Massachusetts at Amherst
December 2022

Bibliography

Books and Articles

Gregory Ablavsky, "The Savage Constitution," *Duke Law Journal*, Vol. 63, No. 5 (February 2014): 999-1090.

Gregory Ablavsky, "Beyond the Indian Commerce Clause," *Yale Law Journal*, Vol. 124, Issue 4 (2015): 1012-1091.

Rolena Adorno, *The Polemics of Possession in Spanish American Narrative*. New Haven: Yale University Press, 2007.

Bayo Akomolafe, *These Wilds Beyond our Fences: Letters to my Daughter on Humanity's Search for Home*. Berkeley: North Atlantic Books, 2017.

Akwesasne Notes, ed., *Basic Call to Consciousness* with an introduction by John Mohawk [1978]. Summertown, TN: Native Voices, 2005.

Danielle Allen and Emily Sneff, "Golden Letters: James Wilson, the Declaration of Independence, and the Sussex Declaration," *The Georgetown Journal of Law and Public Policy*, Vol. 17, No. 1 (Winter 2019), pp. 193-230.

Gary Clayton Anderson, *Ethnic Cleansing and the Indian: The Crime that Should Haunt America*. Norman: University of Oklahoma Press, 2014.

John A. Andrew III, *From Revivals to Removal: Jeremiah Evarts, the Cherokee Nation, and the Search for the Soul of America*. Athens: University of Georgia Press, 1992.

Milner S. Ball, "Constitution, Court, Indian Tribes," *American Bar Foundation Research Journal*, Vol. 12, No. 1 (Winter, 1987), pp. 1-140.

Lundy Bancroft, *Why Does He Do That: Inside the Minds of Angry and Controlling Men*. New York: Berkley, 2002.

Randall E. Barnett, "The People or the State: Chisholm v. Georgia and Popular Sovereignty," *Virginia Law Review*, Vol. 93, No. 7 (November 2007): 1729-1758.

Stuart Banner, *How the Indians Lost their Land: Law and Power on the Frontier*. Cambridge: Harvard University Press, 2005.

Victor N. Baptiste, *Bartolome de Las Casas and Thomas More's Utopia*. Culver City, CA: Labryinthos, 1990.

Albert Jeremiah Beveridge, *The Life of John Marshall* four volumes in two. Boston: Houghton Mifflin, 1944.

John Borrows, *Law's Indigenous Ethics.* Toronto: University of Toronto Press, 2019.

Rizvana Bradley and Denise Ferreira da Silva, "Four Theses on Aesthetics," https://www.e-flux.com/journal/120/416146/four-theses-on-aesthetics/ e-flux Journal #120 (September 2021)

Jean L. Briggs, *Never in Anger.* Cambridge: Harvard University Press, 1970.

Stephen Breyer, "The Cherokee Indians and the Supreme Court," *The Georgia Historical Quarterly*, Vol. 87, No. 3/4 (Fall/Winter 2003), 408-426

Daniel R. Brunstetter, *Tensions of Modernity: Las Casas and His Legacy in the French Enlightenment.* New York: Routledge 2012.

George Bryan, *The Imperialism of John Marshall.* Boston: The Stratford Company, 1924.

Alan Bullock, *Hitler and Stalin: Parallel Lives.* New York: Alfred A. Knopf, 1992.

Joseph C. Burke, "The Cherokee Cases: A Study in Law, Politics, and Morality," *Stanford Law Review*, Vol. 21, No. 3 (February 1969): 500-531.

Collin G. Calloway, *The Indian World of George Washington.* Oxford: Oxford University Press, 2018.

Daniel Castro, *Another Face of Empire.* Durham: Duke University Press, 2007.

Lawrence A. Clayton, *Bartolomé de las Casas and the Conquest of the Americas.* Malden, MA: John Wiley and Sons, 2011.

Robert N. Clinton, "There is No Federal Supremacy Clause for Indian Tribes," *Arizona State Law Journal,* Vol. 34, No. 1 (Spring 2002): 113-260.

Felix S. Cohen, "Original Indian Title," *Minnesota Law Review,* Vol. 32, No. 1 (December 1947): 28-59.

Donald B. Cole, *The Presidency of Andrew Jackson.* Lawrence: University Press of Kansas, 1993.

James H. Cone, *The Cross and the Lynching Tree.* Maryknoll: Orbis Books, 2011.

John Collier, *Indians of the Americas* (abridged version). New York: Mentor Books, 1948.

William Cronon, *Changes in the Land: Indians, Colonists, and the Ecology of New England.* New York: Hill and Wang, 2003.

David Brion Davis, *The Problem of Slavery in the Age of Revolution, 1770-1823.* Oxford: Oxford University Press, 1999.

David Brion Davis, *Inhuman Bondage: The Rise and Fall of Slavery in the New World.* Oxford: Oxford University Press, 2006.

William Dalrymple, *The Anarchy: The East India Company, Corporate Violence, and the Pillage of an Empire.* New York: Bloomsbury Publishing, 2019.

Bartolomé de Las Casas, *In Defense of the Indians* (tr. Stafford Poole, C.M.). DeKalb: Northern Illinois University Press, 1992.

Alexis De Tocqueville, *Democracy in America* (tr. Henry Reeve in two volumes). New York: Scatcherd and Adams, 1839.

Peter d'Errico, *Federal Anti-Indian Law: The Legal Entrapment of Indigenous Peoples*. Santa Barbara: Praeger, 2022.

Peter d'Errico, et al., "Honoring Indian Law and Treaties, Part One" - December 2021, https://www.researchgate.net/publication/357403720_Honoring_Indian_Law_and_Treaties_Part_One_-_Indigenous_Perspectives_podcast

Peter d'Errico, "Restorative Indigenous Justice," *Contemporary Justice Review*, Vol 2, No. 4 (December 1999), 383-395.

Peter d'Errico, "Native Americans in America: A Theoretical and Historical Overview," *Wicazo Sa Review*, Vol. 14, No. 1 (Spring 1999), pp. 7-28.

Peter d'Errico, "Corporate Personality and Human Commodification," *Rethinking Marxism*, Volume 9, Number 2 (Summer 1996/97), pp. 99-113.

Bailey W. Diffie, *Prelude to Empire: Portugal Overseas before Henry the Navigator.* Lincoln: University of Nebraska Press, 1960.

Roxanne Dunbar-Ortiz, *An Indigenous Peoples' History of the United States*. Boston: Beacon Press, 2014.

Sterling E. Edmonds, "The Lawless Law of Nations," *Washington University Law Review*, Vol. 10, No. 3 (January 1925), 171-196.

Walter R. Echo-Hawk, *In the Courts of the Conqueror: The 10 Worst Indian Law Cases Ever Decided.* Golden, Colo: Fulcrum Publ., 2010.

J. H. Elliott, *Empires of the Atlantic World: Britain and Spain in America, 1492-1830.* New Haven: Yale University Press, 2006.

William Ewald, "The Committee of Detail," *Constitutional Commentary*, Vol 28, No. 2 (Fall 2012): 197-286.

William Ewald, "James Wilson and the American Founding," *The Georgetown Journal of Law and Public Policy*, Vol. 17, No. 1 (Winter 2019), 1-22.

Donald L. Fixico, "Documenting Indigenous dispossession," *Science*, Vol. 374, Issue 6567 (28 October 2021), 536-537.

Mark D. Freeland, *Aazheyaadizi: Worldview, Language, and the Logics of Decolonization.* East Lansing: Michigan State University Press, 2021.

Tim Alan Garrison, *The Legal Ideology of Removal.* Athens: University of Georgia Press, 2002.

John J. Gibbons, "The Eleventh Amendment and State Sovereign Immunity: A Reinterpretation," *Columbia Law Review*, Vol. 83, No. 8 (December 1983): 1889-2005.

Dina Gilio-Whitaker, *As Long as the Grass Grows: The Indigenous Fight for Environmental Justice from Colonization to Standing Rock.* Boston: Beacon Press, 2019.

Emilee Gilpin, 15 February 2019, "Urgency in Climate Change Advocacy is Backfiring says Citizen Potawatomi Scientist," *Canada's National Observer*, https://www.nationalobserver.com/2019/02/15/features/urgency-climate-change-advocacy-backfiring-says-citizen-potawatomi-nation (accessed 3 January 2021)

David Graeber, *Possibilities: Essays on Hierarchy, Rebellion, and Desire.* Oakland, CA: AK Press, 2007.

David Graeber and David Wengrow, *The Dawn of Everything: A New History of Humanity.* New York: Farrar, Straus and Giroux, 2021.

Michael D. Green, *The Politics of Indian Removal: Creek Government and Society in Crisis.* Lincoln: University of Nebraska Press, 1985.

Liah Greenfeld, *Mind, Modernity, Madness: The Impact of Culture on Human Experience.* Cambridge: Harvard University Press, 2013.

Liah Greenfeld, *Nationalism and the Mind: Essays on Modern Culture.* Oxford: Oneworld Publications, 2006.

Liah Greenfeld, *The Spirit of Capitalism: Nationalism and Economic Growth.* Cambridge: Harvard University Press, 2001.

Liah Greenfeld, *Nationalism: Five Roads to Modernity.* Cambridge: Harvard University Press, 1992.

Lewis Hanke, *All Mankind is One* [1959]. DeKalb: Northern Illinois University Press, 1974.

Sefano Harney and Fred Moten, *All Incomplete.* Colchester: Minor Compositions, 2021.

Stefano Harney and Fred Moten, *The Undercommons: Fugitive Planning and Black Study*. Wivenhoe: Minor Compositions, 2013.

Roberta Carol Harvey, *The Earth is Red: The Imperialism of the Doctrine of Discovery.* Santa Fe: Sunstone Press, 2021.

Johnann Gottfried von Herder, *Philosophical Writings* translated and edited by Michael N. Forster. Cambridge: Cambridge University Press, 2002.

Katherine Hermes, "Law of Native Americans to 1815," in Michael Grossberg and Christopher Tomlins, *The Cambridge History of Law in America* (Cambridge: Cambridge University Press, 2008): 32-62.

Mary Hershberger, "Mobilizing Women, Anticipating Abolition: The Struggle against Indian Removal in the 1830s," *Journal of American History*, Vol 86, No. 1 (June 1999): 15-40.

Lewis Hyde, *A Primer for Forgetting: Getting Past the Past.* New York: Farrar, Straus, and Giroux, 2019.

Lewis Hyde, *The Gift: How the Creative Spirit Transforms the World.* New York: Vintage, 2019.

Steve Inskeep, *Jacksonland: President Andrew Jackson, Cherokee Chief John Ross, and a great American land grab*. New York: Penguin Press, 2015.

Akira Iriye, *Across the Pacific: An Inner History of American-East Asia Relations* revised edition. Chicago: Imprint Publications, 1992.

Marius Jansen, *The Making of Modern Japan.* Cambridge: Harvard University Press, 2000.

Willie James Jennings, *The Christian Imagination: Theology and the Origins of Race.* New Haven: Yale University Press, 2010.

Peter Jimack, *A History of the Two Indies: A Translated Selection of Writings from Raynal's Histoire philosophique et politique des établissements des Européens dans les Deux Indes.* Hampshire: Ashgate Publishing, 2006.

Eric Kades, "History and Interpretation of the Great Case of Johnson v. M'Intosh," *Law and History Review*, Volume 19, No. 67 (2001): 67-116.

Valarie Kaur, *See No Stranger: A Memoir and Manifesto of Revolutionary Love.* New York: Random House, 2020.

Elie Kedourie, *Nationalism* fourth, expanded edition. Oxford: Blackwell, 1994.

A. J. Langguth, *Driven West: Andrew Jackson and the Trail of Tears to the Civil War*. New York: Simon and Schuster, 2010.

Paul Le Blanc and Michael Yates, *A Freedom Budget for All Americans: Recapturing the Promise of the Civil Rights Movement in the Struggle for Economic Justice Today*. New York, Monthly Review Press, 2013.

Thomas H. Lee, "The Supreme Court of the United States as Quasi-International Tribunal: Reclaiming the Court's Original and Exclusive Jurisdiction over Treaty-Based Suits by Foreign States against States," *Columbia Law Review*, Vol. 104, No. 7 (November 2004): 1765-1885.

Stacy L. Leeds, "The More Things Stay the Same: Waiting on Indian Law's Brown v. Board of Education," *Tulsa Law Review, Vol.* 38, No. 1 (Fall 2002), pp. 73-86

Jill Lepore, *These Truths: A History of the United States.* New York: W. W. Norton, 2018.

Jonathan Levy, *Ages of American Capitalism.* New York: Random House, 2022,

Gerard N. Magliocca, "The Cherokee Removal and the Fourteenth Amendment," *Duke Law Journal*, Vol. 53, No. 3 (December 2003): 875-965.

Barbara Alice Mann, *Iroquoian Women: The Gantowisas*. New York: Peter Lang, 2000.

Charles C. Mann, *1491: New Revelations of the Americas Before Columbus* (second edition). New York: Vintage Books, 2011.

John Marshall, *Life of Washington* in five volumes. Philadelphia: C. P. Wayne, 1805-07.

John Marshall, *Life of Washington* in five volumes. Fredericksburg: The Citizens' Guild, 1926.

Calvin Luther Martin, *The Way of the Human Being.* New Haven: Yale University Press, 1999.

Herbert McCabe, *Law, Love and Language.* London: Continuum, 1968.

Herbert McCabe, *God Matters.* London: Continuum, 1987.

Iain McGilchrist, *The Matter with Things: Our Brains, Our Delusions, and the Unmaking of the World* (in two volumes). London: Perspectiva Press, 2021.

Robert Tracy McKenzie, *We the Fallen People: The Founders and the Future of American Democracy.* Downers Grove: InterVarsity Press, 2021.

William G. McLoughlin, *Cherokee Renascence in the New Republic.* Princeton: Princeton University Press, 1986.

Kent McNeil, *Common Law Aboriginal Title.* Oxford: Clarendon Press, 1989.

Alan McPherson, *The Invaded: How Latin Americans and Their Allies Fought and Ended U.S. Occupations.* Oxford: Oxford University Press, 2014.

Resmaa Menaken, *My Grandmother's Hands: Racialized Trauma and the Pathway to Mending Our Hearts and Bodies.* Las Vegas: Central Recovery Press, 2017.

Resmaa Menaken, *The Quaking of America: An Embodied Guide to Navigating Our Nation's Upheaval and Racial Reckoning.* Las Vegas: Central Recovery Press, 2022.

John Mikhail, "The Necessary and Proper Clauses," *Georgetown Law Journal*, Vol. 102, No. 4 (April 2014): 1045-1132.

John Mikhail, "The Constitution and the Philosophy of Language: Entailment, Implicature, and Implied Powers," *Virginia Law Review*, Vol. 101, No. 4 (June 2014), pp. 1063-1103.

John Mikhail, "Early American Land Companies, and the Original Meaning of 'Ex Post Facto Law'" *The Georgetown Journal of Law and Public Policy*, Vol. 17, No. 1 (Winter 2019), pp. 79-146.

Edwin A. Miles, "After John Marshall's Decision: Worcester v. Georgia and the Nullification Crisis," *The Journal of Southern History*, Vol. 39, No. 4 (November 1973):519-544.

Tiya Miles, "'Circular Reasoning': Recentering Cherokee Women in the Antiremoval Campaigns," *American Quarterly*, Vol. 61, No. 2 (June 2009), pp. 221-243.

Harriet Taylor Mill, *The Enfranchisement of Women* [1851]. London: Trübner and Company, 1868.

Isabel Millar, "Can we forget Foucault? Obscenity and the politics of seduction," *Revista Guillermo de Ockham* Vol. 20, No. 2 (2022), pp. 345-352.

Isabel Millar, *The Psychoanalysis of Artificial Intelligence.* Cham: Palgrave Macmillan, 2021.

Harold Napoleon, *Yuuyaraq: The Way of the Human Being.* Anchorage, AK: The Native Village of Paimiut, 1996.

Susan Neiman, *Learning from the Germans: Race and the Memory of Evil.* New York: Farrar, Straus, and Giroux, 2019.

Melissa K. Nelson, "Time to Indigenize Lands and Water Conservation," 22 December 2020, *Sierra: The National Magazine of the Sierra Club*, https://www.sierraclub.org/sierra/2021-1-january-february/feature/time-indigenize-lands-and-water-conservation (accessed 3 January 2021).

Steven T. Newcomb, *Pagans in the Promised Land: Decoding the Doctrine of Christian Discovery*. Golden, CO: Fulcrum Publishing, 2008.

Steven T. Newcomb, "The Evidence of Christian Nationalism in Federal Indian Law: The Doctrine of Discovery, Johnson v. Mcintosh, and Plenary Power," *N.Y.U. Rev. L. & Soc. Change,* Volume 20, No. 2 (1992-1993), pp. 303-342.

Jill Norgren, *The Cherokee Cases: The Confrontation of Law and Politics*. New York: McGraw-Hill, 1996.

Jeffrey Ostler, *Surviving Genocide: Native Nations and the United States from the American Revolution to Bleeding Kansas*. New Haven: Yale University Press, 2019.

Theda Perdue and Michael D. Green, *The Cherokee Removal: A Brief History with Documents* (second edition). Boston: Bedford/St. Martin's, 2005.

Theda Perdue and Michael D. Green, *The Cherokee Nation and the Trail of Tears*. New York: Viking, 2007.

Richard Peters, *The Case of the Cherokee Nation Against the State of Georgia*. Philadelphia: James Kay, 1831.

Ulrich Bonner Phillips, *Georgia and State Rights: A Study of the Political History of Georgia from the Revolution to the Civil War, with Particular Regard to Federal Relations*. Washington: Government Printing Office: 1902.

Jennifer Pitts, "Empire and Legal Universalisms in the Eighteenth Century," *The American Historical Review*, Vol. 117, No. 1 (February 2012), 92-121.

James E. Pfander, "Rethinking the Supreme Court's Original Jurisdiction in State-Party Cases," *California Law Review*, May, 1994, Vol. 82, No. 3, Symposium: Void for Vagueness (May, 1994), 555-659.

Alisse Portnoy, *Their Right to Speak: Women's Activism in the Indian and Slave Debates*. Cambridge: Harvard University Press, 2005.

Francis Paul Prucha, *The Great Father: The United States Government and the American Indians* (in two volumes). Lincoln: University of Nebraska Press, 1984.

Elizabeth A. Reese, "The Other American Law," *Stanford Law Review*, Vol. 73 (March 2021), 555-636.

Philip Rieff, *The Triumph of the Therapeutic: Uses of Faith after Freud* [1966]. Wilmington: ISI Books, 2006.

Lindsay G. Robertson, *Conquest by Law: How the Discovery of America Dispossessed Indigenous Peoples of their Land.* Oxford: Oxford University Press, 2005.

Marilynne Robinson, *What are we Doing Here?* New York: Farrar, Straus and Giroux, 2018.

John P. Roche, *The History and Impact of Marxist-Leninist Organizational Theory.* Cambridge: Institute for Foreign Policy Analysis, 1984.

Steve Russell, *Sequoyah Rising: Problems in Post-Colonial Tribal Governance.* Durham: Carolina Academic Press, 2010.

Steve Russell, *American Indians Dream: A Movement of Our* Own. No city: no publisher's name, 2014.

Steve Russell, *Lighting the Fire: A Cherokee Journey from Dropout to Professor.* McLean: Miniver Press, 2020.

Marshall Sahlins, *Stone Age Economics.* London: Routledge Classics, 2017.

Philippe Sands, *East West Street: On the Origins of "Genocide" and "Crimes Against Humanity."* New York: Alfred A. Knopf, 2016.

Claudio Saunt, *Unworthy Republic: The Dispossession of Native Americans and the Road to Indian Territory.* New York: W. W. Norton, 2020.

Mark Savage, "The Great Secret about Federal Indian Law--Two Hundred Years in Violation of the Constitution--And the Opinion the Supreme Court Should Have Written to Reveal It," *New York University Review of Law & Social Change*, Vol. 20, No. 2 (1992-1993): 343-372.

Bethany Schneider, "Boudinot's Change: Boudinot, Emerson, and Ross on Cherokee Removal," *English Literary History*, Vol. 75, No. 1 (Spring 2008): 151-177.

Hugh J. Schwartzberg, "One Founding Father, Invisible, with Liberty and Justice for All," presented to the Chicago Literary Club, 28 April 1997, available for download in the club's online archives at http://www.chilit.org/content.aspx?page_id=86&club_id=11539&item_id=25713.

Steven Schwartzberg, "The Lion and the Phoenix: British Policy Toward the 'Greek Question,' 1821-1832," *Middle Eastern Studies*, Volume 24, Numbers 2 and 3 (April and July 1988): 139-177, 287-311

Steven Schwartzberg, "The 'Soft Peace Boys': Presurrender Planning and Japanese Land Reform," *The Journal of American-East Asian Relations*, Vol. 2, No. 2 (Summer 1993), pp. 185-216.

Steven Schwartzberg, *Democracy and U.S. Policy in Latin America during the Truman Years.* Gainesville: University Press of Florida, 2003.

Helen Schucman, *A Course in Miracles* (third edition [originally three volumes in 1976]). Mill Valley, CA: Foundation for Inner Peace, 2007.

Richard Sclove, *Escaping Maya's Palace: Decoding an Ancient Myth to Heal the Hidden Madness of Modern Civilization.* Boston: Karavelle Press, 2022.

Juan Ginés Sepúlveda, twelve point response to Bartolomé de las Casas, text in Kris Lane, ed., *Defending the Conquest: Bernardo de Vargas Machuca's Defense and Discourse of the Western Conquests* (tr. Timothy F. Johnson). University Park, PA: Pennsylvania State University Press, 2010.

Edward Shils, *A Fragment of a Sociological Autobiography.* New Brunswick: Transaction Publishers, 2006.

Edward Shils, *The Virtue of Civility: Selected Essays on Liberalism, Tradition, and Civil Society.* Indianapolis: Liberty Fund, 1997.

Edward Shils, *Tradition.* Chicago: University of Chicago Press, 1981.

Denise Ferreira da Silva, *Unpayable Debt: On the Antipolitical.* London: Sternberg Press, 2022.

Denise Ferreira da Silva, *Toward a Global Idea of Race.* Minneapolis: University of Minnesota Press, 2007.

Denise Ferreira da Silva, "1 (life) ÷ 0 (blackness) = ∞ − ∞ or ∞ / ∞: On Matter Beyond the Equation of Value," e-flux, Journal #79 (February 2017), https://www.e-flux.com/journal/79/94686/1-life-0-blackness-or-on-matter-beyond-the-equation-of-value/

Denise Ferreira da Silva, "On Difference without Separability," 32nd BIENAL DE SÃO PAULO *INCERTEZA VIVA* (7 September - 11 December 2016), pp. 57-65.

Joseph William Singer, "Law and Property," *Northwestern University Law Review*, Vol 86, No. 1 (Fall 1991), pp. 1-40.

Charles Page Smith, *James Wilson: Founding Father, 1742-1798.* Chapel Hill: University of North Carolina Press, 1956.

Georges Sorel, *Reflections on Violence* [1906]. New York: The Free Press, 1950.

Joseph Story, *Commentaries on the Constitution of the United States* (in three volumes). Boston: Hilliard, Gray, and Company, 1833.

Matthew L. Sundquist, "Worcester v. Georgia: A Breakdown in the Separation of Powers, *American Indian Law Review*, Vol. 35, No. 1 (2010-2011): 239-256.

Jacob Taubes, *From Cult to Culture: Fragments Toward a Critique of Historical Reason* (edited by Charlotte Elisheva Fonrobert and Amir Engel). Stanford: Stanford University Press, 2010.

Jacob Taubes, *The Political Theology of Paul* [1993] (edited by Aleida Assmann, et al.). Stanford: Stanford University Press, 2004.

Charles Taylor, *A Secular Age.* Cambridge, MA: Harvard University Press, 2007.

Howard Thurman, *Jesus and the Disinherited* [1949]. Boston: Beacon Press, 1996.

Tink Tinker, "What Are We Going to Do with White People," (Working Copy, 4 March 2021).

Tink Tinker, panel discussion of 14 April 2021 on the volume, Miguel A. De La Torre, et al., editors, *The Colonial Compromise: The Threat of the Gospel to the Indigenous World View* (Fortress Academic Press, 2020), https://www.youtube.com/watch?v=LAzjr_IMRxc (accessed 4 May 2021).

Leon Trotsky, *Terrorism and Communism: A Reply to Karl Kautsky* [1920] (with an introduction by Max Shachtman). Ann Arbor: University of Michigan Press, 1961.

John Trudell, "What it Means to be a Human Being, 15 March 2001, The Women's Building, San Francisco, radio TUC (Time of Useful Consciousness), broadcast quality recordings (two parts): http://www.radio4all.net/files/tuc@tucradio.org/44-2-JohnTrudellONE_2014.mp3. http://www.radio4all.net/files/tuc@tucradio.org/44-2-JohnTrudellTWO_2014.mp3 There is a transcript: https://ratical.org/many_worlds/JohnTrudell/HumanBeing.html#s2

Watanabe Hiroshi, "'They Are Almost the Same as the Ancient Three Dynasties': The West as Seen Through Confucian Eyes in Nineteenth-Century Japan," in Tu Weiming, ed., *Confucian Traditions in East Asian Modernity.* Cambridge: Harvard University Press, 1996: 119-151.

Blake A. Watson, *Buying America from the Indians: Johnson v. McIntosh and the History of Native Land Rights.* Norman: University of Oklahoma Press, 2012.

Sean Wilentz, *No Property in Man: Slavery and Antislavery at the Nation's Founding*. Cambridge: Harvard University Press, 2018.

David E. Wilkins, "Johnson v. M'Intosh Revisited: Through the Eyes of Mitchel v. United States," *American Indian Law Review*, Vol. 19, No. 1 (1994):159-181.

David E. Wilkins and K. Tsianina Lomawaima, *Uneven Ground: American Indian Sovereignty and Federal Law.* Norman: University of Oklahoma Press, 2001.

Rev. angel Kyodo williams, et al., *Radical Dharma: Talking Race, Love, and Liberation.* Berkeley: North Atlantic Books, 2016.

Rev. angel Kyodo williams, *Being Black: Zen and the Art of Living with Fearlessness and Grace.* New York: Viking Compass, 2000.

Terry M. Wildman, *First Nations Version: An Indigenous Translation of the New Testament.* Downers Grove, IL: InterVarsity Press, 2021.

Robert A. Williams, Jr., *The American Indian in Western Legal Thought: The Discourses of Conquest.* Oxford: Oxford University Press, 1990.

James Wilson, *An Account of the Proceedings of the Illinois and Ouabash Land Companies in Pursuance of their Land Purchases made of the Independent Natives, July 5th, 1773 and 18th, October, 1775*. Philadelphia: William Young, 1796.

John Fabian Witt, *Patriots and Cosmopolitans: Hidden Histories of American Law.* Cambridge: Harvard University Press, 2007.

Robert Yazzie, "The Cherokee Nation of Indians, et al., v. Georgia," *Kansas Journal of Law and Public Policy*, Vol. 8, Issue 2 (Winter 1998-1999): 159-173.

Stephen Young, *Indigenous Peoples, Consent and Rights: Troubling Subjects.* London: Routledge, 2020.

Supreme Court Opinions

Chisholm v. Georgia 2 U.S. (2 Dall.) 419 (1793).

Marbury v. Madison, 5 U.S. (1 Cranch) 137 (1803).

Fletcher v. Peck 10 U.S. (6 Cranch) 87 (1810).

Cohens v. Virginia 19 U.S. (6 Wheat.) 264 (1821).

Johnson v. M'Intosh 21 U.S. (8 Wheat.) 543 (1823).

Governor of Georgia v. Madrazo, 26 U.S. (1 Pet.) 110 (1828).

Cherokee Nation v. Georgia U.S. 30 (5 Pet.) 1 (1831).

Worcester v. Georgia 31 U.S. (6 Pet.) 515 (1832).

Mitchel v. United States 34 U.S. 711 (1835).

Dred Scott v. Sandford, 60 U.S. 19 How. 393 (1856).

Bradwell v. The State of Illinois, 83 U.S. (16 Wall.) 130 (1872).

United States v. Kagama, 118 U.S. 375 (1886).

Plessy v. Ferguson, 163 U.S. 537 (1896).

Lone Wolf v. Hitchcock, 187 U.S. 553 (1903).

Principality of Monaco v. Mississippi 292 U.S. 313 (1934).

Korematsu v. United States 323 U.S. 214 (1944).

Tee-Hit-Ton Indians v. United States, 348 U.S. 272 (1955).

United States v. Wheeler 435 U.S. 313 (1978).

United States v. Sioux Nation of Indians, 448 U.S. 371 (1980).

Lyng v. Northwest Indian Cemetery Protective Association, 485 U.S. 439 (1988)

Cotton Petroleum Corporation v. New Mexico 490 U.S. 163 (1989).

Blatchford v. Native Village of Noatak & Circle Village, 501 U.S. 775, 782 (1991).

City of Sherrill v. Oneida Indian Nation 544 U.S. 197 (2005).

Washington State Dept. of Licensing v. Cougar Den, Inc. 188 Wash. 2d 55, 392 p. 3d, 1014, affirmed (2018).

McGirt v. Oklahoma, 2020, https://www.supremecourt.gov/opinions/19pdf/18-9526_9okb.pdf.

Published Documents

John Quincy Adams, Fourth Annual Message to Congress, 2 December 1828, text available at http://millercenter.org/president/jqadams/speeches/speech-3517.

Articles of Confederation, 1 March 1781, http://avalon.law.yale.edu/18th_century/artconf.asp#art9.

The Book of Common Prayer. New York: Church Publishing Incorporated, 2007.

John Catanzariti, et al., editors, *The Papers of Thomas Jefferson*, https://founders.archives.gov/content/volumes#Jefferson.

Constitution of the United States, https://www.archives.gov/founding-docs/constitution-transcript.

Convention on the Prevention and Punishment of the Crime of Genocide, 9 December 1948, https://www.un.org/en/genocideprevention/documents/atrocity-crimes/Doc.1_Convention%20on%20the%20Prevention%20and%20Punishment%20of%20the%20Crime%20of%20Genocide.pdf.

Frances Gardiner Davenport, ed., *European Treaties bearing on the History of the United States and its Dependencies to 1648.* Washington, DC: The Carnegie Institute, 1917.

Max Farrand, ed., *The Records of the Federal Convention of 1787* [1911] (revised edition in four volumes). New Haven: Yale University Press, 1966.

Daniel Feller, Laura-Eve Moss, Thomas Coens, and Erik B. Alexander, editors, *The Papers of Andrew Jackson* (volumes 8-10). Knoxville: The University of Tennessee Press, 2013.

Georgia and the United States, Articles of Agreement and Cession, 24 April 1802, http://amindians.tripod.com/18022.htm.

Kermit L. Hall and Mark David Hall, editors, *The Collected Works of James Wilson* (in two volumes). Indianapolis: Liberty Fund, 2007.

Historical Society of Pennsylvania exhibit, https://hsp.org/history-online/exhibits/constitution-on-display/the-earliest-surviving-version-handwritten-in-1787-by-james-wilson (accessed 26 June 2019).

Charles F. Hobson, editor, *The Papers of John Marshall* (in twelve volumes). Chapel Hill: University of North Carolina Press, 2002.

The House Committee on Indian Affairs, "Removal of Indians," Report No. 227, 24 February 1830, the House of Representatives, 21st Congress, 1st Session.

Andrew Jackson, first annual message to Congress, 8 December 1829, http://millercenter.org/scripps/archive/speeches/detail/3632.

Merrill Jensen, ed., *Ratification of the Constitution by the States* (Madison: Wisconsin Historical Society Press, 1976-).

James Madison to George Washington, 16 April 1787, *Founders Online,* National Archives, https://founders.archives.gov/documents/Washington/04-05-02-0139. [Original source: *The Papers of George Washington,* Confederation Series, vol. 5, *1 February 1787–31 December 1787,* ed. W. W. Abbot. Charlottesville: University Press of Virginia, 1997, pp. 144–150].

Edmund S. Morgan, ed., *Not Your Usual Founding Father: Selected Readings from Benjamin Franklin.* New Haven: Yale University Press, 2006.

Gary E. Moulton, edited and with an introduction, *The Papers of Chief John Ross* in two volumes. Norman: University of Oklahoma Press, 1985

Journals of the Continental Congress, 1774-1789.

Theda Perdue, *Cherokee Editor: The Writings of Elias Boudinot*. Knoxville: University of Tennessee Press, 1983.

Francis Paul Prucha, ed., *Cherokee Removal: The 'William Penn' Essays and Other Writings by Jeremiah Evarts.* Knoxville: University of Tennessee Press, 1981.

Register of Debates in Congress, 1824-37.

James Daniel Richardson, ed., *A Compilation of the Messages and Papers of the Presidents, 1789-1897* in ten volumes. Washington: Government Printing Office, 1896.

Statute of the International Court of Justice, https://www.icj-cij.org/en/statute.

William W. Story, ed., *Life and Letters of Joseph Story* (in two volumes). London: John Chapman, 1851.

"Treaty with the Cherokee," 28 November 1785. | 7 Stat., 18.

"Treaty with the Cherokee," 2 July 1791. | 7 Stat., 39. | Proclamation, 7 February 1792

Dorothy Twohig, et al., editors, *The Papers of George Washington: Presidential Series* (twenty volumes). Charlottesville: University Press of Virginia, 1987-2016.

"From George Washington to James Madison, 31 March 1787," *Founders Online*, National Archives, https://founders.archives.gov/documents/Washington/04-05-02-0111. [Original source: *The Papers of George Washington*, Confederation Series, vol. 5, *1 February 1787–31 December 1787*, ed. W. W. Abbot. Charlottesville: University Press of Virginia, 1997, pp. 114–117].

George Washington, *Message to the Senate of September 17, 1789 Regarding Treaties with Native Americans,* http://avalon.law.yale.edu/18th_century/gw006.asp.

George Washington, "Talk to the Cherokee Nation," 29 August 1796, http://millercenter.org/scripps/archive/speeches/detail/3941.

Robert Morris and James Wilson, proposition to the Illinois and Wabash Companies, 10 May 1791, Digital Law Collections, University of

Oklahoma, https://digital.libraries.ou.edu/IWLC/paper.asp?pID=147&doc_type=Mis.

On Writ of Certiorari to the Supreme Court of Washington, Brief of Amicus Curiae Confederated Tribes and Bands of the Yakama Nation in Support of Respondent, No. 16-1498, *Washington State Dept. of Licensing v. Cougar Den, Inc.*, 188 Wash. 2d 55, 392 p. 3d, 1014, affirmed (2018), https://www.supremecourt.gov/DocketPDF/16/16-1498/64580/20180924115810387_36893%20pdf%20Yakama%20Nation%20br.pdf.

"Notes of the Secret Debates of the Federal Convention of 1787, Taken by the Late Hon Robert Yates, Chief Justice of the State of New York, and One of the Delegates from That State to the Said Convention," https://avalon.law.yale.edu/18th_century/yates.asp.

Notes

[i] James Wilson, Notes of Debate, 26 July 1776, *Journals of the Continental Congress*, Vol. 6, 1774-1789, p. 1078. On Wilson generally, see Kermit L. Hall and Mark David Hall, editors, *The Collected Works of James Wilson* in two volumes (Indianapolis: Liberty Fund, 2007); William Ewald, "James Wilson and the American Founding," *The Georgetown Journal of Law and Public Policy*, Vol. 17, No. 1 (Winter 2019), pp. 1-21; John Mikhail, "The Constitution and the Philosophy of Language: Entailment, Implicature, and Implied Powers," *Virginia Law Review*, Vol. 101, No. 4 (June 2014), pp. 1063-1103.

[ii] "The Bill filed on behalf of the Cherokee Nation vs. The State of Georgia," in Richard Peters, *The Case of the Cherokee Nation Against the State of Georgia* (Philadelphia: James Kay, 1831), p. 3.

[iii] *Johnson v. McIntosh* 21 U.S. (8 Wheat.) 543, 574-77, 587 (1823).

[iv] "all Treaties made, or which shall be made, under the Authority of the United States, shall be the supreme Law of the Land; and the Judges in every State shall be bound thereby, any Thing in the Constitution or Laws of any State to the Contrary notwithstanding" (Article 6). It is this language, in conjunction with the grant of jurisdiction to the Supreme Court in *all* cases arising under treaties, made explicitly a grant/requirement of original jurisdiction in the Supreme Court in *all* cases to which an individual state of the Union is a party (Article 3, Section 2), that I mean when I refer to the Treaty Supremacy Clause. The Constitution of the United States, https://www.archives.gov/founding-docs/constitution-transcript (accessed 24 June 2020).

[v] I am indebted to Tink Tinker for the term "eurochristian."

[vi] See Steven T. Newcomb, *Pagans in the Promised Land: Decoding the Doctrine of Christian Discovery* (Golden, CO: Fulcrum Publishing, 2008), especially pp. 73-102. I am deeply indebted to the clarity with which Newcomb "decodes" and presents *Johnson v. McIntosh* and offers an understanding of the original free and independent existence of the Native peoples. *Johnson v. McIntosh* 21 U.S. (8 Wheat.) 543, 574-77, 587 (1823).

[vii] *Cherokee Nation v. Georgia* U.S. 30 (5 Pet.) 1, 17 (1831).

[viii] *Johnson v. McIntosh* 21 U.S. (8 Wheat.) 543, 574-77, 587 (1823)

[ix] In addition to *Pagans in the Promised Land*, See the extraordinary one-hour documentary film that Newcomb co-produced, "The Doctrine of Discovery: Unmasking the Domination Code," https://vimeo.com/ondemand/dominationcode

[x] The law professor Stacy Leeds notes that "an Indian law *Brown v. Board of Education* decision" will require open discussion of United States notions of racial supremacy and the "perceived inferiority and dependency" of the Native Nations. Stacy L. Leeds, "The More Things Stay the Same: Waiting on Indian Law's Brown v. Board of Education," *Tulsa Law Review, Vol.* 38, No. 1 (Fall 2002), p. 86.

[xi] Peter P. d'Errico, *Federal Anti-Indian Law: The Legal Entrapment of Indigenous Peoples* (Santa Barbara: Praeger, 2022).
[xii] *Vasquez v. Hillery*, 474 U.S. 254, 266 (1986).
[xiii] On the accuracy of the term genocide, see the Introduction of this book and Philippe Sands, *East West Street: On the Origins of "Genocide" and "Crimes Against Humanity"* (New York: Alfred A. Knopf, 2016). I am indebted to the land acknowledgement of the University of Massachusetts at Amherst.
[xiv] Vine Deloria, Jr., *God is Red: A Native View of Religion* (third edition) (New York: Putnam, 2003), p. 75.
[xv] Copy in the possession of the author: Steve Russell, *Lighting the Fire: A Cherokee Journey from Dropout to Professor* (McLean: Miniver Press, 2020).
[xvi] www.schwartzbergforcongress.com.
[xvii] 21 April 1830, United States Senate, 21st Congress, 1st Session, *Register of Debates*, p. 376.
[xviii] Jeremiah Evarts, "What are the People of the United States bound to do in regard to the Indian question," 27 November 1830, text in Francis Paul Prucha, ed., *Cherokee Removal: The 'William Penn' Essays and Other Writings by Jeremiah Evarts* (Knoxville: University of Tennessee Press, 1981), pp. 282-283. See also John A. Andrew III, *From Revivals to Removal: Jeremiah Evarts, the Cherokee Nation, and the Search for the Soul of America* (Athens: University of Georgia Press, 1992).
[xix] On Writ of Certiorari to the Supreme Court of Washington, Brief of Amicus Curiae Confederated Tribes and Bands of the Yakama Nation in Support of Respondent, No. 16-1498, p. 6, *Washington State Dept. of Licensing v. Cougar Den, Inc.*, 188 Wash. 2d 55, 392 p. 3d, 1014, affirmed (2018), https://www.supremecourt.gov/DocketPDF/16/16-1498/64580/20180924115810387_36893%20pdf%20Yakama%20Nation%20br.pdf (accessed 29 July 2020).
[xx] Ibid, p. 5. See Newcomb, *Pagans in the Promised Land*. See also *Johnson v. McIntosh* 21 U.S. (8 Wheat.) 543, 574-77, 587 (1823).
[xxi] Ibid, p. 6. The Yakama Nation is here quoting *Johnson v. McIntosh*.
[xxii] The best treatment of this aspect of the story is in Lindsay G. Robertson, *Conquest by Law: How the Discovery of America Dispossessed Indigenous Peoples of their Land* (Oxford: Oxford University Press, 2005), passim.
[xxiii] For the extent to which the colonists and their heirs and successors were seen by the Native peoples as pursuing a genocidal vision, see Jeffrey Ostler, *Surviving Genocide: Native Nations and the United States from the American Revolution to Bleeding Kansas* (New Haven: Yale University Press, 2019), passim.
[24] Lewis Cass to Andrew Jackson, September 1831, text in Daniel Feller, Laura-Eve Moss, Thomas Coens, and Erik B. Alexander, editors, *The Papers of Andrew Jackson* (Knoxville: The University of Tennessee Press, 2013), Volume 9, p. 541.
[25] 15 April 1830, United States Senate, 21st Congress, 1st Session, *Register of Debates*, p. 336.

[26] The self-deluded self-righteousness of many advocates of removal was perhaps best captured in a report of the House Committee on Indian Affairs of 24 February 1830 which concluded that one of the advantages of removal to the Indians would be that "stimulant, so powerful and important in its effects upon the white man, of a separate and exclusive property in lands, with the privilege of transmitting it to their children." The House Committee on Indian Affairs, "Removal of Indians," Report No. 227, 24 February 1830, p. 26, the House of Representatives, 21st Congress, 1st Session.

[27] The text of Article 7 of the Treaty of 1791 with the Cherokee Nation reads: "The United States solemnly guarantee to the Cherokee nation, all their lands not hereby ceded." "Treaty with the Cherokee," 2 July 1791. | 7 Stat., 39. Article 5 of the 1790 Treaty with the Creek Nation stated: "The United States solemnly guarantee to the Creek Nation, all their lands within the limits of the United States," https://avalon.law.yale.edu/18th_century/cre1790.asp (accessed 14 August 2020). The Treaty with the Choctaw Nation of 1786 specified boundaries and promised perpetual peace and friendship as did the Treaty with the Chickasaw Nation of 1786. "Treaty with the Choctaw," Jan. 3, 1786. | 7 Stat., 21. "Treaty with the Chickasaw," Jan. 10, 1786. | 7 Stat. 24.

[28] 15 May 1830, United States House of Representatives, 21st Congress, 1st Session, *Register of Debates*, p. 1015.

[29] 18 May 1830, United States House of Representatives, 21st Congress, 1st Session, *Register of Debates*, p. 1040.

[30] 19 May 1830, United States House of Representatives, 21st Congress, 1st Session, *Register of Debates*, p. 1060.

[31] John Marshall to Edward Everett, 5 June 1830, in Charles F. Hobson, editor, *The Papers of John Marshall* in twelve volumes (Chapel Hill: University of North Carolina Press, 2002), Vol. 11, p. 379.

[32] Convention on the Prevention and Punishment of the Crime of Genocide, 9 December 1948, https://www.un.org/en/genocideprevention/documents/atrocity-crimes/Doc.1_Convention%20on%20the%20Prevention%20and%20Punishment%20of%20the%20Crime%20of%20Genocide.pdf (accessed 15 September 2019). The Rome Statute of the International Criminal Court, 16 January 2002, https://www.icc-cpi.int/resource-library/documents/rs-eng.pdf (accessed 23 September 2021).

[33] My usage here is indebted to Chancellor James Kent.

[34] Text in Peters, *The Case of the Cherokee Nation*, p. 282

[35] Gary Clayton Anderson, *Ethnic Cleansing and the Indian: The Crime that Should Haunt America* (Norman: University of Oklahoma Press, 2014), pp. 4-5.

[36] Claudio Saunt, *Unworthy Republic: The Dispossession of Native Americans and the Road to Indian Territory* (New York: W. W. Norton, 2020), pp. 308-309.

[37] Ibid.

[38] This calculation is my own. It assumes a mortality rate of 20%.

[39] Ibid.

[40] A. J. Langguth, *Driven West: Andrew Jackson and the Trail of Tears to the Civil War* (New York: Simon and Schuster, 2010), pp. 165-166.

[41] Ibid.

[42] Ibid.

[43] Alexis De Tocqueville, *Democracy in America* tr. Henry Reeve (New York: Scatcherd and Adams, 1839), Volume 1, p. 338.

[44] The House Committee on Indian Affairs, "Removal of Indians," Report No. 227, 24 February 1830, pp. 1-2, the House of Representatives, 21st Congress, 1st Session.

[45] Ibid.

[46] Ibid, p. 3.

[47] Ibid, p. 8.

[48] Ibid, pp. 3-4.

[49] Ibid, pp. 4-5.

[50] *Johnson v. McIntosh* 21 U.S. (8 Wheat.) 543, 574-77, 587 (1823). *Cherokee Nation v. Georgia* U.S. 30 (5 Pet.) 1, 20 (1831).

[51] 18 May 1830, United States House of Representatives, 21st Congress, 1st Session, *Register of Debates*, p. 1045.

[52] The House Committee on Indian Affairs, "Removal of Indians," Report No. 227, 24 February 1830, pp. 6-7, the House of Representatives, 21st Congress, 1st Session.

[53] Ibid, p. 8.

[54] Ibid.

[55] Ibid, p. 17.

[56] Ibid, p. 19.

[57] Ibid, p. 20.

[58] Ibid, p. 21.

[59] Ibid, p. 23.

[60] Ibid, pp. 20, 25.

[61] Deloria, Jr., *God is Red*, especially pp. 200-201. See also John Collier, *Indians of the Americas* (abridged version) (New York: Mentor Books, 1948), especially pp. 7-8.

[62] Valarie Kaur, *See No Stranger: A Memoir and Manifesto of Revolutionary Love* (New York: Random House, 2020).

[63] Herbert McCabe, *God Matters* (London: Continuum, 1987), p. 108

[64] James Wilson, "Chapter III. Of the Law of Nature," in Hall and Hall, eds, *The Collected Works of James Wilson*, Vol. 1, p. 542.

[65] George Washington revealed his hypocrisy in a letter quoted by Walter Echo-Hawk: "notwithstanding the [1763 Royal] Proclamation that restrains [purchases of Native lands] at present...I can never look upon the Proclamation in any other light (but this I say between ourselves) than as a temporary expedient to quiet the Minds of the Indians...Any person therefore who neglects the present opportunity of hunting out good Lands and in some measure marking and distinguishing them for their own (in order to keep others from settling them) will never regain it." Walter R. Echo-Hawk, *In*

the Courts of the Conqueror: The 10 Worst Indian Law Cases Ever Decided (Golden, Colo: Fulcrum Publishing, 2010), p. 59. There is no evidence of analogous hypocrisy on the part of James Wilson, but the fact remains that Wilson was a large land speculator.

[66] Quoted in Langguth, *Driven West*, p. 28.

[67] Ibid.

[68] "The lands that the federal government expropriated in the decade of deportation furnished nearly 160 million pounds of ginned cotton in 1850, equal to 16 percent of the entire crop in the United States." Saunt, *Unworthy Republic*, p. 309.

[69] William G. McLoughlin, *Cherokee Renascence in the New Republic* (Princeton: Princeton University Press, 1986), p. 437.

[70] 26 May 1830, *Journal of the House of Representatives of the United States*, 21st Congress, 1st Session, Volume 23, pp. 729-730; McLoughlin, *Cherokee Renascence*, p. 437

[71] "all Treaties made, or which shall be made, under the Authority of the United States, shall be the supreme Law of the Land; and the Judges in every State shall be bound thereby, any Thing in the Constitution or Laws of any State to the Contrary notwithstanding" (Article 6) It is this language, in conjunction with the grant of jurisdiction to the Supreme Court in *all* cases arising under treaties, made explicitly a grant/requirement of original jurisdiction in the Supreme Court in *all* cases to which an individual state of the Union is a party (Article 3, Section 2), that I mean when I refer to the Treaty Supremacy Clause. The Constitution of the United States, https://www.archives.gov/founding-docs/constitution-transcript (accessed 24 June 2020).

[72] *Johnson v. McIntosh* 21 U.S. (8 Wheat.) 543, 574-77, 587 (1823). Newcomb, *Pagans in the Promised Land,* especially pp. 73-102.

[73] On the papal bulls, see Steven T. Newcomb, "The Evidence of Christian Nationalism in Federal Indian Law: The Doctrine of Discovery, Johnson v. McIntosh, and Plenary Power," *N.Y.U. Rev. L. & Soc. Change,* Volume 20, No. 2 (1992-1993), pp. 310ff. See also Blake A. Watson, *Buying America from the Indians: Johnson v. McIntosh and the History of Native Land Rights* (Norman: University of Oklahoma Press, 2012), pp. 11-26; Robert A. Williams, Jr., *The American Indian in Western Legal Thought: The Discourses of Conquest* (Oxford: Oxford University Press, 1990), passim.

[74] The Bull, *Inter Caetera,* 3 May 1493, in Frances Gardiner Davenport, ed., *European Treaties bearing on the History of the United States and its Dependencies to 1648* (Washington, DC: The Carnegie Institute, 1917), pp. 61-62

[75] The Bull, *Inter Caetera,* 4 May 1493, in Davenport, ed., *European Treaties*, p. 71.

[76] The Bull, *Romans Pontifex*, 8 January 1455, in Davenport, ed., *European Treaties,* p. 23.

[77] On the numbers of petition signatures, see Steve Inskeep, *Jacksonland: President Andrew Jackson, Cherokee Chief John Ross, and a great American land grab* (New York: Penguin Press, 2015).

[78] Senator John Forsyth of Georgia, 15 April 1830, United States Senate, 21st Congress, 1st Session, *Register of Debates*, p. 326.

[79] Ibid, p. 327.

[80] Jeremiah Evarts, "What are the People of the United States bound to do in regard to the Indian question," 27 November 1830, text in Prucha, ed., *Cherokee Removal*, p. 285.

[81] 24 February 1830, United States House of Representatives, 21st Congress, 1st Session, *Register of Debates*, p. 583. 26 May 1830, *Journal of the House of Representatives of the United States*, 21st Congress, 1st Session, Volume 23, pp. 729-730.

[82] Jeremiah Evarts, "What are the People of the United States bound to do in regard to the Indian question," 27 November 1830, text in Prucha, ed., *Cherokee Removal*, pp. 282-283.

[83] Quoted in Saunt, *Unworthy Republic*, p. xix.

[84] Quoted in "Editorial Note" in Hobson, editor, *The Papers of John Marshall*, Vol. 12, p. 48. See George Bryan, *The Imperialism of John Marshall* (Boston: The Stratford Company, 1924).

[85] See, for example, Saunt, *Unworthy Republic*, p. 163.

[86] *Cherokee Nation v. Georgia* U.S. 30 (5 Pet.) 1, 17 (1831).

[87] 15 April 1830, United States Senate, 21st Congress, 1st Session, *Register of Debates*, p. 336.

[88] *Cherokee Nation v. Georgia* U.S. 30 (5 Pet.) 1, 20 (1831).

[89] 15 April 1830, United States Senate, 21st Congress, 1st Session, *Register of Debates*, p. 333.

[90] *Johnson v. McIntosh* 21 U.S. (8 Wheat.) 543, 573 (1823).

[91] *Johnson v. McIntosh* 21 U.S. (8 Wheat.) 543, 573, 577 (1823).

[92] Newcomb, *Pagans in the Promised Land*, especially pp. 73-102.

[93] 15 April 1830, United States Senate, 21st Congress, 1st Session, *Register of Debates*, p. 333.

[94] *Johnson v. McIntosh* 21 U.S. (8 Wheat.) 543, 574 (1823).

[95] *Cherokee Nation v. Georgia* U.S. 30 (5 Pet.) 1, 17 (1831).

[96] 15 April 1830, United States Senate, 21st Congress, 1st Session, *Register of Debates*, p. 333.

[97] *Johnson v. McIntosh* 21 U.S. (8 Wheat.) 543, 574-77, 587 (1823). See also Newcomb, *Pagans in the Promised Land*, especially pp. 73-102.

[98] *Johnson v. M'Intosh* 21 U.S. (8 Wheat.) 543, 587-591 (1823).

[99] Much the same conclusion has been reached by Steven T. Newcomb who writes: "we might say that it was by means of the imaginative processes (thought processes) of Marshall's mind, based on his interpretation of history, that the original rights and existence of the Indians were imaginatively diminished and, to that extent, mentally negated." Newcomb, *Pagans in the Promised Land*, p. 103. As Stuart Banner notes: "If anyone was guilty of 'converting the discovery of an inhabited country into conquest,' it was John Marshall in *Johnson v. M'Intosh*, not the British colonists or their government." Stuart Banner, *How the Indians Lost their Land: Law and Power on the Frontier* (Cambridge: Harvard University Press, 2005), p. 187. See also chapters four and five below.

[100] *Johnson v. McIntosh* 21 U.S. (8 Wheat.) 543, 587, 591-92 (1823)

[101] 15 May 1830, United States House of Representatives, 21st Congress, 1st Session, *Register of Debates*, 1007.

[102] Ibid, p. 1010.

[103] *Johnson v. M'Intosh* 21 U.S. (8 Wheat.) 543, 587-591 (1823). 15 May 1830, United States House of Representatives, 21st Congress, 1st Session, *Register of Debates*, pp. 1010-1011.
[104] Joseph William Singer, "Law and Property," *Northwestern University Law Review*, Vol 86, No. 1 (Fall 1991), p. 30.
[105] *Johnson v. McIntosh* 21 U.S. (8 Wheat.) 543, 591 (1823): "That law which regulates and ought to regulate in general the relations between the conqueror and conquered was incapable of application…"
[106] 9 April 1830, United States Senate, 21st Congress, 1st Session, *Register of Debates*, p. 312.
[107] 15 May 1830, United States House of Representatives, 21st Congress, 1st Session, *Register of Debates*, p. 1008.
[108] *Johnson v. McIntosh* 21 U.S. (8 Wheat.) 543, 563 (1823).
[109] The House Committee on Indian Affairs, "Removal of Indians," Report No. 227, 24 February 1830, p. 8, the House of Representatives, 21st Congress, 1st Session.
[110] Collin G. Calloway, *The Indian World of George Washington* (Oxford: Oxford University Press, 2018), p. 2.
[111] George Washington, *Message to the Senate of September 17, 1789 Regarding Treaties with Native Americans,* http://avalon.law.yale.edu/18th_century/gw006.asp (accessed 22 September 2016).
[112] See Willie James Jennings, *The Christian Imagination: Theology and the Origins of Race* (New Haven: Yale University Press, 2010). See also Bailey W. Diffie, *Prelude to Empire: Portugal Overseas before Henry the Navigator* (Lincoln: University of Nebraska Press, 1960).
[113] My thinking on nationalism and nationality is indebted to Liah Greenfeld, *Nationalism and the Mind: Essays on Modern Culture* (Oxford: Oneworld Publications, 2006). Liah Greenfeld, *Nationalism: Five Roads to Modernity* (Cambridge: Harvard University Press, 1992). Liah Greenfeld, *The Spirit of Capitalism: Nationalism and Economic Growth* (Cambridge: Harvard University Press, 2001). Liah Greenfeld, *Mind, Modernity, Madness: The Impact of Culture on Human Experience* (Cambridge: Harvard University Press, 2013). See also Elie Kedourie, *Nationalism* fourth, expanded edition (Oxford: Blackwell, 1994).
[114] Jennings, *The Christian Imagination*, p. 36.
[115] Tu Weiming, *The Global Significance of Concrete Humanity* (New Delhi: Center for Studies in Civilization, 2010).
[116] See Denise Ferreira da Silva, *Toward a Global Idea of Race* (Minneapolis: University of Minnesota Press, 2007).
[117] "Remarks of James Wilson in the Pennsylvania Convention to Ratify the Constitution of the United States, 1787," in Hall and Hall, editors, *The Collected Works of James Wilson*, Vol. 1, p. 246.
[118] Trotsky's succinct defense of totalitarianism is unrivaled on the antidemocratic left: "The foundations of the militarization of labor are those forms of State compulsion without which the replacement of capitalist economy by the Socialist will forever remain an empty sound. Why do we speak of *militarization?* Of course, this is only an analogy—but an analogy very rich in content. No social organization except the army has ever

considered itself justified in subordinating citizens to itself in such a measure, and to control them by its will on all sides to such a degree, as the State of the proletarian dictatorship considers itself justified in doing, and does. Only the army—just because in its way it used to decide questions of the life or death of nations, States, and ruling classes—was endowed with powers of demanding from each and all complete submission to its problems, aims, regulations and orders." Leon Trotsky, *Terrorism and Communism: A Reply to Karl Kautsky* [1920] with an introduction by Max Shachtman (Ann Arbor: University of Michigan Press, 1961), p. 141.

[119] According to Georges Sorel, who admired Lenin and who was admired in turn by Mussolini: "The bond which I pointed out in the beginning of this inquiry between Socialism and proletarian violence appears to us now in all its strength. It is to violence that Socialism owes those high ethical values by means of which it brings *salvation* to the modern world." Georges Sorel, *Reflections on Violence* [1906] (New York: The Free Press, 1950), p. 249. See also John P. Roche, *The History and Impact of Marxist-Leninist Organizational Theory* (Cambridge: Institute for Foreign Policy Analysis, 1984) and Alan Bullock, *Hitler and Stalin: Parallel Lives* (New York: Alfred A. Knopf, 1992).

[120] Bill Clinton, inaugural address, 20 January 1997, *Public Papers of the Presidents of the United States, William J. Clinton, 1997* (in two volumes) (Washington: United States Government Printing Office, 1998), Vol. 1, p. 44.

[121] The nearly 4 million U.S. slaves in 1860, "were worth a combined $3 billion… Three billion dollars was triple the value of the entire U.S. industrial capital stock in 1860." Jonathan Levy, *Ages of American Capitalism* (New York: Random House, 2022), p. 154. d'Errico, *Federal Anti-Indian Law,* especially the "Call to Consciousness," pp. 164-87.

[122] *Johnson v. McIntosh* 21 U.S. (8 Wheat.) 543, 574-77, 587 (1823). *Cherokee Nation v. Georgia* U.S. 30 (5 Pet.) 1, 17 (1831).

[123] *Cherokee Nation v. Georgia* U.S. 30 (5 Pet.) 1, 17 (1831).

[124] Milner S. Ball, "Constitution, Court, Indian Tribes," *American Bar Foundation Research Journal,* Vol. 12, No. 1 (Winter, 1987), pp. 60-61.

[125] *Johnson v. McIntosh* 21 U.S. (8 Wheat.) 543, 574-77 (1823).

[126] Article 6, Clause 2, the Constitution of the United States.

[127] d'Errico, *Federal Anti-Indian Law,* p. 54.

[128] James Wilson, "Introductory Lecture. Of the Study of the Law in the United States," in Hall and Hall, editors, *The Collected Works of James Wilson,* Vol. 1, p. 446

[129] Jeremiah Evarts, "Present State of the Indian Question," 24 November 1830, text in Prucha, ed., *Cherokee Removal,* p. 281.

[130] Jeremiah Evarts, Essay No. XXIV, 19 December 1829, text in Prucha, ed., *Cherokee Removal,* p. 195.

[131] Jeremiah Evarts, "Present State of the Indian Question," 24 November 1830, text in Prucha, ed., *Cherokee Removal,* pp. 279-280.

[132] 9 April 1830, United States Senate, 21st Congress, 1st Session, *Register of Debates,* p. 309.

[133] Ibid, p. 312.

[134] Ibid.

[135] Ibid, p. 313.

[136] Ibid.

[137] Ibid, p. 314.

[138] Ibid, p. 315.

[139] Ibid, p. 316.

[140] Ibid.

[141] Ibid, p. 320.

[142] 15 April 1830, United States Senate, 21st Congress, 1st Session, *Register of Debates*, p. 325.

[143] Ibid, p. 326.

[144] 15 April 1830, United States Senate, 21st Congress, 1st Session, *Register of Debates*, p. 325.

[145] Ibid, p. 333.

[146] Ibid, p. 336.

[147] Ibid.

[148] Ibid, p. 339.

[149] 17 April 1830, United States Senate, 21st Congress, 1st Session, *Register of Debates*, p. 344.

[150] Ibid.

[151] Ibid, p. 345.

[152] Ibid, p. 348.

[153] Ibid, p. 350.

[154] Ibid, p. 355.

[155] Ibid, p. 357.

[156] *Worcester v. Georgia* 31 U.S. (6 Pet.) 515, 553-54 (1832).

[157] 20 April 1830, United States Senate, 21st Congress, 1st Session, *Register of Debates*, p. 359.

[158] Ibid, p. 361.

[159] Ibid.

[160] Ibid, p. 364.

[161] 21 April 1830, United States Senate, 21st Congress, 1st Session, *Register of Debates*, p. 376.

[162] McLoughlin, *Cherokee Renascence*, p. 437.

[163] Langguth, *Driven West*, p. 248.

[164] 15 May 1830, United States House of Representatives, 21st Congress, 1st Session, *Register of Debates*, p. 994.

[165] Ibid, p. 997.

[166] Ibid, p. 999.

[167] Ibid, p. 1000.

[168] Ibid, p. 1002.

[169] Ibid.
[170] Ibid, p. 1003.
[171] Ibid, pp. 1005-1006.
[172] Ibid, p. 1006.
[173] Ibid, p. 1007.
[174] Ibid, p. 1008.
[175] Ibid, p. 1009.
[176] Ibid, p. 1010.
[177] Ibid, p. 1012.
[178] Ibid, p. 1014.
[179] Ibid.
[180] Ibid.
[181] Ibid, p. 1015. The Latin is: "faithful guardian of the matter."
[182] 17 May 1830, United States House of Representatives, 21st Congress, 1st Session, *Register of Debates*, p. 1016.
[183] Ibid, p. 1017.
[184] Ibid.
[185] Ibid, pp. 1017-1018.
[186] Ibid, p. 1018.
[187] Ibid, p. 1019.
[188] Ibid, p. 1020.
[189] Ibid, p. 1022.
[190] Ibid.
[191] Ibid.
[192] Ibid, p. 1023. Cadmus, in Greek mythology, was a Phoenician prince credited with introducing the alphabet to the Greeks.
[193] Ibid, p. 1028.
[194] Ibid, p. 1030.
[195] Ibid, p. 1031.
[196] Ibid.
[197] Ibid.
[198] 17 May 1830, United States House of Representatives, 21st Congress, 1st Session, *Register of Debates*, p. 1033.
[199] Ibid. Foster is here confusing the Articles of Confederation with the Constitution.
[200] Ibid.
[201] Ibid, p. 1034.
[202] Ibid, p. 1035.
[203] Ibid, p. 1036.
[204] Ibid, p. 1037.
[205] 18 May 1830, United States House of Representatives, 21st Congress, 1st Session, *Register of Debates*, p. 1038.

[206] Ibid, p. 1040.
[207] Ibid, p. 1043.
[208] Ibid, p. 1045.
[209] Ibid.
[210] Ibid.
[211] Ibid, p. 1047.
[212] Ibid, p. 1048.
[213] Ibid, p. 1049.
[214] 19 May 1830, United States House of Representatives, 21st Congress, 1st Session, *Register of Debates*, p. 1051.
[215] Ibid, p. 1060.
[216] Ibid, p. 1061.
[217] Ibid, p. 1070.
[218] Ibid, p. 1071.
[219] Ibid, p. 1073.
[220] Ibid, p. 1079.
[221] Ibid, p. 1080.
[222] Ibid, p. 1081.
[223] Ibid, p. 1083.
[224] Ibid, p. 1086.
[225] Ibid.
[226] Ibid, p. 1093.
[227] Ibid, p. 1095.
[228] Ibid, p. 1098.
[229] Ibid.
[230] Ibid, p. 1103.
[231] Ibid.
[232] Ibid, p. 1105.
[233] Ibid, p. 1106.
[234] Ibid, p. 1107.
[235] Ibid.
[236] Ibid.
[237] Ibid, p. 1108.
[238] Ibid, p. 1110.
[239] Ibid, pp. 1111-1112.
[240] Ibid, p. 1113.
[241] 24 May 1830, United States House of Representatives, 21st Congress, 1st Session, *Register of Debates*, p. 1122.
[242] Ibid, p. 1123.
[243] Ibid, p. 1128.
[244] Ibid, p. 1132.

[245] Ibid.

[246] Ibid, p. 1133.

[247] Ibid.

[248] 25 May 1830, *Journal of the House of Representatives of the United States*, 21st Congress, 1st Session, Volume 23, pp. 721-722.

[249] 26 May 1830, *Journal of the House of Representatives of the United States*, 21st Congress, 1st Session, Volume 23, pp. 727-728.

[250] Ibid, pp. 729-730.

[251] The House Committee on Indian Affairs, "Removal of Indians," Report No. 227, 24 February 1830, p. 31, the House of Representatives, 21st Congress, 1st Session. Act of May 28, 1830, ch 148, 4 Stat, 412.

[252] Act of May 28, 1830, ch 148, 4 Stat, 412.

[253] *Lone Wolf v. Hitchcock*, 187 U.S. 553 (1903).

[254] *Lone Wolf v. Hitchcock*, 187 U.S. 553, 564 (1903).

[255] Langguth, *Driven West*, p. 145; Perdue and Green, *The Cherokee Nation and the Trail of Tears*, p. 86.

[256] https://en.wikipedia.org/wiki/Gabriel_Duvall#Dissents (accessed 18 September 2016).

[257] Justice Johnson maintained that the "absolute proprietorship of their soil" was maintained by "the tribes to the west of Georgia" *Fletcher v. Peck* 10 U.S. (6 Cranch) 87, 146-47 (1810).

[258] *Mitchel v. United States* 34 U.S. 711, 746 (1835). David E. Wilkins, "Johnson v. M'Intosh Revisited: Through the Eyes of Mitchel v. United States," *American Indian Law Review*, Vol. 19, No. 1 (1994), pp. 159-181.

[259] "The Bill filed on behalf of the Cherokee Nation vs. The State of Georgia," in Peters, *The Case of the Cherokee Nation*, p. 3.

[260] Ibid, p. 4.

[261] Ibid, pp. 5-9. The text of Article 11 reads in part: "If any citizen or inhabitant of the United States, or of either of the territorial districts of the United States, shall go into any town, settlement or territory belonging to the Cherokees, and shall there commit any crime upon, or trespass against the person or property of any peaceable and friendly Indian or Indians, which if committed within the jurisdiction of any state, or within the jurisdiction of either of the said districts, against a citizen or white inhabitant thereof, would be punishable by the laws of such state or district, such offender or offenders, shall be subject to the same punishment, and shall be proceeded against in the same manner as if the offence had been committed within the jurisdiction of the state or district to which he or they may belong, against a citizen or white inhabitant thereof." The text of Article 7 reads: "The United States solemnly guarantee to the Cherokee nation, all their lands not hereby ceded." "Treaty with the Cherokee," 2 July 1791. | 7 Stat., 39. | Proclamation, 7 February 1792, http://digital.library.okstate.edu/kappler/vol2/treaties/che0029.htm.

[262] "The Bill filed on behalf of the Cherokee Nation vs. The State of Georgia," in Peters, *The Case of the Cherokee Nation*, p. 12.

[263] Ibid, p. 16.

[264] Ibid.

[265] Ibid, p. 17.

[266] Ibid, p. 18.

[267] Ibid, pp. 19-20.

[268] Ibid, p. 22.

[269] Ibid, p. 28.

[270] Ibid, p. 29.

[271] Ibid, p. 30.

[272] I am indebted to Steve Newcomb for this observation.

[273] Newcomb, *Pagans in the Promised Land.*

[274] Deloria, *God is Red,* especially pp. 200-201. Collier, *Indians of the Americas,* especially pp. 7-8. See also the Epilogue below.

[275] On the concept of "civility"—understood, as a first approximation, as the virtue of the citizen and not merely as politeness—see Edward Shils, *The Virtue of Civility: Selected Essays on Liberalism, Tradition, and Civil Society* (Indianapolis: Liberty Fund, 1997).

[276] *Cherokee Nation v. Georgia* U.S. 30 (5 Pet.) 1, 17 (1831).

[277] Steve Russell, *Sequoyah Rising: Problems in Post-Colonial Tribal Governance* (Durham: Carolina Academic Press, 2010), pp. 156-157.

[278] Newcomb, *Pagans in the Promised Land,* especially pp. 73-102. *Johnson v. McIntosh* 21 U.S. (8 Wheat.) 543, 574-77, 587 (1823).

[279] Saunt, *Unworthy Republic*, p. 163.

[280] Banner, *How the Indians Lost their Land*, p. 220.

[281] Williams, Jr., *The American Indian in Western Legal Thought*, p. 317.

[282] "Editorial Note" in Hobson, editor, *The Papers of John Marshall,* Vol. 9, p. 282.

[283] "This is not a property right, but amounts to a right of occupancy which the sovereign grants and protects against intrusion by third parties, but which right of occupancy may be terminated and such lands fully disposed of by the sovereign itself without any legally enforceable obligation to compensate the Indians." *Tee-Hit-Ton Indians v. United States*, 348 U.S. 272, 279-280 (1955).

[284] McLoughlin, *Cherokee Renascence*, p. 270.

[285] Williams, Jr., *The American Indian in Western Legal Thought,* p. 269.

[286] Dina Gilio-Whitaker, *As Long as the Grass Grows: The Indigenous Fight for Environmental Justice from Colonization to Standing Rock* (Boston: Beacon Press, 2019).

[287] Article 6, Clause 2, the Constitution of the United States.

[288] *Cherokee Nation v. Georgia*, 30 U.S. 1, 60, 80 (1831).

[289] Albert Jeremiah Beveridge, *The Life of John Marshall* (four volumes in two) (Boston: Houghton Mifflin, 1944), Volume 4, p. 546.

[290] James Wilson, "Considerations on the Nature and Extent of the Legislative Authority of the British Parliament," 1774, in Hall and Hall, eds., *The Collected Works of James Wilson*, Vol. 1, pp. 4-5.

[291] James Wilson, Notes of Debate, 26 July 1776, *Journals of the Continental Congress*, Vol. 6, 1774-1789, p. 1078.

[292] James Wilson, "Chapter IV. Of the Law of Nations," in Hall and Hall, editors, *The Collected Works of James Wilson*, Vol. 1, p. 532.

[293] Charles Page Smith, *James Wilson: Founding Father, 1742-1798* (Chapel Hill: University of North Carolina Press, 1956), p.72.

[294] Robert N. Clinton, "There is No Federal Supremacy Clause for Indian Tribes," *Arizona State Law Journal*, Vol. 34, No. 1 (Spring 2002), p. 147. See also Mark Savage, "The Great Secret about Federal Indian Law--Two Hundred Years in Violation of the Constitution--And the Opinion the Supreme Court Should Have Written to Reveal It," *New York University Review of Law & Social Change*, Vol. 20, No. 2 (1992-1993), pp. 343-372.

[295] John Quincy Adams, Fourth Annual Message to Congress, 2 December 1828, text available at http://millercenter.org/president/jqadams/speeches/speech-3517.

[296] Ulrich Bonner Phillips, *Georgia and State Rights: A Study of the Political History of Georgia from the Revolution to the Civil War, with Particular Regard to Federal Relations* (Washington: Government Printing Office: 1902), p. 48.

[297] Peters, *The Case of the Cherokee Nation*.

[298] "Strangely absent from Chief Justice Marshall's opinion is an explicit discussion of a related (but different) jurisdictional claim that one of the Cherokee's lawyers had made. The first paragraph of art. 3 says the 'judicial power of the United States' also shall extend to cases 'arising under... Treaties.' The Cherokees had argued that their case 'arises under a treaty.' Consequently paragraph one, they said, extended the federal judicial power to the case; paragraph two provides original jurisdiction in the Supreme Court. Chief Justice Marshall did not describe the flaw, if any, in this jurisdictional logic." Stephen Breyer, "The Cherokee Indians and the Supreme Court," *The Georgia Historical Quarterly*, Vol. 87, No. 3/4 (Fall/Winter 2003), p. 416.

[299] "Argument of Mr. Sergeant," in Peters, *The Case of the Cherokee Nation*, pp. 56-57.

[300] "Argument of Mr. Wirt," in Peters, *The Case of the Cherokee Nation*, pp. 95-96.

[301] *Johnson v. McIntosh* 21 U.S. (8 Wheat.) 543, 574-77, 588 (1823). See also Newcomb, *Pagans in the Promised Land*, especially pp. 73-102.

[302] "Argument of Mr. Sergeant," in Peters, *The Case of the Cherokee Nation*, p. 44.

[303] *Johnson v. McIntosh* 21 U.S. (8 Wheat.) 543, 591-92 (1823).

[304] *Johnson v. McIntosh* 21 U.S. (8 Wheat.) 543, 587, 591-92 (1823)

[305] *Johnson v. McIntosh* 21 U.S. (8 Wheat.) 543, 591-92 (1823).

[306] 21 April 1830, United States Senate, 21st Congress, 1st Session, *Register of Debates*, p. 376.

[307] James Wilson, Notes of Debate, 26 July 1776, *Journals of the Continental Congress*, Vol. 6, 1774-1789, p. 1078.

[308] "Argument of Mr. Wirt," in Peters, *The Case of the Cherokee Nation*, p. 110.

[309] "Argument of Mr. Sergeant," in Peters, *The Case of the Cherokee Nation*, p. 45.

[310] Ibid.

[311] *Johnson v. McIntosh* 21 U.S. (8 Wheat.) 543, 587, 591-92 (1823).

[312] *Worcester v. Georgia* 31 U.S. (6 Pet.) 515, 544 (1832).

[313] "Argument of Mr. Wirt," in Peters, *The Case of the Cherokee Nation*, p. 115.

[314] Ibid.

[315] James Wilson, Notes of Debate, 26 July 1776, *Journals of the Continental Congress*, Vol. 6, 1774-1789, p. 1078. John Catanzariti, et al., editors, *The Papers of Thomas Jefferson*, Vol. 25, p. 272.

[316] *Johnson v. M'Intosh* 21 U.S. (8 Wheat.) 543, 587-591 (1823).

[317] Newcomb, *Pagans in the Promised Land*, p. 103. Banner, *How the Indians Lost their Land*, p. 187.

[318] *Johnson v. McIntosh* 21 U.S. (8 Wheat.) 543, 587-588 (1823)

[319] Behind the words of the royal charter of Rhode Island in 1662, one can see an early exchange between the native peoples and the colonists as having been a foundation of life for the latter: "They the said John Clerk, Benjamin Arnold, &c. and the rest of the *purchasers* and inhabitants of our island, called Rhode Island, and the rest of the colony of Providence plantations, did transplant themselves into the midst of *the Indian nations*, who, as we are informed, *are* the *most potent princes* and *people* of all that country, where, by the good providence of God upon their labor and industry, they have not only been preserved to admiration, but have increased and prospered, *and are seized and possessed, by purchase and consent of said Natives*, to their full content, of such lands, rivers, harbours, and roads, as are very convenient both for plantations, and building ships." Quoted in Wharton, *Plain Facts*, p. 17

[320] *Worcester v. Georgia* 31 U.S. (6 Pet.) 515, 560 (1832).

[321] John Catanzariti, et al., editors, *The Papers of Thomas Jefferson*, Vol. 25, p. 272.

[322] "Argument of Mr. Wirt," in Peters, *The Case of the Cherokee Nation*, p. 116.

[323] Compare: John Marshall, *Life of Washington* (in five volumes) (Philadelphia: C. P. Wayne, 1805-07), Vol. 1, pp. 308-09; John Marshall, *Life of Washington* (in five volumes) (Fredericksburg: The Citizens' Guild, 1926), Vol. 1, p. 252. Conceivably someone other than Marshall was responsible for the excision, though this seems unlikely.

[324] Quoted in Banner, *How the Indians Lost their Land*, p. 189.

[325] William Wirt, "The Seneca Lands," 26 April 1821, in Robert Farnham, *Official Opinions of the Attorneys General of the United States* (Washington:1852), Volume 1, pp. 466-67. I am indebted to Peter d'Errico for directing me to this source.

[326] *Johnson v. McIntosh* 21 U.S. (8 Wheat.) 543, 587-588 (1823).

[327] Wirt, "The Seneca Lands," *Official Opinions of the Attorneys General of the United States*, Volume 1, pp. 466-67.

[328] 15 May 1830, United States House of Representatives, 21st Congress, 1st Session, *Register of Debates*, pp. 1010-1011.

[329] Wirt, "The Seneca Lands," *Official Opinions of the Attorneys General of the United States*, Volume 1, pp. 466-67.

[330] William Wirt, "Georgia and the Treaty of Indian Spring," 28 July 1828, in Robert Farnham, *Official Opinions of the Attorneys General of the United States* (Washington:1852), Volume 2, pp. 132-33.

[331] *Cherokee Nation v. Georgia* U.S. 30 (5 Pet.) 1, 17 (1831). The Supreme Court's decision in *Principality of Monaco v. Mississippi* 292 U.S. 313 (1934) extended the mistake in *Cherokee Nation* to treaties with foreign states generally. See Thomas H. Lee, "The Supreme Court of the United States as Quasi-International Tribunal: Reclaiming the Court's Original and Exclusive Jurisdiction over Treaty-Based Suits by Foreign States against States," *Columbia Law Review*, Vol. 104, No. 7 (November 2004), pp. 1765-1885. See also John J. Gibbons, "The Eleventh Amendment and State Sovereign Immunity: A Reinterpretation," *Columbia Law Review*, Vol. 83, No. 8 (December 1983), pp. 1889-2005.

[332] Ibid.

[333] *Cherokee Nation v. Georgia* U.S. 30 (5 Pet.) 1, 17 (1831).

[334] *Johnson v. McIntosh* 21 U.S. (8 Wheat.) 543, 573 (1823).

[335] *Cherokee Nation v. Georgia* U.S. 30 (5 Pet.) 1, 17 (1831).

[336] *Worcester v. Georgia* 31 U.S. (6 Pet.) 515, 559-60 (1832).

[337] *Johnson v. McIntosh* 21 U.S. (8 Wheat.) 543, 590 (1823). Emphasis added.

[338] *Johnson v. McIntosh* 21 U.S. (8 Wheat.) 543, 590 (1823). *Worcester v. Georgia* 31 U.S. (6 Pet.) 515, 549 (1832).

[339] *Johnson v. McIntosh* 21 U.S. (8 Wheat.) 543, 591 (1823).

[340] Ibid.

[341] *Johnson v. McIntosh* 21 U.S. (8 Wheat.) 543, 596-97 (1823).

[342] *Johnson v. McIntosh* 21 U.S. (8 Wheat.) 543, 604 (1823).

[343] "Argument of Mr. Sergeant," in Peters, *The Case of the Cherokee Nation*, p. 44.

[344] David E. Wilkins and K. Tsianina Lomawaima, *Uneven Ground: American Indian Sovereignty and Federal Law* (Norman: University of Oklahoma Press, 2001), p. 21.

[345] *Johnson v. McIntosh* 21 U.S. (8 Wheat) 543, 584-585 (1823).

[346] *Worcester v. Georgia* 31 U.S. (6 Pet.) 515, 543-44 (1832). Emphasis added.

[347] *Worcester v. Georgia* 31 U.S. (6 Pet.) 515, 549 (1832). Emphasis added.

[348] Ibid.

[349] *Cherokee Nation v. Georgia* U.S. 30 (5 Pet.) 1, 17 (1831).

[350] *Worcester v. Georgia* 31 U.S. (6 Pet.) 515, 580 (1832).

[351] *Cherokee Nation v. Georgia* U.S. 30 (5 Pet.) 1, 17 (1831).

[352] *Johnson v. McIntosh* 21 U.S. (8 Wheat) 543, 584-585 (1823).

[353] Quoted in Henry Storrs, 15 May 1830, United States House of Representatives, 21st Congress, 1st Session, *Register of Debates*, p. 1009.

[354] The Treaty with the Choctaw of 1786 specified boundaries and promised perpetual peace and friendship as did the Treaty with the Chickasaw of 1786. "Treaty with the Choctaw," Jan. 3, 1786. | 7 Stat., 21. "Treaty with the Chickasaw," Jan. 10, 1786. | 7 Stat. 24.

[355] *Johnson v. McIntosh* 21 U.S. (8 Wheat) 543, 584-585 (1823).

[356] The House Committee on Indian Affairs, "Removal of Indians," Report No. 227, 24 February 1830, p. 8, the House of Representatives, 21st Congress, 1st Session.

[357] The House Committee on Indian Affairs, "Removal of Indians," Report No. 227, 24 February 1830, pp. 4-5, the House of Representatives, 21st Congress, 1st Session.

[358] "Argument of Mr. Wirt," in Peters, *The Case of the Cherokee Nation*, p. 86.

[359] "Argument of Mr. Sergeant," in Peters, *The Case of the Cherokee Nation*, p. 50.

[360] The House Committee on Indian Affairs, "Removal of Indians," Report No. 227, 24 February 1830, p. 8, the House of Representatives, 21st Congress, 1st Session.

[361] *United States v. Kagama*, 118 U.S. 375, 381-382 (1886).

[362] *Johnson v. McIntosh* 21 U.S. (8 Wheat.) 543, 573 (1823).

[363] "Editorial Note" in Hobson, ed., *The Papers of John Marshall*, Vol. 12, p. 50.

[364] "Argument of Mr. Wirt," in Peters, *The Case of the Cherokee Nation*, p. 125. The actual wording of *Johnson* is that the Indians "were admitted to be the rightful occupants of the soil, with a legal as well as just claim to retain possession of it, and to use it according to their own discretion."

[365] "Argument of Mr. Wirt," in Peters, *The Case of the Cherokee Nation*, p. 128.

[366] Ibid, p. 141.

[367] Ibid, p. 144.

[368] Ibid, p. 148.

[369] Hobson, ed., *The Papers of John Marshall*, Volume 11, pp. 380-81.

[370] What appear to be notes from a message of William Wirt's of 22 September 1830 in the Ross Papers, indicate that "Wirt personally had strong doubts about the Cherokees being considered a foreign nation, but [Daniel] Webster communicated to him through Jeremiah Evarts that there was a chance this way." And similar notes from a message of Wirt's of 15 November 1830 indicated that John Sergeant also had doubts on this point. Only jurist James Kent's opinion on the subject led them to give an appeal to the Supreme Court's original jurisdiction a try. Gary E. Moulton, edited and with an introduction, *The Papers of Chief John Ross* (in two volumes) (Norman: University of Oklahoma Press, 1985), Vol. 1, pp. 199-200, 205.

[371] Article 2, Section 3 of the Constitution, http://www.archives.gov/exhibits/charters/constitution_transcript.html (accessed 24 September 2016).

[372] "Argument of Mr. Wirt," in Peters, *The Case of the Cherokee Nation*, p. 155.

[373] Ibid, pp. 156-157.

[374] John Marshall to Joseph Story, 12 October 1828, in Hobson, ed., *The Papers of John Marshall*, Vol. 12, p. 178.

[375] *Cherokee Nation v. Georgia* U.S. 30 (5 Pet.) 1, 21 (1831).

[376] *Cherokee Nation v. Georgia* U.S. 30 (5 Pet.) 1, 22 (1831).
[377] *Cherokee Nation v. Georgia* U.S. 30 (5 Pet.) 1, 25 (1831).
[378] *Cherokee Nation v. Georgia* U.S. 30 (5 Pet.) 1, 32 (1831).
[379] *Cherokee Nation v. Georgia* U.S. 30 (5 Pet.) 1, 44 (1831).
[380] Quoted in Garrison, *The Legal Ideology of Removal*, p. 149.
[381] Quoted in "Editorial Note" in Hobson, ed., *The Papers of John Marshall*, Vol. 12, p. 52.
[382] Quoted in Ibid.
[383] Ibid, p. 53.
[384] Quoted in Ibid, p. 53.
[385] *Cherokee Nation v. Georgia* U.S. 30 (5 Pet.) 1, 53 (1831). I am grateful to Konya Lafferty for introducing me to this dissent.
[386] *Cherokee Nation v. Georgia* U.S. 30 (5 Pet.) 1, 54 (1831).
[387] *Cherokee Nation v. Georgia* U.S. 30 (5 Pet.) 1, 55 (1831).
[388] Ibid.
[389] *Cherokee Nation v. Georgia* U.S. 30 (5 Pet.) 1, 60 (1831).
[390] *Cherokee Nation v. Georgia* U.S. 30 (5 Pet.) 1, 63 (1831).
[391] *Cherokee Nation v. Georgia* U.S. 30 (5 Pet.) 1, 64 (1831).
[392] *Cherokee Nation v. Georgia* U.S. 30 (5 Pet.) 1, 70 (1831).
[393] *Cherokee Nation v. Georgia* U.S. 30 (5 Pet.) 1, 74 (1831).
[394] *Cherokee Nation v. Georgia* U.S. 30 (5 Pet.) 1, 75 (1831).
[395] *Cherokee Nation v. Georgia* U.S. 30 (5 Pet.) 1, 80 (1831).
[396] *Cherokee Nation v. Georgia* U.S. 30 (5 Pet.) 1, 12-13 (1831).
[397] Quoted in Beveridge, *The Life of John Marshall*, Volume 3-4, p. 544.
[398] *Cherokee Nation v. Georgia* U.S. 30 (5 Pet.) 1, 17 (1831).
[399] Ibid.
[400] *Cherokee Nation v. Georgia* U.S. 30 (5 Pet.) 1, 18 (1831).
[401] See Katherine Hermes, "Law of Native Americans to 1815," in Michael Grossberg and Christopher Tomlins, *The Cambridge History of Law in America* (Cambridge: Cambridge University Press, 2008), pp. 32-62.
[402] *Cherokee Nation v. Georgia* U.S. 30 (5 Pet.) 1, 19 (1831).
[403] "Argument of Mr. Sergeant," in Peters, *The Case of the Cherokee Nation*, pp. 47-49.
[404] *Cherokee Nation v. Georgia* U.S. 30 (5 Pet.) 1, 19 (1831).
[405] "Argument of Mr. Sergeant," in Peters, *The Case of the Cherokee Nation*, pp. 56-57.
[406] d'Errico, *Federal Anti-Indian Law*, p. 54.
[407] James E. Pfander, "Rethinking the Supreme Court's Original Jurisdiction in State-Party Cases," *California Law Review*, May, 1994, Vol. 82, No. 3, Symposium: Void for Vagueness (May, 1994), p. 562.
[408] *Cohens v. Virginia*, 19 U.S. (6 Wheat.) 264, 380 (1821).
[409] Constitution of the United States, https://www.archives.gov/founding-docs/constitution-transcript.

[410] *Marbury v. Madison*, 5 U.S. (1 Cranch) 137, 173-74 (1803). By this reasoning, one of Marshall's assertions in *Marbury*—that the Congress does not have the right to establish that cases in which the Constitution indicated that at least appellate jurisdiction must exist are cases that could by federal law be placed under the original jurisdiction of the Supreme Court—is mistaken. To use Marshall's terms, it denies "operation" to the language, explicitly stated, that grants Congress the right to make "exceptions" in cases in which neither a state nor the United States is a party and in which ambassadors, or other public ministers and consuls, are not affected.

[411] Pfander, "Rethinking the Supreme Court's Original Jurisdiction in State-Party Cases," p. 558.

[412] Pfander, "Rethinking the Supreme Court's Original Jurisdiction in State-Party Cases," p. 619.

[413] "Remarks of James Wilson in the Pennsylvania Convention to Ratify the Constitution of the United States, 1787," in Hall and Hall, editors, *The Collected Works of James Wilson*, Vol. 1, p. 246.

[414] *Cohens v. Virginia*, 19 U.S. (6 Wheat.) 264, 378, 393-94 (1821).

[415] Pfander, "Rethinking the Supreme Court's Original Jurisdiction in State-Party Cases," p. 614.

[416] *Governor of Georgia v. Madrazo*, 26 U.S. (1 Pet.) 110, 124. (1828).

[417] d'Errico, *Federal Anti-Indian Law*, p. 56.

[418] "Treaty with the Cherokee," 28 November 1785. | 7 Stat., 18. "Treaty with the Cherokee," 2 July 1791. | 7 Stat., 39. | Proclamation, 7 February 1792.

[419] William Wirt, "Georgia and the Treaty of Indian Spring," 28 July 1828, in Robert Farnham, *Official Opinions of the Attorneys General of the United States* (Washington: 1852), Volume 2, pp. 132-33.

[420] "Treaty with the Cherokee," 2 July 1791. | 7 Stat., 39. | Proclamation, 7 February 1792, http://legisworks.org/sal/7/stats/STATUTE-7-Pg39.pdf (accessed 7 May 2019).

[421] *Cherokee Nation v. Georgia* U.S. 30 (5 Pet.) 1, 80 (1831).

[422] "Argument of Mr. Sergeant," in Peters, *The Case of the Cherokee Nation*, pp. 56-57.

[423] Joseph Story to Sarah Story, 4 March 1832, in William W. Story, ed., *Life and Letters of Joseph Story* (in two volumes) (London: John Chapman, 1851), Vol. 2, p. 87.

[424] Joseph Story, *Commentaries on the Constitution of the United States* (in three volumes) (Boston: Hilliard, Gray, and Company, 1833), Vol. 1 pp. 135-36.

[425] John Marshall, *Life of Washington* (in five volume) (Philadelphia: C. P. Wayne, 1805-07).

[426] Joseph C. Burke, "The Cherokee Cases: A Study in Law, Politics, and Morality," *Stanford Law Review*, Vol. 21, No. 3 (February 1969), pp. 507, 500-531.

[427] Quoted in Donald B. Cole, *The Presidency of Andrew Jackson* (Lawrence: University Press of Kansas, 1993), p. 141.

[428] Edwin A. Miles, "After John Marshall's Decision: Worcester v. Georgia and the Nullification Crisis," *The Journal of Southern History*, Vol. 39, No. 4 (November 1973), pp. 532, 519-544.

[429] Cole, *The Presidency of Andrew Jackson*, pp. 150-151.

[430] Quoted in Matthew L. Sundquist, "Worcester v. Georgia: A Breakdown in the Separation of Powers, *American Indian Law Review*, Vol. 35, No. 1 (2010-2011), pp. 246, 239-255.

[431] "Editorial Note" in Hobson, editor, *The Papers of John Marshall*, Vol. 12, p. 156.

[432] For a study of the tension between positive international law and natural law conceptions of international legal personality, and their influence on the creation of the modern state of Greece, see Steven Schwartzberg, "The Lion and the Phoenix: British Policy Toward the 'Greek Question,' 1821-1832," *Middle Eastern Studies*, Volume 24, Numbers 2 and 3 (April and July 1988), pp. 139-177, 287-311

[433] *Worcester v. Georgia* 31 U.S. (6 Pet.) 515, 561 (1832).

[434] *Cherokee Nation v. Georgia* U.S. 30 (5 Pet.) 1, 16 (1831).

[435] *Cherokee Nation v. Georgia* U.S. 30 (5 Pet.) 1, 19 (1831).

[436] James Wilson, "Of Man, as a Member of the Great Commonwealth of Nations," in Hall and Hall, editors, *The Collected Works of James Wilson*, Vol. 1, pp. 686-688.

[437] Quoted in Garrison, *The Legal Ideology of Removal*, p. 149.

[438] Elias Boudinot, *The Cherokee Phoenix*, 16 April 1831, quoted in Bethany Schneider, "Boudinot's Change: Boudinot, Emerson, and Ross on Cherokee Removal," *English Literary History*, Vol. 75, No. 1 (Spring 2008), pp. 151-177.

[439] Quoted in Jill Norgren, *The Cherokee Cases: The Confrontation of Law and Politics* (New York: McGraw-Hill, 1996), p. 110.

[440] *Worcester v. Georgia*, 31 U.S. 515, 561-62 (1832).

[441] *Cherokee Nation v. Georgia* U.S. 30 (5 Pet.) 1, 20 (1831).

[442] Quoted in Norgren, *The Cherokee Cases*, p. 122.

[443] Norgren, *The Cherokee Cases*, p. 123.

[444] *Cherokee Nation v. Georgia* U.S. 30 (5 Pet.) 1, 17 (1831).

[445] See Gerard N. Magliocca, "The Cherokee Removal and the Fourteenth Amendment," *Duke Law Journal*, Vol. 53, No. 3 (December 2003), pp. 875-965.

[446] Andrew, *From Revivals to Removal*, p. 262.

[447] Norgren, *The Cherokee Cases*, p. 124.

[448] Quoted in Langguth, *Driven West*, p. 197; Perdue and Green, *The Cherokee Nation and the Trail of Tears*, p. 98.

[449] Perdue and Green, *The Cherokee Nation and the Trail of Tears*, pp. 97-99.

[450] Quoted in Perdue and Green, *The Cherokee Nation and the Trail of Tears*, pp. 101-102.

[451] http://avalon.law.yale.edu/19th_century/ordnull.asp.

[452] https://www.loc.gov/rr/program/bib/ourdocs/Nullification.html.

[453] Miles, "After John Marshall's Decision," p. 534.

[454] Norgren, *The Cherokee Cases*, pp. 128, 130. Quoted in Miles, "After John Marshall's Decision," p. 541.

[455] Quoted in Burke, "The Cherokee Cases," p. 530.

[456] Langguth, *Driven West*, pp. 214-215.

[457] Quoted in Perdue and Green, *The Cherokee Nation and the Trail of Tears*, p. 104.

[458] Langguth, *Driven West*, pp. 214-234, quotation p. 234.

[459] Quoted in Langguth, *Driven West*, p. 239

[460] Langguth, *Driven West*, p. 239; Perdue and Green, *The Cherokee Nation and the Trail of Tears*, p. 113.

[461] Langguth, *Driven West*, pp. 268-69.

[462] Watson, *Buying America from the Indians*, pp. 330-31.

[463] Quoted in Perdue and Green, *The Cherokee Nation and the Trail of Tears*, p. 121.

[464] Quoted in Langguth, *Driven West*, p. 244.

[465] Langguth, *Driven West*, p. 255.

[466] Quoted in Langguth, *Driven West*, p. 280.

[467] Quoted in Perdue and Green, *The Cherokee Nation and the Trail of Tears*, pp. 123-124.

[468] Quoted in Langguth, *Driven West*, p. 281.

[469] Perdue and Green, *The Cherokee Nation and the Trail of Tears*, pp. 126-127.

[470] Saunt, *Unworthy Republic*, pp. 277-78.

[471] Russell, *Sequoyah Rising*, p. 12.

[472] Perdue and Green, *The Cherokee Nation and the Trail of Tears*, p. 139.

[473] Robertson, *Conquest by Law*, pp. 44 and passim.

[474] James Wilson, *An Account of the Proceedings of the Illinois and Ouabash Land Companies in Pursuance of their Land Purchases made of the Independent Natives, July 5th, 1773 and 18th, October, 1775* (Philadelphia: William Young, 1796), p. 33, https://digital.library.pitt.edu/islandora/object/pitt%3A31735054850270/viewer#page/1/mode/2up

[475] Professor Danielle Allen and doctoral candidate Emily Sneff have written: "No other American, in any context, in the years from 1776 to 1793—not in urban centers, nor in smaller towns—worked as consistently and assiduously as Wilson to place the Declaration of Independence at the heart of the new nation's self-understanding." Danielle Allen and Emily Sneff, "Golden Letters: James Wilson, the Declaration of Independence, and the Sussex Declaration," *The Georgetown Journal of Law and Public Policy*, Vol. 17, No. 1 (Winter 2019), pp. 193-230.

[476] Farrand, *Records of the Federal Convention of 1787*, Vol 2, p. 29-30.

[477] John M. Harlan, "James Wilson and the Formation of the Constitution," *American Law Review*, Vol. 34 (July-August 1900), p. 483.

[478] James Wilson, "Of Man, as a Member of the Great Commonwealth of Nations," in Hall and Hall, editors, *The Collected Works of James Wilson*, Vol. 1, pp. 674-675.

[479] Ibid.

[480] Ibid.

[481] James Wilson, "Chapter IV. Of the Law of Nations," in Hall and Hall, editors, *The Collected Works of James Wilson*, Vol. 1, p. 547.

[482] *Foster & Elam v. Neilson*, 27 U.S. 253, 306-307 (1829). Emphasis added.

[483] See James Wilson, *Chisholm v. Georgia* 2 U.S. (2 Dall.) 419, 462 (1793).

[484] https://www.archives.gov/founding-docs/declaration-transcript.

[485] James Wilson, 7 December 1787, "Proceedings and debates of the convention," Merrill Jensen, et al., eds, Ratification of the Constitution by the States: Pennsylvania (1976), pp. 517-18. http://digital.library.wisc.edu/1711.dl/History.DHRCv2 (accessed 27 November 2019).

[486] James Madison, 19 June 1788, *The Documentary History of the Ratification of the Constitution: Virginia*, Volume 10, p. 1409, http://digicoll.library.wisc.edu/cgi-bin/History/History-idx?type=turn&entity=History.DHRCv10.p0267&id=History.DHRCv10&isize=M (accessed 21 August 2020).

[487] An argument has been made that this constitutional mechanism should be reclaimed which does a persuasive job of criticizing the Supreme Court's decision in *Principality of Monaco v. Mississippi* 292 U.S. 313 (1934) but without recognizing the need to reverse *Cherokee Nation* and without any apparent awareness of Wilson's jurisprudence. See Thomas H. Lee, "The Supreme Court of the United States as Quasi-International Tribunal: Reclaiming the Court's Original and Exclusive Jurisdiction over Treaty-Based Suits by Foreign States against States," *Columbia Law Review*, Vol. 104, No. 7 (November 2004), pp. 1765-1885. Confronted with opposition to the Constitution on this score in the Virginia ratifying convention, James Madison waffled and seemed to claim—in spite of the clear text of the Constitution—that individuals could not sue states, an interpretation that Madison was joined in by John Marshall. There is even evidence that Madison altered the text of his notes of the constitutional convention in an effort to obscure the related issue of the convention's understanding of the Constitution's prohibition on ex post facto laws. See John Mikhail, "Early American Land Companies, and the Original Meaning of 'Ex Post Facto Law'" *The Georgetown Journal of Law and Public Policy*, Vol. 17, No. 1 (Winter 2019), pp. 79-146; especially p. 125 on state suability. For more on Madison and Marshall's position, see John J. Gibbons, "The Eleventh Amendment and State Sovereign Immunity: A Reinterpretation," *Columbia Law Review*, Vol. 83, No. 8 (December 1983), pp. 1905-09.

[488] 30 November 1787, "Proceedings and debates of the convention," Merrill Jensen, et al., eds, Ratification of the Constitution by the States: Pennsylvania (1976), p. 518. http://digital.library.wisc.edu/1711.dl/History.DHRCv2.

[489] *The Documentary History of the Ratification of the Constitution: Virginia*, Volume 10, p. 1639, http://digicoll.library.wisc.edu/cgi-bin/History/History-idx?type=goto&id=History.DHRCv10&isize=M&submit=Go+to+page&page=1639.

[490] Deloria, *God is Red*, pp. 47-48.

[491] James Wilson, "Considerations on the Nature and Extent of the Legislative Authority of the British Parliament," 1774, text in Hall and Hall, editors, *The Collected Works of James Wilson,* Vol. 1, p. 4.

[492] *Chisholm v. Georgia* 2 U.S. (2 Dall.) 419, 471 (1793).

[493] *Chisholm v. Georgia* 2 U.S. (2 Dall.) 419, 457 (1793).

[494] *Chisholm v. Georgia* 2 U.S. (2 Dall.) 419, 456 (1793).

[495] Randall E. Barnett, "The People or the State: Chisholm v. Georgia and Popular Sovereignty," *Virginia Law Review,* Vol. 93, No. 7 (November 2007), pp. 1729, 1758.

[496] John Mikhail, "The Necessary and Proper Clauses," *Georgetown Law Journal,* Vol. 102, No. 4 (April 2014), pp. 1045-1132.

[497] Quoted in Wilson, "Considerations on the Bank of North America," 1785, in Hall and Hall, eds., *The Collected Works of James Wilson,* Vol. 1, p. 67.

[498] The Declaration of Independence, https://www.archives.gov/founding-docs/declaration-transcript (accessed 14 November 2020).

[499] Farrand, ed., *The Records of the Federal Convention,* Vol. 1, pp. 166-67.

[500] "From George Washington to James Madison, 31 March 1787," *Founders Online,* National Archives, https://founders.archives.gov/documents/Washington/04-05-02-0111. [Original source: *The Papers of George Washington,* Confederation Series, vol. 5, *1 February 1787–31 December 1787,* ed. W. W. Abbot. Charlottesville: University Press of Virginia, 1997, pp. 114–117].

[501] "To George Washington from James Madison, 16 April 1787," *Founders Online,* National Archives, https://founders.archives.gov/documents/Washington/04-05-02-0139. [Original source: *The Papers of George Washington,* Confederation Series, vol. 5, *1 February 1787–31 December 1787,* ed. W. W. Abbot. Charlottesville: University Press of Virginia, 1997, pp. 144–150].

[502] "Notes of the Secret Debates of the Federal Convention of 1787, Taken by the Late Hon Robert Yates, Chief Justice of the State of New York, and One of the Delegates from That State to the Said Convention," https://avalon.law.yale.edu/18th_century/yates.asp, accessed 14 April 2020). Emphasis added.

[503] Quoted in Mikhail, "The Necessary and Proper Clauses," p. 1073.

[504] John Mikhail, "The Constitution and the Philosophy of Language: Entailment, Implicature, and Implied Powers," *Virginia Law Review,* Vol. 101, No. 4 (June 2014), p. 1098.

[505] Ibid, pp. 1098-1100.

[506] Farrand, *Records of the Federal Convention of 1787,* Vol 2, pp. 28-29.

[507] James E. Pfander, "Rethinking the Supreme Court's Original Jurisdiction in State-Party Cases," *California Law Review,* May, 1994, Vol. 82, No. 3, Symposium: Void for Vagueness (May, 1994), p. 590n145.

[508] Pfander, "Rethinking the Supreme Court's Original Jurisdiction in State-Party Cases," pp. 593-94.

[509] Pfander, "Rethinking the Supreme Court's Original Jurisdiction in State-Party Cases," p. 618.

[510] Farrand, *Records of the Federal Convention of 1787*, Vol 2, p. 389.

[511] Ibid, p. 390.

[512] Ibid, p. 431.

[513] See the sources and quotes referred to in Pfander, "Rethinking the Supreme Court's Original Jurisdiction in State-Party Cases," p. 645n376.

[514] *Chisholm v. Georgia* 2 U.S. (2 Dall.) 419, 457 (1793).

[515] This was a problem that Wilson had thought had a "plain and easy" answer: "But say the gentlemen, the sovereignty of the states is destroyed, if they should be engaged in a controversy with the United States, because a suitor in court must acknowledge the jurisdiction of that court, and it is not the custom of sovereigns to suffer their names to be made use of in this manner. The answer is plain and easy. The government of each state ought to be subordinate to the government of the United States." James Wilson, 7 December 1787, "Proceedings and debates of the convention," Merrill Jensen, et al., eds, Ratification of the Constitution by the States: Pennsylvania (1976), p. 518. http://digital.library.wisc.edu/1711.dl/History.DHRCv2 (accessed 27 November 2019). See also, Phillips, *Georgia and State Rights*, pp. 24-28.

[516] John J. Gibbons, "The Eleventh Amendment and State Sovereign Immunity: A Reinterpretation," *Columbia Law Review*, Vol. 83, No. 8 (December 1983), p. 1894.

[517] Mark David Hall, "Biographical Essay: History of James Wilson's Law Lectures," in Hall and Hall, editors, *The Collected Works of James Wilson*, Vol. 1, p. 403.

[518] James Wilson, "Introductory Lecture. Of the Study of the Law in the United States," in Hall and Hall, editors, *The Collected Works of James Wilson*, Vol. 1, pp. 431-432.

[519] Ibid, pp. 440-441.

[520] Ibid, 452.

[521] James Wilson, "Plan," in Hall and Hall, editors, *The Collected Works of James Wilson*, Vol. 1, p. 456.

[522] James Wilson, "Chapter II. Of the General Principles of Law and Obligation," in Hall and Hall, editors, *The Collected Works of James Wilson*, Vol. 1, pp. 494-496.

[523] James Wilson, "Chapter III. Of the Law of Nature," in Hall and Hall, editors, *The Collected Works of James Wilson*, Vol. 1, p. 500.

[524] Ibid, pp. 505-506.

[525] Ibid, p. 507.

[526] Ibid, p. 509.

[527] Ibid, p. 515.

[528] Ibid, p. 517.

[529] Ibid, p. 518.

[530] Ibid, p. 523.

[531] James Wilson, "Chapter IV. Of the Law of Nations," in Hall and Hall, editors, *The Collected Works of James Wilson*, Vol. 1, pp. 539-545.

[532] Ibid, pp. 541-542.

[533] See Edward Shils, *The Virtue of Civility: Selected Essays on Liberalism, Tradition, and Civil Society* (Indianapolis: Liberty Fund, 1997). "I am probably the only social scientist (!) who asserts that there is a concern for the common good simultaneously experienced in many individuals, in some, even many politicians, and in many ordinary persons, local civic leaders, etc. I do not argue that the collective self-consciousness of the society predominates in all their actions or that it has a high position of precedence in the outlook and conduct of the large majority. I argue that it exists to some extent in most large societies and not least in the United States, even at present when my belief that this is so among my own fellow-countrymen is put under tense strain. Most social scientists attribute all action to self-enhancement, self-protection, the exploration and deception of others—'strategies' is the common and revealing word. Yet, I insist that this is not the case, and I am staking the final vindications of my intellectual history or rather assessment of my life-long wrestling and skirmishing with the world on behalf of the truth about itself." Edward Shils, *A Fragment of a Sociological Autobiography* ed. Steven Grosby (New Brunswick: Transaction Publishers, 2006), p. 148.

[534] James Wilson, "Chapter IV. Of the Law of Nations," in Hall and Hall, editors, *The Collected Works of James Wilson*, Vol. 1, p. 543.

[535] James Wilson, "Chapter IV. Of the Law of Nations," in Hall and Hall, editors, *The Collected Works of James Wilson*, Vol. 1, p. 544.

[536] William Ewald, "James Wilson and the American Founding," *The Georgetown Journal of Law and Public Policy*, Vol. 17, No. 1 (Winter 2019), p. 17.

[537] The only exception Wilson admitted to the American people's joint tenancy in the sovereignty were "African slaves" who might be considered as subjects. *Chisholm v. Georgia* 2 U.S. (2 Dall.) 419, 471 (1793). Wilson appears to have thought that the Constitution's implicit grant of authority to the Congress to end the importation of slaves in 1808 (Article 1, Section 9, Clause 1) would bring slavery in the United States to a gradual end. Sean Wilentz, *No Property in Man: Slavery and Antislavery at the Nation's Founding* (Cambridge: Harvard University Press, 2018), pp. 132-133.

[538] On 22 August 1787, Edmund Randolph of Virginia addressed the convention on what he saw as a dilemma between agreeing to the importation of slaves which "would revolt the Quakers, the Methodists, and many others in the States having no slaves. On the other hand, two States might be lost to the Union." On 25 August 1787, Hugh Williamson of North Carolina offered a related calculus: "both in opinion & practice he was, against slavery; but thought it more in favor of humanity, from a view of all circumstances, to let in S— C— & Georgia on those terms, than to exclude them from the Union." Farrand, ed., *The Records of the Federal Convention of 1787*, Vol. 2, pp. 374, 415-416.

[539] James Wilson, "Of the Natural Rights of Individuals," in Hall and Hall, editors, *The Collected Works of James* Wilson, Vol. 2, p. 1077.

[540] Ibid.

[541] James Wilson, "Chapter IV. Of the Law of Nations," in Hall and Hall, editors, *The Collected Works of James Wilson*, Vol. 1, p. 545.

[542] George Washington, "Talk to the Cherokee Nation," 29 August 1796, http://millercenter.org/scripps/archive/speeches/detail/3941.

[543] Ibid.

[544] Quoted in J. H. Elliott, *Empires of the Atlantic World: Britain and Spain in America, 1492-1830* (New Haven: Yale University Press, 2006), p. 11.

[545] Ostler, *Surviving Genocide*, p. 2.

[546] Ostler, *Surviving Genocide*, p. 97.

[547] Ostler, *Surviving Genocide*, p. 122.

[548] McLoughlin, *Cherokee Renascence*, p. 171.

[549] McLoughlin, *Cherokee Renascence*, p. 295.

[550] Theda Perdue and Michael D. Green, *The Cherokee Removal: A Brief History with Documents* second edition (Boston: Bedford/St. Martin's, 2005), p. 50.

[551] Langguth, *Driven West*, p. 71; McLoughlin, *Cherokee Renascence*, p. 278; Congressman Edward Everett of Massachusetts, 19 May 1830, United States House of Representatives, 21st Congress, 1st Session, *Register of Debates*, p. 1071.

[552] Quoted in Langguth, *Driven West*, p. 166.

[553] Quoted in McLoughlin, *Cherokee Renascence*, p. 288.

[554] Russell, *Sequoyah Rising*, pp. 48, 148,

[555] 15 April 1830, United States Senate, 21st Congress, 1st Session, *Register of Debates*, p. 333.

[556] *Johnson v. McIntosh* 21 U.S. (8 Wheat.) 543, 574-77, 587 (1823).

[557] *Cherokee Nation v. Georgia* U.S. 30 (5 Pet.) 1, 15 (1831).

[558] *Lyng v. Northwest Indian Cemetery Protective Association*, 485 U.S. 439, 440 (1988).

[559] *Oneida County v. Oneida Indian Nation*, 470 U.S. 226 (1985). *City of Sherrill v. Oneida Indian Nation*, 544 U.S. 197 (2005).

[560] *Tee-Hit-Ton Indians v. United States*, 348 U.S. 272, 279-280 (1955).

[561] https://www.nps.gov/articles/000/dawes-act.htm (accessed 19 March 2021). Donald L. Fixico, "Documenting Indigenous dispossession," *Science*, Vol. 374, Issue 6567 (28 October 2021), pp. 536-537.

[562] Richard Henry Pratt, founder of the Carlisle Indian Industrial School, quoted in d'Errico, *Federal Anti-Indian Law*, p. 28.

[563] *McGirt v. Oklahoma*, 2020, https://www.supremecourt.gov/opinions/19pdf/18-9526_9okb.pdf.

[564] Treaty with the Apache, 1 July 1852, https://avalon.law.yale.edu/19th_century/apa1852.asp (accessed 25 June 2021). This treaty contains the phrase that the Apache people were "under the laws, jurisdiction, and government of the United States of America," as if intending that the law of conquest would apply, while actually depending on the Apache to govern themselves and relying upon a treaty to effect that

object. Even through the filter of the dishonesty of the American side, one can see an obligation on the United States, if it were to pass any law affecting the Apache, to do so only if it was "conducive to the prosperity and happiness of said Indians," and promising, "this treaty is to receive a liberal construction, at all times and in all places, to the end that the said Apache Indians shall not be held responsible for the conduct of others, and that the government of the United States shall so legislate and act as to secure the permanent prosperity and happiness of said Indians." Herb Yazzie, "Renounce Racist Christian Discovery Doctrine," *Navajo Times,* 24 May 2021, https://navajotimes.com/opinion/columns/guest-column-renounce-racist-christian-discovery-doctrine/ (accessed 29 June 2021). https://en.wikipedia.org/wiki/Oak_Flat_(Arizona).

[565] For an extensive and incisive critique of modern civilization grounded in the ideas of psychospiritual development conveyed in the Hindu classic, *The Mahabharata,* as well as in contemporary science, see Richard Sclove, *Escaping Maya's Palace: Decoding an Ancient Myth to Heal the Hidden Madness of Modern Civilization* (Boston: Karavelle Press, 2022).

[566] The Fort Laramie Treaty of 1868, https://avalon.law.yale.edu/19th_century/nt001.asp (accessed 7 July 2021). See also, Native Knowledge 360, "Treaties Still Matter: The Dakota Access Pipeline," https://americanindian.si.edu/nk360/plains-treaties/dapl.

[567] See Jeniffer Solis, "Will Thacker Pass be another Keystone?," 16 September 2021, *Nevada Current,* https://www.nevadacurrent.com/2021/09/16/will-thacker-pass-be-another-keystone/.

[568] For background and links to the texts of some of the relevant treaties, see: https://www.mprnews.org/story/2016/02/01/explaining-minnesota-ojibwe-treaties (accessed 9 August 2021). See also https://mncourts.libguides.com/c.php?g=509384&p=3483460.

[569] Peter d'Errico, et al., "Honoring Indian Law and Treaties, Part One" - December 2021, https://www.researchgate.net/publication/357403720_Honoring_Indian_Law_and_Treaties_Part_One_-_Indigenous_Perspectives_podcast (accessed 9 January 2022). See also the White Earth Band of Ojibwe in Tribal Court, Civil Case No. GC 21-0428, Plaintiffs' Response to Motion to Dismiss, https://whiteearth.com/assets/files/programs/judicial/cases/Manoomin v DNR Plaintiff's Response to Motion to Dismiss 8-15-21.pdf.

[570] See Tink Tinker, panel discussion of 14 April 2021 on the volume, Miguel A. De La Torre, et al., editors, *The Colonial Compromise: The Threat of the Gospel to the Indigenous World View* (Fortress Academic Press, 2020), https://www.youtube.com/watch?v=LAzjr_IMRxc.

[571] White Earth Band of Ojibwe Court of Appeals, Opinion of the Court, Manoomin v. DNR, Case No. AP21-0516, 10 March 2022, p. 17, https://turtletalk.blog/2022/03/21/white-earth-ojibwe-appellate-court-dismissed-manoomin-suit-against-minnesota-dnr/.

[572] Supplemental brief, Case No. AP21-0516, 6 April 2022, https://turtletalk.files.wordpress.com/2022/04/white-earth-manoomin-supplemental-brief-4-6-2022.pdf.

[573] Freeland, *Aazheyaadizi,* p. 61.

[574] Peters, *The Case of the Cherokee Nation*. Joseph Story quoted in Burke, "The Cherokee Cases," p. 518.

[575] John Marshall to Edward Everett, 5 June 1830, *The Papers of John Marshall*, Vol. 11, pp. 378-379.

[576] Bartolomé de Las Casas, *In Defense of the Indians* (tr. Stafford Poole, C.M.) (DeKalb: Northern Illinois University Press, 1992), p. 355.

[577] Las Casas, *In Defense of the Indians*, pp. 82-83.

[578] Elliott, *Empires of the Atlantic World*, p. 64.

[579] Jill Lepore, *These Truths: A History of the United States* (New York: W. W. Norton, 2018), p. 28.

[580] "He argued that slavery was contrary to natural law, for it deprived people of individual liberty which was a right conceived by God as an essential attribute of human beings, and since that was the natural state of man, then slavery had to be an aberration." Daniel Castro, *Another Face of Empire* (Durham: Duke University Press, 2007), p. 37. Before becoming an opponent of slavery, Las Casas came to rue having once suggested that African slaves could ease the burden being imposed on the Indians in the New World. Rolena Adorno, *The Polemics of Possession in Spanish American Narrative* (New Haven: Yale University Press, 2007), p. 67.

[581] Quoted in Adorno, *The Polemics of Possession in Spanish American Narrative*, p. 87.

[582] George Handley, letter of 19 February 1788, quoted in Merrill Jensen, ed., Ratification of the Constitution by the states: Delaware, New Jersey, Georgia, Connecticut (1978), p. 288, http://digicoll.library.wisc.edu/cgi-bin/History/History-idx?type=turn&entity=History.DHRCv3.p0292&id=History.DHRCv3&isize=M&q1=Indian.

[583] 3 August 1787, *Journals of the Continental Congress*, Volume 33, p. 462.

[584] 13 July 1787, *Journals of the Continental Congress*, Volume 33, pp. 340-341.

[585] Gregory Ablavsky, "The Savage Constitution," *Duke Law Journal*, Vol. 63, No. 5 (February 2014), p. 1032.

[586] 3 August 1787, *Journals of the Continental Congress*, Volume 33, p. 457.

[587] Ibid, pp. 457-459. Emphasis added.

[588] Articles of Confederation, 1 March 1781, http://avalon.law.yale.edu/18th_century/artconf.asp#art9.

[589] The Constitution of the United States.

[590] Merrill Jensen, ed., Ratification of the Constitution by the States: Delaware, New Jersey, Georgia, Connecticut (1978), p. 289, http://digicoll.library.wisc.edu/cgi-bin/History/History-idx?type=turn&entity=History.DHRCv3.p0292&id=History.DHRCv3&isize=M&q1=Indian.

[591] https://avalon.law.yale.edu/18th_century/cre1790.asp.

[592] Phillips, *Georgia and State Rights*, p. 48.

[593] This episode is examined at greater length later in this chapter.

[594] The closest anyone in the debate in Congress came to Marshall's concept of "domestic dependent nations" was Edward Everett who quoted an 1814 letter from John Quincy

Adams, James Bayard, Henry Clay, and Albert Gallatin, the American envoys then negotiating peace with Great Britain at Ghent. This letter represented perhaps the first official effort to repudiate the legal position of the Constitution's framers. In this letter, the envoys sought to respond to British charges that the United States was now, for the first time, adopting a stance toward the Native peoples that broke with America's own precedents: "If the United States had now asserted that the Indians within their boundaries, who have acknowledged the United States as their only protectors, were their subjects, living only at their sufferance on their lands, far from being the first in making that assertion, they would only have followed the example of the principles uniformly and invariably asserted in substance, and frequently avowed in express terms by the British Government itself... From the rigor of this system, however, as practised by Great Britain and all the other European powers in America, the humane and liberal policy of the United States has voluntarily relaxed. A celebrated writer on the law of nations, to whose authority British jurists have taken particular satisfaction in appealing, after stating, in the most explicit manner, the legitimacy of colonial settlements in America, to the exclusion of all rights of uncivilized Indian tribes, has taken occasion to praise the first settlers of New England and the founder of Pennsylvania, in having purchased of the Indians the lands they resolved to cultivate, notwithstanding their being furnished with a charter from their sovereign. It is this example which the United States, since they became, by their independence, the sovereigns of the territory, have adopted and organized into a political system. Under that system, the Indians residing within the United States are so far independent that they live under their own customs, and not under the laws of the United States; that their rights upon the lands where they inhabit or hunt are secured to them by boundaries defined in amicable treaties between the United States and themselves; and that, whenever these boundaries are varied, it is also by amicable and voluntary treaties, by which they receive from the United States ample compensation for every right they have to the lands ceded by them." Quoted by Congressman Edward Everett of Massachusetts, 19 May 1830, United States House of Representatives, 21st Congress, 1st Session, *Register of Debates*, p. 1059.

595 Quoted in George Chalmers, *Opinions of Eminent Lawyers, On Various Points of English Jurisprudence, Chiefly Concerning the Colonies, Fisheries, and Commerce of Great Britain* (London: Reed and Hunter, 1814), p. 195.

596 "Significantly, Wilson and Tench Coxe were given 300 shares of the Indiana Company shortly after *Plain Facts* appeared, suggesting that one or both of them may have had a hand in composing it. Wilson also apparently helped arrange for the Illinois-Wabash Company to purchase and distribute 200 copies of the pamphlet in the summer of 1781.... If one reads Wilson's *Chisholm* opinion alongside *Plain Facts*, for example, it becomes apparent that they share a common perspective on vindicating natural rights against the unscrupulous actions of dishonest states. Conversely, knowledgeable insiders such as Madison, Randolph, Lewis, and Rawle probably perceived Wilson's opinion to be at least indirectly related to his stake in the land companies' claims." John

Mikhail, "Early American Land Companies, and the Original Meaning of 'Ex Post Facto Law'" *The Georgetown Journal of Law and Public Policy*, Vol. 17, No. 1 (Winter 2019), pp. 117-118, 127.

[597] "The opinion of the Attorney and Solicitor General, Pratt and Yorke, have been adduced to prove that in the opinion of those great law officers, the Indian grant could convey a title to the soil without a patent emanating from the Crown. The opinion of those persons would certainly be of great authority on such a question, and we were not a little surprised when it was read, at the doctrine it seemed to advance. An opinion so contrary to the whole practice of the Crown and to the uniform opinions given on all other occasions by its great law officers ought to be very explicit and accompanied by the circumstances under which it was given, and to which it was applied before we can be assured that it is properly understood. In a pamphlet written for the purpose of asserting the Indian title, styled "*Plain Facts*," the same opinion is quoted, and is said to relate to purchases made in the East Indies. It is, of course, entirely inapplicable to purchases made in America. Chalmers, in whose collection this opinion is found, does not say to whom it applies, but there is reason to believe that the author of 'Plain Facts' is, in this respect, correct." *Johnson v. McIntosh* 21 U.S. (8 Wheat.) 543, 599 (1823).

[598] *Johnson v. McIntosh* 21 U.S. (8 Wheat.) 543, 591-92 (1823).

[599] Samuel Wharton, *Plain Facts: Being an Examination Into the Rights of the Indian Nations of America, to their respective Countries* (Philadelphia: R. Aitken, 1781), pp. 4-6. "Avid ravishers of other's riches. They leave their country to inundate ours." —Racine.

[600] *Cherokee Nation v. Georgia* U.S. 30 (5 Pet.) 1, 20 (1831).

[601] "Treaty with the Cherokee," 28 November 1785. | 7 Stat., 18. "Treaty with the Cherokee," 2 July 1791. | 7 Stat., 39. | Proclamation, 7 February 1792.

[602] *Cherokee Nation v. Georgia* U.S. 30 (5 Pet.) 1, 17 (1831).

[603] *Cherokee Nation v. Georgia* U.S. 30 (5 Pet.) 1, 20 (1831).

[604] Ibid.

[605] Ibid.

[606] Michael D. Green, *The Politics of Indian Removal: Creek Government and Society in Crisis* (Lincoln: University of Nebraska Press, 1985), p. 125.

[607] Green, *The Politics of Indian Removal*, p. 130.

[608] Quoted in Green, *The Politics of Indian Removal*, p. 133.

[609] John Quincy Adams to the Congress, 5 February 1827, text in James Daniel Richardson, ed., *A Compilation of the Messages and Papers of the Presidents, 1789-1897* (in ten volumes) (Washington: Government Printing Office, 1896), Vol. 2, p. 373. There is an online version: http://babel.hathitrust.org/cgi/pt?id=pst.000015229304;_view=1up;seq=399.

[610] Green, *The Politics of Indian Removal*, p. 133.

[611] Green, *The Politics of Indian Removal*, pp. 138-139.

[612] "Constitution of the Cherokee Nation," 26 July 1827, text in Theda Perdue and Michael D. Green, *The Cherokee Removal: A Brief History with Documents* (second edition) (Boston: Bedford/St. Martin's, 2005), p. 60.

[613] Ibid.

[614] Quoted in Perdue and Green, *The Cherokee Removal*, p. 75.

[615] Perdue and Green, *The Cherokee Nation and the Trail of Tears*, p. 55. For the text of the Articles of Agreement and Cession, 24 April 1802 (Feb. 11, 2017), http://amindians.tripod.com/18022.htm.

[616] Senator John Forsyth of Georgia, 15 April 1830, United States Senate, 21st Congress, 1st Session, *Register of Debates*, p. 330.

[617] Tim Alan Garrison, *The Legal Ideology of Removal* (Athens: University of Georgia Press, 2002), p. 14.

[618] American State Papers, House of Representatives, 17th Congress, 1st Session, Indian Affairs: Volume 2, p. 260, No. 177. "Extinguishment of the Indian Title to Land in Georgia." I am grateful to Peter d'Errico for a copy of this document.

[619] William G. McLoughlin, *Cherokee Renascence in the New Republic* (Princeton: Princeton University Press, 1986), pp. 303-305.

[620] Perdue and Green, *The Cherokee Nation and the Trail of Tears*, p. 56.

[621] McLoughlin, *Cherokee Renascence*, pp. 307-308.

[622] McLoughlin, *Cherokee Renascence*, pp. 408-409.

[623] John Quincy Adams, Fourth Annual Message to Congress, 2 December 1828, text available at http://millercenter.org/president/jqadams/speeches/speech-3517.

[624] Quoted in Langguth, *Driven West*, p. 239

[625] Quoted in Saunt, *Unworthy Republic*, p. xix.

[626] Andrew Jackson, first annual message to Congress, 8 December 1829, http://millercenter.org/scripps/archive/speeches/detail/3632 (accessed 4 March 2011).

[627] Donald B. Cole, *The Presidency of Andrew Jackson* (Lawrence: University Press of Kansas, 1993), p. 291n51.

[628] "An attempt is making in the Eastern States to create a great deal of sympathy for this people; and the attempt is making, so far as I can discover, by what is termed the 'Christian party in politics.'" Senator John Forsyth of Georgia, 15 April 1830, United States Senate, 21st Congress, 1st Session, *Register of Debates*, p. 32.

[629] 19 May 1830, United States House of Representatives, 21st Congress, 1st Session, *Register of Debates*, p. 1080.

[630] David Brion Davis, *Inhuman Bondage: The Rise and Fall of Slavery in the New World* (Oxford: Oxford University Press, 2006), p. 76.

[631] Quoted in Silva, *Toward a Global Idea of Race*, p. 101 [italics added by Silva].

[632] John Forsyth, 15 April 1830, United States Senate, 21st Congress, 1st Session, *Register of Debates*, p. 333. Andrew Jackson, first annual message to Congress, 8 December 1829, http://millercenter.org/scripps/archive/speeches/detail/3632 (accessed 4 March 2011).

[633] For just such a "we're all guilty of original sin" account—one that mistakenly asserts that "A decided majority of white Americans supported the policy championed by 'the People's President'"—and that tries to blame "democracy" for the genocide rather than a corrupt "states' rights"-based political elite and their appeasers—see Robert Tracy

McKenzie, *We the Fallen People: The Founders and the Future of American Democracy* (Downers Grove: InterVarsity Press, 2021), p. 259.

[634] 15 May 1830, United States House of Representatives, 21st Congress, 1st Session, *Register of Debates*, p. 1006.

[635] See Steven T. Newcomb, *Pagans in the Promised Land*, passim.

[636] Michael D. Green, *The Politics of Indian Removal: Creek Government and Society in Crisis* (Lincoln: University of Nebraska Press, 1985), p. 133.

[637] Quoted in Andrew, *From Revivals to Removal*, p. 143.

[638] Quoted in Langguth, *Driven West*, p. 179.

[639] On "legal positivism," with its notion that law is the command of a sovereign backed by force, see the entry in the Stanford Encyclopedia of Philosophy: https://plato.stanford.edu/entries/legal-positivism/ (accessed 4 December 2019).

[640] Jennifer Pitts, "Empire and Legal Universalisms in the Eighteenth Century," *The American Historical Review*, Vol. 117, No. 1 (February 2012), p. 95.

[641] Ibid, p. 110.

[642] Quoted in William Dalrymple, *The Anarchy: The East India Company, Corporate Violence, and the Pillage of an Empire* (New York: Bloomsbury Publishing, 2019), p. 309.

[643] 18 May 1830, United States House of Representatives, 21st Congress, 1st Session, *Register of Debates*, p. 1049.

[644] See Kent McNeil, *Common Law Aboriginal Title* (Oxford: Clarendon Press, 1989), pp. 84-85, 229, 246.

[645] *Johnson v. McIntosh* 21 U.S. (8 Wheat.) 543, 574-77 (1823). John Catanzariti, et al., editors, *The Papers of Thomas Jefferson*, Vol. 25, p. 272.

[646] See Gregory Ablavsky, "Beyond the Indian Commerce Clause," *Yale Law Journal*, Vol. 124, Issue 4 (2015): 1012-1091.

[647] David Brion Davis, *The Problem of Slavery in the Age of Revolution, 1770-1823* (Oxford: Oxford University Press, 1999), p. 16.

[648] Mary Hershberger, "Mobilizing Women, Anticipating Abolition: The Struggle against Indian Removal in the 1830s," *Journal of American History*, Vol 86, No. 1 (June 1999), pp. 15-40.

[649] Quoted in Mary Hershberger, "Mobilizing Women, Anticipating Abolition," p. 39.

[650] Quoted in Hershberger, "Mobilizing Women, Anticipating Abolition," p. 26.

[651] Quoted in Hershberger, "Mobilizing Women, Anticipating Abolition," pp. 26-27.

[652] Alisse Portnoy, *Their Right to Speak: Women's Activism in the Indian and Slave Debates* (Cambridge: Harvard University Press, 2005), p. 3.

[653] Quoted in Tiya Miles, "'Circular Reasoning': Recentering Cherokee Women in the Antiremoval Campaigns," *American Quarterly*, Vol. 61, No. 2 (June 2009), p. 221.

[654] Miles, "'Circular Reasoning,'" pp. 222, 229.

[655] Elizabeth A. Reese, "The Other American Law," *Stanford Law Review*, Vol. 73 (March 2021), p. 636.

[656] *United States v. Wheeler* 435 U.S. 313, 323 (1978).

[657] *McGirt v. Oklahoma,* 2020, https://www.supremecourt.gov/opinions/19pdf/18-9526_9okb.pdf.

[658] Henfield's Case, Whart.St.Tr. 49 (1793).

[659] John Trudell, "What it Means to be a Human Being," 15 March 2001, The Women's Building, San Francisco, radio TUC (Time of Useful Consciousness) (two parts): http://www.radio4all.net/files/tuc@tucradio.org/44-2-JohnTrudellONE_2014.mp3. http://www.radio4all.net/files/tuc@tucradio.org/44-2-JohnTrudellTWO_2014.mp3 There is a transcript: https://ratical.org/many_worlds/JohnTrudell/HumanBeing.html#s2.

[660] Ibid.

[661] John Trudell, quoted in "Native Lives Matter," https://www.facebook.com/nativelivesmatter1/posts/john-trudell-when-columbus-got-off-the-boatwhen-columbus-got-off-the-boat-he-ask/1683044438397154/.

[662] Quoted in Lewis Hanke, *All Mankind is One* [1959] (DeKalb: Northern Illinois University Press, 1974), p. 84.

[663] Quoted in Lawrence A. Clayton, *Bartolomé de las Casas and the Conquest of the Americas* (Malden, MA: John Wiley and Sons, 2011), p. 134.

[664] Juan Ginés Sepúlveda, twelve point response to Bartolomé de las Casas, text in Kris Lane, ed., *Defending the Conquest: Bernardo de Vargas Machuca's Defense and Discourse of the Western Conquests* (tr. Timothy F. Johnson) (University Park, PA: Pennsylvania State University Press, 2010), p. 51.

[665] In addition to Trudell's work, see Deloria, *God is Red,* especially pp. 295-296.

[666] John Trudell, quoted in https://www.native-americans-online.com/native-american-warriors.html (accessed 23 October 2022)

[667] Roberta Carol Harvey, *The Earth is Red: The Imperialism of the Doctrine of Discovery* (Santa Fe: Sunstone Press, 2021), p. 6.

[668] Jennings, *The Christian Imagination,* pp. 24 and passim.

[669] Calvin Luther Martin, *The Way of the Human Being* (New Haven: Yale University Press, 1999). Harold Napoleon, *Yuuyaraq: The Way of the Human Being* (Anchorage, AK: The Native Village of Paimiut, 1996).

[670] See Noam Chomsky and Robert Pollin, *Climate Crisis and the Global Green New Deal* (New York: Verso, 2020).

[671] The ideas in this paragraph are drawn from two video interviews with John Trudell, https://www.youtube.com/watch?v=180vRsMmqNI&fbclid=IwAR0fYIFwtyahqy3F2Qyx9JyLl3nIXfELxmblojzNnbp8LTnX6siiCsuwIyI, and https://www.youtube.com/watch?fbclid=IwAR0jTFPGPeFnVbTAj4ICw77NFHu5SAb1QlcN_vkcTVlflqAcipz8C9XTqT4&v=5yuUQzN-G2w&feature=youtu.be.

[672] Some of my formulations here are drawn from observations by Kyle Powys Whyte as quoted in Emilee Gilpin, 15 February 2019, "Urgency in Climate Change Advocacy is Backfiring says Citizen Potawatomi Scientist," *Canada's National Observer,* https://www.nationalobserver.com/2019/02/15/features/urgency-climate-change-advocacy-backfiring-says-citizen-potawatomi-nation.

---

[673] For an example of relatively successful American "leadership," see Steven Schwartzberg, "The 'Soft Peace Boys': Presurrender Planning and Japanese Land Reform," *The Journal of American-East Asian Relations*, Vol. 2, No. 2 (Summer 1993), pp. 185-216. See also Steven Schwartzberg, *Democracy and U.S. Policy in Latin America during the Truman Years* (Gainesville: University Press of Florida, 2003).

[674] I was first introduced to this concept of "domination free zones" by Steve Newcomb.

[675] See Russell, *Sequoyah Rising* and Steve Russell, *American Indians Dream: A Movement of Our* Own (n.c.: n.p., 2014).

[676] I first began to think seriously about this idea after reading: Melissa K. Nelson, "Time to Indigenize Lands and Water Conservation," 22 December 2020, *Sierra: the National Magazine of the Sierra Club*, https://www.sierraclub.org/sierra/2021-1-january-february/feature/time-indigenize-lands-and-water-conservation.

[677] Akwesasne Notes, ed. *Basic Call to Consciousness* [1978] (Summertown, TN: Book Publishing Company, 2005), pp. 90-91. d'Errico, *Federal Anti-Indian Law*, p. 166.

[678] Quoted in Emilee Gilpin, 15 February 2019, "Urgency in Climate Change Advocacy is Backfiring says Citizen Potawatomi Scientist," *Canada's National Observer*, https://www.nationalobserver.com/2019/02/15/features/urgency-climate-change-advocacy-backfiring-says-citizen-potawatomi-nation.

[679] Mark D. Freeland, *Aazheyaadizi: Worldview, Language, and the Logics of Decolonization* (East Lansing: Michigan State University Press, 2021), p. 126.

[680] Ibid.

[681] Deloria, *God is Red*, p. 75.

[682] Melissa K. Nelson, "Time to Indigenize Lands and Water Conservation," 22 December 2020, *Sierra: the National Magazine of the Sierra Club*, https://www.sierraclub.org/sierra/2021-1-january-february/feature/time-indigenize-lands-and-water-conservation.

[683] On the counterproductive consequences of some American efforts at coercive democracy promotion in Latin America, and for a history of how some of these efforts came to be discontinued, at least for a time, in part on the basis of American popular support for the national sovereignty of others, see Alan McPherson, *The Invaded: How Latin Americans and Their Allies Fought and Ended U.S. Occupations* (Oxford: Oxford University Press, 2014).

[684] https://franciscantradition.org/francis-of-assisi-early-documents/the-saint/the-sacred-exchange-between-saint-francis-and-lady-poverty/984-fa-ed-1-page-537.

[685] Timothy Radcliffe, *What is the Point of Being a Christian?* (London: Continuum, 2005), p. 134.

[686] John S. Mbiti, *African Religions and Philosophy* (second edition) (Oxford: Heinemann, 1989), p. 141.

[687] My thinking on the ego has been influenced by a book of mystical spirituality in which belief in the existence of the ego is presented as the great antagonist of knowledge of who we really are: Helen Schucman, *A Course in Miracles* (third edition [originally three volumes in 1976]) (Mill Valley, CA: Foundation for Inner Peace, 2007), especially 100-

103. My thinking on tradition, and its importance to society as seen in the sociological tradition, has been influenced by Edward Shils, *Tradition* (Chicago: University of Chicago Press, 1981). From a related angle, the cultural critic Philip Rieff has poignantly asked, what previous culture has ever attempted to see to it that no ego is hurt? This is, according to Rieff, the focus of "psychological" or "therapeutic" man for whom nothing is at stake beyond a sense of well-being with which to pursue "impulse release" and the psychological adjustments that facilitate it. Philip Rieff, *The Triumph of the Therapeutic: Uses of Faith after Freud* [1966] (Wilmington: ISI Books, 2006), pp. xii, 10, 21.

[688] Marshall Sahlins, *Stone Age Economics* (London: Routledge Classics, 2017). Lewis Hyde, *The Gift: How the Creative Spirit Transforms the World* (New York: Vintage, 2019).

[689] See David Graeber, *Possibilities: Essays on Hierarchy, Rebellion, and Desire* (Oakland, CA: AK Press, 2007).

[690] David Graeber and David Wengrow, *The Dawn of Everything: A New History of Humanity* (New York: Farrar, Straus and Giroux, 2021).

[691] Graeber and Wengrow, *The Dawn of Everything,* pp. 39-40.

[692] Graeber and Wengrow, *The Dawn of Everything,* p. 41.

[693] Graeber and Wengrow, *The Dawn of Everything,* pp. 40-41.

[694] See, for example, Tu Weiming, *The Global Significance of Concrete Humanity* (New Delhi: Center for Studies in Civilization, 2010), especially pp. 112-129.

[695] See Victor N. Baptiste, *Bartolome de Las Casas and Thomas More's Utopia* (Culver City, CA: Labryinthos, 1990).

[696] Graeber and Wengrow, *The Dawn of Everything,* pp. 44.

[697] Graeber and Wengrow, *The Dawn of Everything,* pp. 44-45.

[698] Graeber and Wengrow, *The Dawn of Everything,* p. 508.

[699] Graeber and Wengrow, *The Dawn of Everything,* p. 510.

[700] Benjamin Franklin, "Remarks Concerning the Savages of North-America," ca. 1783, Edmund S. Morgan, ed., *Not Your Usual Founding Father: Selected Readings from Benjamin Franklin* (New Haven: Yale University Press, 2006), pp. 52-53.

[701] Iain McGilchrist, *The Matter with Things: Our Brains, Our Delusions, and the Unmaking of the World* in two volumes (London: Perspectiva Press, 2021).

[702] Isabel Millar, "Can we forget Foucault? Obscenity and the politics of seduction," *Revista Guillermo de Ockham* Vol. 20, No. 2 (2022), pp. 351. See also Isabel Millar, *The Psychoanalysis of Artificial Intelligence* (Cham: Palgrave Macmillan, 2021).

[703] *Chisholm v. Georgia* 2 U.S. (2 Dall.) 419, 462-63 (1793).

[704] This is the theme of my first book: Schwartzberg, *Democracy and U.S. Policy in Latin America during the Truman Years,* which stressed what I called the "civility" of American imperialism. This "civility" is at the heart of the legitimacy claimed by the invader state. Without it, or so I think, the lands of the continent could never have been stolen. It was far more important in that ongoing process of thieving than the greed involved was. Without a belief that the United States was serving the common good (a belief rooted

ultimately in religious conceptions), the self-deluded self-righteousness that was needed could never have been mustered.

[705] The somewhat different experience of the Native Nations original to that part of Turtle Island currently claimed as the "sovereign territory" of Canada is worth stressing in this regard. See Elder Larry McDermott, John Borrows, Aimée Craft, Larry Innes, and Rayanna Seymour-Hourie, "Demystifying the Doctrine of Discovery," 28 October 2020, https://www.youtube.com/watch?v=OMilOvNHyow (accessed 23 February 2022).

[706] Harriet Taylor Mill, *The Enfranchisement of Women* [1851] (London: Trübner and Company, 1868), pp. 7-8.

[707] Stefano Harney and Fred Moten, *The Undercommons: Fugitive Planning and Black Study* (Wivenhoe: Minor Compositions, 2013), pp. 98-99.

[708] This paragraph is made up of quotations and close paraphrases drawn from Stefano Harney and Fred Moten, *All Incomplete* (Colchester: Minor Compositions, 2021), especially pp. 68, 120-123, 129, 155, 167.

[709] Harney and Moten, *All Incomplete*, p. 68.

[710] Harney and Moten, *All Incomplete*, p. 155.

[711] Harney and Moten, *All Incomplete*, p. 167.

[712] It remains true that the conscience is a ubiquitous presence in every known culture. See Marilynne Robinson, *What are we Doing Here?* (New York: Farrar, Straus and Giroux, 2018), especially pp. 3-16.

[713] I am deeply indebted to the Rev. angel Kyodo williams' writing and speaking on blackness and on embodied social justice. Rev. angel Kyodo williams, *Being Black: Zen and the Art of Living with Fearlessness and Grace* (New York: Viking Compass, 2000). See also Bayo Akomolafe, *These Wilds Beyond our Fences: Letters to my Daughter on Humanity's Search for Home* (Berkeley: North Atlantic Books, 2017). See also Resmaa Menaken, *My Grandmother's Hands: Racialized Trauma and the Pathway to Mending Our Hearts and Bodies* (Las Vegas: Central Recovery Press, 2017); Resmaa Menaken, *The Quaking of America: An Embodied Guide to Navigating Our Nation's Upheaval and Racial Reckoning* (Las Vegas: Central Recovery Press, 2022).

[714] Denise Ferreira da Silva, *Unpayable Debt: On the Antipolitical* (London: Sternberg Press, 2022), pp. 168-69.

[715] I am indebted to Marilyn Charles for her use of the concept of prosody, including the importance of the mother's heartbeat to the developing child in utero.

[716] See "How your gut bacteria influences your behaviour, emotions and thinking," on "Quirks and Quarks with Bob McDonald," CBC Radio, 22 March 2019, https://www.cbc.ca/radio/quirks/july-27-2019-shopping-for-souvenirs-on-an-asteroid-new-cambrian-explosion-fossils-and-more-1.5065927/how-your-gut-bacteria-influences-your-behaviour-emotions-and-thinking-1.5065955 (accessed 17 October 2019).

[717] Denise Ferreira da Silva, *Toward a Global Idea of Race*, passim.

[718] Denise Ferreira da Silva, "On Difference without Separability," 32nd BIENAL DE SÃO PAULO *INCERTEZA VIVA* (7 September - 11 December 2016), p. 64.

[719] Silva, "On Difference without Separability," pp. 64-65.
[720] James H. Cone, *The Cross and the Lynching Tree* (Maryknoll: Orbis Books, 2011), p. 2. See also Howard Thurman, *Jesus and the Disinherited* [1949] (Boston: Beacon Press, 1996).
[721] Valarie Kaur, *See No Stranger: A Memoir and Manifesto of Revolutionary Love* (New York: Random House, 2020).
[722] Russell, *Sequoyah Rising*, p. 170.
[723] Ibid, 172.
[724] Ibid, p. 88.
[725] John Borrows, *Law's Indigenous Ethics* (Toronto: University of Toronto Press, 2019), pp. 3-5.
[726] Tink Tinker, "What Are We Going to Do with White People," (Working Copy, 4 March 2021), graciously shared with the author by Professor Tinker.
[727] Among the Inuit, the non-racial term Qallunaat is the term for white people. See the collaboration between filmmaker Mark Sandiford and Inuit writer and satirist Zebedee Nungak, "Qallunaat!: Why White People Are Funny," 2006, https://www.nfb.ca/film/qallunaat_why_white_people_are_funny/ (accessed 2 February 2022).
[728] I have been deeply moved in this regard by a series of interviews with the Wampanoag medicine man John Peters (Slow Turtle):
Slow Turtle - Part 1
https://www.youtube.com/watch?v=rZl7LKc9hos&list=WL&index=32&t=0s
Slow Turtle - Part 2
https://www.youtube.com/watch?v=UZ8Acrrljsw&list=WL&index=30&t=0s
Slow Turtle - Part 3
https://www.youtube.com/watch?v=T3kQ5ffVE8I&list=WL&index=31&t=0s
Slow Turtle - Part 4
https://www.youtube.com/watch?v=Riv1pygh7ho&list=WL&index=33&t=1s
Slow Turtle - Part 5
https://www.youtube.com/watch?v=9x8KSTAIqfM&list=WL&index=29&t=0s
[729] I am indebted to JoDe Goudy from whom I first heard this answer: "We are of creation." I have since heard this answer from Resmaa Menakem as well.
[730] Deloria, *God is Red*, pp. 59, 193.
[731] Sterling E. Edmonds, "The Lawless Law of Nations," *Washington University Law Review*, Vol. 10, No. 3 (January 1925), 171-196. I am grateful to Steve Newcomb for calling my attention to this article.
[732] Stephen Young, *Indigenous Peoples, Consent and Rights: Troubling Subjects* (London: Routledge, 2020), p. 214.
[733] Those who want more information on the rigging of "federal Indian law" are referred to d'Errico, *Federal Anti-Indian Law*.
[734] Young, *Indigenous Peoples*, p. 217.
[735] Peter d'Errico, "Restorative Indigenous Justice," *Contemporary Justice Review*, Vol 2, No. 4 (December 1999), pp. 383-84.

[736] John Trudell, "What it Means to be a Human Being, 15 March 2001, https://ratical.org/many_worlds/JohnTrudell/HumanBeing.html#s2.
[737] Peter d'Errico, "Restorative Indigenous Justice," pp. 383-84.
[738] "Cheap grace is the grace we bestow on ourselves. Cheap grace is the preaching of forgiveness without requiring repentance, baptism without church discipline, Communion without confession.... Cheap grace is grace without discipleship, grace without the cross, grace without Jesus Christ, living and incarnate." Dietrich Bonhoeffer, *The Cost of Discipleship*, https://tdbi.org/dietrich-bonhoeffer/notable-quotes/.
[739] Luke 19:8.
[740] See "It's Time To Get Ready | Chief Oren Lyons (Faithkeeper Of The Wolf Clan)," https://youtu.be/EzUpOpNR6aE.
[741] Tu Weiming, "Spiritual Humanism: An Emerging Global Discourse, 18 December 2015," https://www.youtube.com/watch?v=Ya-jsyg6c_I.
[742] George Manuel, *The Fourth World: An Indian Reality* [1974] (Minneapolis: University of Minnesota Press, 2019), pp. 264-265. I am grateful to Peter d'Errico for introducing me to this work.
[743] See the discussions of recent South African history, and of the history of some of the relations between the Cheyenne and the United States, in Lewis Hyde, *A Primer for Forgetting: Getting Past the Past* (New York: Farrar, Straus, and Giroux, 2019), especially pp. 169-186, 237-250.
[744] Jacob Taubes, "Religion and the Future of Psychoanalysis" [1957], in Jacob Taubes, *From Cult to Culture: Fragments Toward a Critique of Historical Reason* (edited by Charlotte Elisheva Fonrobert and Amir Engel) (Stanford: Stanford University Press, 2010), p. 336. See also Jacob Taubes, *The Political Theology of Paul* [1993] (edited by Aleida Assmann, et al.) (Stanford: Stanford University Press, 2004).
[745] See Deloria, *God is Red*, especially pp. 200-201. I have also learned much from Barbara Alice Mann, *Iroquoian Women: The Gantowisas* (New York: Peter Lang, 2000).
[746] For an example of this kind of listening in preaching, see Fred Moten, "This is How we Fellowship," 19 January 2020, https://www.trinitywallstreet.org/video/1115am-sermon-dr-fred-moten.
[747] Terry M. Wildman, *First Nations Version: An Indigenous Translation of the New Testament* (Downers Grove, IL: InterVarsity Press, 2021).
[748] Cone, *The Cross and the Lynching Tree*, p. 2. See also Howard Thurman, *Jesus and the Disinherited* [1949] (Boston: Beacon Press, 1996).
[749] John 1:3
[750] See the related discussion in McGilchrist, *The Matter with Things*, Vol. 2, pp. 1193-1304.
[751] Johnann Gottfried von Herder, *Philosophical Writings* (translated and edited by Michael N. Forster) (Cambridge: Cambridge University Press, 2002), p. 381.
[752] Herder, *Philosophical Writings*, p. 424.
[753] Senator John Forsyth of Georgia, 15 April 1830, United States Senate, 21st Congress, 1st Session, *Register of Debates*, p. 32.

[754] The Episcopal Church, *The Book of Common Prayer* (New York: Church Publishing Incorporated, 2007), pp. 362-63.

[755] Radcliffe, *What is the Point of Being a Christian?*, p. 175.

[756] Charles Taylor, *A Secular Age* (Cambridge, MA: Harvard University Press, 2007), p. 371.

[757] Taylor, *A Secular Age*, p. 637.

[758] Rev. angel Kyodo Williams, et al., *Radical Dharma: Talking Race, Love, and Liberation* (Berkeley: North Atlantic Books, 2016).

[759] See: http://charterforcompassion.org/. Signatories include Karen Armstrong, the Dalai Lama, Desmond Tutu, Ali Gomaa, Sadhvi Chaitanya, Tu Weiming, and tens of thousands of others.

[760] Tu Weiming, "Spiritual Humanism: Self, Community, Earth, and Heaven: 24th World Congress of Philosophy, Wang Yangming Lecture," 18 August 2018, https://www.youtube.com/watch?v=oTiPiMaroY0.

[761] Quoted in Tu, *The Global Significance of Concrete Humanity*, p. 243.

[762] Harney and Moten, *The Undercommons*, pp. 98-99.

[763] Kaur, *See No Stranger*.

[764] See Herbert McCabe, *Law, Love and Language* (London: Continuum, 1968), especially p. 25.

[765] See Susan Neiman, *Learning from the Germans: Race and the Memory of Evil* (New York: Farrar, Straus, and Giroux, 2019).

[766] See Steven Schwartzberg, "The 'Soft Peace Boys': Presurrender Planning and Japanese Land Reform," *The Journal of American-East Asian Relations*, Vol. 2, No. 2 (Summer 1993), pp. 185-216, https://www.researchgate.net/publication/273601891.

[767] Susan Raffo, "Embodying Impact," 27 January 2021, https://www.susanraffo.com/blog/embodying-impact.

[768] See Collier, *Indians of the Americas*, pp. 7-8.

Index